VOLUME TWO
DESOLATION & DESTRUCTION
IN THE LAST DAYS

WARNINGS FROM THE PROPHETS

Compiled by Arlene Kay Butler

ISBN #0-9660284-2-2

Published & Distributed by Nelson Book
HC-61 Box 1056
Malta, ID   83342
1-800-388-4512

Italics have been added by the author. Quotes have been verified from the original source or through the Infobase Collector's Library. For future revisions if there are any suggestions, or additions you would like to suggest please contact the publisher.

Additional copies may be ordered from the above address.

TABLE OF CONTENTS

PUBLISHER'S FOREWORD

The three volumes in this series are a partial fulfillment of the publisher's thirty-year quest to better understand the glorious times surrounding the Second Coming of the Lord Jesus Christ.

Additional quotes by the apostles and prophets concerning the future events of our times may be submitted with primary source documentation to the publisher for possible inclusion in an expanded version of this work at the following address: Nelson Book, HC 61, Box 1056, Malta, ID 83342.

I would like to express sincere thanks to Arlene Kay Butler for her tireless efforts over the past seven years in compiling these quotes.

Zeldon Nelson
Publisher & President of Nelson Book

PREFACE

The words of the Lord and the prophets are beautiful! In these books I do not interpret them nor comment on them. They speak for themselves! The book only contains quotes from apostles, prophets, and the scriptures. The quotes are organized under subject in different chapters. Due to the overlap of subject matter, the quotes could not be organized within the chapter into more defined subjects. The quotes in each chapter are organized chronologically according to the date the individual was sustained as an apostle, i.e. beginning with Joseph Smith and ending with the newest sustained apostle. This also helps provide a time perspective. The "Apostle and Prophet List" gives the date an apostle was ordained. Due to copyright restrictions, some quotes are condensed and say "See" before the reference indicating a need to refer to the original source for full information.

In the 1986 Priesthood Manual it states: "The Lord has revealed a great deal concerning his Second Coming, and he expects his Saints to search out and understand the signs of the times (p. 210-211)."

When I started I had no thought of compiling a book, but desired to understand the last days. As I read every book available on the subject instead of the events and doctrines becoming plainer, I found that the fog became even thicker. I determined that it might be more understandable if I could read just what the prophets, apostles, and scriptures had said on the subject. So I started collecting quotes and organizing them on my computer according to subject. When I obtained the gospel CD-Rom, I was able to thoroughly research by methodically scanning every key word imaginable checking tens of thousands of quotes.

President Lorenzo Snow tells us: "Knowledge helps us withstand difficulties. God bless this people is my prayer continually, especially in the obtaining of knowledge and intelligence from heaven, so that we may be able to withstand the difficulties, trials, and afflictions which may arise in our path." (Teachings of Lorenzo Snow, p.30, October 5, 1889.)

In 2 Nephi 25:7-8 it says "in the days that the prophecies of Isaiah shall be fulfilled men will know of a surety, at the times when they shall come to pass", and " I know that they shall be of great worth unto them in the last days; for in that day shall they understand them".

I hope this book will help you understand the events surrounding the "Great and dreadful day of the Lord", and as you read you will be filled with a sense of joy and hope for truly it is a "Great Day" for the saints. I am grateful to my Heavenly Father, for his love, guidance, and protection, and allowing "a small and weak thing" to contribute to His work (Joel 2:28-29).

Arlene Kay Butler

INTRODUCTION

As you study this book you might wonder if the incredible prophecies of the last days will really happen. Be assured: "God will not disappoint you in these the last days; he will not disappoint the wicked, he will not disappoint the devils in hell, nor the angels of God in the heaven will not be disappointed with regard to the fulfilment of the revelations; whatever may be the unbelief of this generation it will make no difference with regard to the fulfilment of the revelations of God and the predictions of his servants." (Wilford Woodruff, Journal of Discourses, Vol. 21, p. 300, August 1, 1880.)

President Benson has declared the prophecies are not only future, but have been and are being fulfilled. "I solemnly declare that the Lord has established His latter-day kingdom upon the earth in fulfillment of prophecies uttered by His ancient prophets and Apostles. Holy angels have again communed with men on the earth. God has again revealed Himself from heaven and restored to the earth His holy priesthood with power to administer in all the sacred ordinances necessary for the exaltation of His children. His Church has been reestablished among men with all the spiritual gifts enjoyed anciently. All this is done in preparation for Christ's second coming. The great and dreadful day of the Lord is near at hand. In preparation for this great event and as a means of escaping the impending judgments, inspired messengers have gone forth to the nations of the earth carrying this testimony and warning." (Ezra Taft Benson, Teachings of Ezra Taft Benson, p. 19, Stockholm Sweden Area Conference, 18 August 1974.)

Why and how will these events occur? "The signs of both heaven and earth all indicate the coming of the Son of man, which is near at the door. No man knows the day or the hour when Christ will come, but the generation is clearly pointed out, the fig tree is leafing, and great changes are near at hand. Great Babylon is coming in remembrance before God, and the Lord has called upon the inhabitants of the earth who are very wicked, to repent of their sins and turn unto him. The generation in which we live is a wicked and an adulterous generation, and wickedness and abomination of every kind are increasing, and the earth has commenced to groan under the evil practices of man. The heavens are in pain over the disobedience and unrighteousness of the children of men, and the angels, we are told, are waiting in their places in the temple for the time to come when they will be called upon to go forth and reap down the earth. Judgments await the world, but they heed not, and apparently do not care. With fire and sword the Lord will plead with all flesh, and as the prophet has said respecting this event, 'the slain of the Lord will be many;' and these things will overtake the world in an hour when they expect them not, when they will be crying peace, but alas, peace will have departed from them, and they left to devour and destroy each other. All these things are foretold and many of them are written in these revelations given in our day, and they are already being fulfilled before our eyes; and they will continue to be fulfilled, until all that is spoken of shall have come to pass." (Wilford Woodruff, JD, Vol. 19, p. 362-364, June 30, 1878.)

How should we feel and respond as the foretold disasters occur? "I would like to suggest, in today's vernacular, two attitude adjustments. First, we need to overcome fatalism. We know the prophecies of the future. We know the final outcome. We know the world collectively will not repent and consequently the last days will be filled with much pain and suffering. Therefore, we could throw up our hands and do nothing but pray for the end to come so the millennial reign could begin. To do so would forfeit our right to participate in the grand event we are all awaiting. We must all become players in the winding-up scene, not spectators. We must do all we can to prevent calamities, and then do everything possible to assist and comfort the victims of tragedies that do occur . . .

The second attitude adjustment is to not allow ourselves to find satisfaction in calamities of the last days. Sometimes we tend to take joy in seeing the natural consequences of sin unfold. We might feel some vindication for being ignored by most of the world and persecuted and berated by others . . .

As the last days unfold, we will see all the prophecies fulfilled. We will see today's problems compounded, and we will see new challenges scarcely imaginable at this time. We must reach out to those who are suffering from these events. We must not become fatalistic or judgmental—even if we warn the people in the world sometimes a thousand times and they heed us not." (Glenn L. Pace, Conference Report, Oct. 1990, Ensign, Nov. 1990, p. 8-9.)

When will they begin in earnest? "Do you think there is calamity abroad now among the people? Not much. All we have yet heard and all we have experienced is scarcely a preface to the sermon that is going to be preached. When the testimony of the Elders ceases to be given, and the Lord says to them, 'Come home; I will now preach my own sermons to the nations of the earth,' all you now know can scarcely be called a preface to the sermon that will be preached with fire and sword, tempests, earthquakes, hail, rain, thunders and lightnings, and fearful destruction." (Brigham Young, JD, Vol. 8, p. 123, July 15, 1860.)

When will they cease? "In the very nature of things, the signs of the times will not cease until the Lord comes. Those that involve chaos and commotion and distress of nations will continue in the future with even greater destructive force. Men's hearts will fail them for fear in greater degree hereafter than heretofore. Wars will get worse. Moments of armistice and peace will be less stable. Viewed in the perspective of years, all worldly things will degenerate. There will be an increasing polarization of views. There will be more apostasy from the Church, more summer saints and sunshine patriots who will be won over to the cause of the adversary. . . .While the faithful saints get better and better, and cleave more firmly to the heaven-sent standards, the world will get worse and worse and will cleave to the policies and views of Lucifer." (Bruce R. McConkie, The Millennial Messiah, p. 404.)

Why doesn't the world understand and 'wake up and repent' as the prophecies are fulfilled? "They belong only to the people of God, to those who have entered into the everlasting covenant, to those who have received the Holy Ghost, and who understand the things of God; for 'no man knoweth the things of God, but by the Spirit of God.' But this work will go on; the Saints will be gathered, and temples will be built, and Israel will be redeemed, and the kingdoms of this world will become more and more divided; and the sects and parties of Christendom will become more and more contentious even than they are today. Infidelity will increase, for the Spirit of God is being withdrawn from them, because they receive not the truth when it is presented to them. And nation will rise against nation, and kingdom against kingdom, and people against people. War will be poured out eventually upon all nations; the only place where there will be peace and safety will be in the Zion of God. The judgments we read of in the revelations will all be poured out just as the Prophets have predicted and just as John the beloved has declared. All the woes that John saw are bound to be poured out upon the inhabitants of the earth; every word will be fulfilled, not one jot or tittle will pass away without its fulfillment." (Charles W. Penrose, JD, Vol. 24, p. 217-218, May 18, 1883.)

The Lord is our Redeemer and friend. Through the trials we face remember we can rely upon the Lord because: "The Lord is in control. He knows the end from the beginning. He has given us adequate instruction that, if followed, will see us safely through any crisis. His purposes will be fulfilled, and someday we will understand the eternal reasons for all of these events." (M. Russell Ballard, The Friend, Sept 1995, p. 1, adapted from October 1992 Conference Report.)

CHAPTER ONE

DESTRUCTION

"The destroyer of the Gentiles is on his way to overthrow governments, to destroy dynasties, to lay waste thrones, kingdoms and empires, to spread abroad anarchy and desolation, and to cause war, famine and bloodshed to overspread the earth."
(John Taylor, JD 23:63, April 9, 1882.)

Joseph Smith, History of the Church, Vol. 1, p. 13.

"He (Heavenly Messenger) informed me of great judgments which were coming upon the earth, with great desolations by famine, sword, and pestilence; and that these grievous judgments would come on the earth in this generation."

Joseph Smith, History of the Church, Vol. 6, p. 26.

"Isaiah, in his 24th chapter, gives something of an account of the calamities and judgments which shall come upon the heads of the Gentile nations, and this because they have transgressed the laws, changed the ordinance, and broken the everlasting covenant. The Apostle Paul says to his Roman brethren, that if the Gentiles do not continue in the goodness of God, they, like the house of Israel, should be cutoff. Though Babylon says, 'I sit as a queen, and am no widow, and shall see no sorrow,' the Revelator says, 'Therefore shall her plagues come in one day, death and mourning and famine; and she shall be utterly burned with fire, for strong is the Lord God who judgeth her.'"

Teachings of the Prophet Joseph Smith, Section Two, 1834–37, p. 87.

"The servants of God will not have gone over the nations of the Gentiles, with a warning voice, until the destroying angel will commence to waste the inhabitants of the earth, and as the prophet hath said, 'It shall be a vexation to hear the report.'"

Teachings of the Prophet Joseph Smith, Section Four, 1839–42, p. 160-161.

"Wars are at hand; we must not delay; but are not required to sacrifice. We ought to have the building up of Zion as our greatest object. When wars come, we shall have to flee to Zion. The cry is to make haste. The last revelation says, Ye shall not have time to have gone over the earth, until these things come. It will come as did the cholera, war, fires, and earthquakes; one pestilence after another, until the Ancient of Days comes, then judgment will be given to the Saints . . .

Look to the Presidency and receive instruction. Every man who is afraid, covetous, will be taken in a snare. The time is soon coming, when no man will have any peace but in Zion and her stakes.

I saw men hunting the lives of their own sons, and brother murdering brother, women killing

1

their own daughters, and daughters seeking the lives of their mothers. I saw armies arrayed against armies. I saw blood, desolation, fires. The Son of man has said that the mother shall be against the daughters, and the daughter against the mother. These things are at our doors. They will follow the Saints of God from city to city. Satan will rage, and the spirit of the devil is now enraged. I know not how soon these things will take place; but with a view of them, shall I cry peace? No; I will lift up my voice and testify of them. How long you will have good crops, and the famine be kept off, I do not know; when the fig tree leaves, know then that the summer is nigh at hand."

Teachings of the Prophet Joseph Smith, Section Five, 1842–43, p. 280.
"He (Mr. Redding) has not seen the sign of the Son of Man, as foretold by Jesus; neither has any man, nor will any man, until after the sun shall have been darkened and the moon bathed in blood; for the Lord hath not shown me any such sign; and as the prophet saith, so it must be—'Surely the Lord God will do nothing, but He revealeth His secret unto His servants the prophets.' (See Amos 3:7.)"

Teachings of the Prophet Joseph Smith, Section Six, 1843-44, p. 286.
"There will be wars and rumors of wars, signs in the heavens above and on the earth beneath, the sun turned into darkness and the moon to blood, earthquakes in divers places, the seas heaving beyond their bounds; then will appear one grand sign of the Son of Man in heaven. But what will the world do? They will say it is a planet, a comet, etc. But the Son of Man will come as the sign of the coming of the Son of Man, which will be as the light of the morning cometh out of the east."

Teachings of the Prophet Joseph Smith, Section Six, 1843-44, p. 305.
"The Lord deals with this people as a tender parent with a child, communicating light and intelligence and the knowledge of his ways as they can bear it. The inhabitants of the earth are asleep; they know not the day of their visitation. The Lord hath set the bow in the cloud for a sign that while it shall be seen, seed time and harvest, summer and winter shall not fail; but when it shall disappear woe to that generation, for behold the end cometh quickly."

Teachings of the Prophet Joseph Smith, Section Six, 1843-44, p. 321.
"The world is reserved unto burning in the last days. He shall send Elijah the prophet, and he shall reveal the covenants of the fathers in relation to the children, and the covenants of the children in relation to the fathers.
Four destroying angels holding power over the four quarters of the earth until the servants of God are sealed in their foreheads, which signifies sealing the blessing upon their heads, meaning the everlasting covenant, thereby making their calling and election made sure. When a seal is put upon the father and mother, it secures their posterity, so that they cannot be lost, but will be saved by virtue of the covenant of their father and mother."

Teachings of the Prophet Joseph Smith, Section Six, 1843-44, p. 328.
"I prophesy, in the name of the Lord God of Israel, anguish and wrath and tribulation and the withdrawing of the Spirit of God from the earth await this generation, until they are visited with utter

desolation. This generation is as corrupt as the generation of the Jews that crucified Christ; and if He were here today, and should preach the same doctrine He did then, they would put Him to death."

Teachings of the Prophet Joseph Smith, Section Six, 1843-44, p. 340.

"I have asked of the Lord concerning His coming; and while asking the Lord, He gave a sign and said, 'In the days of Noah I set a bow in the heavens as a sign and token that in any year that the bow should be seen the Lord would not come; but there should be seed time and harvest during that year: but whenever you see the bow withdrawn, it shall be a token that there shall be famine, pestilence, and great distress among the nations, and that the coming of the Messiah is not far distant.'"

Brigham Young, Messages of the First Presidency, Vol. 2, p. 211, December 10, 1856.

"Their long, hypocritical players, lip-service, pretended piety and idolatrous worship, have become an abomination before Him; wherefore will He proceed to bring upon them the judgments which have been foretold by His servants the Prophets, and great will be the desolation thereof. Their great and mighty nations, empires, and kingdoms, with all the pride, pomp and power thereof, will be broken and crumbled in pieces, and come to nought. Their cities will become a howling waste, a solitary place, wherein shall be found the wolf and the vulture, and no man shall be found an inhabitant therein. Yea, verily, He will empty the earth of the wicked, and those who work abominations in His sight, so shall the kingdoms of this world become the kingdoms of our Lord and His Christ, so shall the Lord prepare the way for His coming, and reign upon the earth."

Brigham Young, Journal of Discourses, Vol. 2, p. 178, February 18, 1855.

"In the progress of the age in which we live, we discern the fulfillment of prophecy, and the preparation for the second coming of our Lord and Savior to dwell upon the earth. We expect that the refuge of lies will be swept away, and that city, nation, government, or kingdom which serves not God, and gives no heed to the principles of truth and religion, will be utterly wasted away and destroyed."

Brigham Young, Journal of Discourses, Vol. 8, p. 123, July 15, 1860.

"'Do you think there is calamity abroad now among the people?' Not much. All we have yet heard and all we have experienced is scarcely a preface to the sermon that is going to be preached. When the testimony of the Elders ceases to be given, and the Lord says to them, 'Come home; I will now preach my own sermons to the nations of the earth,' all you now know can scarcely be called a preface to the sermon that will be preached with fire and sword, tempests, earthquakes, hail, rain, thunders and lightnings, and fearful destruction. What matters the destruction of a few railway cars? You will hear of magnificent cities, now idolized by the people, sinking in the earth, entombing the inhabitants. The sea will heave itself beyond its bounds, engulfing mighty cities. Famine will spread over the nations, and nation will rise up against nation, kingdom against kingdom, and states against states, in our own country and in foreign lands; and they will destroy each other, caring not for the blood and lives of their neighbours, of their families, or for their own lives. They will be like the Jaredites who preceded the Nephites upon this continent, and will destroy each other to the last man, through the anger that the Devil will place in their hearts, because they have rejected the words of life and are given over to Satan to do whatever he listeth to do with them. You may think that the little you hear of now is grievous; yet the faithful of God's people will see days that will cause them to close their eyes because of the sorrow that will come upon the wicked nations. The hearts of the faithful will be filled with pain and anguish for them."

Brigham Young, Journal of Discourses, Vol. 9, p. 365, August 31, 1862.

"If any people reject the Gospel, God will destroy that people or nation. The majority of the people of the world declare that Joseph Smith was not called of God. If they know that, then are they safe in rejecting his testimony. I know that he was called of God, and this I know by the revelations of Jesus Christ to me, and by the testimony of the Holy Ghost."

Brigham Young, Journal of Discourses, Vol. 9, p. 366-367, August 31, 1862.

"What do we now see abroad? Confusion in all the ramifications of society. In the days of the great tower of Babel God confounded their language, and spread confusion and dismay among them, and ultimately scattered them to the four winds of heaven. The confusion will be no less great in these days, and the destruction of human life will be so great that but few men will be left."

Prophecy of Heber C. Kimball, Deseret News, May 23, 1931.

"The judgments of God will be poured out upon the wicked to that extent that our Elders from far and near will be called home, or, in other words, the Gospel will be taken from the Gentiles and later on will be carried to the Jews. The western boundaries of the state of Missouri will be swept so clean of its inhabitants that as President Young tells us, 'When you return to that place there will not be so much as a yellow dog to wag his tail.' Before that day comes, however, the Saints will be put to tests that will try the integrity of the best of them."

Heber C. Kimball, Journal of Discourses, Vol. 4, p. 224, February 8, 1857.

"I know the character of the human family and the course that many men and women are taking; they are making a desolation and taking a course to bring destruction upon their root; they are following a course that would ultimately depopulate the earth. All will come to that, if they do not take a course of continual increase for ever and for ever."

Heber C. Kimball, Journal of Discourses, Vol. 6, p. 66, November 22, 1857.

"We have invited the nations to receive the truth, but they will not, nor let us go to them; and now God is going to compel them to come in by famine, war, and every kind of desolation; and they will come faster than we can provide for them. Then let us awake, and not lie down and sleep, and go home and act as though we had not heard anything."

Parley P. Pratt, Millennial Star, Vol. 1, p. 258, February 1841.

"We are nowhere given to understand that all the stars will fall or even many of them: but only 'as a fig tree casteth her untimely figs when she is shaken with a mighty wind.' The stars which will fall to the earth, are fragments, which have been broken off from the earth from time to time, in mighty convulsions of nature. Some in the days of Enoch, some perhaps in the days of Peleg, some with the ten tribes, and some at the crucifixion of the Messiah. These all must be restored again at the 'times of restitution of all things.' This will restore the ten tribes of Israel; and also bring again Zion, even Enoch's city. It will bring back the tree of life which is in the midst of the paradise of God; that you and I may partake of it. (See Rev 2:7.) When these fragments (some of which are vastly larger than the present earth) are brought back and joined to this earth, it will cause a convulsion of all nature; the graves of the Saints will be opened, and rise from the dead; while the mountains will flow down, the valleys rise, the sea retire to its own place, the islands and continents will be removed, and earth be rolled together as a scroll. The earth will be many times larger than it is now."

Orson Pratt, Journal of Discourses, Vol. 2, p. 286-287, January 7, 1855.

"'Thou shalt be visited of the Lord of hosts with thunder, and with earthquake, and great noise, with storm and tempest, and the flame of devouring fire.' This verse has reference to what follows in the next—'And the multitude of all the nations that fight against Ariel, even all that fight against her and her munition, and that distress her, shall be as a dream of a night vision. It shall even be as when an hungry man dreameth, and, behold, he eateth; but he awaketh, and his soul is empty: or as when a thirsty man dreameth, and, behold, he drinketh; but he awaketh, and, behold, he is faint, and his soul hath appetite: so shall the multitude of all the nations be, that fight against Mount Zion.' Here you perceive is another thing taken up by the Prophet in connection with the whispering of the words of that nation out of the dust; immediately following that remarkable event there was to be a dreadful destruction, not upon Ariel—not upon Israel—but upon the multitude of all the nations of the earth that should fight against Mount Zion. Three things, then, are declared in succession—one is the destruction of a nation, another the speaking of their words out of the dust in the ears of the living, and the third that which immediately follows, namely, the destruction of all the nations of the earth that should fight against Mount Zion; this latter event has not yet been fulfilled; but is just as sure to be fulfilled as the other portions of the prophecy that have taken place; just as sure as the Book of Mormon has whispered out of the dust, and spoken in the ears of this generation, in fulfillment of the words of the Prophet Isaiah, so sure will the Lord of hosts visit the multitude of all the nations of the earth, that fight against Mount Zion, with thunder, and earthquake, and with the flame of devouring fire, and they shall be as the dream of a night vision, they shall pass away from the face of the earth and be as chaff blown to the four winds of heaven, and no place shall be found for them."

Orson Pratt, Journal of Discourses, Vol. 2, p. 294, January 7, 1855.

"That is what we look for, for the union of the heavens and the earth; we are dwelling here, separate from our brethren in heaven; we want to get back to them, and they to us, and we want to be united, and accomplish what the Lord intends to be accomplished in the last days; and before we get through with it, we shall see greater wonders and signs than that little transaction of bringing Israel out of Egypt; that will almost be entirely forgotten among the great displays of His power in the last days."

Orson Pratt, Journal of Discourses, Vol. 14, p. 65-66, March 26, 1871.

"And as these judgments come, kingdoms and thrones will be cast down and overturned. Empire will war with empire, kingdom with kingdom, and city with city, and there will be one general revolution throughout the earth, the Jews fleeing to their own country, desolation coming upon the wicked, with the swiftness of whirlwinds and fury poured out, recollect, as it was poured out on the Egyptians."

Orson Pratt, Journal of Discourses, Vol. 15, p. 330-331, January 26, 1873.

"Where shall these great and severe judgments begin? Upon what people does the Lord intend to commence this great work of vengeance? Upon the people who profess to know his name and still blaspheme it in the midst of his house. They are the ones designated for some of the most terrible judgments of the latter days. This should be a warning to the Latter-day Saints; an not only those who are parents, but those who are children should diligently consider whether they are numbered among those who are mentioned in the 10th paragraph, which I have read. Upon my house, saith the Lord, shall it begin, first upon those among you who have professed my name and have not known me and have blasphemed against me in the midst of my house."

Orson Pratt, Journal of Discourses, Vol. 15, p. 332-333, January 26, 1873.

"The Lord says that through the united testimonies of those who believed in this work he would condemn this generation, that he would send forth a desolating scourge, and it should be poured out upon the inhabitants of the earth until the earth should be empty and desolate inasmuch as its inhabitants would not repent of their sins. The Lord informed us on that occasion that it should be with the inhabitants of the whole earth as it was with the inhabitants of Jerusalem in ancient times, that is, as he spoke concerning their destruction and his word was verified, so should they be verified at this time in relation to the inhabitants of the earth in the latter days. Consequently we see from these revelations, that the judgments of the Almighty are to be universal—upon all the earth desolation and destruction, a day of vengeance and burning and sore calamity until the inhabitants are wasted away and the earth made empty and desolate."

Orson Pratt, Journal of Discourses, Vol. 15, p. 334, January 26, 1873.

"Here we perceive how long the Lord will bear with the people—all the day long, stretching forth his hand, pleading with them by the voice of lightnings, thunders, earthquakes, great hailstorms, famines, pestilences of every kind, and by the voice of mercy and judgment, yet they will not repent, but will harden their hearts when all these things go forth among them, from nation to nation, people to people, and from kingdom to kingdom, and they will refuse the message of salvation. It is true that the Lord has not yet spoken by the voice of thunders, calling upon the people form the ends of the earth, saying, 'Repent and prepare for the great day of the Lord,' but such an event will come; and when it does come it will not be a mere ordinary, common thunderstorm, such as we experience occasionally, extending only over a small extent of country, but the Lord will cause the thunders to utter their voices from the ends of the earth until they sound in the ears of all that live, and these thunders shall use the very words here predicted—'Repent O ye inhabitants of the earth, and prepare the way of the Lord, prepare yourselves for the great day of the Lord.' These words will be distinctly heard by every soul that lives, whether in America, Asia, Africa, Europe, or upon the islands of the sea. And not only the thunders, but the lightings will utter forth their voices in the ears of all that live, saying, 'Repent, for the great day of the Lord is come.' Besides the voices of thunder and lightning, the Lord himself, before he comes in his glory, will speak by his own voice out of heaven in the ears of all that live, commanding them to repent and to prepare for his coming. I do not know how the Lord will send forth his voice so as to make all the people on the four quarters of the globe hear it, for the loudest sound that we can produce only extends over a small area, a few miles at most; but the Lord has power to make his voice heard by all that live on the four quarters of the earth, and when he fulfills this prediction, all that live will literally hear the words that are here named; and the wicked will perish out of the earth as they did in the days of Noah, and so far as they are concerned the earth will be made empty and desolate."

Orson Pratt, Journal of Discourses, Vol. 15, p. 338, January 26, 1873.

"If you want to know about the time when the sun and moon are to be darkened, and when the stars will no longer give any light, and when there will be total darkness over all the face of the earth, here is an event predicted so that you can not mistake. When you see the nations of the earth, especially the heathen nations, and also those north of Jerusalem—the great nation of Russia and other nations on the continent of Asia, together with many in Europe, gather up against Jerusalem after the Jews have returned and rebuilt their city and Temple, and when their armies become exceeding great multitudes in the valley of decision, then you may look for the Lord to come down with his mighty ones, and for the constellations of heaven to be darkened."

Orson Pratt, Journal of Discourses, Vol. 16, p. 327, December 28, 1873.

"After the testimonies of the servants of God among the nations comes the testimony of many judgments, which will be poured upon the nations, such as earthquakes, wars, the sea heaving beyond its bounds, and a variety of calamities which shall make the hearts of all the wicked fail them for fear. After these great judgments are poured upon the nations of the earth, then will be fulfilled the words which I have read, 'and angels will fly through the midst of heaven sounding the trump of God, saying prepare ye, prepare ye, O inhabitants of the earth, for the judgment of our God is come, behold and lo! the Bridegroom cometh, go yet out to meet him.' After these angels have flown through the midst of heaven calling upon the inhabitants of the earth to prepare for the coming of the Bridegroom, seven more angels are to sound their trumps. The first one sounds, and his proclamation is concerning great Babylon, 'who has made all nations drink of the wine of the wrath of her fornication, concerning her who sits upon many waters, who has her dominion among many nations, kindreds, tongues and people, behold she is the tares of all the earth, she is bound in bundles, her bands are made strong, no man can loose them, therefore she is ready to be burned, and he shall sound his trump both long and loud, and all nations shall hear it.'"

Orson Pratt, Journal of Discourses, Vol. 18, p. 314-315, December 3, 1876.

"Since the day that Isaiah lived and prophesied among the people, you will admit, with me, that there never has been a universal destruction of all the wicked and the transgressors from off the face of the earth. There have been scores of millions of sinners upon the earth since the utterance of this prophecy to the present time, but the wholesale destruction spoken of has never taken place. You will all admit with me also that the signs which are to appear in the heavens, about the time of this universal destruction of the wicked, have not yet taken place. We are told not only that the sun shall be darkened in his going forth, but the stars shall refuse their shining. If only the sun were to be darkened, the heathen nations, that could not account for it, might say it had reference to some great eclipse, such as has occurred in different ages; but when they find that all the stars of heaven withhold their light, and there is not even so much as a glimmer of light, and the sun too becomes as black as sackcloth, they cannot impute it to be an eclipse, for an eclipse would not destroy the light of the stars that are scattered over the concave of heaven. We are also told, in connection with this, that the earth is to be affected as well as the heavenly bodies; it is to roll to and fro like a drunken man, the mountains are to be broken down, and the whole earth is to be dissolved. No such thing has ever taken place since the day this prophecy was uttered; it is therefore yet to be fulfilled."

Orson Pratt, Journal of Discourses, Vol. 18, p. 339-340, February 25, 1877.

"We read that the four beasts, representing the powers of the earth, will exist at the time of the coming of the Ancient of Days. And that the fourth beast, represented by the Roman Empire and the kingdoms that have grown out of it, will be 'slain and his body destroyed and given to the burning flame.' Here then we can read the destiny of that portion of the inhabitants of the earth constituting the fourth beast: or, in other words, the destiny of the kingdoms of Europe, who were to arise and grow out of that fourth power. We can read the final destiny of the kingdoms of Europe, namely, Germany, France, Italy, Spain, Portugal, Scandinavia, and the great northern power, Russia, Austria and Prussia, and all those various nations, that more particularly pertain to this great iron power that once so cruelly oppressed the people; its 'body shall be destroyed and given to the burning flame,' which signifies the nature of the judgment that will befall them. According to other prophecies, contained in Daniel, a succession of judgments, great and terrible in their nature, will overtake them, before the ire spoken of comes. Nation will rise against nation in war, kingdom against kingdom: or in the language of Isaiah, 'Behold, the Lord will come with fire, and with his chariots like a whirlwind, to render his anger with fury, and with his chariots like a whirlwind, to render his anger with fury, and his rebuke with flames of fire. For by fire and by his sword will the Lord plead with all flesh; and the slain of the Lord shall be many.'

It seems then that the body of the fourth power is to be given to the burning flame, that signifies the utter extinction of that power from the face of the earth. The heathen nations representing the other three beasts, will not then be destroyed: but their lives are to be prolonged, and their dominion is to be taken away. Though their lives will be prolonged, yet they will not have power to rule and govern, only as they are permitted. If you will read from the beginning of the 36th to the end of the 39th chapters of Ezekiel, you find much said, in regard to the heathen nations. 'And the heathen shall know that I am the Lord,' etc. But the fourth power represents the nations of modern Christendom. They have not the privilege of the heathen, in having their lives prolonged. Why? Does the speaker mean to say that modern Christendom is more wicked than the heathen? Yes; the people of Christendom possess more light and knowledge than the heathen, and therefore, they are under the greater condemnation; for according to the light and knowledge they severally have, will they be judged. The more enlightened nations, so called, are rejecting the Gospel message which is being sent to them by divine authority; and for that reason their utter destruction is inevitable, and, as had been decreed, they must pass away. Their lives will not be prolonged. Not only the kingdoms and governments of Europe, and the western portion of Asia are to be thus visited, but also those who have grown out of these kingdoms, and that have emigrated to this western hemisphere and elsewhere."

Orson Pratt, Journal of Discourses, Vol. 19, p. 358-359, June 16, 1878.

"But such testimony will not always be unto salvation. It will be the testimony of judgment that will overwhelm them, in a time, too, they think not of; a time when they will be crying all is peace and safety—lo! sudden destruction is at their doors; and thus the Scriptural saying will be literally fulfilled, 'As the days of Noah were, so shall also the coming of the Son of Man be,' etc. When that unfortunate, but disobedient and wicked people, the Ante-diluvians, were sinking in the waters, they could then say, 'I know that Noah is a Prophet, and that the message he has declared in our ears for these many years is divine.' But alas! it was too late; they rejected the message, paying heedless regard to it as well as to him who preached the Gospel to them; they would not call upon God in all honesty of heart, but they considered Noah deceived; they obeyed not, and were destroyed by the mighty flood."

Orson Pratt, Journal of Discourses, Vol. 20, p. 153-154, March 9, 1879.

"It is because of this, of the light that the nations have in their midst, which they will not receive that the Lord will visit them first; and when he has visited and overthrown them, he will lay his hand heavily upon the heathen nations in Asia, and also those who are in Africa, and they will be visited with severe judgment, but they will not be utterly destroyed."

Orson Pratt, Journal of Discourses, Vol. 21, p. 279-280, June 20, 1880.

"It is our God that will cleanse the earth from wickedness. 'A fire shall devour before him, and it shall be very tempestuous round about him.' He it is that will speak and the wicked shall melt away. He it is that will cause violent whirlwinds to go forth and destroy this, that, or the other city, according to his own will. He it is that will send forth pestilence and plague, and will perform all that has been spoken by the mouth of his prophets, concerning the destruction that is to take place in the latter days."

John Taylor, Journal of Discourses, Vol. 6, p. 24, November 1, 1857.

"Why is it that thrones will be cast down, empires dissolved, nations destroyed, and confusion and distress cover all people, as the Prophets have spoken? Because the Spirit of the Lord will be withdrawn from the nations in consequence of their wickedness, and they will be left to their own folly."

John Taylor, Journal of Discourses, Vol. 17, p. 5, February 1, 1874.

"This nation and other nations will be overthrown, not because of their virtue, but because of their corruption and iniquity. The time will come, for the prophecies will be fulfilled, when kingdoms will be destroyed, thrones cast down and the powers of the earth shaken, and God's wrath will be kindled against the nations of the earth, and it is for us to maintain correct principles, political, religious and social, and to feel towards all men as God feels."

John Taylor, Journal of Discourses, Vol. 18, p. 332, December 31, 1876.

"When the people shall have been gathered in fulfillment of this prophecy, judgments will again be visited upon the wicked, as a necessary consequence. Will such visitations really take place? Yes, I know that this part, too, of the Lord's designs will be fulfilled, for God revealed it to me long, long ago. We need not be too anxious for the destruction of the wicked, for it will be indeed terrible when it comes, it will make every feeling man weep for sorrow over the trouble and affliction that will come."

John Taylor, Journal of Discourses, Vol. 19, p. 307, April 8, 1878.

"Will this people grow and increase? Yes. And the time will come—it is not now, we are not prepared for it—when calamity and trouble and bloodshed, confusion and strife will spread among all the nations of the earth. The time will come, and is not far distant, when those who will not take up the sword to fight against their neighbors, will have to flee to Zion for safety. That was true some time ago, and it is nearer its fulfillment by a great many years than at the time it was first uttered."

John Taylor, Journal of Discourses, Vol. 20, p. 47, August 4, 1878.

"And I have thought sometimes that if the people did not understand that God ruled, they would find out by and by; for I believe that all these things are used by the Lord to bring the people to reflection. And if I read my Bible aright, judgments are first to begin at the house of God. And if judgments are to commence at the house of God, where are the wicked and ungodly to appear? There is a terrible time approaching the nations of the earth, and also this nation, worse than has ever entered into the heart of man to conceive of—war, bloodshed and desolation, mourning and misery, pestilence, famine and earthquakes, and all those calamities spoken of by the prophets will most assuredly be fulfilled, and they are nearer by forty years than they were forty years ago."

John Taylor, Journal of Discourses, Vol. 20, p. 118, January 6, 1879.

"Does he destroy them for their good sometimes? Yes. After Noah had preached the Gospel to the antediluvian world, and after their cup of iniquity was full, and Zion and her cities had fled, then followed the judgments of God; then came desolation and destruction. And why this wholesale sweeping out of existence of humanity? To stop them from propagating a corrupt species. Was not that right? Yes it was. He said, I will cut them off; I will prepare a prison for them, in which they shall be confined for generations, where they shall not have power to propagate their species; for these pure spirits in the eternal world shall not be contaminated with their corruptions: I will take them off the earth, and I will raise up another people. And he did do it. What then? He was still merciful. When Jesus was put to death in the flesh, he remembered them. 'He went,' said Peter, 'and preached unto the spirits in prison, which sometimes were disobedient, when once the long-suffering of God waited in the days of Noah, etc.' What did he preach? The Gospel."

John Taylor, Journal of Discourses, Vol. 23, p. 61-63, April 9, 1882.

"I also say to other nations of the earth, that unless they repent of their crimes, their iniquities and abominations, their thrones will be overturned, their kingdoms and governments overthrown, and their lands made desolate. This is not only my saying, but it is the saying of those ancient prophets which they themselves profess to believe; for God will speedily have a controversy with the nations of the earth, and, as I stated before, the destroyer of the Gentiles is on his way to overthrow governments, to destroy dynasties, to lay waste thrones, kingdoms and empires, to spread abroad anarchy and desolation, and to cause war, famine and bloodshed to overspread the earth."

John Taylor, Journal of Discourses, Vol. 24, p. 199-200, June 18, 1883.

"The world, as I have said, is full of confusion, and there will be worse confusion by and by. We had a great war upon this continent some years ago; but there will yet be wars pass through these United States, and through other nations, until it will be mournful to hear the report of the bloodshed, the sorrow and trouble that will be caused thereby, as also by pestilence, famine and earthquake, and the waves of the sea heaving themselves beyond their bounds, and storms and tempests, etc.."

John W. Taylor, Collected Discourses, Vol. 5, October 7, 1898.

"I tell you my brethren and sisters and friends that God never poured out His judgments upon the children of men in any age of the world except for the breaking of the moral law."

John Taylor, The Government of God, Chapter 7.

"The Lord has given laws, and although he has not forced man to keep them, nor coerced his will, yet he has punished him for disobedience, as a father would a son. A father of a child can teach that child correct principles; but unless he controls or confines the body, he cannot force that child to observe them; he can punish him for disobedience, however, and thus exert a moral or physical influence over him. Our Father does the same. He punished the inhabitants of Sodom and Gomorrah, Babylon, Nineveh, Jerusalem, and many other cities, and will punish the world on the same principle."

John Taylor, The Government of God, Chapter 11.

"Some people talk about the world being burned up, about plagues, pestilence, famine, storm, and ruin, and all these things being instantaneous. Now it would not be just for the Lord to punish the inhabitants of the earth without warning. For if the world are ignorant of God, they cannot altogether be blamed for it; if they are made the dupes of false systems, and false principles, they cannot help it; many of them are doing as well as they can, while, as we have before stated, it would be unjust for the world to continue as it is. It would at the same time be as unjust to punish the inhabitants of the world for things that they are ignorant of, or for things over which they have no control. Before the Lord destroyed the inhabitants of the old world, he sent Enoch and Noah to warn them. Before the Lord destroyed Sodom and Gomorrah, he sent Lot into their midst. Before the Children of Israel were carried captive to Babylon, they were warned of it by the Prophets; and before Jerusalem was destroyed, the inhabitants had the testimony of our Lord, and his Disciples. And so will it be in the last days; and as it is the world that is concerned, the world will have to be warned."

John Taylor, The Government of God, Chapter 11.

"Before the Lord destroyed the old world, he directed Noah to prepare an ark; before the cities of Sodom and Gomorrah were destroyed, he told Lot to 'flee to the mountains,' before Jerusalem was destroyed, Jesus gave his disciples warning, and told the to 'flee out of it;' and before the destruction of the world, a message is sent; after this, the nations will be judged, for God is now preparing his own kingdom for his own reign, and will not be thwarted by any conflicting influence, or opposing power. The testimony of God if first to be made known, the standard is to be raised, the Gospel of the kingdom is to be preached to all nations, the world is to be warned, and then come the troubles. The whole world is in confusion, morally, politically, and religiously; but a voice was to be heard, 'come out of her, me people, that you partake not of her sins, and that ye receive not of her plagues.' John saw an angel having the everlasting Gospel to preach to every nation, kindred, people, and tongue. And afterwards there was another cried, 'Babylon is fallen.' Isaiah, after describing some of the most terrible calamities that should overtake that people, says, 'The noise of a multitude in the mountains, like as of a great people; a tumultuous noise of the kingdoms of nations gathered together: the Lord of hosts mustereth the host of the battle . . . Pangs shall take hold of them, and they shall be in pain, as a woman that travaileth.' That 'the day of the Lord cometh, cruel both with wrath and fierce anger, to lay the land desolate, and shall destroy the sinners thereof out of it; for the stars of heaven, and the constellations thereof, shall not give their light: the sun shall be darkened in his going forth; and the moon shall not cause her light to shine. And I will punish the world for their evil, and the wicked for their iniquity, and I will cause the arrogance of the proud to cease, and will lay low the haughtiness of the terrible. I will make a man more precious than fine gold.' (Isaiah 13:4-12) After enumerating may other things concerning Babylon and Assyria, as types of things to come, he says, 'This is the purpose that is purposed upon the whole earth: and this is the hand that is stretched out upon all the nations.' (Isaiah 14:26) He says again, 'Behold the Lord maketh the earth empty, and maketh it waste, and turneth it upside down, and scattereth abroad the inhabitants thereof. And it shall be, as with the people, so with the priest; as with the servant, so with his master . . . The land shall be utterly emptied, and utterly spoiled: for the Lord hath spoken his word . . . The earth also is defiled under the inhabitants thereof, because they have transgressed the laws, changed the ordinance, broken the everlasting covenant.' (Isaiah 24:1-5) From the above, it would seem that terrible judgments await the inhabitants of the world; that there will be a general destruction; the world will be full of war and confusion, the nations of the earth will be convulsed, and the wicked hurled out of it. Jesus said, when on the earth, 'For nation shall rise against nation, and kingdom against kingdom; and there shall be famine and pestilences and earthquakes in divers places; men's hearts shall fail them for fear of those things that are coming on the earth.'"

John Taylor, The Government of God, Chapter 11.

"The spirit of the Lord will be withdrawn from the nations, and after rejecting the truth, they will be left in darkness to grope their way, and being full of the spirit of wickedness, they will rage and war against each other, and finally, after dreadful struggles, plagues, pestilence, famine, etc., instigated by the powers of darkness, there will be a great gathering of the nations against Jerusalem, for they will be infuriated against its inhabitants, and mighty hosts will assemble, so that they will be like a cloud to cover the land, and the Lord will appear himself to the deliverance of his people, and the destruction of the wicked."

John Taylor, The Gospel Kingdom, p. 79-80.

"It is for us to learn this lesson and to find out that there is a God who rules in heaven, and that he manages, directs and controls the affairs of the human family. We are not our own rulers. We are all the children of God. He is our Father and has a right to direct us, not only us, but has a perfect right to direct and control the affairs of all the human family that exist upon the face of the earth for they are all his offspring. Now, he feels kindly towards them and knows what kind of people they are, and also what we are, and he would do everything he could for them even if in his almighty wisdom he has to kill them off in order to save them. He destroyed the antediluvian world on that account, because they were not filling the measure of their creation. They had corrupted themselves to such an extent that it would have been an injustice to the spirits in the eternal worlds if they had to come through such a corrupt lineage to be subject to all the trouble incident thereunto. And therefore God destroyed them. He cut off the cities of Sodom and Gomorrah in consequence of their corruptions, and by and by he will shake all the inhabitants of the earth, he will shake thrones and will overturn empires and desolate the land and lay millions of the human family in the dust. Plagues and pestilence will stalk through the earth because of the iniquities of men, because of some of these corruptions . . . namely, the perversion of the laws of nature between the sexes, and the damnable murders that exist among men. (JD, 21:113-116, November 28, 1879.)"

Wilford Woodruff-History of His Life and Labors, p. 393.

"The judgments of God will now begin to rest more fully upon this nation and will be increased upon it, year by year. Calamities will come speedily upon it and it will be visited with thunder, lightning, storms, whirlwinds, floods, pestilence, plagues, war and devouring fire; and the wicked will slay the wicked until the wicked are wasted away."

Wilford Woodruff, Journal of Discourses, Vol. 10, p. 16, July 27, 1862.

"War is only one of the troubles that the United States are going to receive; and I can further testify, that there is no nation that will escape the judgments of the Almighty. There is no ear but what has to be penetrated with the sound of the Gospel of Christ; and by-and-by the Elders of Israel will be taken from those nations where they are now preaching, and there will be another set of Missionaries sent amongst the people; there will be the voice of lightning, the noise of war, and of all those judgments which have been enumerated and prophesied of since the beginning of time, and they will go forth among the nations until the land is cleansed from the abominations that now reign upon the face of the earth."

Wilford Woodruff, Journal of Discourses, Vol. 10, p. 219, June 2, 1863.

"The Lord God has spoken through his Prophet; his words have been recorded, and he is backing up the testimony of his servants in fulfillment of his word; and the end is not yet. War and distress of nations has only just commenced, and famine and pestilence will follow on the heels of war, and there will be great mourning, and weeping, and lamentations in the land, and no power can stay the work of desolation and utter overthrow of the wicked."

Wilford Woodruff, Journal of Discourses, Vol. 14, p. 2-3, January 1, 1871.

"This is the work of the Lord, and all the Scriptures, from the beginning of Genesis to the end of Revelations point to this day as one of great interest to all the human family; although as one said of old, 'As it was in the days of Noah and of Lot, so shall it be in the days of the coming of the Son of Man.' In those days they were marrying and giving in marriage, and when Noah went into the Ark, and when Lot fled out of Sodom, the inhabitants of the earth through their unbelief were ignorant of the destruction awaiting them."

Wilford Woodruff, Journal of Discourses, Vol. 21, p. 126-127, June 6, 1880.

"What the Lord has spoken concerning our nation, and concerning the nations of the earth, notwithstanding that the unbelief of the world may be great, notwithstanding that they may reject the word of God and seek to put the servants of god to death—will all be fulfilled. War, pestilence, famine, earthquakes and storms await this generation. These calamities will overtake the world as God lives, and no power can prevent them."

Wilford Woodruff, Journal of Discourses, Vol. 22, p. 207, January 9, 1881.

"We have been under the necessity of carrying this Gospel to the generation in which we live. The Lord has never sent judgments upon any generation which we have any knowledge of until he has raised up prophets and inspired men to warn the inhabitants of the earth. This is the course the Lord has dealt with all men from the days of Father Adam to the present time."

Wilford Woodruff, Collected Discourses, Vol. 3, June 12-13, 1892.

"Behold what is taking place in the earth today! It really seems as if the day had almost dawned upon us when there is no other place of safety for the human family than the land of Zion. Three elements—fire, water and wind—seem to have been chosen to go forth on a mission to visit the nations. Cities are burned up, and floods and whirlwinds sweep away towns and villages and the inhabitants are destroyed. Are not these things all proclaimed by the revelations of God? They are, and they will come to pass."

Discourses of Wilford Woodruff, p. 230.

"God has held the angels of destruction for many years, lest they should reap down the wheat with the tares. But I want to tell you now, that those angels have left the portals of heaven, and they stand over this people and this nation now, and are hovering over the earth waiting to pour out the judgments. And from this very day they shall be poured out. Calamities and troubles are increasing in the earth, and there is a meaning to these things . . . Great changes are at our doors. The next 20 years will see mighty changes among the nations of the Earth."

The Discourses of Wilford Woodruff, p. 251.

"What is the matter with the world today? What has created this change that we see coming over the world? Why these terrible earthquakes, tornadoes, and judgments? What is the meaning of all these mighty events that are taking place? The meaning is, these angels that have been held for many years in the temple of our God have got their liberty to go out and commence their mission and their work in the earth, and they are here today in the earth. I feel bold in saying this to the Latter-day Saints. There is a meaning in these judgments. The word of the Lord cannot fall unfulfilled. If you want to know what is coming to pass, read the revelations of St. John, read the Book of Mormon and the book of Doctrine and Covenants, and these things are at our doors." (October 8, 1894.)

Teachings of Lorenzo Snow, p. 150.

"The wicked will destroy themselves. Our object is the temporal salvation of the people as much as it is for their spiritual salvation. By and by the nations will be broken up on account of their wickedness. The Latter-day Saints are not going to move upon them with their little army; they will destroy themselves with their wickedness and immorality. They will contend and quarrel one with another, state after state and nation after nation, until they are broken up, and thousands, tens of thousands, and hundreds of thousands will undoubtedly come and seek protection at the hands of the servants of God, as much so as in the days of Joseph when he was called upon to lay a plan for the salvation of the house of Israel. (14 January 1872)"

Erastus Snow, Journal of Discourses, Vol. 16, p. 206, September 14, 1873.

"Thus we learn, my friends, that the warning voice of God will go forth among the nations, and he will warn them by his servants; and by thunder, by lightning, by earthquake, by great hailstorms and by devouring fire; by the voice of judgment and by the voice of mercy; by the voice of angels and by the voice of his servants the Prophets; he will warn them by gathering out the righteous from among the wicked, and those who will not heed these warnings will be visited with sore judgments until the earth is swept as with the besom of destruction; and those who remain, in all the nations, tongues and kingdoms of the world, will heed the voice of warning and will accept the salvation sent unto them by the Lord through his servants."

Jedediah M. Grant, Journal of Discourses, Vol. 2, p. 147-148, April 2, 1854.

"The Prophet stood in his own house when he told several of us of the night the visions of heaven were opened to him, in which he saw the American continent drenched in blood, and he saw nation rising up against nation. He also saw the father shed the blood of the son, and the son the blood of the father; the mother put to death the daughter, and the daughter the mother; and natural affection forsook the hearts of the wicked; for he saw that the Spirit of God should be withdrawn from the inhabitants of the earth, in consequence of which there should be blood upon the face of the whole earth, except among the people of the Most High. The Prophet gazed upon the scene his vision presented, until his heart sickened, and he besought the Lord to close it up again.

When we hear of war in foreign lands—when we hear of the revolutions among nations afar off, we necessarily infer that distresses incident to war and the hottest of the battle will not come nigh unto us. It is natural for man to make favorable conclusions as to his own safety, when danger threatens, but the Prophet saw in the vision, that war and distress of nations will not only occur in Europe, in Asia, and in the islands of the sea, but he saw it upon the American Continent—in the region of country where he first introduced the doctrine of the Son of God; so we may look for calamity in our own borders, in our own nation, as well as in the nations of foreign climes.

Some think, because of the peculiar situation of the country of the United States—the government being so well organized, little or no difficulty will ever come upon this continent, notwithstanding the European wars. Allow me to tell you in relation to that—when the Spirit of the Lord is powerfully manifested in any of the Elders of Israel, the first thing that is presented to his mind is the shedding of the blood of the Prophet, and those who did the deed.

It is no matter how much they deal in compromised measures, or how often they try to adjust difficulties that thicken around them—it is a stern fact that the people of the United States have shed the blood of the Prophets, driven out the Saints of God, rejected the Priesthood, and set at naught the holy Gospel; and the result of rejecting the Gospel has been, in every age, a visitation from the chastening hand of the Almighty—which chastisement will be administered in proportion to the magnitude and enormity of their crimes."

George Q. Cannon, Deseret Evening News, Sept. 21, 1895.

"The wicked will be destroyed, according to the words of all the Prophets, and the righteous only will survive. There will be a cleansing of the earth from the wicked as great in its place as the cleansing of the earth by the flood that came in the days of Noah, though this time it will be by fire. Malachi says the day will come when the wicked shall be ashes under the soles of the feet of the righteous.

Already, as I have said, you can see the operation of this cleansing process among us. The wicked are gradually being purged from among us. It is not very perceptible; we have got to think about it and call it to mind to become aware of it; but we can become aware of it if we will reflect. And this will be more and more the case as the power of God increases and the responsibility of the Latter-day Saints becomes greater.

Therefore, I am looking for destructions and for judgments; I am looking for the cleansing power of God among us as well as among the nations of the earth, in order that the foundation of that great and glorious time shall be laid when Jesus shall reign upon the earth."

George Q. Cannon, Juvenile Instructor, Vol. 18, p. 200, July 1, 1883.

"So with all the calamities that are taking place. They are attributed to every cause but the true one. For instance, these dreadful cyclones of which we read in every issue of the daily papers which are so destructive in their effects upon life and property are undoubtedly a part of those judgments which God inspired His servants to foretell. But who, outside of the members of this Church, looks upon them as a fulfillment of the word of God? Who thinks that the predictions of the Elders of this Church are being fulfilled in these destructive storms? Who imagines that the shedding of the blood of a mighty Prophet and of faithful followers of Jesus Christ, or the mobbing and persecuting and driving out of the people of God, has anything to do with the occurrence of these dreadful disasters? Yet, they are a part of those calamities which the Lord has said He will pour out upon the people if they do not repent."

George Q. Cannon, Juvenile Instructor, Vol. 26, p. 693, Nov. 15, 1891.

"The time is not far distant when great judgments will be poured out upon the wicked inhabitants of the earth. Every Prophet who has looked forward to our day has seen and predicted that the wicked would be destroyed. Their destruction means the destruction of Satan's power. The righteous will be left, and because of their righteousness the Lord will have mercy upon them; they, exercising their agency in the right direction, will bring down His blessings upon them to such an extent that Satan will be bound."

George Q. Cannon, Gospel Truth, Vol. 1, p. 47.

"The scriptures inform us that there will be earthquakes and other terrible calamities given unto man for the accomplishment of the purposes of the Almighty; but they do not lead us to expect that repentance and an acknowledgment of the hand and the power of the Lord, on the part of mankind, will follow these visitations. They intimate, on the contrary, that feelings directly the opposite of these will be indulged in and that men will feel more like cursing God and dying than repenting."

George Q. Cannon, Journal of Discourses, Vol. 25, p. 283-285, August 24, 1884.

"When the wickedness and corruptions of men shall have provoked the anger of the Almighty in these latter days as they did in the days before the flood, the Lord will come out of His hiding place to vex the nations of the earth, and then there will be a time of trouble, a time of sorrow such as has not been from the beginning of the world, and we are told, never shall be again. Men may think they can trample upon human rights and upon correct principles, and do things which are contrary to the law and order of God, and to the principles of truth, integrity, equity, justice, and righteousness; but they cannot do this with impunity, for the Lord has said that He will smite the wicked, and with the breath of His nostrils He will slay them. The earth shall be emptied of the wicked, and a place prepared, in the due time of the Lord, for those who fear Him, as He has designed from before the foundation of the world."

George Q. Cannon, Collected Discourses, Vol. 1, June 16, 1889.

"We are living in the last days. There is every indication that the words of the Lord are being fulfilled concerning judgments and calamities, wars and destructions. These things must come, and they will not be poured out without cause. God never punishes a people without first sending some message of warning to them. He never did in ancient days. . . .He has sent His messengers now to the nations of the earth . . .That day is coming and the judgments will be poured out. But will they be poured out without cause? No, they will not. It is because men reject God; it is because they will not accept the salvation that He proffers to them; it is because they will harden their hearts and reject the testimonies they might receive—it is on this account that these calamities will come. Yet when they do come those who witness them will not perceive in them the hand of God, and they will ask for signs. This was the characteristic of the generation in which the Savior lived. They wanted a sign. Although He was going among the people performing great and mighty works, they asked him for a sign. . . .So it is always. Men ask for signs, and yet there are the greatest signs taking place at the present time. If they would but open their eyes to see and their hearts to understand they might perceive that the words of the Prophets are being fulfilled."

Hyrum M. Smith, Doctrine and Covenants Commentary, Sec. 45, p. 268-269.

"The expression 'signs in the heavens', such as the darkening of sun and moon, and the falling of stars, when used metaphorically, means the overthrow of kingdoms and the fall of potentates. But the last days will also be marked by strange phenomena in the sky."

Hyrum M. Smith, Doctrine and Covenants Commentary, Sec. 87, p. 537–538.

"Not only by sword and cannon were the inhabitants of the earth to be called upon to mourn because of their iniquity, but even the elements were to become angry, and by famine, plague, and the vivid lightnings and thunder, earthquakes and other disturbances, the inhabitants of the earth are to feel the wrath, and indignation, and chastening hand of the Almighty. We have discovered in another revelation (Sec. 43) that the thunders shall utter their voices from the ends of the earth in a manner never witnessed before. This will come after the testimonies of the elders of Israel have been declared."

George Albert Smith, Conference Report, April 1950, p. 169.

"It will not be long until calamities will overtake the human family unless there is speedy repentance. It will not be long before those who are scattered over the face of the earth by millions will die like flies because of what will come."

Charles W. Penrose, Millennial Star, Vol. 21, p. 582, September 10, 1859.

"Through the rejection of this Gospel, which `shall be preached to all the world as a witness' of the coming of Christ, the world will increase in confusion, doubt, and horrible strife. As the upright in heart, the meek of the earth, withdraw from their midst, so will the Spirit of God also be withdrawn from them. The darkness upon their minds in relation to eternal things will become blacker, nations will engage in frightful and bloody warfare, the crimes which are now becoming so frequent will be of continual occurrence, the ties that bind together families and kindred will be disregarded and violated, the passions of human nature will be put to the vilest uses, the very elements around will seem to be affected by the national and social convulsions that will agitate the world, and storms, earthquakes, and appalling disasters by sea and land will cause terror and dismay among the people; new diseases will silently eat their ghastly way through the ranks of the wicked; the earth, soaked with gore and defiled with the filthiness of her inhabitants, will begin to withhold her fruits in their season; the waves of the sea will heave themselves beyond their bounds, and all things will be in commotion; and in the midst of all these calamities, the master-minds among nations will be taken away, and fear will take hold of the hearts of all men."

Orson F. Whitney, Saturday Night Thoughts, p. 187.

"*The Divine Purpose*—And what is the intent—the ultimate purpose of it all? Destruction? No, a thousand times no, except in so far as destruction must precede reconstruction, and is necessary to preserve what is worth preserving. The world's welfare is the object in view. God's wrath, however fiercely it burns, is not on the same plane with petty human anger. His work and his glory is 'to bring to pass the immortality and eternal life of man.' If, in the process, he uses the powers of destruction, as well as those of construction—for 'all power' is his, 'in heaven and in earth'—it is because such a course has become necessary and is for the best. However severe his chastisements, we can rest assured that hatred of humanity has no place in the heart of Him who 'so loved the world' that he 'gave his Only Begotten Son' to save it from eternal damnation.

Why Calamities Come—Calamities do not come upon the world merely to scourge the wicked and avenge the wrongs of the righteous. The primal aim of divine punishment is to purify, and if possible save those upon whom the 'Great Avenger' lays a chastening hand. His object is to bring sinners to repentance, to throw down the barriers that prevent men from coming to Christ, and turn into the upward path those bent upon pursuing the downward road. The Gospel saves all who are willing to be saved, and who show their willingness by their obedience, their faith by their works. It also aims to save the unwilling and disobedient—here if possible, and if not here, then hereafter. Wars and other woes are sent to put a stop to men's evil practices, lest they add sin to sin and pile up guilt to their greater condemnation. To be swept off the earth and ministered to in the spirit world, is not the worst fate that can befall the wicked. Omnipotence wields the powers of destruction in such a way as to make of them instruments of salvation. It may seem cruel, but in reality it is kind."

Joseph Fielding Smith, The Signs of the Times, p. 96.

"Does this sound terrible? The Lord is merciful, always merciful, and do you not think it is a merciful act, if people become so filled with disease and corruption through sin, and when they have turned away from God, and they are teaching their posterity all the evil which they themselves know, for the Lord to remove them from the face of the earth so they will not contaminate the generations yet to come and lead them to eternal destruction? What is life, anyway? We are here for a little while in this world, to receive experience. We are taught to keep the commandments of the Lord. We are here to be tried and proved to see what kind of stuff we are made of; and here is a people rebellious, and filled with corruption brought upon them through iniquity. Should they be permitted to corrupt the souls of unborn generations which would come through their lineage? Should they be permitted to rob their posterity of the greatest gift of God—eternal life? Is it not better to sweep the wicked and cleanse the earth rather than to bring eternal destruction upon thousands, yes millions, and have them shut out of the kingdom of God? In the destruction of the wicked, God is merciful both to them and to the unborn generations."

Joseph Fielding Smith Jr., Doctrines of Salvation, Vol. 3, p. 7.

"After the testimony of the elders will come wrath and indignation upon the people. . . .All things shall be in commotion . . .These things shall follow the testimony of the elders . . . when the people of the world reject them and drive them from their borders."

Joseph Fielding Smith Jr., Doctrines of Salvation, Vol. 3, p. 29.

"Now, that was a calamity which came upon the world, when the Lord decreed that he would withhold his spirit from the inhabitants of the earth. He had no reference to the Holy Ghost, because they never had the gift of the Holy Ghost, but he had reference to the light of truth, or Spirit of Christ, which would lead them to the truth, if they would heed it. This spirit he was withdrawing from them because of their wickedness, and the withdrawal of his spirit would bring upon them these calamities—the pestilences, the plagues, and all the rest . . . including bloodshed, and war."

Joseph Fielding Smith Jr., Doctrines of Salvation, Vol. 3, p. 42-43.

"These things the Lord said through his Prophet in warnings that have come to the people of this nation and other lands. The Lord says the wicked will not repent, and because they will not repent he has decreed wars to come upon them, and the wicked shall slay the wicked, and thus the earth will be cleansed, as we read in the 24th chapter of Isaiah, until there shall be few men left."

Ezra Taft Benson, Conference Report, Ensign, May 1989, p. 4-7.

"The Doctrine and Covenants tells us that the Book of Mormon is the 'record of a fallen people.' (D&C 20:9) Why did they fall? This is one of the major messages of the Book of Mormon. Mormon gives the answer in the closing chapters of the book in these words: 'Behold, the pride of this nation, or the people of the Nephites, hath proven their destruction.' (Moroni 8:27.) And then, lest we miss that momentous Book of Mormon message from that fallen people, the Lord warns us in the Doctrine and Covenants, 'Beware of pride, lest ye become as the Nephites of old.' (D&C 38:39.) . . .

The scriptures abound with evidences of the severe consequences of the sin of pride to individuals, groups, cities, and nations. 'Pride goeth before destruction' (Proverbs 16:18). It destroyed the Nephite nation and the city of Sodom . . .

Pride results in secret combinations which are built up to get power, gain and glory of the world. This fruit of the sin of pride, namely secret combinations, brought down both the Jaredite and the Nephite civilizations and has been and will yet be the cause of the fall of many nations."

Teachings of Ezra Taft Benson, p. 73-74.

"The voice of warning is unto all people by the mouths of His servants (see D&C 1:4). If this voice is not heeded, the angels of destruction will increasingly go forth, and the chastening hand of Almighty God will be felt upon the nations, as decreed, until a full end thereof will be the result. Wars, devastation, and untold suffering will be your lot except you turn unto the Lord in humble repentance. Destruction even more terrible and far-reaching than attended the last great war will come with certainty unless rulers and people alike repent and cease their evil and godless ways. God will not be mocked (D&C 63:58). He will not permit the sins of sexual immorality, secret murderous combinations, the killing of the unborn, and disregard for all His holy commandments and the messages of His servants to go unheeded without grievous punishment for such wickedness. The nations of the world cannot endure in sin. The way of escape is clear. The immutable laws of God remain steadfastly in the heavens above. When men and nations refuse to abide by them, the penalty must follow. They will be wasted away. Sin demands punishment. (This Nation Shall Endure, p. 111.)"

Marion G. Romney, Conference Report, April 1950, p. 83.

"It is only a question of time, unless people repent of their sins, until war will come, not only war but pestilence will come, until the human family disappears from the world. There is only one way to enjoy peace and happiness in this world,—repent and turn to the Lord. That is the only way."

Bruce R. McConkie, Conference Report, Ensign, May 1979, p. 92-93.

"Be it remembered that tribulations lie ahead. There will be wars in one nation and kingdom after another until war is poured out upon all nations and two hundred million men of war mass their armaments at Armageddon. Peace has been taken from the earth, the angels of destruction have begun their work, and their swords shall not be sheathed until the Prince of Peace comes to destroy the wicked and usher in the great Millennium.

There will be earthquakes and floods and famines. The waves of the sea shall heave themselves beyond their bounds, the clouds shall withhold their rain, and the crops of the earth shall wither and die. There will be plagues and pestilence and disease and death. An overflowing scourge shall cover the earth and a desolating sickness shall sweep the land. Flies shall take hold of the inhabitants of the earth, and maggots shall come in upon them (see D&C 29:14-20). 'Their flesh shall fall from off their bones, and their eyes from their sockets' (D&C 29:19).

Bands of Gadianton robbers will infest every nation, immorality and murder and crime will increase, and it will seem as though every man's hand is against his brother."

Also see Bruce R. McConkie, The Millennial Messiah, p. 380-381.

Bruce R. McConkie, The Millennial Messiah, p. 385.

"'And the shapes of the locusts were like unto horses prepared unto battle; and on their heads were as it were crowns like gold, and their faces were as the faces of men. And they had hair as the hair of women, and their teeth were as the teeth of lions. And they had breastplates, as it were breastplates of iron; and the sound of their wings was the sound of chariots of many horses running to battle. And they had tails like unto scorpions, and there were stings in their tails: and their power was to hurt men five months.'

John is seeing warfare and armaments so foreign to his experience that he has no language to describe to the people of his day the horror and destructive power of it all."

See Bruce R. McConkie, The Millennial Messiah, p. 411-412.

"From this account (D&C 133:49) we conclude that the stars shall fall from heaven at the time of his arrival rather than before. . . .It will seem to men on earth as though the stars . . . are falling because the earth reels. The great fixed stars will continue in their assigned orbits and spheres."

Bruce R. McConkie, A New Witness for the Articles of Faith, p. 637.

"Near to and almost concurrent with the Second Coming, there will be certain promised signs and wonders that exceed and excel any like events of the past. These may appropriately be collated under the following headings: (1) Manifestations of blood, and fire, and vapors of smoke. (2) The sun shall be darkened and the moon turned into blood. (3) The stars shall hurl themselves from heaven. (4) The rainbow shall cease to appear in the mists and rains of heaven. (5) The sign of the Son of Man shall make its appearance. (6) A mighty earthquake, beyond anything of the past, shall shake the very foundations of the earth."

SCRIPTURAL REFERENCES

Isaiah 6:9-13

9 And he said, Go, and tell this people, Hear ye indeed, but understand not; and see ye indeed, but perceive not.

10 Make the heart of this people fat, and make their ears heavy, and shut their eyes; lest they see with their eyes, and hear with their ears, and understand with their heart, and convert, and be healed.

11 Then said I, Lord, how long? And he answered, Until the cities be wasted without inhabitant, and the houses without man, and the land be utterly desolate,

12 And the LORD have removed men far away, and there be a great forsaking in the midst of the land.

13 But yet in it shall be a tenth, and it shall return, and shall be eaten: as a teil tree, and as an oak, whose substance is in them, when they cast their leaves: so the holy seed shall be the substance thereof.

Isaiah 10:17-20

17 And the light of Israel shall be for a fire, and his Holy One for a flame: and it shall burn and devour his thorns and his briers in one day;

18 And shall consume the glory of his forest, and of his fruitful field, both soul and body: and they shall be as when a standardbearer fainteth.

19 And the rest of the trees of his forest shall be few, that a child may write them.

20 ¶ And it shall come to pass in that day, [that] the remnant of Israel, and such as are escaped of the house of Jacob, shall no more again stay upon him that smote them; but shall stay upon the LORD, the Holy One of Israel, in truth.

Isaiah 10:22-27

22 For though thy people Israel be as the sand of the sea, yet a remnant of them shall return: the consumption decreed shall overflow with righteousness.

23 For the Lord GOD of hosts shall make a consumption, even determined, in the midst of all the land.

24 Therefore thus saith the Lord GOD of hosts, O my people that dwellest in Zion, be not afraid of the Assyrian: he shall smite thee with a rod, and shall lift up his staff against thee, after the manner of Egypt.

25 For yet a very little while, and the indignation shall cease, and mine anger in their destruction.

26 And the LORD of hosts shall stir up a scourge for him according to the slaughter of Midian at the rock of Oreb: and as his rod was upon the sea, so shall he lift it up after the manner of Egypt.

27 And it shall come to pass in that day, that his burden shall be taken away from off thy shoulder, and his yoke from off thy neck, and the yoke shall be destroyed because of the anointing.

Isaiah 13:4-11

4 The noise of a multitude in the mountains, like as of a great people; a tumultuous noise of the kingdoms of nations gathered together: the LORD of hosts mustereth the host of the battle.

5 They come from a far country, from the end of heaven, even the LORD, and the weapons of his indignation, to destroy the whole land.

6 Howl ye; for the day of the LORD is at hand; it shall come as a destruction from the Almighty.

7 Therefore shall all hands be faint, and every man's heart shall melt:

8 And they shall be afraid: pangs and sorrows shall take hold of them; they shall be in pain as a woman that travaileth: they shall be amazed one at another; their faces shall be as flames.

9 Behold, the day of the LORD cometh, cruel both with wrath and fierce anger, to lay the land desolate: and he shall destroy the sinners thereof out of it.

10 For the stars of heaven and the constellations thereof shall not give their light: the sun shall be darkened in his going forth, and the moon shall not cause her light to shine.

11 And I will punish the world for their evil, and the wicked for their iniquity; and I will cause the arrogancy of the proud to cease, and will lay low the haughtiness of the terrible.

Isaiah 18:7

7 In that time shall the present be brought unto the LORD of hosts of a people scattered and peeled, and from a people terrible from their beginning hitherto; a nation meted out and trodden under foot, whose land the rivers have spoiled, to the place of the name of the LORD of hosts, the mount Zion.

Isaiah 24:1-6

1 Behold, the LORD maketh the earth empty, and maketh it waste, and turneth it upside down, and scattereth abroad the inhabitants thereof.

2 And it shall be, as with the people, so with the priest; as with the servant, so with his master; as with the maid, so with her mistress; as with the buyer, so with the seller; as with the lender, so with the borrower; as with the taker of usury, so with the giver of usury to him.

3 The land shall be utterly emptied, and utterly spoiled: for the LORD hath spoken this word.

4 The earth mourneth and fadeth away, the world languisheth and fadeth away, the haughty people of the earth do languish.

5 The earth also is defiled under the inhabitants thereof; because they have transgressed the laws, changed the ordinance, broken the everlasting covenant.

6 Therefore hath the curse devoured the earth, and they that dwell therein are desolate: therefore the inhabitants of the earth are burned, and few men left.

Isaiah 34:2-5

2 For the indignation of the LORD is upon all nations, and his fury upon all their armies: he hath utterly destroyed them, he hath delivered them to the slaughter.

3 Their slain also shall be cast out, and their stink shall come up out of their carcases, and the mountains shall be melted with their blood.

4 And all the host of heaven shall be dissolved, and the heavens shall be rolled together as a scroll: and all their host shall fall down, as the leaf falleth off from the vine, and as a falling fig from the fig tree.

5 For my sword shall be bathed in heaven: behold, it shall come down upon Idumea, and upon the people of my curse, to judgment.

Isaiah 51:6

6 Lift up your eyes to the heavens, and look upon the earth beneath: for the heavens shall vanish away like smoke, and the earth shall wax old like a garment, and they that dwell therein shall die in like manner: but my salvation shall be for ever, and my righteousness shall not be abolished.

Isaiah 66:15-16

15 For, behold, the LORD will come with fire, and with his chariots like a whirlwind, to render his anger with fury, and his rebuke with flames of fire.

16 For by fire and by his sword will the LORD plead with all flesh: and the slain of the LORD shall be many.

Jeremiah 25:30-33

30 Therefore prophesy thou against them all these words, and say unto them, The LORD shall roar from on high, and utter his voice from his holy habitation; he shall mightily roar upon his habitation; he shall give a shout, as they that tread the grapes, against all the inhabitants of the earth.

31 A noise shall come even to the ends of the earth; for the LORD hath a controversy with the nations, he will plead with all flesh; he will give them that are wicked to the sword, saith the LORD.

32 Thus saith the LORD of hosts, Behold, evil shall go forth from nation to nation, and a great whirlwind shall be raised up from the coasts of the earth.

33 And the slain of the LORD shall be at that day from one end of the earth even unto the other end of the earth: they shall not be lamented, neither gathered, nor buried; they shall be dung upon the ground.

Jeremiah 25:37-38

37 And the peaceable habitations are cut down because of the fierce anger of the LORD.

38 He hath forsaken his covert, as the lion: for their land is desolate because of the fierceness of the oppressor, and because of his fierce anger.

Jeremiah 46:20-21

20 Egypt is like a very fair heifer, but destruction cometh; it cometh out of the north.

21 Also her hired men are in the midst of her like fatted bullocks; for they also are turned back, and are fled away together: they did not stand, because the day of their calamity was come upon them, and the time of their visitation.

Jeremiah 46:24

24 The daughter of Egypt shall be confounded; she shall be delivered into the hand of the people of the north.

Jeremiah 51:6

6 Flee out of the midst of Babylon, and deliver every man his soul: be not cut off in her iniquity; for this is the time of the LORD's vengeance; he will render unto her a recompence.

Ezekiel 6:11-12

11 Thus saith the Lord GOD; Smite with thine hand, and stamp with thy foot, and say, Alas for all the evil abominations of the house of Israel! for they shall fall by the sword, by the famine, and by the pestilence.

12 He that is far off shall die of the pestilence; and he that is near shall fall by the sword; and he that remaineth and is besieged shall die by the famine: thus will I accomplish my fury upon them.

Joel 2:30-32

30 And I will shew wonders in the heavens and in the earth, blood, and fire, and pillars of smoke.

31 The sun shall be turned into darkness, and the moon into blood, before the great and the terrible day of the Lord come.

32 And it shall come to pass, that whosoever shall call on the name of the Lord shall be delivered: for in mount Zion and in Jerusalem shall be deliverance, as the Lord hath said, and in the remnant whom the Lord shall call.

Micah 1:3-4

3 For, behold, the LORD cometh forth out of his place, and will come down, and tread upon the high places of the earth.

4 And the mountains shall be molten under him, and the valleys shall be cleft, as wax before the fire, [and] as the waters [that are] poured down a steep place.

Zephaniah 3:6-8

6 I have cut off the nations: their towers are desolate; I made their streets waste, that none passeth by: their cities are destroyed, so that there is no man, that there is none inhabitant.

7 I said, Surely thou wilt fear me, thou wilt receive instruction; so their dwelling should not be cut off, howsoever I punished them: but they rose early, and corrupted all their doings.

8 Therefore wait ye upon me, saith the LORD, until the day that I rise up to the prey: for my determination is to gather the nations, that I may assemble the kingdoms, to pour upon them mine indignation, even all my fierce anger: for all the earth shall be devoured with the fire of my jealousy.

Haggai 2:6-7

6 For thus saith the LORD of hosts; Yet once, it [is] a little while, and I will shake the heavens, and the earth, and the sea, and the dry [land];

7 And I will shake all nations, and the desire of all nations shall come: and I will fill this house with glory, saith the LORD of hosts.

Malachi 4:1-3

1 For, behold, the day cometh, that shall burn as an oven; and all the proud, yea, and all that do wickedly, shall be stubble: and the day that cometh shall burn them up, saith the LORD of hosts, that it shall leave them neither root nor branch.

2 But unto you that fear my name shall the Sun of righteousness arise with healing in his wings; and ye shall go forth, and grow up as calves of the stall.

3 And ye shall tread down the wicked; for they shall be ashes under the soles of your feet in the day that I shall do this, saith the LORD of hosts.

JST Matthew 1:28-30

28 And they shall hear of wars, and rumors of wars.

29 Behold I speak for mine elect's sake; for nation shall rise against nation, and kingdom against kingdom; there shall be famines, and pestilences, and earthquakes, in divers places.

30 And again, because iniquity shall abound, the love of men shall wax cold; but he that shall not be overcome, the same shall be saved.

JST Matthew 1:33-36

33 And immediately after the tribulation of those days, the sun shall be darkened, and the moon shall not give her light, and the stars shall fall from heaven, and the powers of heaven shall be shaken.

34 Verily, I say unto you, this generation, in which these things shall be shown forth, shall not pass away until all I have told you shall be fulfilled.

35 Although, the days will come, that heaven and earth shall pass away; yet my words shall not pass away, but all shall be fulfilled.

36 And, as I said before, after the tribulation of those days, and the powers of the heavens shall be shaken, then shall appear the sign of the Son of Man in heaven, and then shall all the tribes of the earth mourn; and they shall see the Son of Man coming in the clouds of heaven, with power and great glory;

Mark 13:8

8 For nation shall rise against nation, and kingdom against kingdom: and there shall be earthquakes in divers places, and there shall be famines and troubles: these are the beginnings of sorrows.

Mark 13:24-26

24 But in those days, after that tribulation, the sun shall be darkened, and the moon shall not give her light,

25 And the stars of heaven shall fall, and the powers that are in heaven shall be shaken.

26 And then shall they see the Son of man coming in the clouds with great power and glory.

JST Mark 13:32-38

32 And they shall hear of wars and rumors of wars. Behold, I speak unto you for mine elect's sake.

33 For nation shall rise against nation, and kingdom against kingdom;

34 There shall be famines, and pestilences, and earthquakes in divers places.

35 And again, because iniquity shall abound, the love of men shall wax cold; but he who shall not be overcome, the same shall be saved.

36 And again this gospel of the kingdom shall be preached in all the world, for a witness unto all nations, and then shall the end come, or the destruction of the wicked.

37 And again shall the abomination of desolation, spoken of by Daniel the prophet, be fulfilled.

38 And immediately after the tribulation of those days, the sun shall be darkened, and the moon shall

not give her light, and the stars shall fall from heaven, and the powers of heaven shall be shaken. JST

Luke 21:9-11

9 But when ye shall hear of wars and commotions, be not terrified: for these things must first come to pass; but the end is not by and by.

10 Then said he unto them, Nation shall rise against nation, and kingdom against kingdom:

11 And great earthquakes shall be in divers places, and famines, and pestilences; and fearful sights and great signs shall there be from heaven.

JST Luke 21:24-25

24 Now these things he spake unto them, concerning the destruction of Jerusalem. And then his disciples asked him, saying, Master, tell us concerning thy coming?

25 And he answered them, and said, In the generation in which the times of the Gentiles shall be fulfilled, there shall be signs in the sun, and in the moon, and in the stars; and upon the earth distress of nations with perplexity, like the sea and the waves roaring. The earth also shall be troubled, and the waters of the great deep;

Luke 21:26

26 Men's hearts failing them for fear, and for looking after those things which are coming on the earth: for the powers of heaven shall be shaken.

Acts 2:19-21

19 And I will shew wonders in heaven above, and signs in the earth beneath; blood, and fire, and vapour of smoke:

20 The sun shall be turned into darkness, and the moon into blood, before that great and notable day of the Lord come:

21 And it shall come to pass, that whosoever shall call on the name of the Lord shall be saved.

1 Thessalonians 5:2-6

2 For yourselves know perfectly that the day of the Lord so cometh as a thief in the night.

3 For when they shall say, Peace and safety; then sudden destruction cometh upon them, as travail upon a woman with child; and they shall not escape.

4 But ye, brethren, are not in darkness, that that day should overtake you as a thief.

5 Ye are all the children of light, and the children of the day: we are not of the night, nor of darkness.

6 Therefore let us not sleep, as do others; but let us watch and be sober.

JST 2 Thess 2:8

8 And then shall that wicked one be revealed, whom the Lord shall consume with the spirit of his mouth, and shall destroy with the brightness of his coming.

Revelation 6:12-17

12 And I beheld when he had opened the sixth seal, and, lo, there was a great earthquake; and the sun became black as sackcloth of hair, and the moon became as blood;

13 And the stars of heaven fell unto the earth, even as a fig tree casteth her untimely figs, when she is shaken of a mighty wind.

14 And the heaven departed as a scroll when it is rolled together; and every mountain and island were moved out of their places.

15 And the kings of the earth, and the great men, and the rich men, and the chief captains, and the mighty men, and every bondman, and every free man, hid themselves in the dens and in the rocks of the mountains;

16 And said to the mountains and rocks, Fall on us, and hide us from the face of him that sitteth on the throne, and from the wrath of the Lamb:

17 For the great day of his wrath is come; and who shall be able to stand?

Revelation 8:Heading-13

John sees fire and desolation poured out during the seventh seal and preceding the Second Coming.

1 And when he had opened the seventh seal, there was silence in heaven about the space of half an hour.

2 And I saw the seven angels which stood before God; and to them were given seven trumpets.

3 And another angel came and stood at the altar, having a golden censer; and there was given unto him much incense, that he should offer it with the prayers of all saints upon the golden altar which was before the throne.

4 And the smoke of the incense, which came with the prayers of the saints, ascended up before God out of the angel's hand.

5 And the angel took the censer, and filled it with fire of the altar, and cast it into the earth: and there were voices, and thunderings, and lightnings, and an earthquake.

6 And the seven angels which had the seven trumpets prepared themselves to sound.

7 The first angel sounded, and there followed hail and fire mingled with blood, and they were cast upon the earth: and the third part of trees was burnt up, and all green grass was burnt up.

8 And the second angel sounded, and as it were a great mountain burning with fire was cast into the sea: and the third part of the sea became blood;

9 And the third part of the creatures which were in the sea, and had life, died; and the third part of the ships were destroyed.

10 And the third angel sounded, and there fell a great star from heaven, burning as it were a lamp, and it fell upon the third part of the rivers, and upon the fountains of waters;

11 And the name of the star is called Wormwood: and the third part of the waters became wormwood; and many men died of the waters, because they were made bitter.

12 And the fourth angel sounded, and the third part of the sun was smitten, and the third part of the moon, and the third part of the stars; so as the third part of them was darkened, and the day shone not for a third part of it, and the night likewise.

13 And I beheld, and heard an angel flying through the midst of heaven, saying with a loud voice, Woe, woe, woe, to the inhabiters of the earth by reason of the other voices of the trumpet of the three angels, which are yet to sound!

Destruction

Revelation 11:18

18 And the nations were angry, and thy wrath is come, and the time of the dead, that they should be judged, and that thou shouldest give reward unto thy servants the prophets, and to the saints, and them that fear thy name, small and great; and shouldest destroy them which destroy the earth.

Revelation 15:1-8

1 And I saw another sign in heaven, great and marvellous, seven angels having the seven last plagues; for in them is filled up the wrath of God.

2 And I saw as it were a sea of glass mingled with fire: and them that had gotten the victory over the beast, and over his image, and over his mark, and over the number of his name, stand on the sea of glass, having the harps of God.

3 And they sing the song of Moses the servant of God, and the song of the Lamb, saying, Great and marvellous are thy works, Lord God Almighty; just and true are thy ways, thou King of saints.

4 Who shall not fear thee, O Lord, and glorify thy name? for thou only art holy: for all nations shall come and worship before thee; for thy judgments are made manifest.

5 And after that I looked, and, behold, the temple of the tabernacle of the testimony in heaven was opened:

6 And the seven angels came out of the temple, having the seven plagues, clothed in pure and white linen, and having their breasts girded with golden girdles.

7 And one of the four beasts gave unto the seven angels seven golden vials full of the wrath of God, who liveth for ever and ever.

8 And the temple was filled with smoke from the glory of God, and from his power; and no man was able to enter into the temple, till the seven plagues of the seven angels were fulfilled.

Revelation 18:4-10

4 And I heard another voice from heaven, saying, Come out of her, my people, that ye be not partakers of her sins, and that ye receive not of her plagues.

5 For her sins have reached unto heaven, and God hath remembered her iniquities.

6 Reward her even as she rewarded you, and double unto her double according to her works: in the cup which she hath filled fill to her double.

7 How much she hath glorified herself, and lived deliciously, so much torment and sorrow give her: for she saith in her heart, I sit a queen, and am no widow, and shall see no sorrow.

8 Therefore shall her plagues come in one day, death, and mourning, and famine; and she shall be utterly burned with fire: for strong is the Lord God who judgeth her.

9 And the kings of the earth, who have committed fornication and lived deliciously with her, shall bewail her, and lament for her, when they shall see the smoke of her burning,

10 Standing afar off for the fear of her torment, saying, Alas, alas, that great city Babylon, that mighty city! for in one hour is thy judgment come.

2 Nephi 6:14-15

14 And behold, according to the words of the prophet, the Messiah will set himself again the second

time to recover them; wherefore, he will manifest himself unto them in power and great glory, unto the destruction of their enemies, when that day cometh when they shall believe in him; and none will he destroy that believe in him.

15 And they that believe not in him shall be destroyed, both by fire, and by tempest, and by earthquakes, and by bloodsheds, and by pestilence, and by famine. And they shall know that the Lord is God, the Holy One of Israel.

2 Nephi 25:9

9 And as one generation hath been destroyed among the Jews because of iniquity, even so have they been destroyed from generation to generation according to their iniquities; and never hath any of them been destroyed save it were foretold them by the prophets of the Lord.

2 Nephi 26:5-6

5 And they that kill the prophets, and the saints, the depths of the earth shall swallow them up, saith the Lord of Hosts; and mountains shall cover them, and whirlwinds shall carry them away, and buildings shall fall upon them and crush them to pieces and grind them to powder.

6 And they shall be visited with thunderings, and lightnings, and earthquakes, and all manner of destructions, for the fire of the anger of the Lord shall be kindled against them, and they shall be as stubble, and the day that cometh shall consume them, saith the Lord of Hosts.

2 Nephi 26:10-11

10 And when these things have passed away a speedy destruction cometh unto my people; for, notwithstanding the pains of my soul, I have seen it; wherefore, I know that it shall come to pass; and they sell themselves for naught; for, for the reward of their pride and their foolishness they shall reap destruction; for because they yield unto the devil and choose works of darkness rather than light, therefore they must go down to hell.

11 For the Spirit of the Lord will not always strive with man. And when the Spirit ceaseth to strive with man then cometh speedy destruction, and this grieveth my soul.

2 Nephi 26:18-19

18 Wherefore, as those who have been destroyed have been destroyed speedily; and the multitude of their terrible ones shall be as chaff that passeth away—yea, thus saith the Lord God: It shall be at an instant, suddenly—

19 And it shall come to pass, that those who have dwindled in unbelief shall be smitten by the hand of the Gentiles.

2 Nephi 27:1-2

1 But, behold, in the last days, or in the days of the Gentiles—yea, behold all the nations of the Gentiles and also the Jews, both those who shall come upon this land and those who shall be upon other lands, yea, even upon all the lands of the earth, behold, they will be drunken with iniquity and all manner of abominations—

2 And when that day shall come they shall be visited of the Lord of Hosts, with thunder and with

earthquake, and with a great noise, and with storm, and with tempest, and with the flame of devouring fire.

2 Nephi 30:1-2

1 And now behold, my beloved brethren, I would speak unto you; for I, Nephi, would not suffer that ye should suppose that ye are more righteous than the Gentiles shall be. For behold, except ye shall keep the commandments of God ye shall all likewise perish; and because of the words which have been spoken ye need not suppose that the Gentiles are utterly destroyed.

2 For behold, I say unto you that as many of the Gentiles as will repent are the covenant people of the Lord; and as many of the Jews as will not repent shall be cast off; for the Lord covenanteth with none save it be with them that repent and believe in his Son, who is the Holy One of Israel.

Mosiah 29:27

27 And if the time comes that the voice of the people doth choose iniquity, then is the time that the judgments of God will come upon you; yea, then is the time he will visit you with great destruction even as he has hitherto visited this land.

Alma 1:12

12 But Alma said unto him: Behold, this is the first time that priestcraft has been introduced among this people. And behold, thou art not only guilty of priestcraft, but hast endeavored to enforce it by the sword; and were priestcraft to be enforced among this people it would prove their entire destruction.

Alma 9:12-13

12 Behold, now I say unto you that he commandeth you to repent; and except ye repent, ye can in nowise inherit the kingdom of God. But behold, this is not all—he has commanded you to repent, or he will utterly destroy you from off the face of the earth; yea, he will visit you in his anger, and in his fierce anger he will not turn away.

13 Behold, do ye not remember the words which he spake unto Lehi, saying that: Inasmuch as ye shall keep my commandments, ye shall prosper in the land? And again it is said that: Inasmuch as ye will not keep my commandments ye shall be cut off from the presence of the Lord.

Alma 10:22-23

22 Yea, and I say unto you that if it were not for the prayers of the righteous, who are now in the land, that ye would even now be visited with utter destruction; yet it would not be by flood, as were the people in the days of Noah, but it would be by famine, and by pestilence, and the sword.

23 But it is by the prayers of the righteous that ye are spared; now therefore, if ye will cast out the righteous from among you then will not the Lord stay his hand; but in his fierce anger he will come out against you; then ye shall be smitten by famine, and by pestilence, and by the sword; and the time is soon at hand except ye repent.

Alma 10:27

27 And now behold, I say unto you, that the foundation of the destruction of this people is beginning

to be laid by the unrighteousness of your lawyers and your judges.

Alma 37:22

22 For behold, the Lord saw that his people began to work in darkness, yea, work secret murders and abominations; therefore the Lord said, if they did not repent they should be destroyed from off the face of the earth.

Alma 37:25-31

25 I will bring forth out of darkness unto light all their secret works and their abominations; and except they repent I will destroy them from off the face of the earth; and I will bring to light all their secrets and abominations, unto every nation that shall hereafter possess the land.

26 And now, my son, we see that they did not repent; therefore they have been destroyed, and thus far the word of God has been fulfilled; yea, their secret abominations have been brought out of darkness and made known unto us.

27 And now, my son, I command you that ye retain all their oaths, and their covenants, and their agreements in their secret abominations; yea, and all their signs and their wonders ye shall keep from this people, that they know them not, lest peradventure they should fall into darkness also and be destroyed.

28 For behold, there is a curse upon all this land, that destruction shall come upon all those workers of darkness, according to the power of God, when they are fully ripe; therefore I desire that this people might not be destroyed.

29 Therefore ye shall keep these secret plans of their oaths and their covenants from this people, and only their wickedness and their murders and their abominations shall ye make known unto them; and ye shall teach them to abhor such wickedness and abominations and murders; and ye shall also teach them that these people were destroyed on account of their wickedness and abominations and their murders.

30 For behold, they murdered all the prophets of the Lord who came among them to declare unto them concerning their iniquities; and the blood of those whom they murdered did cry unto the Lord their God for vengeance upon those who were their murderers; and thus the judgments of God did come upon these workers of darkness and secret combinations.

31 Yea, and cursed be the land forever and ever unto those workers of darkness and secret combinations, even unto destruction, except they repent before they are fully ripe.

Alma 51:16

16 For it was his first care to put an end to such contentions and dissensions among the people; for behold, this had been hitherto a cause of all their destruction. And it came to pass that it was granted according to the voice of the people.

Helaman 8:1-10

1 And now it came to pass that when Nephi had said these words, behold, there were men who were judges, who also belonged to the secret band of Gadianton, and they were angry, and they cried out against him, saying unto the people: Why do ye not seize upon this man and bring him forth, that he

may be condemned according to the crime which he has done?

2 Why seest thou this man, and hearest him revile against this people and against our law?

3 For behold, Nephi had spoken unto them concerning the corruptness of their law; yea, many things did Nephi speak which cannot be written; and nothing did he speak which was contrary to the commandments of God.

4 And those judges were angry with him because he spake plainly unto them concerning their secret works of darkness; nevertheless, they durst not lay their own hands upon him, for they feared the people lest they should cry out against them.

5 Therefore they did cry unto the people, saying: Why do you suffer this man to revile against us? For behold he doth condemn all this people, even unto destruction; yea, and also that these our great cities shall be taken from us, that we shall have no place in them.

6 And now we know that this is impossible, for behold, we are powerful, and our cities great, therefore our enemies can have no power over us.

7 And it came to pass that thus they did stir up the people to anger against Nephi, and raised contentions among them; for there were some who did cry out: Let this man alone, for he is a good man, and those things which he saith will surely come to pass except we repent;

8 Yea, behold, all the judgments will come upon us which he has testified unto us; for we know that he has testified aright unto us concerning our iniquities. And behold they are many, and he knoweth as well all things which shall befall us as he knoweth of our iniquities;

9 Yea, and behold, if he had not been a prophet he could not have testified concerning those things.

10 And it came to pass that those people who sought to destroy Nephi were compelled because of their fear, that they did not lay their hands on him; therefore he began again to speak unto them, seeing that he had gained favor in the eyes of some, insomuch that the remainder of them did fear.

Helaman 12:3

3 And thus we see that except the Lord doth chasten his people with many afflictions, yea, except he doth visit them with death and with terror, and with famine and with all manner of pestilence, they will not remember him.

Helaman 13:6

6 Yea, heavy destruction awaiteth this people, and it surely cometh unto this people, and nothing can save this people save it be repentance and faith on the Lord Jesus Christ, who surely shall come into the world, and shall suffer many things and shall be slain for his people.

3 Nephi 9:9

9 And behold, that great city Jacobugath, which was inhabited by the people of king Jacob, have I caused to be burned with fire because of their sins and their wickedness, which was above all the wickedness of the whole earth, because of their secret murders and combinations; for it was they that did destroy the peace of my people and the government of the land; therefore I did cause them to be burned, to destroy them from before my face, that the blood of the prophets and the saints should not come up unto me any more against them.

3 Nephi 9:12

12 And many great destructions have I caused to come upon this land, and upon this people, because of their wickedness and their abominations.

3 Nephi 21:14-21

14 Yea, wo be unto the Gentiles except they repent; for it shall come to pass in that day, saith the Father, that I will cut off thy horses out of the midst of thee, and I will destroy thy chariots;

15 And I will cut off the cities of thy land, and throw down all thy strongholds;

16 And I will cut off witchcrafts out of thy land, and thou shalt have no more soothsayers;

17 Thy graven images I will also cut off, and thy standing images out of the midst of thee, and thou shalt no more worship the works of thy hands;

18 And I will pluck up thy groves out of the midst of thee; so will I destroy thy cities.

19 And it shall come to pass that all lyings, and deceivings, and envyings, and strifes, and priestcrafts, and whoredoms, shall be done away.

20 For it shall come to pass, saith the Father, that at that day whosoever will not repent and come unto my Beloved Son, them will I cut off from among my people, O house of Israel;

21 And I will execute vengeance and fury upon them, even as upon the heathen, such as they have not heard.

Mormon 4:5

5 But, behold, the judgments of God will overtake the wicked; and it is by the wicked that the wicked are punished; for it is the wicked that stir up the hearts of the children of men unto bloodshed.

Ether 8:23

23 Wherefore, O ye Gentiles, it is wisdom in God that these things should be shown unto you, that thereby ye may repent of your sins, and suffer not that these murderous combinations shall get above you, which are built up to get power and gain—and the work, yea, even the work of destruction come upon you, yea, even the sword of the justice of the Eternal God shall fall upon you, to your overthrow and destruction if ye shall suffer these things to be.

Ether 9:28-30

28 And there came prophets in the land again, crying repentance unto them—that they must prepare the way of the Lord or there should come a curse upon the face of the land; yea, even there should be a great famine, in which they should be destroyed if they did not repent.

29 But the people believed not the words of the prophets, but they cast them out; and some of them they cast into pits and left them to perish. And it came to pass that they did all these things according to the commandment of the king, Heth.

30 And it came to pass that there began to be a great dearth upon the land, and the inhabitants began to be destroyed exceedingly fast because of the dearth, for there was no rain upon the face of the earth.

Ether 11:7
7 And they hearkened not unto the voice of the Lord, because of their wicked combinations; wherefore, there began to be wars and contentions in all the land, and also many famines and pestilences, insomuch that there was a great destruction, such an one as never had been known upon the face of the earth; and all this came to pass in the days of Shiblom.

Ether 14:25
25 And thus we see that the Lord did visit them in the fulness of his wrath, and their wickedness and abominations had prepared a way for their everlasting destruction.

Moroni 8:27
27 Behold, my son, I will write unto you again if I go not out soon against the Lamanites. Behold, the pride of this nation, or the people of the Nephites, hath proven their destruction except they should repent.

D&C 1:17
17 Wherefore, I the Lord, knowing the calamity which should come upon the inhabitants of the earth, called upon my servant Joseph Smith, Jun., and spake unto him from heaven, and gave him commandments;

D&C 29:14-20
14 But, behold, I say unto you that before this great day shall come the sun shall be darkened, and the moon shall be turned into blood, and the stars shall fall from heaven, and there shall be greater signs in heaven above and in the earth beneath;
15 And there shall be weeping and wailing among the hosts of men;
16 And there shall be a great hailstorm sent forth to destroy the crops of the earth.
17 And it shall come to pass, because of the wickedness of the world, that I will take vengeance upon the wicked, for they will not repent; for the cup of mine indignation is full; for behold, my blood shall not cleanse them if they hear me not.
18 Wherefore, I the Lord God will send forth flies upon the face of the earth, which shall take hold of the inhabitants thereof, and shall eat their flesh, and shall cause maggots to come in upon them;
19 And their tongues shall be stayed that they shall not utter against me; and their flesh shall fall from off their bones, and their eyes from their sockets;
20 And it shall come to pass that the beasts of the forest and the fowls of the air shall devour them up.

D&C 34:9
9 But before that great day shall come, the sun shall be darkened, and the moon be turned into blood; and the stars shall refuse their shining, and some shall fall, and great destructions await the wicked.

D&C 38:8
8 But the day soon cometh that ye shall see me, and know that I am; for the veil of darkness shall

soon be rent, and he that is not purified shall not abide the day.

D&C 38:11-13

11 For all flesh is corrupted before me; and the powers of darkness prevail upon the earth, among the children of men, in the presence of all the hosts of heaven—

12 Which causeth silence to reign, and all eternity is pained, and the angels are waiting the great command to reap down the earth, to gather the tares that they may be burned; and, behold, the enemy is combined.

13 And now I show unto you a mystery, a thing which is had in secret chambers, to bring to pass even your destruction in process of time, and ye knew it not;

D&C 43:25-26

25 How oft have I called upon you by the mouth of my servants, and by the ministering of angels, and by mine own voice, and by the voice of thunderings, and by the voice of lightnings, and by the voice of tempests, and by the voice of earthquakes, and great hailstorms, and by the voice of famines and pestilences of every kind, and by the great sound of a trump, and by the voice of judgment, and by the voice of mercy all the day long, and by the voice of glory and honor and the riches of eternal life, and would have saved you with an everlasting salvation, but ye would not!

26 Behold, the day has come, when the cup of the wrath of mine indignation is full.

D&C 45:19

19 But, verily I say unto you, that desolation shall come upon this generation as a thief in the night, and this people shall be destroyed and scattered among all nations.

D&C 45:30-33

30 And in that generation shall the times of the Gentiles be fulfilled.

31 And there shall be men standing in that generation, that shall not pass until they shall see an overflowing scourge; for a desolating sickness shall cover the land.

32 But my disciples shall stand in holy places, and shall not be moved; but among the wicked, men shall lift up their voices and curse God and die.

33 And there shall be earthquakes also in divers places, and many desolations; yet men will harden their hearts against me, and they will take up the sword, one against another, and they will kill one another.

D&C 45:40-42

40 And they shall see signs and wonders, for they shall be shown forth in the heavens above, and in the earth beneath.

41 And they shall behold blood, and fire, and vapors of smoke.

42 And before the day of the Lord shall come, the sun shall be darkened, and the moon be turned into blood, and the stars fall from heaven.

D&C 61:5

5 For I, the Lord, have decreed in mine anger many destructions upon the waters; yea, and especially upon these waters.

D&C 63:6

6 Wherefore, verily I say, let the wicked take heed, and let the rebellious fear and tremble; and let the unbelieving hold their lips, for the day of wrath shall come upon them as a whirlwind, and all flesh shall know that I am God.

D&C: 63:33-37

33 I have sworn in my wrath, and decreed wars upon the face of the earth, and the wicked shall slay the wicked, and fear shall come upon every man;

34 And the saints also shall hardly escape; nevertheless, I, the Lord, am with them, and will come down in heaven from the presence of my Father and consume the wicked with unquenchable fire.

35 And behold, this is not yet, but by and by.

36 Wherefore, seeing that I, the Lord, have decreed all these things upon the face of the earth, I will that my saints should be assembled upon the land of Zion;

37 And that every man should take righteousness in his hands and faithfulness upon his loins, and lift a warning voice unto the inhabitants of the earth; and declare both by word and by flight that desolation shall come upon the wicked.

D&C 84:118-119

118 For, with you saith the Lord Almighty, I will rend their kingdoms; I will not only shake the earth, but the starry heavens shall tremble.

119 For I, the Lord, have put forth my hand to exert the powers of heaven; ye cannot see it now, yet a little while and ye shall see it, and know that I am, and that I will come and reign with my people.

D&C 87:6

6 And thus, with the sword and by bloodshed the inhabitants of the earth shall mourn; and with famine, and plague, and earthquake, and the thunder of heaven, and the fierce and vivid lightning also, shall the inhabitants of the earth be made to feel the wrath, and indignation, and chastening hand of an Almighty God, until the consumption decreed hath made a full end of all nations;

D&C 88:84-91

84 Therefore, tarry ye, and labor diligently, that you may be perfected in your ministry to go forth among the Gentiles for the last time, as many as the mouth of the Lord shall name, to bind up the law and seal up the testimony, and to prepare the saints for the hour of judgment which is to come;

85 That their souls may escape the wrath of God, the desolation of abomination which awaits the wicked, both in this world and in the world to come. Verily, I say unto you, let those who are not the first elders continue in the vineyard until the mouth of the Lord shall call them, for their time is not yet come; their garments are not clean from the blood of this generation.

86 Abide ye in the liberty wherewith ye are made free; entangle not yourselves in sin, but let your

hands be clean, until the Lord comes.

87 For not many days hence and the earth shall tremble and reel to and fro as a drunken man; and the sun shall hide his face, and shall refuse to give light; and the moon shall be bathed in blood; and the stars shall become exceedingly angry, and shall cast themselves down as a fig that falleth from off a fig-tree.

88 And after your testimony cometh wrath and indignation upon the people.

89 For after your testimony cometh the testimony of earthquakes, that shall cause groanings in the midst of her, and men shall fall upon the ground and shall not be able to stand.

90 And also cometh the testimony of the voice of thunderings, and the voice of lightnings, and the voice of tempests, and the voice of the waves of the sea heaving themselves beyond their bounds.

91 And all things shall be in commotion; and surely, men's hearts shall fail them; for fear shall come upon all people.

D&C 97:22

22 For behold, and lo, vengeance cometh speedily upon the ungodly as the whirlwind; and who shall escape it?

D&C 101:25

25 And also that of element shall melt with fervent heat; and all things shall become new, that my knowledge and glory may dwell upon all the earth.

D&C 105:15

15 Behold, the destroyer I have sent forth to destroy and lay waste mine enemies; and not many years hence they shall not be left to pollute mine heritage, and to blaspheme my name upon the lands which I have consecrated for the gathering together of my saints.

D&C 112:24-26

24 Behold, vengeance cometh speedily upon the inhabitants of the earth, a day of wrath, a day of burning, a day of desolation, of weeping, of mourning, and of lamentation; and as a whirlwind it shall come upon all the face of the earth, saith the Lord.

25 And upon my house shall it begin, and from my house shall it go forth, saith the Lord;

26 First among those among you, saith the Lord, who have professed to know my name and have not known me, and have blasphemed against me in the midst of my house, saith the Lord.

D&C 121:12

12 And also that God hath set his hand and seal to change the times and seasons, and to blind their minds, that they may not understand his marvelous workings; that he may prove them also and take them in their own craftiness;

D&C 133:22-24

22 And it shall be a voice as the voice of many waters, and as the voice of a great thunder, which shall break down the mountains, and the valleys shall not be found.

23 He shall command the great deep, and it shall be driven back into the north countries, and the islands shall become one land;

24 And the land of Jerusalem and the land of Zion shall be turned back into their own place, and the earth shall be like as it was in the days before it was divided.

Moses 7:61

61 And the day shall come that the earth shall rest, but before that day the heavens shall be darkened, and a veil of darkness shall cover the earth; and the heavens shall shake, and also the earth; and great tribulations shall be among the children of men, but my people will I preserve;

Moses 7:65-66

65 And it came to pass that Enoch saw the day of the coming of the Son of Man, in the last days, to dwell on the earth in righteousness for the space of a thousand years;

66 But before that day he saw great tribulations among the wicked; and he also saw the sea, that it was troubled, and men's hearts failing them, looking forth with fear for the judgments of the Almighty God, which should come upon the wicked.

Joseph Smith-History 1:37

37 For behold, the day cometh that shall burn as an oven, and all the proud, yea, and all that do wickedly shall burn as stubble; for they that come shall burn them, saith the Lord of Hosts, that it shall leave them neither root nor branch.

Joseph Smith-History 1:45

45 He commenced, and again related the very same things which he had done at his first visit, without the least variation; which having done, he informed me of great judgments which were coming upon the earth, with great desolations by famine, sword, and pestilence; and that these grievous judgments would come on the earth in this generation. Having related these things, he again ascended as he had done before.

Also see Revelation chapters 8-11, 16.

WAR

Joseph Smith, History of the Church, Vol. 6, p. 199.

"The great Washington, soon after the foregoing faithful admonition for the common welfare of his nation, further advised Congress that 'among the many interesting objects which will engage your attention, that of providing for the common defense will merit particular regard. To be prepared for war is one of the most effectual means of preserving peace.'"

Orson Pratt, Journal of Discourses, Vol. 7, p. 185, July 10, 1859.

"There must be the interposition of the Almighty to make a change among the nations of the earth before this church can be established among all the nations and kingdoms of the Gentiles. This change will probably be brought about by war overturning all the governments and kingdoms of the Gentiles."

Orson Pratt, Journal of Discourses, Vol. 7, p. 185-186, July 10, 1859.

"This war that is now taking place will not result in that dreadful extinction that is foretold in the Book of Mormon, and which will rage among all the nations and kingdoms of the Gentiles, or, in other words, among the nations of Christendom. The one is a war preparatory to the proclamation of the Gospel; the other is a war of terrible destruction, which will not better the condition of those who escape. The wars that are now taking place will have a tendency, in some measure, to open the way for the Elders of the Church of Jesus Christ to go and establish the Church and kingdom of God among those nations."

Orson Pratt, Journal of Discourses, Vol. 7, p. 188, July 10, 1859.

"By-and-by, when the Lord has made bare his arm in signs, in great wonders, and in mighty deeds, through the instrumentality of his servants the Seventies, and though the instrumentality of the churches that shall be built up, and the nations and kingdoms of the earth have been faithfully and fully warned, and the Lord has fulfilled and accomplished all things that have been written in the Book of Mormon, and in other revelations pertaining to the preaching of the Gospel to the nations of the Gentiles and to the nations of Israel, by-and-by the Spirit of God will entirely withdraw from those Gentile nations, and leave them to themselves. Then they will find something else to do besides warring against the Saints in their midst—besides raising their sword and fighting against the Lamb of God; for then war will commence in earnest, and such a war as probably never entered into the hearts of men in our age to conceive of. No nation of the Gentiles upon the face of the whole earth but what will be engaged in deadly war, except the Latter-day Kingdom. They will be fighting one against another. And when that day comes, the Jews will flee to Jerusalem, and those nations will almost use one another up, and those of them who are left will be burned; for that will be the last sweeping judgment that is to go over the earth to cleanse it from wickedness. That is the day spoken of in this book—And I saw there were wars and rumours of wars among the Gentiles, and the angel said to me, Behold the wrath of God is upon the mother of harlots; and when that day comes, then shall the work of the Father commence in preparing the way to gather in all his covenant people, and then great Babylon will come down."

Orson Pratt, Journal of Discourses, Vol. 18, p. 341, February 25, 1877.

"If a war of this description should take place, who would carry on his business in safety? Who would feel safe to put his crops in the ground or to carry on any enterprise? There would be fleeing from one State to another, and general confusion would exist throughout the whole Republic. Such eventually is to be the condition of this whole nation, if the people do not repent of their wickedness; and such a state of affairs means no more or less than the complete overthrow of the nation, and not only of this nation, but the nations of Europe, which form the feet and toes of that great image."

Orson Pratt, Journal of Discourses, Vol. 20, p. 150-151, March 9, 1879.

"On the other hand, if you do not receive it, the Lord, who is long suffering, will, after he has borne with the people all the day long, withdraw his servants from your midst. When that day shall come there shall be wars, not such wars has have come in centuries and years that are past and gone, but a desolating war. When I say desolating, I mean that it will lay these European nations in waste. Cities will be left vacated, without inhabitants. The people will be destroyed by the sword of their own hands. Not only this but many other cities will be burned; for when contending armies are wrought up with terrible anger, without the Spirit of God upon them, when they have not that spirit of humanity that now characterizes many of the wars amongst the nations, when they are left to themselves, there will be no quarter given, no prisoners taken, but a war of destruction, of desolation, of the burning of the cities and villages, until the land is laid desolate. That is another thing that will come before the coming of the Son of Man."

George Q. Cannon, Gospel Truth, Vol. 1, p. 57.

"War is one of the scourges which man, by his sinfulness, has brought upon himself. There is one way—and but one way—to avert it and that is for the people to obey God's commands, through whose power alone can this and other threatened evils be stayed. This is too simple for the great men of the earth to believe. Like their class in every preceding generation they view such a proposition as ridiculous and treat it with contempt, practically asserting by their actions that they consider their wisdom and plans as being infinitely superior to the Lord's. The day will come when they will see their folly and be constrained to acknowledge it; but in the most of instances it will be when they will not have the power to avail themselves of the knowledge."

Joseph F. Smith, Gospel Doctrine, p. 416.

"We know that the spirit of strife and contention exists to an alarming extent among all the people of the world. Why does it exist? Because they are not one with God, nor with Christ. They have not entered into the true fold, and the result is they do not possess the spirit of the true Shepherd sufficiently to govern and control their acts in the ways of peace and righteousness. Thus they contend and strive one against another, and at last nation rises up against nation in fulfillment of the predictions of the prophets of God that war should be poured out upon all nations. I don't want you to think I believe that God has designed or willed that war should come among the people of the world, that the nations of the world should be divided against one another in war, and engaged in the destruction of each? God did not design or cause this. It is deplorable to the heavens that such a condition should exist among men, but the conditions do exist, and men precipitate war and destruction upon themselves because of their wickedness, and that because they will not abide in God's truth, walk in his love, and seek to establish and maintain peace instead of strife and contention in the world. (CR, Oct.1914, p. 8.)"

Joseph F. Smith, Gospel Doctrine, p. 418.

"So, I repeat, there is but one remedy that can prevent men from going to war, when they feel disposed to do it, and that is the Spirit of God, which inspires to love, and not to hatred, which leads unto all truth, and not unto error, which inclines the children of God to pay deference to him and to his laws and to esteem them as above all other things in the world.

The Lord has told us that these wars would come. We have not been ignorant that they were pending, and that they were likely to burst out upon the nations of the earth at any time. We have been looking for the fulfilment of the words of the Lord that they would come. Why? Because the Lord wanted it? No; not by any means. Was it because the Lord predestined it, or designed it, in any degree? No, not at all. Why? It was for the reason that men did not hearken unto the Lord God, and he foreknew the results that would follow, because of men, and because of the nations of the earth; and therefore he was able to predict what would befall them, and came upon them in consequence of their own acts, and not because he has willed it upon them, for they are but suffering and reaping the results of their own actions."

Joseph F. Smith, Gospel Doctrine, p. 419.

"Well, my sisters, 'peace on earth, and good will to men,' is our slogan. That is our principle. That is the principle of the gospel of Jesus Christ. And while I think it is wrong, wickedly wrong, to force war upon any nation, or upon any people, I believe it is righteous and just for every people to defend their own lives and their own liberties, and their own homes, with the last drop of their blood. I believe it is right, and I believe that the Lord will sustain any people in defending their own liberty to worship God according to the dictates of their conscience, any people trying to preserve their wives and their children from the ravages of the war. But we do not want to be brought into the necessity of having to defend ourselves."

Heber J. Grant, Messages of the First Presidency, Vol. 6, p. 90.

"We further declare that God is grieved by war and that He will hold subject to the eternal punishments of His will those who wage it unrighteously."

Heber J. Grant, Messages of the First Presidency, Vol. 6, p. 158, April 6, 1942.

"Thus the Church is and must be against war. The Church itself cannot wage war, unless and until the Lord shall issue new commands. It cannot regard war as a righteous means of settling international disputes; these should and could be settled—the nations agreeing—by peaceful negotiation and adjustment."

Hyrum M. Smith, Doctrine and Covenants Commentary, Sec. 45, p. 264.

"41. Blood, fire, and vapors of smoke. Evidently referring to the destructive agencies of modern warfare and their death-dealing effects—'blood.' This is another sign. There have been wars before (v. 26), but the armed conflicts immediately preceding the coming of our Savior in glory will be more destructive than any previous wars."

Hyrum M. Smith, Doctrine and Covenants Commentary, Sec. 63, p. 379.
"The Latter-day Saints are forbidden to make war in order to secure a gathering-place, and especially such a sacred place as that in which the greatest of all God's temples is to be located. They are not forbidden to defend their lives, their homes, their loved ones, their liberty and country, against murderers and thieves, but they are forbidden to be the aggressors."

George Albert Smith, Conference Report, October 1946, p. 149.
"I fear that the time is coming, . . . unless we can call the people of this world to repent of their sins and turn from the error of their ways, that the great war that has just passed will be an insignificant thing, as far as calamity is concerned, compared to that which is before us. And we can avoid it if we will; if we will each do our part, it can be prevented."

George Albert Smith, Conference Report, April 1950, p. 5.
"When we realize the uncertainty that exists in the world today realize that the strongest nations of the earth as well as the weaker ones are arming to the teeth preparing for war, we may know that it is only a question of time, unless they repent of their sins and turn to God, that war will come, and not only war, but pestilence and other destruction, until the human family will disappear from the earth."

Charles W. Penrose, Conference Report, April 1917, p. 20.
"The Lord does not want us to inculcate the spirit of war nor the spirit of bloodshed. In fact he has commanded us not to shed blood, but there are times and seasons, as we can find in the history of the world, in Bible and the Book of Mormon, when it is justifiable and right and proper and the duty of men to go forth in the defense of their homes and their families and maintain their privileges and rights by force of arms."

David O. McKay, Conference Report, April 1969, p. 5.
"Christ came to bring peace. Rejection of his way of life has made strife and contention rampant. Man, not the Lord, has brought deadly conflicts and subsequent misery. Wars spring from wickedness of unrighteous leaders. Not until freedom triumphs and a just peace comes may we hope for the end of wars and for goodwill among men."

David O. McKay, Gospel Ideals, p. 278.
"Again, misguided leaders of nations, worshiping the god of materialism, have brought on World War II, and unless the nations avoid the evil things which caused this war, there will be a World War III even more destructive, more terrible than the present murderous conflict. Like causes produce like effects."

David O. McKay, Gospel Ideals, p. 287.

"There are, however, two conditions which may justify a truly Christian man to enter—mind you, I say enter, not begin—a war: (1) an attempt to dominate and to deprive another of his free agency, and (2) loyalty to his country. Possibly there is a third, viz., defense of a weak nation that is being unjustly crushed by a strong, ruthless one."

Harold B. Lee, Church News, June 6, 1953, p. 4.

"The task of your generation for the next half century, it seems clear to me, is to build a faith in God sufficiently strong in the hearts of civilized people so as to forbid the use of the marvelous developments of science to the destruction of our civilization.

A few years ago at Stanford University, I heard an address by Dr. Robert Maynard Hutchins of the University of Chicago pleading for world peace. He closed his appeal by the declaration that there was no such thing as the 'secret' of the atomic bomb because every major nation knew how and given the materials and the financial ability would be manufacturing atomic bombs. He then warned: 'There must never be another world war, for another such war could mean the end of all civilization.'"

Bruce R. McConkie, Doctrinal New Testament Commentary, Vol. 3, p. 512.

"After showing John the woes that would befall mankind before the Second Coming (Rev. 6:9-17; 7; 8:1-13.), the Lord by an angelic ministrant promised three more woes, which were to attend and usher in the reign of the Great King. (Rev. 8:13.) The first of these was the unbelievably destructive series of wars leading up to the final great holocaust. (Rev. 9:1-12.) The second was the final great war itself in which one-third of the hosts of men should be slain. (Rev. 9:12-21; 10; 11:1-14.) And now the third woe is to be the destruction of the remainder of the wicked when the vineyard is burned by divine power and the earth changes from its telestial to its terrestrial state. In destructive power and effect this woe is to surpass all others many times over."

Neal A. Maxwell, Sermons Not Spoken, p. 66.

"Section 87 (D&C) also speaks of 'wars' (verse 1), suggesting not one war but a continuum of conflict. Thus, like chapter 24 of Matthew, this scripture covered things both imminent and distant. Furthermore, verse 4 speaks of a time . . . 'after many days' . . . when slaves would rise against their masters. True, some slaves fought in the Civil War, but these words may suggest something of far greater portent.

So too with verse 5, which speaks about 'the remnants' on the land, the seed of Jacob who will rise up to 'vex the Gentiles'; an intriguing and sobering prophecy, obviously involving developments far beyond the events of the American Civil War.

SCRIPTURAL REFERENCES

Jeremiah 50:8-9

8 Remove out of the midst of Babylon, and go forth out of the land of the Chaldeans, and be as the he goats before the flocks.

9 For, lo, I will raise and cause to come up against Babylon an assembly of great nations from the north country: and they shall set themselves in array against her; from thence she shall be taken: their arrows shall be as of a mighty expert man; none shall return in vain.

Daniel 11:40-45

40 And at the time of the end shall the king of the south push at him: and the king of the north shall come against him like a whirlwind, with chariots, and with horsemen, and with many ships; and he shall enter into the countries, and shall overflow and pass over.

41 He shall enter also into the glorious land, and many countries shall be overthrown: but these shall escape out of his hand, even Edom, and Moab, and the chief of the children of Ammon.

42 He shall stretch forth his hand also upon the countries: and the land of Egypt shall not escape.

43 But he shall have power over the treasures of gold and of silver, and over all the precious things of Egypt: and the Libyans and the Ethiopians shall be at his steps.

44 But tidings out of the east and out of the north shall trouble him: therefore he shall go forth with great fury to destroy, and utterly to make away many.

45 And he shall plant the tabernacles of his palace between the seas in the glorious holy mountain; yet he shall come to his end, and none shall help him.

Matthew 24:6-8

6 And ye shall hear of wars and rumours of wars: see that ye be not troubled: for all these things must come to pass, but the end is not yet.

7 For nation shall rise against nation, and kingdom against kingdom: and there shall be famines, and pestilences, and earthquakes, in divers places.

8 All these are the beginning of sorrows.

JST Matthew 24:25

25 And ye also shall hear of wars, and rumors of wars; see that ye be not troubled; for all I have told you must come to pass. But the end is not yet.

Mark 13:7-8

7 And when ye shall hear of wars and rumours of wars, be ye not troubled: for such things must needs be; but the end shall not be yet.

8 For nation shall rise against nation, and kingdom against kingdom: and there shall be earthquakes in divers places, and there shall be famines and troubles: these are the beginnings of sorrows.

Luke 21:9-10

9 But when ye shall hear of wars and commotions, be not terrified: for these things must first come to pass; but the end is not by and by.

10 Then said he unto them, Nation shall rise against nation, and kingdom against kingdom:

Revelation 9:13-18

13 And the sixth angel sounded, and I heard a voice from the four horns of the golden altar which is before God,

14 Saying to the sixth angel which had the trumpet, Loose the four angels which are bound in the great river Euphrates.

15 And the four angels were loosed, which were prepared for an hour, and a day, and a month, and a year, for to slay the third part of men.

16 And the number of the army of the horsemen were two hundred thousand thousand: and I heard the number of them.

17 And thus I saw the horses in the vision, and them that sat on them, having breastplates of fire, and of jacinth, and brimstone: and the heads of the horses were as the heads of lions; and out of their mouths issued fire and smoke and brimstone.

18 By these three was the third part of men killed, by the fire, and by the smoke, and by the brimstone, which issued out of their mouths.

1 Nephi 14:15-16

15 And it came to pass that I beheld that the wrath of God was poured out upon that great and abominable church, insomuch that there were wars and rumors of wars among all the nations and kindreds of the earth.

16 And as there began to be wars and rumors of wars among all the nations which belonged to the mother of abominations, the angel spake unto me, saying: Behold, the wrath of God is upon the mother of harlots; and behold, thou seest all these things—

1 Nephi 22:13-14

13 And the blood of that great and abominable church, which is the whore of all the earth, shall turn upon their own heads; for they shall war among themselves, and the sword of their own hands shall fall upon their own heads, and they shall be drunken with their own blood.

14 And every nation which shall war against thee, O house of Israel, shall be turned one against another, and they shall fall into the pit which they digged to ensnare the people of the Lord. And all that fight against Zion shall be destroyed, and that great whore, who hath perverted the right ways of the Lord, yea, that great and abominable church, shall tumble to the dust and great shall be the fall of it.

2 Nephi 1:10-12

10 But behold, when the time cometh that they shall dwindle in unbelief, after they have received so great blessings from the hand of the Lord—having a knowledge of the creation of the earth, and all men, knowing the great and marvelous works of the Lord from the creation of the world; having

power given them to do all things by faith; having all the commandments from the beginning, and having been brought by his infinite goodness into this precious land of promise—behold, I say, if the day shall come that they will reject the Holy One of Israel, the true Messiah, their Redeemer and their God, behold, the judgments of him that is just shall rest upon them.

11 Yea, he will bring other nations unto them, and he will give unto them power, and he will take away from them the lands of their possessions, and he will cause them to be scattered and smitten.

12 Yea, as one generation passeth to another there shall be bloodsheds, and great visitations among them; wherefore, my sons, I would that ye would remember; yea, I would that ye would hearken unto my words.

Alma 43:45-47

45 Nevertheless, the Nephites were inspired by a better cause, for they were not fighting for monarchy nor power but they were fighting for their homes and their liberties, their wives and their children, and their all, yea, for their rites of worship and their church.

46 And they were doing that which they felt was the duty which they owed to their God; for the Lord had said unto them, and also unto their fathers, that: Inasmuch as ye are not guilty of the first offense, neither the second, ye shall not suffer yourselves to be slain by the hands of your enemies.

47 And again, the Lord has said that: Ye shall defend your families even unto bloodshed. Therefore for this cause were the Nephites contending with the Lamanites, to defend themselves, and their families, and their lands, their country, and their rights, and their religion.

3 Nephi 20:19-20

19 For I will make my people with whom the Father hath covenanted, yea, I will make thy horn iron, and I will make thy hoofs brass. And thou shalt beat in pieces many people; and I will consecrate their gain unto the Lord, and their substance unto the Lord of the whole earth. And behold, I am he who doeth it.

20 And it shall come to pass, saith the Father, that the sword of my justice shall hang over them at that day; and except they repent it shall fall upon them, saith the Father, yea, even upon all the nations of the Gentiles.

Mormon 8:30

30 And there shall also be heard of wars, rumors of wars, and earthquakes in divers places.

D&C 1:35

35 For I am no respecter of persons, and will that all men shall know that the day speedily cometh; the hour is not yet, but is nigh at hand, when peace shall be taken from the earth, and the devil shall have power over his own dominion.

D&C 38:29

29 Ye hear of wars in far countries, and you say that there will soon be great wars in far countries, but ye know not the hearts of men in your own land.

D&C 45:63

63 Ye hear of wars in foreign lands; but, behold, I say unto you, they are nigh, even at your doors, and not many years hence ye shall hear of wars in your own lands.

D&C 45:66-70

66 And it shall be called the New Jerusalem, a land of peace, a city of refuge, a place of safety for the saints of the Most High God;

67 And the glory of the Lord shall be there, and the terror of the Lord also shall be there, insomuch that the wicked will not come unto it, and it shall be called Zion.

68 And it shall come to pass among the wicked, that every man that will not take his sword against his neighbor must needs flee unto Zion for safety.

69 And there shall be gathered unto it out of every nation under heaven; and it shall be the only people that shall not be at war one with another.

70 And it shall be said among the wicked: Let us not go up to battle against Zion, for the inhabitants of Zion are terrible; wherefore we cannot stand.

D&C 87:1-5

1 Verily, thus saith the Lord concerning the wars that will shortly come to pass, beginning at the rebellion of South Carolina, which will eventually terminate in the death and misery of many souls;

2 And the time will come that war will be poured out upon all nations, beginning at this place.

3 For behold, the Southern States shall be divided against the Northern States, and the Southern States will call on other nations, even the nation of Great Britain, as it is called, and they shall also call upon other nations, in order to defend themselves against other nations; and then war shall be poured out upon all nations.

4 And it shall come to pass, after many days, slaves shall rise up against their masters, who shall be marshaled and disciplined for war.

5 And it shall come to pass also that the remnants who are left of the land will marshal themselves, and shall become exceedingly angry, and shall vex the Gentiles with a sore vexation.

D&C 98:16-17

16 Therefore, renounce war and proclaim peace, and seek diligently to turn the hearts of the children to their fathers, and the hearts of the fathers to the children;

17 And again, the hearts of the Jews unto the prophets, and the prophets unto the Jews; lest I come and smite the whole earth with a curse, and all flesh be consumed before me.

D&C 98:33-38

33 And again, this is the law that I gave unto mine ancients, that they should not go out unto battle against any nation, kindred, tongue, or people, save I, the Lord, commanded them.

34 And if any nation, tongue, or people should proclaim war against them, they should first lift a standard of peace unto that people, nation, or tongue;

35 And if that people did not accept the offering of peace, neither the second nor the third time, they should bring these testimonies before the Lord;

36 Then I, the Lord, would give unto them a commandment, and justify them in going out to battle against that nation, tongue, or people.

37 And I, the Lord, would fight their battles, and their children's battles, and their children's children's, until they had avenged themselves on all their enemies, to the third and fourth generation.

38 Behold, this is an ensample unto all people, saith the Lord your God, for justification before me.

Moses 6:15

15 And the children of men were numerous upon all the face of the land. And in those days Satan had great dominion among men, and raged in their hearts; and from thenceforth came wars and bloodshed; and a man's hand was against his own brother, in administering death, because of secret works, seeking for power.

EARTHQUAKES

Orson Pratt, Journal of Discourses, Vol. 14, p. 328, February 11, 1872.

"What is it that has disrupted and apparently thrown the western continent into such terrible convulsion as to place the rocks on edge and rend them asunder? If they would inquire into these things it would be no marvel to them to find the remains of the ancient arts of men sunk far beneath the surface of the earth. I would say to them that, peradventure, they may yet find, when the Lord shall again convulse this continent, as he assuredly will do, throwing down the mountains and raising up the valleys, at the time of his second coming, for then, says the prophet Isaiah, the mountains shall flow down at his presence. Then, says the prophet David, the hills and the mountains shall melt like wax before the presence of the Lord. I say when this great and terrible convulsion shall come we may find cities rising, as it were, from the bowels of the earth, disgorged and brought to the surface. It need not surprise the inhabitants who then live to see cities brought up from the depths of the lakes and from the depths of great waters; to see mountains removed from their places and uncovering ancient cities that have been covered up for generations. All it needs then is a convulsion, a terrible catastrophe of nature to produce the effects that are sometimes ascribed to long ages of the slow working of the elements."

John Taylor, Journal of Discourses, Vol. 21, p. 59-61, September 21, 1878.

"What do we know about the calamities that are to come? I can tell you that while we have peace today and everything runs smoothly and quietly on, the day is not far distant before the Lord will arise to shake terribly the earth, and it will be felt in this nation more keenly and more severely than any of you have seen it by a great deal, and I know it, and I bear testimony to it."

Jedediah M. Grant, Journal of Discourses, Vol. 2, p. 146, April 2, 1854.

"This is a fact the Saints have known for many years—that the Gods in yonder heavens have something to do with these revolutions; the angels, those holy beings who are sent from the heavens to the earth to minister in the destiny of nations, have something to do in these mighty revolutions and convulsions that shake creation almost to its centre."

Joseph Fielding Smith, The Signs of the Times, p. 170.

"You can see what a terrible condition it is going to be; and the Jews besieged, not only in Jerusalem but, of course, throughout Palestine are in the siege; and when they are about to go under, then the Lord comes. There will be the great earthquake. The earthquake will not be only in Palestine. There will not be merely the separation of the Mount of Olives, to form a valley that the Jews may escape, but the whole earth is going to be shaken."

Bruce R. McConkie, Mormon Doctrine, "Earthquakes", p. 212.

"Earthquakes are given as one of the signs of the times; they foreshadow the Second Coming. By them the testimony of the Lord's power is borne to the people of the earth, and when the glorious Second Coming itself arrives there will be a great earthquake."

Bruce R. McConkie, The Millennial Messiah, p. 412-413.
"Earthquakes . . . and are destined to increase both in number and intensity in the last days."

Also see The Millennial Messiah, p. 620-621.

M. Russell Ballard, Conference Report, Ensign, November 1992, p. 31.
"These are difficult times, when the forces of nature seem to be unleashing a flood of 'famines, and pestilences, and earthquakes, in divers places.'
Recently, I read a newspaper article that cited statistics from the U.S. Geological Survey indicating that earthquakes around the world are increasing in frequency and intensity. According to the article, only two major earthquakes, earthquakes measuring at least six on the Richter scale, occured during the 1920s. In the 1930s the number increased to five, and then decreased to four during the 1940s. But in the 1950s, nine major earthquakes occured, followed by fifteen during the 1960s, forty-six during the 1970s, and fifty-two during the 1980s. Already almost as many major earthquakes have occurred during the 1990s as during the entire decade of the 1980s."

SCRIPTURAL REFERENCES

Ezekiel 38:18-20
18 And it shall come to pass at the same time when Gog shall come against the land of Israel, saith the Lord GOD, that my fury shall come up in my face.
19 For in my jealousy and in the fire of my wrath have I spoken, Surely in that day there shall be a great shaking in the land of Israel;
20 So that the fishes of the sea, and the fowls of the heaven, and the beasts of the field, and all creeping things that creep upon the earth, and all the men that are upon the face of the earth, shall shake at my presence, and the mountains shall be thrown down, and the steep places shall fall, and every wall shall fall to the ground.

Joel 3:16
16 The LORD also shall roar out of Zion, and utter his voice from Jerusalem; and the heavens and the earth shall shake: but the LORD will be the hope of his people, and the strength of the children of Israel.

Zechariah 14:4-5
4 And his feet shall stand in that day upon the mount of Olives, which is before Jerusalem on the east, and the mount of Olives shall cleave in the midst thereof toward the east and toward the west, and there shall be a very great valley; and half of the mountain shall remove toward the north, and half of it toward the south.
5 And ye shall flee to the valley of the mountains; for the valley of the mountains shall reach unto Azal: yea, ye shall flee, like as ye fled from before the earthquake in the days of Uzziah king of Judah: and the LORD my God shall come, and all the saints with thee.

Luke 21:9-11
9 But when ye shall hear of wars and commotions, be not terrified: for these things must first come to pass; but the end is not by and by.
10 Then said he unto them, Nation shall rise against nation, and kingdom against kingdom:
11 And great earthquakes shall be in divers places, and famines, and pestilences; and fearful sights and great signs shall there be from heaven.

Revelation 6:12
12 And I beheld when he had opened the sixth seal, and, lo, there was a great earthquake; and the sun became black as sackcloth of hair, and the moon became as blood;

Revelation 6:14
14 And the heaven departed as a scroll when it is rolled together; and every mountain and island were moved out of their places.

Destruction

Revelation 8:5-6

5 And the angel took the censer, and filled it with fire of the altar, and cast it into the earth: and there were voices, and thunderings, and lightnings, and an earthquake.

6 And the seven angels which had the seven trumpets prepared themselves to sound.

Revelation 11:12-14

12 And they heard a great voice from heaven saying unto them, Come up hither. And they ascended up to heaven in a cloud; and their enemies beheld them.

13 And the same hour was there a great earthquake, and the tenth part of the city fell, and in the earthquake were slain of men seven thousand: and the remnant were affrighted, and gave glory to the God of heaven.

14 The second woe is past; and, behold, the third woe cometh quickly.

Revelation 11:19

19 And the temple of God was opened in heaven, and there was seen in his temple the ark of his testament: and there were lightnings, and voices, and thunderings, and an earthquake, and great hail.

Revelation 16:17-20

17 And the seventh angel poured out his vial into the air; and there came a great voice out of the temple of heaven, from the throne, saying, It is done.

18 And there were voices, and thunders, and lightnings; and there was a great earthquake, such as was not since men were upon the earth, so mighty an earthquake, and so great.

19 And the great city was divided into three parts, and the cities of the nations fell: and great Babylon came in remembrance before God, to give unto her the cup of the wine of the fierceness of his wrath.

20 And every island fled away, and the mountains were not found.

2 Nephi 12:19-21

19 And they shall go into the holes of the rocks, and into the caves of the earth, for the fear of the Lord shall come upon them and the glory of his majesty shall smite them, when he ariseth to shake terribly the earth.

20 In that day a man shall cast his idols of silver, and his idols of gold, which he hath made for himself to worship, to the moles and to the bats;

21 To go into the clefts of the rocks, and into the tops of the ragged rocks, for the fear of the Lord shall come upon them and the majesty of his glory shall smite them, when he ariseth to shake terribly the earth.

2 Nephi 27:1-2

1 But, behold, in the last days, or in the days of the Gentiles—yea, behold all the nations of the Gentiles and also the Jews, both those who shall come upon this land and those who shall be upon other lands, yea, even upon all the lands of the earth, behold, they will be drunken with iniquity and all manner of abominations—

2 And when that day shall come they shall be visited of the Lord of Hosts, with thunder and with

earthquake, and with a great noise, and with storm, and with tempest, and with the flame of devouring fire.

D&C 29:13

13 For a trump shall sound both long and loud, even as upon Mount Sinai, and all the earth shall quake, and they shall come forth—yea, even the dead which died in me, to receive a crown of righteousness, and to be clothed upon, even as I am, to be with me, that we may be one.

D&C 45:48

48 And then shall the Lord set his foot upon this mount, and it shall cleave in twain, and the earth shall tremble, and reel to and fro, and the heavens also shall shake.

D&C 84:118

118 For, with you saith the Lord Almighty, I will rend their kingdoms; I will not only shake the earth, but the starry heavens shall tremble.

D&C 88:89

89 For after your testimony cometh the testimony of earthquakes, that shall cause groanings in the midst of her, and men shall fall upon the ground and shall not be able to stand.

SCOURGE/PLAGUES

Teachings of the Prophet Joseph Smith, Section One, 1830–34, p. 17.

"The city of Zion spoken of by David, in the one hundred and second Psalm, will be built upon the land of America, 'And the ransomed of the Lord shall return, and come to Zion with songs and everlasting joy upon their heads.' (Isaiah 35:10); and then they will be delivered from the overflowing scourge that shall pass through the land. . . .

I declare unto you the warning which the Lord has commanded me to declare unto this generation, remembering that the eyes of my Maker are upon me, and that to Him I am accountable for every word I say, wishing nothing worse to my fellowmen than their eternal salvation; therefore, 'Fear God, and give glory to Him, for the hour of His judgment is come.' Repent ye, repent ye, and embrace the everlasting covenant, and flee to Zion, before the overflowing scourge overtake you, for there are those now living upon the earth whose eyes shall not be closed in death until they see all these things, which I have spoken, fulfilled. (DHC 1:312-316.)"

Teachings of the Prophet Joseph Smith, Section Four, 1839–42, p. 200.

"The speaker, before closing, called upon the assembly before him to humble themselves in faith before God, and in mighty prayer and fasting to call upon the name of the Lord, until the elements were purified over our heads, and the earth sanctified under our feet, that the inhabitants of this city may escape the power of disease and pestilence, and the destroyer that rideth upon the face of the earth, and that the Holy Spirit of God may rest upon this vast multitude."

Brigham Young, Journal of Discourses, Vol. 15, p. 193-195, October 8, 1872.

"I refer to a revelation given in the year 1833, called the Word of Wisdom. We fail to obey it today, and we shall fail tomorrow unless we make a short turn and determine in our own minds that we will obey it. How many of us have disregarded that revelation, in every particular? It is to be found on page 240 of the Doctrine and Covenants, and it shadows to me that a time will come in the midst of this people when a desolating scourge will pass through our ranks, and the destroying angel will be in our midst as he was in Egypt when he slew all the firstborn of the Egyptians. God says 'The destroying angel shall pass by' and shall not harm you if you will observe to do these things. Now if we believe this revelation, and I take it for granted that we do, though I may choose to doubt in my own case and some others, yet I assume that as a people we believe it; but what assurance have we that that angel will pass us by unless we do observe it? No more than the children of Israel would have had if they had failed to mark their doors and lintels with the blood of a lamb, as Moses had commanded them. What effect would a failure to comply with this commandment have had on them? Would the Destroyer have passed by the firstborn of Israel? I know not; I think the firstborn of Israel would have been slain as well as the first born of Egypt. That was a revelation given by the Lord to Moses for the salvation of Israel; the Word of Wisdom is a revelation given by the Lord to Joseph Smith for the salvation of this people, and if we disobey we have no more assurance than Israel had that the destroying angel will pass through our ranks and leave us unscathed."

Orson Hyde, Journal of Discourses, Vol. 7, p. 110, July 4, 1853.

"If the United States have been guilty of a great dereliction of duty in not making an effort to redress the sufferings and wrongs of the 'Mormons,' and the 'Mormons' have said that this inaction and indifference on the part of the Government in relation to their grievances will draw upon the nation a scourge and chastisement from God, we have no more idea that the great purposes and designs of the Creator will be changed in relation to this nation, in consequence of this merited chastisement, than the purposes and designs of a father to rear up his son in honour, integrity, and truth will become changed by the infliction of chastisement for some transgression or misdemeanour."

Orson Pratt, Journal of Discourses, Vol. 15, p. 339-340, January 26, 1873.

"This gives a clue to the time when the seven angels will sound. They will not sound their trumpets in the evening of the sixth thousand years, but when the six thousand years shall have passed away from the creation, and the morning of the seventh has commenced, then these great events will happen. Jesus does not come immediately at the commencement of the seventh thousand years, but as there was a work in the beginning which he performed on the seventh day, such as planting the garden and placing men therein, so there will be a certain work to be performed in the beginning of the seventh thousand years, namely, the resurrection and redemption of man, including the heathen nations and those people in prison who have died without the law and have been punished for their sins. When the Lord has caused these seven angels to sound their trumps, he will bring about all these purposes which he has ordained, and which must be accomplished in that morning. Before Jesus appears in the clouds of heaven they are to sound to prepare the way of the Lord before his coming. What will take place when they sound? I will tell you some few things.

When the first angel sounds there will come upon the inhabitants of the earth a great hailstorm mingled with fire and blood, and so severe will be this storm of fire and blood, that one-third of the trees will be destroyed, and all the green grass will be burned up. The second angel will sound his trump, and the Lord will pour out his judgments upon the water, and a third part of the sea will become blood, and in consequence of the corruption thereof one-third part of all the animals living in the sea will die.

When the third angel sounds his trump, John says he saw a star fall from heaven to earth, burning as it were like a lamp, and it fell upon the fountains and rivers of water, and they were turned into bitterness, and the name of the star was called 'Wormwood,' and great were the numbers of the people who perished and died because of the bitterness of the waters.

The fourth angel will sound his trump and certain judgments will follow. By and by the fifth angel will sound his trump, and an angel will descend holding the key of what is termed the bottomless pit, and he will open the door of this pit, and there shall issue therefrom certain terrible creatures called locusts. And it will be given unto them to torment men five months—the time which is to intervene between the sounding of the fifth and sixth trumpets, and during that time these awful creatures, such as neither we nor our forefathers, in all the generations before us, have ever seen on the earth, will torment the wicked. These creatures have wings, hair like women, teeth like lions, tails like scorpions, and with their stings they will torment the wicked for five months. But it will not be given unto them to destroy men, only to torment them. That will be a terrible judgment. They will have a king over them, whose name in the Greek tongue is 'Apollyon,' in other words the devil. He has power over them and with them, and commands these awful beings, and they go forth and torment the inhabitants of the earth, but are not permitted to kill them. Men in those days will seek for death, but it will flee from them, although they will greatly desire it on account of the terrible torment they endure.

When the Lord permits the devil to go forth and torment people he has considerable power. You can see this in the case of Job. When the devil stirred up the Lord to torment Job, the devil was permitted to go and strike Job with pestilence, with sore boils, and to make him feel sorrow, pain and distress. Said the devil to the Lord, 'He will curse you to your face,' and to prove whether he would or not Job was sorely smitten and afflicted; and so will men be afflicted by these awful creatures which will issue from the bottomless pit, and are under his command.

By and by the sixth angel sounds his trumpet, and what will take place? The powers around the great river Euphrates in Asia will be loosed, and they will come forth riding on horses, and the number of them is two hundred thousand thousand, that is two hundred millions—a great and tremendous army, greater than the inhabitants of the earth ever saw before. Who will be with them? This same class of beings with animals such as the earth never saw nor heard of, only as they heard of them in the revelations of St. John. Animals with brimstone and fire issuing from their mouths, having tails like serpents, and heads to their tails, and with these one-third part of the inhabitants of the earth are to be destroyed. How long will it be before they are destroyed? There will be at least a year pass away between the sounding of the sixth and seventh trumpets. This great army is prepared for a day, and an hour, a month and a year. Now I have named some of the judgments, not all, that will transpire before the coming of the Son of Man. Let me refer in a few words to some of the last ones that will come before Jesus makes his appearance, called the seven last plagues. I shall only refer to a few of them.

One of the four beasts gives vials filled with the wrath of God to the seen Angels that came out of the Temple and Tabernacle in heaven, and these vials are to be poured out upon the earth. We find that the inhabitants are to be visited with greater judgments than what they have been heretofore, so much so that when the second Angel pours out his vial upon the great waters, instead of a third part of them becoming blood, they all become as the blood of a dead man; and there shall not any living thing be preserved in the great mass of waters on our globe, but everything living in the sea will perish, the whole ocean becoming as the blood of a dead man. Quite a difference between the blood of a dead man and the blood that comes from a living man—one is very nauseous when compared with the other. No wonder then that everything having life in the sea should perish.

A third Angel pours out his vial on the fountains and rivers, and they also become blood. You have already learned that when the third Angel sounded his trump the third part of the waters become bitter with wormwood, and it was accompanied by certain judgments not universal, but when the last plagues are poured out the fountains and rivers of water, and the ocean become blood. Does this cause the people to repent? One would imagine that all the earth would repent when they see judgments of this kind; yet we are told that for all this the people will blaspheme God, because of their plagues, sores and pains, and the calamities they have to endure. They are given up the hardness of heart, the Spirit of God is withdrawn from them, and instead of repenting of their evil deeds, their murders, sorceries, whoredoms, idolatries, thefts and various crimes that are mentioned, they continue in their wickedness, and judgment after judgment is poured upon them until they are consumed.

When the rivers and fountains are turned into blood, a certain Angel cries out saying, 'Thou art righteous, O Lord, which art and wast and shall be, because thou hast judged thus. For they have shed the blood of Saints and Prophets, and thou hast given them blood to drink, for they are worthy.' This shows that there will be Prophets in those days and that these people will shed their blood. A great many people think there are to be no more Prophets; but the Prophets have their blood shed in those days, and God will give the wicked blood to drink."

Orson Pratt, Journal of Discourses, Vol. 18, p. 227, August 26, 1876.

"These plagues named in John's revelations, will take place literally—'The Lord God will curse the waters of the great deep, and they shall be turned into blood.' 'The sea shall become as the blood of a dead man, and every living thing in the sea shall be destroyed.' And the time will come, when the seven angels having the seven last trumps will sound their trumps literally, and the sound thereof will be heard among the nations, just preparatory to the coming of the Son of Man; and all the judgments foretold by John, which are to succeed the sound of each of the seven trumpets, will be fulfilled literally upon the earth in their times and seasons. And the wicked will gnaw their tongues for peace and will curse God, wishing to die because of their pain. These are they who repented not when the gospel was preached to them and who became hardened in their iniquities, which were overflowing, in order that God might visit them according to all that had been spoken by the mouths of his ancient Prophets."

Hyrum M. Smith, Doctrine and Covenants Commentary, Sec. 5, p. 28.

"19. A desolating scourge. The consequence of the rejection of the testimony of the Prophet and the three witnesses would be 'a desolating scourge,' in the form of pestilence, floods, earthquakes, wars, etc., until the final destruction by the coming of Christ."

Hyrum M. Smith, Doctrine and Covenants Commentary, Sec. 29, p. 152.

"'And this shall be the plague wherewith the Lord will smite all the people that have fought against Jerusalem; Their flesh shall consume away while they stand upon their feet, and their eyes shall consume away in their holes, and their tongues shall consume away in their mouth.' (Zech. 14:12.) there is no promise that this great plague of hail, destruction and disease shall be confined to any one section of the earth. It is a calamity which will come upon the wicked because they will not repent. We may well believe that in addition to the plague of flies there shall be included in this prediction the plague of microbes, or bacilli, new to the scientific world and with which they will not be able to cope, much of which will be the result of impure lives."

J. Reuben Clark, Jr., Conference Report, October 1952, p. 85.

"I do not know when the Lord is coming. I have no idea about it. But I do know this, that the signs we have today are the signs which he said would precede his coming. Similar signs have been in other days and he did not come. But these signs we do now have, and if the Lord's prophecies, the prophecies of his servants shall come true, and they will, we shall have more than one plague against which to preserve ourselves, against which we shall want to call all the faith that we can possess, to buttress our call to our Heavenly Father for his sustaining power, his comfort, his consolation, and for the healing influences of his Spirit."

Bruce R. McConkie, Mormon Doctrine, "Signs of the Times", p. 725.

"Despite medical advances, people are to suffer from diseases, plagues, and pestilences of undreamed proportions in the last days. . . .New and unheard of diseases will attack the human system . . .The plagues and pestilences of the past will be as nothing compared to what is yet to be."

See Bruce R. McConkie, The Millennial Messiah, p. 389.

"Our setting for the slaughter of the two prophets in Jerusalem and for the seven last plagues is not only in the seventh seal, but also just before and during the time when the seventh angel is announcing the plague of burning and destruction that will usher in the Second Coming."

Bruce R. McConkie, A New Witness for the Articles of Faith, p. 636.

"In those days, which shall be in the beginning of the seventh thousand years, as explained in The Millennial Messiah, the Lord will pour out the seven last plagues. These are: (1) a noisome and grievous sore; (2) the seas become blood and their life dies; (3) all water turns to blood and is diseased; (4) the sun scorches men and the earth; (5) darkness, pain, and sores in the kingdoms of the world; (6) false miracles as the world prepares for Armageddon; and (7) war, upheavals of nature, and the fall of Babylon."

SCRIPTURAL REFERENCES

Isaiah 28:15
15 Because ye have said, We have made a covenant with death, and with hell are we at agreement; when the overflowing scourge shall pass through, it shall not come unto us: for we have made lies our refuge, and under falsehood have we hid ourselves:

Isaiah 28:18
18 And your covenant with death shall be disannulled, and your agreement with hell shall not stand; when the overflowing scourge shall pass through, then ye shall be trodden down by it.

Zechariah 14:12
12 And this shall be the plague wherewith the LORD will smite all the people that have fought against Jerusalem; Their flesh shall consume away while they stand upon their feet, and their eyes shall consume away in their holes, and their tongue shall consume away in their mouth.

Zechariah 14:15-18
15 And so shall be the plague of the horse, of the mule, of the camel, and of the ass, and of all the beasts that shall be in these tents, as this plague.
16 And it shall come to pass, that every one that is left of all the nations which came against Jerusalem shall even go up from year to year to worship the King, the LORD of hosts, and to keep the feast of tabernacles.
17 And it shall be, that whoso will not come up of all the families of the earth unto Jerusalem to worship the King, the Lord of hosts, even upon them shall be no rain.
18 And if the family of Egypt go not up, and come not, that have no rain; there shall be the plague, wherewith the Lord will smite the heathen that come not up to keep the feast of tabernacles.

Revelation 9:20
20 And the rest of the men which were not killed by these plagues yet repented not of the works of their hands, that they should not worship devils, and idols of gold, and silver, and brass, and stone, and of wood: which neither can see, nor hear, nor walk:

Revelation 16:21
21 And there fell upon men a great hail out of heaven, every stone about the weight of a talent: and men blasphemed God because of the plague of the hail; for the plague thereof was exceeding great.

Revelation 18:4
4 And I heard another voice from heaven, saying, Come out of her, my people, that ye be not partakers of her sins, and that ye receive not of her plagues.

Revelation 18:8
8 Therefore shall her plagues come in one day, death, and mourning, and famine; and she shall be utterly burned with fire: for strong is the Lord God who judgeth her.

Revelation 21:9
9 And there came unto me one of the seven angels which had the seven vials full of the seven last plagues, and talked with me, saying, Come hither, I will shew thee the bride, the Lamb's wife.

3 Nephi 20:28
28 And they shall be a scourge unto the people of this land. Nevertheless, when they shall have received the fulness of my gospel, then if they shall harden their hearts against me I will return their iniquities upon their own heads, saith the Father.

D&C 5:18-19
18 And their testimony shall also go forth unto the condemnation of this generation if they harden their hearts against them;
19 For a desolating scourge shall go forth among the inhabitants of the earth, and shall continue to be poured out from time to time, if they repent not, until the earth is empty, and the inhabitants thereof are consumed away and utterly destroyed by the brightness of my coming.

D&C 84:54-59
54 And your minds in times past have been darkened because of unbelief, and because you have treated lightly the things you have received—
55 Which vanity and unbelief have brought the whole church under condemnation.
56 And this condemnation resteth upon the children of Zion, even all.
57 And they shall remain under this condemnation until they repent and remember the new covenant, even the Book of Mormon and the former commandments which I have given them, not only to say, but to do according to that which I have written—
58 That they may bring forth fruit meet for their Father's kingdom; otherwise there remaineth a scourge and judgment to be poured out upon the children of Zion.
59 For shall the children of the kingdom pollute my holy land? Verily, I say unto you, Nay.
D&C 84:96-97
96 For I, the Almighty, have laid my hands upon the nations, to scourge them for their wickedness.
97 And plagues shall go forth, and they shall not be taken from the earth until I have completed my work, which shall be cut short in righteousness—

D&C 97:22-26
22 For behold, and lo, vengeance cometh speedily upon the ungodly as the whirlwind; and who shall escape it?
23 The Lord's scourge shall pass over by night and by day, and the report thereof shall vex all people; yea, it shall not be stayed until the Lord come;
24 For the indignation of the Lord is kindled against their abominations and all their wicked works.

25 Nevertheless, Zion shall escape if she observe to do all things whatsoever I have commanded her. 26 But if she observe not to do whatsoever I have commanded her, I will visit her according to all her works, with sore affliction, with pestilence, with plague, with sword, with vengeance, with devouring fire.

FAMINE

Teachings of the Prophet Joseph Smith, Section Six, 1843–44, p. 340.

"I have asked of the Lord concerning His coming; and while asking the Lord, He gave a sign and said, 'In the days of Noah I set a bow in the heavens as a sign and token that in any year that the bow should be seen the Lord would not come; but there should be seed time and harvest during that year: but whenever you see the bow withdrawn, it shall be a token that there shall be famine, pestilence, and great distress among the nations, and that the coming of the Messiah is not far distant.'"

Brigham Young, Journal of Discourses, Vol. 12, p. 241-242, July 25, 1868.

"I have never promised a famine to the Latter-day Saints, if we will do half right. You have never heard it drop from my lips that a famine would come upon this people. There never will, if we will only do half right, and we expect to do better than that."

Heber C. Kimball, Journal of Discourses, Vol. 5, p. 20-21, April 6, 1857.

"When we have stored away our grain we are safe, independent of the world, in case of famine, are we not? Yes, we are; for, in that case we will have the means for subsistence in our own hands. When the famines begin upon the earth, we shall be very apt to feel them first.

If judgments must need begin at the house of God, and if the righteous scarcely are saved, how will it be with the wicked? Am I looking for famines? Yes, the most terrible and severe that have ever come upon the nations of the earth."

John Taylor, The Gospel Kingdom, p. 349.

"So, knowing that there are other judgments in store for the whole earth, we will venture a prediction, and that shall be storm and hail enough to cause a famine, and show the whole of the earth that Jesus Christ, and not the Mormons, vexes the nation. Enough of the present generation shall see, hear, and feel it, to be witnesses that the servants of God tell the truth."

Joseph F. Smith, Collected Discourses, Vol. 3, July 16, 1893.

"My brethren and sisters, we were taught here this morning, the Scriptures being quoted, that troublous times will come upon the children of men, that their hearts will fail them for fear of the difficulties and sorrows that threaten them, and it is needful for this people to prepare themselves for these events that they may be as Joseph in the land of Egypt, when famine shall come, and when pestilence shall stalk abroad in the earth, when tempests and storms shall sweep cities, and when devastating fire shall consume all before it, that there may be found 'corn in Egypt,' and the people shall say, 'Come, let us go up to the mountain of the Lord's house.' The world today will laugh at you if you talk about a famine in this land. Why, they say, such a thing is absolutely impossible. We are so connected and bound together with the iron rails, and by navigation, that it is utterly impossible for any section of the country to be left destitute, because there will be abundance of food somewhere, and the railroads can speedily take from the lands that teem with plenty to the lands that are impoverished. But notwithstanding this, we hear very frequently of famine in the land. Only a few years ago, in Russia, people died by the thousands from famine, and from the pestilence that followed it. Ship load after ship load of provisions were sent from America to the starving ones in that land, but did it prevent the famine? No, because that which we did was but a mite compared with the great necessities of the people. A few days ago we read of the farmers in the western portion of Kansas famishing for the necessaries of life, and this in our own land! But I am not here to try to scare anybody with famine, although the Lord has revealed through His servants that famine is one of the scourges that He will send upon the inhabitants of the earth in the last days, and as the Lord lives, He will send it in His time. As the Lord blessed the earth in the beginning, and caused it to be fruitful and bring forth for man, so sure can He put His curse upon it, as He did upon the land of Canaan and caused it to be barren and unfruitful: and so sure can He send the devouring insect, to sweep the earth of the crops that are upon it, and He can scourge the nations that boast of their wealth, and of their power to resist the providences of God. He can teach them a lesson when He wills; and when the time comes, as God lives, He will teach them a lesson, however little they may believe it possible for Him to do it. It is as easy for Him to send famine in this bountiful land of ours as it is for Him to send the cyclone; and it is just as easy for Him to send the devouring element of fire, which consumed Chicago a number of years ago, and which is now from time to time devastating cities, as it is to send famine, or the cyclone. I believe in the almighty power of God, and in His justice, and mercy; and I have unlimited faith in the words that He has spoken by inspired men."

Ezra Taft Benson, Conference Report, April 1969, p. 12.
    "A major reason why there is famine in some parts of the world is because evil men have used the vehicle of government to abridge the freedom that men need to produce abundantly."

Teachings of Ezra Taft Benson, p. 265.
    "Should the Lord decide at this time to cleanse the Church—and the need for that cleansing seems to be increasing—a famine in this land of one year's duration could wipe out a large percentage of slothful members, including some ward and stake officers. Yet we cannot say we have not been warned."

SCRIPTURAL REFERENCES

Helaman 11:4-7

4 O Lord, do not suffer that this people shall be destroyed by the sword; but O Lord, rather let there be a famine in the land, to stir them up in remembrance of the Lord their God, and perhaps they will repent and turn unto thee.

5 And so it was done, according to the words of Nephi. And there was a great famine upon the land, among all the people of Nephi. And thus in the seventy and fourth year the famine did continue, and the work of destruction did cease by the sword but became sore by famine.

6 And this work of destruction did also continue in the seventy and fifth year. For the earth was smitten that it was dry, and did not yield forth grain in the season of grain; and the whole earth was smitten, even among the Lamanites as well as among the Nephites, so that they were smitten that they did perish by thousands in the more wicked parts of the land.

7 And it came to pass that the people saw that they were about to perish by famine, and they began to remember the Lord their God; and they began to remember the words of Nephi.

Ether 9:28

28 And there came prophets in the land again, crying repentance unto them—that they must prepare the way of the Lord or there should come a curse upon the face of the land; yea, even there should be a great famine, in which they should be destroyed if they did not repent.

Ether 9:35

35 And it came to pass that when they had humbled themselves sufficiently before the Lord he did send rain upon the face of the earth; and the people began to revive again, and there began to be fruit in the north countries, and in all the countries round about. And the Lord did show forth his power unto them in preserving them from famine.

D&C 89:12-15

12 Yea, flesh also of beasts and of the fowls of the air, I, the Lord, have ordained for the use of man with thanksgiving; nevertheless they are to be used sparingly;

13 And it is pleasing unto me that they should not be used, only in times of winter, or of cold, or famine.

14 All grain is ordained for the use of man and of beasts, to be the staff of life, not only for man but for the beasts of the field, and the fowls of heaven, and all wild animals that run or creep on the earth;

15 And these hath God made for the use of man only in times of famine and excess of hunger.

FIRE

Teachings of the Prophet Joseph Smith, Section Two, 1834-37, p. 100.

"Now men cannot have any possible grounds to say that this is figurative, or that it does not mean what it says; for he is now explaining what He had previously spoken in parables; and according to this language, the end of the world is the destruction of the wicked, the harvest and the end of the world have an allusion directly to the human family in the last days, instead of the earth, as many have imagined; and that which shall precede the coming of the Son of Man, and the restitution of all things spoken of by the mouth of all the holy prophets since the world began; and the angels are to have something to do in this great work, for they are the reapers. As, therefore, the tares are gathered and burned in the fire, so shall it be in the end of the world; that is, as the servants of God go forth warning the nations, both priests and people, and as they harden their hearts and reject the light of truth, these first being delivered over to the buffetings of Satan, and the law and the testimony being closed up, as it was in the case of the Jews, they are left in darkness, and delivered over unto the day of burning; thus being bound up by their creeds, and their bands being made strong by their priests, are prepared for the fulfilment of the saying of the Savior—The Son of Man shall send forth His angels, and gather out of His Kingdom all things that offend, and them which do iniquity, and shall cast them into a furnace of fire, there shall be wailing and gnashing of teeth.' We understand that the work of gathering together of the wheat into barns, or garners, is to take place while the tares are being bound over, and preparing for the day of burning; that after the day of burnings, the righteous shall shine forth like the sun, in the Kingdom of their Father. Who hath ears to hear, let him hear."

Brigham Young, Journal of Discourses, Vol. 13, p. 314, April 17, 1870.

"The Lord has said that He will never again destroy the world by a flood. What will the next great catastrophe be? It will be fire: He will cleanse the earth as by fire, and will purify and make it holy, and prepare it for the habitation of His Saints."

Orson Pratt, Millennial Star, *A Prophetic Warning to the Inhabitants of Great Britain,* Vol. 19, p. 680-681, October 24, 1857.

"But if you will not, as a nation, repent, and unite yourselves with God's kingdom, then the days are near at hand, when the righteous shall be gathered out of your midst: and woe unto you when that day shall come! For it shall be a day of vengeance upon the British nation; and your armies shall perish; your maritime forces shall cease; your cities shall be ravaged, burned, and made desolate, and your strongholds shall be thrown down; the poor shall rise against the rich, and their storehouses and their fine mansions shall be pillaged, their merchandise, and their gold, and their silver, and their rich treasures, shall be plundered; then shall the Lords, the Nobles, and the merchants of the land, and all in high places, be brought down, and shall sit in the dust, and howl for the miseries that shall be upon them; and they that trade by sea shall lament and mourn; for their traffic shall cease. And thus shall the Lord Almighty visit you, because of your great wickedness in rejecting His servants and His kingdom; and if you continue to harden your hearts, your remnants which shall be left, shall be consumed as the dry stubble before the devouring flame, and all the land shall be cleansed by the fire of the Lord, that the filthiness thereof may no more come up before Him."

Orson Pratt, Journal of Discourses, Vol. 20, p. 10-11, June 23, 1878.

"When therefore, we read that the earth was once depopulated, except a few individuals, who were saved in the ark, why should it be thought a thing incredible that the Lord should again depopulate our globe, not by a flood, but by devouring fire. It may be said that we cannot see how a universal fire can prevail over the face of the earth. There are various ways by which this could be accomplished. How did the Lord cause fire in ancient times to break out among the children of Israel, when they transgressed his holy laws, and when they murmured and complained against God? Fire was sent forth from his presence we are told, rested upon the tabernacle; he was in the tabernacle, and his cloud was over the tabernacle; and fire went forth from this centre, or the place where the Lord chose to manifest and show forth his glory, and it destroyed many of the people. You may say, 'But this was a supernatural fire that proceeded from the presence of God, from the tabernacle, consuming thousands of transgressors.' I would ask, cannot the same Being who was able to produce this destruction by fire upon a few thousand individuals cause it to be more extensive and more universal in its operation? Has he not the same power to produce a supernatural fire over all the earth; even to the consuming of 'all the proud, yea, and all that do wickedly;' burning them up literally their bodies becoming as 'ashes,' as a farmer would set fire and burn up the stubble of his fields? Well, you say, 'If we admit that the first was supernatural, that God did actually burn the transgressors among Israel by fire, we are willing to admit that the same Being that could do this upon a small scale, could perform a similar work on a universal scale.' But then, perhaps the Lord may not see proper to do this work of burning in the latter-days altogether upon a supernatural principle; he may, perhaps, bring it about by certain physical forces or laws, by certain changes that may be wrought upon our elements; for the Lord holds in his own hands all the elements, and not only those of this little globe of ours, but all the elements that compose the universe; they are in his hands, he can give instructions and they are made subservient in the accomplishing of his great and wise purposes. Now, there is in the very air which we breathe, and which all animated beings, more or less, breathe, and by which they live—a principle of heat; and when this heat in its latent form is evolved, or comes forth from the constituents of the atmosphere, would there not be a sufficient amount to produce this revolution upon the earth? Is there not sufficient heat not only to burn up the wicked and the proud, but to cause the very elements of our globe to melt by its intensity? thus fulfilling another prophecy which says, 'the hills melted like wax at the presence of the Lord;' and yet another prophecy, which says, the mountains shall flow down at His presence like melted substance; run like rivers, in consequence of the intensity of the heat, connected with the elements of which our atmosphere and mountains are composed."

Orson Pratt, Journal of Discourses, Vol. 20, p. 11-14, June 23, 1878.

"It is not for us, unless we have some definite instructions by the word of God, to tell how He is going to accomplish His great purposes. It is sufficient for us to know that he will do it. We are told this burning is to be universal, so far as all the proud, and all that do wickedly are concerned. It seems, then, it is to be one of the last destructions of the wicked. Prior to this there will be numerous destructions, by way of earthquakes, plagues, hailstorms, wars, etc., that will prevail and that will sweep away millions from the face of our globe. But the great judgment that is to cleanse the earth from all sin, is to be by the element of fire, 'But,' inquires one, 'do you think there will be many in that day, that will be proud and wicked? Will they not be mostly converted, and consequently escape this great conflagration, as Noah escaped being drowned?' I will answer this by repeating another prophecy, that now occurs to my mind, recorded in the 24th chapter of Isaiah. This man of God saw the period of time when the earth should real to a fro like a drunken man; and he saw that glorious day when the Lord of Hosts shall be about to reign in Zion and Jerusalem. And among other things he saw in vision was that the earth became defiled under the inhabitants thereof; 'because,' says the Prophet, 'they have transgressed the laws, changed the ordinance, broken the everlasting covenant.' Plainly showing that they were to be a corrupt people; a people who, for instance, would change the ordinance of baptism from immersion to sprinkling or pouring, or doing it away altogether, and in the same manner changing the various ordinances of the Gospel from the original form in which the Lord revealed them. He says, through the mouth of His Prophet, that the people who should be guilty of this great wickedness should be visited with fire; 'the inhabitants of the earth are burned and few men left.' This is a little more definite. We learned through Malachi, that they should be destroyed both root and branch—no branch of wickedness, no roots of wickedness left; but it does not give us the proportion, between the righteous and the wicked. But Isaiah gives us a little further clue to this matter. To the query, how many are to be overtaken by this last great judgment, Isaiah would answer, 'the inhabitants of the earth are burned and few men left.' What, only a few persons to be converted, only a few to receive the true Gospel, and be prepared for the coming of the Bridegroom; only a few people to escape this awful desolation? So says the Prophet Isaiah; that is, few in comparison to the great and numerous population of our globe. Even some few millions would be few compared with the twelve hundred millions that inhabit the earth. Isaiah, in the same chapter, in describing the glory of his personal reign on the earth, says that 'Then the moon shall be confounded and the sun ashamed,' because of the superior light that will attend the presence of the being who is to reign in Zion and Jerusalem. The Lord causes the natural light of the sun and the heat thereof; he causes the natural light of the other luminaries that twinkle in yonder heavens, and also the heat which proceeds from their bodies. Now, if he can produce such intense heat by such bodies as our sun; if he can cause the surrounding worlds to be heated and to receive a certain temperature by the radiation of light and heat; if the sun can produce such a high temperature on our earth, existing some 90 millions of miles away, who not the Lord be able to produce a greater light and heat if necessary to sweep off the wicked, and to cause the earth in a moment, as it were, to feel the power of heat, even to its melting like wax before his presence? But, you may ask, 'why not this heat destroy the righteous, as well as the wicked? Have not the righteous often times been burned at the stake? have they not been consumed to ashes, by the power of the wicked? And why should this intense heat, of which you are speaking, which is to destroy the wicked root and branch, not affect the righteous as well?' Let us explain. Before this day of burning there will be no righteous on the earth. Not one? No, not one. 'What is to become of them?' The Apostle Paul informs us that, 'The Lord himself shall descend from heaven with a shout, with the voice of the Archangel, and with the trump of God; and the dead in Christ shall rise first. Then we, which are alive and remain, shall be caught up together with them in the clouds to meet the Lord in the air.'"

68

Joseph Fielding Smith, The Way to Perfection, p. 285.

"In this warning Peter calls attention to the destruction of the world in the flood, and says that at the coming of Christ—which scoffers would postpone, or deny—there shall come another cleansing of the earth; but the second time by fire. Is not the condition among the people today similar to that in the days of Noah? Did the people believe and repent then? Can you make men, save with few exceptions, believe today that there is any danger? Do you believe the Lord when he said one hundred years ago: 'For I am no respecter of persons, and will that all men shall know that the day speedily cometh; the hour is not yet, but is nigh at hand, when peace shall be taken from the earth, and the devil shall have power over his own dominion'? (D&C 1:35.) 'And behold, and lo, I come quickly to judgment, to convince all of their ungodly deeds which they have committed against me, as it is written of men in the volume of the book.' (D&C 99:5.) 'Prepare ye, prepare ye for that which is to come, for the Lord is nigh; and the anger of the Lord is kindled, and his word is bathed in heaven, and it shall fall upon the inhabitants of the earth.' (D&C 1:12-13.) 'Verily, I say unto you, this generation, in which these things shall be shown forth, shall not pass away until all I have told you shall be fulfilled.' (P.G.P., Writings of J.S., 1:34.)"

Bruce R. McConkie, The Millennial Messiah, p. 525.

"At the Second Coming when the same literal fire burns over all the earth. The wicked shall be consumed and the righteous shall be as though they walked in the furnace of Nebuchadnezzar."

SCRIPTURAL REFERENCES

1 Nephi 22:15-19

15 For behold, saith the prophet, the time cometh speedily that Satan shall have no more power over the hearts of the children of men; for the day soon cometh that all the proud and they who do wickedly shall be as stubble; and the day cometh that they must be burned.

16 For the time soon cometh that the fulness of the wrath of God shall be poured out upon all the children of men; for he will not suffer that the wicked shall destroy the righteous.

17 Wherefore, he will preserve the righteous by his power, even if it so be that the fulness of his wrath must come, and the righteous be preserved, even unto the destruction of their enemies by fire. Wherefore, the righteous need not fear; for thus saith the prophet, they shall be saved, even if it so be as by fire.

18 Behold, my brethren, I say unto you, that these things must shortly come; yea, even blood, and fire, and vapor of smoke must come; and it must needs be upon the face of this earth; and it cometh unto men according to the flesh if it so be that they will harden their hearts against the Holy One of Israel.

19 For behold, the righteous shall not perish; for the time surely must come that all they who fight against Zion shall be cut off.

2 Nephi 26:4

4 Wherefore, all those who are proud, and that do wickedly, the day that cometh shall burn them up, saith the Lord of Hosts, for they shall be as stubble.

2 Nephi 30:10

10 For the time speedily cometh that the Lord God shall cause a great division among the people, and the wicked will he destroy; and he will spare his people, yea, even if it so be that he must destroy the wicked by fire.

Helaman 13:12-14

12 Yea, wo unto this great city of Zarahemla; for behold, it is because of those who are righteous that it is saved; yea, wo unto this great city, for I perceive, saith the Lord, that there are many, yea, even the more part of this great city, that will harden their hearts against me, saith the Lord.

13 But blessed are they who will repent, for them will I spare. But behold, if it were not for the righteous who are in this great city, behold, I would cause that fire should come down out of heaven and destroy it.

14 But behold, it is for the righteous' sake that it is spared. But behold, the time cometh, saith the Lord, that when ye shall cast out the righteous from among you, then shall ye be ripe for destruction; yea, wo be unto this great city, because of the wickedness and abominations which are in her.

3 Nephi 9:11

11 And because they did cast them all out, that there were none righteous among them, I did send down fire and destroy them, that their wickedness and abominations might be hid from before my face, that the blood of the prophets and the saints whom I sent among them might not cry unto me

from the ground against them.

3 Nephi 25:1-3

1 For behold, the day cometh that shall burn as an oven; and all the proud, yea, and all that do wickedly, shall be stubble; and the day that cometh shall burn them up, saith the Lord of Hosts, that it shall leave them neither root nor branch.

2 But unto you that fear my name, shall the Son of Righteousness arise with healing in his wings; and ye shall go forth and grow up as calves in the stall.

3 And ye shall tread down the wicked; for they shall be ashes under the soles of your feet in the day that I shall do this, saith the Lord of Hosts.

D&C 64:24

24 For after today cometh the burning—this is speaking after the manner of the Lord—for verily I say, tomorrow all the proud and they that do wickedly shall be as stubble; and I will burn them up, for I am the Lord of Hosts; and I will not spare any that remain in Babylon.

WHEN RIPE IN INIQUITY

Brigham Young, Journal of Discourses, Vol. 2, p. 311, July 8, 1855.
"'When the wicked rule the people mourn,' and when the corruption of a people bears down the scale in favor of wickedness, that people is nigh unto destruction."

Heber C. Kimball, Journal of Discourses, Vol. 6, p. 126, December 13, 1857.
"Let me tell you the world is ripe, and there are no saving principles within them, with a very few exceptions; and they will gather out, and the rest of mankind are ready for destruction, for they will have no salt to save them. I know the day is right at hand when men will forfeit their Priesthood and turn against us and against the covenants they have made, and they will be destroyed as Judas was."

Orson Hyde, Journal of Discourses, Vol. 2, p. 206, March 18, 1855.
"Nations shall be cut off when they are ripe in iniquity. But they are not ripe in iniquity, until they kill my servants, and cast out my people;—then will I visit them in my anger, and vex them in my displeasure, and cut off their bitter branches. A desolating sickness shall cover the land. (See Book of Covenants.) Famine shall sorely oppress them—confusion and war shall make their hearts to faint, and their knees to tremble."

Orson Pratt, Journal of Discourses, Vol. 17, p. 286, September 20, 1874.
"To show more fully the time when this book should be brought to light, let me say that it is a latter-day work, and to prove it, I will read the following verses. 'The poor among men shall rejoice in the Holy One of Israel, for the terrible one is brought to naught, and the scorner is consumed, and all that watch for iniquity are cut off; all that make a man an offender for a word, or that lay a snare for him that reproveth in the gate, or that turn aside the just for a thing of naught.' All these are to be cut off. When? When they have heard the words of this book, when the proclamation has been sounded in their ears. When they are become fully ripened in iniquity, they will be cut off according to the declaration of the Prophet Isaiah. But their times must first be fulfilled; their fulness must come in, before these terrible judgments and destructions shall lay waste the nations of the Gentiles."

Wilford Woodruff, Journal of Discourses, Vol. 5, p. 269, September 27, 1857.
"You have all the blessings which the celestial kingdom and laws of God impart unto men on the earth, while the Gentile nations have suffered ruin, wickedness, and abominations of every kind to increase in their midst until they are ripe for destruction. Do they not thirst for the blood of the Saints and every man who is righteous? Do they not delight in wickedness? They are full of wrath and anger, and they are ripe for the damnation of hell. Yes, the nations of the earth are ripe today."

Wilford Woodruff, Journal of Discourses, Vol. 7, p. 105, January 10, 1858.
"This nation is ripe in iniquity, and the destroying angels are at their doors; and I am as sure that the scourges will follow as I am that the servants of god have borne a true and faithful testimony

unto them. I know what the consequence will be of the world rejecting the truth, for I have the testimony of Jesus and the Spirit of God within me; and therefore I say, Let us look well to our ways, remember our covenants, our duties, and our prayers; and I do hope and pray that the Elders in Great Salt Lake City will not, in the midst of their recreations, neglect their prayers or their duties before the Lord, nor permit any thing to stand between them and the building up the kingdom of God."

Wilford Woodruff, Journal of Discourses, Vol. 17, p. 246-247, October 9, 1874.

"This nations and other nations will war with the Saints of God until their cup is full; and when they become ripened in iniquity the Lord Almighty will cut them off, and the judgments of the Most High God will follow the testimony of the Elders of Israel."

Wilford Woodruff, Journal of Discourses, Vol. 18, p. 128, October 8, 1875.

"The whole earth is ripe in iniquity; and these inspired men, these Elders of Israel, have been commanded of the Almighty to go forth and warn the world, that their garments may be clear of the blood of all men.

I tell you that God will not disappoint Zion or Babylon, the heavens or the earth, in regard to the judgements which he has promised in these last days, but every one of them will have its fulfillment upon the heads of the children of men; and when they are fully ripened in iniquity the nations of the earth will be swept away as with the besom of destruction."

Wilford Woodruff, Collected Discourses, Vol. 2, April 6, 1890.

" Whenever a nation is ripened in iniquity, the Lord raises up prophets and inspired men and they are sent forth to warn that nation, and when they have warned the people and given unto them the word of the Lord, that word will not fall unfulfilled. . . .You may trace this through the whole history of the world until the present hour and you will find that that God who sits enthroned on high has governed and controlled all these things. He will do the same today."

Erastus Snow, Journal of Discourses, Vol. 25, p. 73, February 24, 1884.

"For the wicked have their agency as well as the righteous, and God will not deprive them of it. He wills not that any be deprived of their agency. If people will work wickedness; if they will violate their covenants; if they will foreswear themselves; if they will trample under foot the constitution and institutions of our common country, (which they are sworn to defend and maintain) in their over-zeal to destroy the Saints, they must have their agency so to do. They must have the privilege of working out their own salvation, or their own damnation. They must fill up the cup of their iniquity; otherwise, how will the Lord be justified in wasting them away and destroying them out of the earth, except they first fill up the cup of their iniquity."

Erastus Snow, Journal of Discourses, Vol. 25, p. 196, May 31, 1884.

"The Gospel exalts those who receive it, and brings condemnation and destruction upon those who refuse to obey it. But without the Gospel being sent out by authority and power from God, the inhabitants of the earth could not be ripened for destruction. We read in many places in the Scriptures concerning the destruction of the wicked in the last days. But we read also in other

Scriptures, that the Lord destroys them only when they are ripe in their iniquity. Jesus, in prophesying of His second coming, and the destruction that shall fall upon the wicked, speaks in this wise—that they shall fill up the cup of their iniquity. This principle we see referred to and illustrated in the days of Abraham. The Lord promised unto him the land of Canaan for an everlasting possession. Nevertheless, his seed must be brought into bondage in Egypt, and remain there until those who dwelt in the land of Canaan had filled up the cup of their iniquity. The people were not yet ripe for destruction, and therefore the Lord could not displace them and put Abraham and his seed in possession of his land."

Jedediah M. Grant, Journal of Discourses, Vol. 2, p. 146, April 2, 1854.

"The world is in commotion, and the hearts of men fail them for fear of the impending storm that threatens to enshroud all nations in its black mantle. Treaties of peace may be made, and war will stop for a season, but there are certain decrees of the Gods, and certain bounds fixed, and laws and edicts passed the high courts of heaven, beyond which the nations cannot pass; and when the Almighty decrees the wicked shall slay the wicked, strong nations may interfere, peace conventions may become rife in the world and exert their influence to sheath the sword of war, and make treaties of peace to calm the troubled surface of all Europe, to no effect; the war cloud is still booming o'er the heavens, darkening the earth, and threatening the world with desolation."

Heber J. Grant, Messages of the First Presidency, Vol. 6, p. 99, June 9, 1940.

"We are not given the step-by-step backsliding of this Jareditic civilization till it reached the social and governmental chaos the record sets out, but those steps seem wholly clear from the results. Put into modern terms, we can understand them. First there was a forsaking of the righteous life, and the working of wickedness; then must have come the extortion and oppression of the poor by the rich; then retaliation and reprisal by the poor against the rich; then would come a cry to share the wealth which should belong to all; then the easy belief that society owed every man a living whether he worked or not; then the keeping of a great body of idlers; then when community revenues failed to do this, as they always have failed and always will fail, a self-helping by one to the goods of his neighbor; and finally when the neighbor resisted, as resist he must, or starve with his family, then death to the neighbor and all that belonged to him. This was the decreed 'fulness of iniquity.'"

Hyrum M. Smith, Doctrine and Covenants Commentary, Sec. 18, p. 83.

"6. Ripening in iniquity. As fruit, when ripe, falls, so the world, when ripened in iniquity, is destroyed. The Lord, therefore, commanded His servants to preach repentance, to avert destruction. The most conspicuous sin of the world in this age, as when Paul wrote his letter to the Romans (Rom. 1:26), is unchastity. Consequently, the voice of the Church has been raised against that sin with more emphasis than against any other evil."

Joseph Fielding Smith, Church History and Modern Revelation, Vol 2, p. 110.

"The Lord threatened destruction to great cities if they in their iniquity rejected his truth. This destruction, evidently is to come when their cup is full. Desolation awaited them and the hour of their judgment would come.

Joseph Fielding Smith, Answers to Gospel Questions, Vol. 2, p. 109.

"The millennium will come when the Lord decides that the cup of iniquity is full. He will come to cleanse the earth, and in that day the veil of the covering of the temple 'which hideth the earth, shall be taken off, and all flesh shall see me together,' said the Lord."

Joseph Fielding Smith Jr., Doctrines of Salvation, Vol. 3, p. 3.

"I get annoyed sometimes at some of our elders who when speaking say the Lord will come when we all become righteous enough to receive him. The Lord is not going to wait for us to get righteous. When he gets ready to come, he is going to come—when the cup of iniquity is full—and if we are not righteous then, it will be just too bad for us, for we will be classed among the ungodly, and we will be as stubble to be swept off the face of the earth."

Bruce R. McConkie, A New Witness for the Articles of Faith, p. 608.

"'Mine indignation is soon to be poured out without measure upon all nations; and this will I do when the cup of their iniquity is full.' When men become again as they were in Noah's day, they again will be destroyed, this time by the fires that consume every corruptible thing."

SCRIPTURAL REFERENCES

2 Nephi 28:16
16 Wo unto them that turn aside the just for a thing of naught and revile against that which is good, and say that it is of no worth! For the day shall come that the Lord God will speedily visit the inhabitants of the earth; and in that day that they are fully ripe in iniquity they shall perish.

Alma 10:19
19 Yea, well did Mosiah say, who was our last king, when he was about to deliver up the kingdom, having no one to confer it upon, causing that this people should be governed by their own voices—yea, well did he say that if the time should come that the voice of this people should choose iniquity, that is, if the time should come that this people should fall into transgression, they would be ripe for destruction.

Alma 10:22-23
22 Yea, and I say unto you that if it were not for the prayers of the righteous, who are now in the land, that ye would even now be visited with utter destruction; yet it would not be by flood, as were the people in the days of Noah, but it would be by famine, and by pestilence, and the sword.
23 But it is by the prayers of the righteous that ye are spared; now therefore, if ye will cast out the righteous from among you then will not the Lord stay his hand; but in his fierce anger he will come out against you; then ye shall be smitten by famine, and by pestilence, and by the sword; and the time is soon at hand except ye repent.

Alma 37:28-31
28 For behold, there is a curse upon all this land, that destruction shall come upon all those workers of darkness, according to the power of God, when they are fully ripe; therefore I desire that this people might not be destroyed.
29 Therefore ye shall keep these secret plans of their oaths and their covenants from this people, and only their wickedness and their murders and their abominations shall ye make known unto them; and ye shall teach them to abhor such wickedness and abominations and murders; and ye shall also teach them that these people were destroyed on account of their wickedness and abominations and their murders.
30 For behold, they murdered all the prophets of the Lord who came among them to declare unto them concerning their iniquities; and the blood of those whom they murdered did cry unto the Lord their God for vengeance upon those who were their murderers; and thus the judgments of God did come upon these workers of darkness and secret combinations.
31 Yea, and cursed be the land forever and ever unto those workers of darkness and secret combinations, even unto destruction, except they repent before they are fully ripe.

Alma 45:16
16 And he said: Thus saith the Lord God—Cursed shall be the land, yea, this land, unto every nation, kindred, tongue, and people, unto destruction, which do wickedly, when they are fully ripe; and as

I have said so shall it be; for this is the cursing and the blessing of God upon the land, for the Lord cannot look upon sin with the least degree of allowance.

Helaman 5:2-3

2 For as their laws and their governments were established by the voice of the people, and they who chose evil were more numerous than they who chose good, therefore they were ripening for destruction, for the laws had become corrupted.

3 Yea, and this was not all; they were a stiffnecked people, insomuch that they could not be governed by the law nor justice, save it were to their destruction.

Helaman 11:37

37 And it came to pass in the eighty and fifth year they did wax stronger and stronger in their pride, and in their wickedness; and thus they were ripening again for destruction.

Helaman 13:12-14

12 Yea, wo unto this great city of Zarahemla; for behold, it is because of those who are righteous that it is saved; yea, wo unto this great city, for I perceive, saith the Lord, that there are many, yea, even the more part of this great city, that will harden their hearts against me, saith the Lord.

13 But blessed are they who will repent, for them will I spare. But behold, if it were not for the righteous who are in this great city, behold, I would cause that fire should come down out of heaven and destroy it.

14 But behold, it is for the righteous' sake that it is spared. But behold, the time cometh, saith the Lord, that when ye shall cast out the righteous from among you, then shall ye be ripe for destruction; yea, wo be unto this great city, because of the wickedness and abominations which are in her.

3 Nephi 9:11

11 And because they did cast them all out, that there were none righteous among them, I did send down fire and destroy them, that their wickedness and abominations might be hid from before my face, that the blood of the prophets and the saints whom I sent among them might not cry unto me from the ground against them.

Ether 2:9-11

9 And now, we can behold the decrees of God concerning this land, that it is a land of promise; and whatsoever nation shall possess it shall serve God, or they shall be swept off when the fulness of his wrath shall come upon them. And the fulness of his wrath cometh upon them when they are ripened in iniquity.

10 For behold, this is a land which is choice above all other lands; wherefore he that doth possess it shall serve God or shall be swept off; for it is the everlasting decree of God. And it is not until the fulness of iniquity among the children of the land, that they are swept off.

11 And this cometh unto you, O ye Gentiles, that ye may know the decrees of God—that ye may repent, and not continue in your iniquities until the fulness come, that ye may not bring down the fulness of the wrath of God upon you as the inhabitants of the land have hitherto done.

Ether 2:15

15 And the brother of Jared repented of the evil which he had done, and did call upon the name of the Lord for his brethren who were with him. And the Lord said unto him: I will forgive thee and thy brethren of their sins; but thou shalt not sin any more, for ye shall remember that my Spirit will not always strive with man; wherefore, if ye will sin until ye are fully ripe ye shall be cut off from the presence of the Lord. And these are my thoughts upon the land which I shall give you for your inheritance; for it shall be a land choice above all other lands.

Ether 9:20

20 And thus the Lord did pour out his blessings upon this land, which was choice above all other lands; and he commanded that whoso should possess the land should possess it unto the Lord, or they should be destroyed when they were ripened in iniquity; for upon such, saith the Lord: I will pour out the fulness of my wrath.

D&C 29:8-9

8 Wherefore the decree hath gone forth from the Father that they shall be gathered in unto one place upon the face of this land, to prepare their hearts and be prepared in all things against the day when tribulation and desolation are sent forth upon the wicked.
9 For the hour is nigh and the day soon at hand when the earth is ripe; and all the proud and they that do wickedly shall be as stubble; and I will burn them up, saith the Lord of Hosts, that wickedness shall not be upon the earth;

D&C 101:11

11 Mine indignation is soon to be poured out without measure upon all nations; and this will I do when the cup of their iniquity is full.

CHAPTER TWO

PROPHECIES OF THE JEWS & JERUSALEM

"Judah must return, Jerusalem must be rebuilt, and the temple, and water come out from under the temple, and the waters of the Dead Sea be healed. It will take some time to rebuild the walls of the city and the temple, etc.; and all this must be done before the Son of Man will make his appearance." (Teachings of the Prophet Joseph Smith, Sec. 6, p. 286.)

Joseph Smith, History of the Church, Vol. 2, Introduction, p. 29.

"Acting, then, under the divine authority restored to earth by the Prophet Moses, this Apostolic delegation—as well as the Apostle first sent—from the summit of Mount Olivet blessed the land, and again dedicated it for the return of the Jews. It is not strange, therefore, to those who look upon such a movement as Zionism in connection with faith in God's great latter-day work, to see this spirit now moving upon the minds of the Jewish people prompting their return to the land of their fathers. It is but the breath of God upon their souls turning their hearts to the promises made to the fathers. It is but the fulfillment in part of one of the many prophecies of the Book of Mormon relating to the gathering of Israel, viz: 'It shall come to pass that the Lord God shall commence His work among all nations, kindreds, tongues, and people, to bring about the restoration of the keys of authority to gather Israel from the four quarters of the earth', and the exercise of that divine authority, though unrecognized as yet by the world, is the real cause of this movement Palestine-ward by the Jews."

Joseph Smith, History of the Church, Vol. 4, Introduction, p. 31.

"The mission appointed to Elders Orson Hyde and John E. Page, of the quorum of the Twelve, to Jerusalem, was second in importance only to that appointed to the rest of the Twelve to Great Britain. John E. Page utterly failed to fulfill his appointment, notwithstanding the frequent urging and reproofs of the Prophet. He never left the shores of America, and finally returned to Nauvoo to be severely censured for his lack of faith and energy. Orson Hyde, on the contrary, in the midst of many hardships, persevered in his journey to the Holy Land, until he succeeded in accomplishing that which had been appointed unto him. Elder Hyde it appears, was a descendant of the tribe of Judah; and sometime after the Prophet had become acquainted with him, most probably in the year 1832, in the course of pronouncing a blessing upon him, said, 'In due time thou shalt go to Jerusalem, the land of thy fathers, and be a watchman unto the house of Israel; and by thy hand shall the Most High do a great work, which shall prepare the way and greatly facilitate the gathering together of that people.' It was in fulfillment of this prediction upon his head that he had been called upon this mission to Jerusalem, to dedicate the land of Palestine by apostolic authority, preparatory to the return of the Jews and other of the tribes of Israel to that land of promise. This mission he fully accomplished. An account of his journey and of his beautiful and powerful prayer of dedication will be found in his letters published in this volume."

Joseph Smith, History of the Church, Vol. 4, Introduction, p. 33.

"The age has come when the promises of the Lord to Israel must be fulfilled; and hence an apostle of the new dispensation of the Gospel is sent by divine authority to dedicate the land of Palestine preparatory to the return of Israel to his promised inheritance. After which follows this strange and world-wide movement among the Jews looking to the re-establishment of 'Jewish nationalism on a modern basis in Palestine.' What other relationship can exist between the mission of the Apostle Orson Hyde and this world-wide movement among the Jews for the re-establishment of Israel in Palestine, but the relationship of cause to effect—under, of course, the larger fact that the set time for the restoration of Israel has come? The apostle's mission to Jerusalem for the purpose of dedicating that land, preparatory to the return of Israel, was without doubt part of the general program for the restoration of Israel to their lands and to the favor and blessing of God."

Joseph Smith, History of the Church, Vol. 4, p. 211.

"It will be necessary here to make a few observations on the doctrine set forth in the above quotation, and it is generally supposed that sacrifice was entirely done away when the Great Sacrifice [i.e., the sacrifice of the Lord Jesus] was offered up, and that there will be no necessity for the ordinance of sacrifice in future; but those who assert this are certainly not acquainted with the duties, privileges and authority of the priesthood, or with the Prophets.

The offering of sacrifice has ever been connected and forms a part of the duties of the Priesthood. It began with the Priesthood, and will be continued until after the coming of Christ, from generation to generation. We frequently have mention made of the offering of sacrifice by the servants of the Most High in ancient days, prior to the law of Moses; which ordinances will be continued when the Priesthood is restored with all its authority, power and blessings.

Elijah was the last Prophet that held the keys of the Priesthood, and who will, before the last dispensation, restore the authority and deliver the keys of the Priesthood, in order that all the ordinances may be attended to in righteousness. It is true that the Savior had authority and power to bestow this blessing; but the sons of Levi were too prejudiced. 'And I will send Elijah the Prophet before the great and terrible day of the Lord,' etc. Why send Elijah? Because he holds the keys of the authority to administer in all the ordinances of the Priesthood; and without the authority is given, the ordinances could not be administered in righteousness.

It is a very prevalent opinion that the sacrifices which were offered were entirely consumed. This was not the case; if you read Leviticus, second chap., second and third verses, you will observe that the priests took a part as a memorial and offered it up before the Lord, while the remainder was kept for the maintenance of the priests; so that the offerings and sacrifices are not all consumed upon the altar--but the blood is sprinkled, and the fat and certain other portions are consumed.

These sacrifices, as well as every ordinance belonging to the Priesthood, will, when the Temple of the Lord shall be built, and the sons of Levi be purified, be fully restored and attended to in all their powers, ramifications, and blessings. This ever did and ever will exist when the powers of the Melchisedek Priesthood are sufficiently manifest; else how can the restitution of all things spoken of by the holy Prophets be brought to pass?It is not to be understood that the law of Moses will be established again with all its rites and variety of ceremonies; this has never been spoken of by the Prophets; but those things which existed prior to Moses' day, namely, sacrifice, will be continued."

Teachings of the Prophet Joseph Smith, Section Four, 1839–42, p. 173.

"These sacrifices, as well as every ordinance belonging to the Priesthood, will, when the Temple of the Lord shall be built, and the sons of Levi be purified, be fully restored and attended to in all their powers, ramifications, and blessings. This ever did and ever will exist when the powers of the Melchizedek Priesthood are sufficiently manifest; else how can the restitution of all things spoken of by the Holy Prophets be brought to pass? It is not to be understood that the law of Moses will be established again with all its rites and variety of ceremonies; this has never been spoken of by the prophets; but those things which existed prior to Moses' day, namely, sacrifice, will be continued.

It may be asked by some, what necessity for sacrifice, since the Great Sacrifice was offered? In answer to which, if repentance, baptism, and faith existed prior to the days of Christ, what necessity for them since that time?"

Teachings of the Prophet Joseph Smith, Section Six, 1843–44, p. 286.

"Judah must return, Jerusalem must be rebuilt, and the temple, and water come out from under the temple, and the waters of the Dead Sea be healed. It will take some time to rebuild the walls of the city and the temple, etc.; and all this must be done before the Son of Man will make his appearance."

Brigham Young, Messages of the First Presidency, Vol. 1, p. 257.

"To such an extreme will this great division finally extend, that the nations of the old world will combine to oppose these things by military force. They will send a great army to Palestine, against the Jews; and they will besiege their city, and will reduce the inhabitants of Jerusalem to the greatest extreme of distress and misery. Then will commence a struggle in which the fate of nations and empires will be suspended on a single battle. . . .

In that day the Lord will pour upon the inhabitants of Jerusalem the spirit of grace and supplication, and they shall look upon the Messiah whom they have pierced. For lo! he will descend from heaven, as the defender of the Jews: and to complete their victory. His feet will stand in that day upon the Mount of Olives, which shall cleave in asunder at his presence, and remove one half to the north, and the other to the south; thus forming a great valley where the mountain now stands.

The earth will quake around him, while storm and tempest, hail and plague, are mingled with the clash of arms, the roar of artillery, the shouts of victory, and the groans of the wounded and dying.

In that day all who are in the siege, both against Judea and against Jerusalem, shall be cut in pieces; though all the people of the earth should be gathered together against it.

This signal victory on the part of the Jews, so unlooked for by the nations, and attended with the personal advent of Messiah, and the accompanying events, will change the whole order of things in Europe and Asia, in regard to political and religious organization, and government.
The Jews as a nation become holy from that day forward; and their city and sanctuary becomes holy. There also the Messiah establishes his throne, and seat of government.

Jerusalem then becomes the seat of empire, and the great centre and capital of the old world.
All the families of the land shall then go up to Jerusalem once a year, to worship the King, the Lord of Hosts, and to keep the feast of Tabernacles.

Those who refuse to go up, shall have no rain, but shall be smitten with dearth and famine. And if the family of Egypt go not up (as it never rains there) they shall be smitten with the plague. And thus all things shall be fulfilled according to the words of the holy prophets of old, and the word of the Lord which is now revealed, to confirm and fulfil them.

In short the kings, rulers, priests and people of Europe, and of the old world, shall know this once that there is a God in Israel, who, as in days of old, can utter his Voice, and it shall be obeyed."

Brigham Young, Journal of Discourses, Vol. 2, p. 142, December, 3, 1854.

"Jerusalem is not to be redeemed by the soft still voice of the preacher of the Gospel of peace. Why? Because they were once the blessed of the Lord, the chosen of the Lord, the promised seed. They were the people from among whom should spring the Messiah; and salvation could be found only through that tribe. The Messiah came through them, and they killed him; and they will be the last of all the seed of Abraham to have the privilege of receiving the New and Everlasting Covenant. You may hand out to them gold, you may feed and clothe them, but it is impossible to convert the Jews, until the Lord God Almighty does it."

Brigham Young, Journal of Discourses, Vol. 4, p. 352, June 7, 1857.

"We have also got to assist in rebuilding Jerusalem; for, as brother Kimball has said, if it is built up, we have got to assist in doing it."

Brigham Young, Journal of Discourses, Vol. 11, p. 279, December 23, 1866.

"The decree has gone forth from the Almighty that they cannot have the benefit of the atonement until they gather to Jerusalem, for they said, let his blood be upon us and upon our children, consequently, they cannot believe in him until his second coming. We have a great desire for their welfare, and are looking for the time soon to come when they will gather to Jerusalem, build up the city and the land of Palestine, and prepare for the coming of the Messiah."

Discourses of Brigham Young, p. 121.

"Jerusalem is not to be redeemed by our going there and preaching to the inhabitants. It will be redeemed by the high hand of the Almighty. It will be given into the possession of the ancient Israelites by the power of God, and by the pouring out of his judgments."

Discourses of Brigham Young, p. 122.

"When the Savior visits Jerusalem, and the Jews look upon him, and see the wounds in his hands and in his side and in his feet, they will then know that they have persecuted and put to death the true Messiah, and then they will acknowledge him, but not till then. They have confounded his first and second coming, expecting his first coming to be as a mighty prince instead of as a servant. They will go back by and by to Jerusalem and own their Lord and Master. We have no feelings against them."

Parley P. Pratt, A Voice of Warning, p. 49.

"John, in his 11th chapter of Revelations, gives us many more particulars concerning this same event. He informs us that, after the city and temple are rebuilt by the Jews, the Gentiles will tread it under foot forty and two months, during which time there will be two prophets continually prophesying and working mighty miracles.

And it seems that the Gentile army shall be hindered from utterly destroying and overthrowing the city, while these two prophets continue. But, after a struggle of three years and a half, they at length succeed in destroying these two prophets, and then overrunning much of the city; they send gifts to each other because of the death of the two prophets; and in the meantime will not allow their dead bodies to be put in graves; but suffer them to lie in the streets of Jerusalem three days and a half, during which the armies of the Gentiles, consisting of many kindreds, tongues and nations, passing through the city, plundering the Jews see their dead bodies lying in the street.

But, after three days and a half on a sudden, the spirit of life from God enters them, and they will arise and stand upon their feet, and great fear will fall upon them that see them. And then they shall hear a voice from heaven saying, 'Come up hither,' and they will ascend up to heaven in a cloud, and their enemies beholding them."

Orson Pratt, Journal of Discourses, Vol. 7, p. 187-188, July 10, 1859.

"By-and-by, after you have fulfilled your missions to the nations of the Gentiles, and there will not any more of them repent,—that is, when you have fully accomplished all that is required of you in relation to them, you will have another mission, and so will the Twelve, and that is to the house of Israel that may be among those nations; I mean the literal descendants of Jacob—the Jews, and the descendants of the other tribes that may be scattered among those nations. There are some from the ten tribes among them; but the body of the ten tribes are in the north country. You will find a few among all these Gentile nations: you will have to direct your attention to them after you have fulfilled your mission among the Gentiles, and their times are fulfilled. You will have something to do among the Jews, and then will be a time of great power, such as you and I have not dreamed of. Indeed, we could not, with our narrow comprehensions of mind, perceive the power that will then follow. The Lord has told it in a revelation in the Book of Doctrine and Covenants. He has told us, before the rise of this Church, that in bringing forth this Gospel, it is a light that could not be hid in darkness: therefore, He says I must bring the fulness of my Gospel from among the Gentiles to the house of Israel; or, this light of the fulness of my Gospel will, as it were, be covered up and hid in darkness in many respects, and will not shine with that brilliancy, power, and greatness: it will not appear in that magnitude that it will when I bring it from the midst of the Gentiles to my people, O house of Israel. Again, the Lord says, in another revelation in the Book of Doctrine and Covenants, that when we have preached the Gospel faithfully to the Gentile nations, then cometh the day of my power; and we already know what the Psalmist says in regard to that day—'My people shall be willing in the day of my power.' The house of Israel have been unwilling in many generations past to receive the Gospel; but in the day of his power, you Seventies, that will go forth among the nations of Gentiles to hunt out the literal descendants of Jacob, will be armed with that glory, power, and majesty and clothed upon from on high to that degree that no power on earth can stay you; and then, in that day, the seed of Jacob will be willing to receive the testimony of the Gospel. Then many of the Jews will believe, although many of that nation will gather to Jerusalem in unbelief. But the Book of Mormon has told us that the main part of them will believe while yet scattered. They will receive your testimony and gather to Jerusalem; and because of your testimony, the Gentile believers will gather to Zion; and because of your testimony, all the elect of God, of whatever nation, tongue, and people, will be gathered out year after year; and by-and-by, the great and last gathering will be done through instrumentality of angels. There will be two, as it were, grinding at a mill; the faithful one will be taken, and the other will be left: there will be two, as it were, sleeping in one bed; one will be picked up by the angels, and the other will be left; and the remnant of the children of god scattered abroad on all the face of the earth will receive their last gathering by the angels. But between this and that day there will be ship-load after ship-load gathering continually of the elect of God, of the Israel of God, and of the covenant people of the Lord to Zion and Jerusalem."

Orson Pratt, Journal of Discourses, Vol. 14, p. 274-275, April 9, 1871.

"'The Lord whom ye seek shall suddenly come to his temple, but who shall abide the day of his coming? Who shall stand when he appears? For he is like the refiner's fire and like fuller's soap. He shall sit as a refiner and purifier of silver upon the sons of Levi; that they may offer an offering unto the Lord in righteousness. Then shall the offering of Judah and Jerusalem be pleasant unto the Lord as in days of old and as in former years.' The Lord intends to have a temple not only in Zion, but, according to this, in old Jerusalem; and he intends that the sons of Levi shall receive their blessings—the blessings of their priesthood that were conferred upon them in that temple; and he is determined that the ministers in that temple shall be purified as gold and silver is purified, and he is determined to sit as a refiner's fire in the midst of that temple."

Orson Pratt, Journal of Discourses. Vol. 16, p. 152, August 16, 1873.

"Will the waters be divided? O yes. We are told, in the prophecies of Isaiah, that when the house of Israel shall return to their own country, he will strike the river Nile, in the seven great channels, by which it enters into the Mediterranean Sea. Instead of taking them above these seven different channels, he will make a road through the seven channels of the river Nile; and the people of Israel will go again dry shod, as they did anciently. In the eleventh chapter of Isaiah, and the 15th verse, we read that 'the Lord shall utterly destroy the tongue of the Egyptian Sea,' not the main body of the sea. Those who are acquainted with the north portion of the Red Sea know there are two prongs, one is called the tongue of the Egyptian Sea; and the children of Israel shall go through dry shod, and through the seven channels of the river Nile, as did Israel in the day that they came up out of the land of Egypt."

Orson Pratt, Journal of Discourses, Vol. 16, p. 183, August 31, 1873.

"We may go beyond this life, to the next, and we shall find that the honors conferred by God upon these twelve sons are continued there. Christians believe that there will be a holy Jerusalem come down from God out of heaven, which will be prepared as a bride adorned for her husband. This holy city which will descend from God out of heaven, will have a wall round it, and in this wall there will be a certain number of the most beautiful gates—three on the north, three on the south, three on the east and three on the west. Each of these gates will be made of one pearl—a precious stone most beautiful to look upon. On each of these gates there will be a certain name—one will have inscribed upon it the name of Judah, another Levi, another Simeon, and so on until the whole twelve gates will be named after the twelve sons of Jacob and his four polygamic wives; thus we see that, instead of the Lord calling them bastards, and forbidding them to enter the congregation of the Lord until the tenth generation, he honors them above all people, making them the most conspicuous in the holy city, having their names written on its very gates."

Orson Pratt, Journal of Discourses, Vol. 18, p. 64-65, July 25, 1875.

"The Jews dispersed among the Gentiles will not come and sing in the height of Zion, or but very few of them, they will go to Jerusalem. Some of them will believe in the true Messiah, and thousands of the more righteous, whose fathers did not consent to the shedding of the blood of the Son of God, will receive the Gospel before they gather from among the nations. Many of them, however, will not receive the Gospel, but seeing that others are going to Jerusalem they will go also; and when they get back to Palestine, to the place where their ancient Jerusalem stood, and see a certain portion of the believing Jews endeavoring to fulfill and carry out the prophecies, they also will take hold and assist in the same work. At the same time they will have their synagogues, in which they will preach against Jesus of Nazareth, 'that impostor,' as they call him, who was crucified by their fathers. After awhile, when tens of thousands of them have gathered and rebuilt their Temple, and re-established Jerusalem upon its own heap, the Lord will send forth amongst them a tremendous scourge. What will be the nature of that scourge? The nations that live in the regions round about Jerusalem will gather up like a cloud, and cover all that land round about Jerusalem. They will come into the Valley of Jehoshaphat, east of Jerusalem, and they will lay siege to the city. What then? The Lord will raise up two great Prophets, they are called witnesses, in the Revelations of St. John. Will they have much power? Yes, during the days of their prophesying they will have power to smite those who undertake to destroy them, and until their testimonies are fulfilled they will be able to keep at bay all those nations besieging Jerusalem, so that they will not have power to take that city. How long will that be? Three and a half years, so says John the Revelator. If any man hurt them, they shall have power to bring upon that man, nation or army, the various plagues that are there written. They will have power to smite the earth with plague and famine, and to turn the rivers of water into blood. And when they have fulfilled their prophecy, then the nations that have been lying before Jerusalem so long, waiting for an opportunity to destroy the city, will succeed in killing these two Prophets, and their bodies, says John's revelations, will lie in the streets of Jerusalem three days and a half after they are killed. What rejoicing there will be over the death of these men! Those who have been waiting so long and anxiously for this to take place, will no doubt send gifts one to another, and if the telegraph wires are not destroyed, they will telegraph to the uttermost parts of the earth that they have succeeded in killing the two men who had so long tormented them with plagues, turning the waters into blood, etc. But by and by, right in the midst of their rejoicing, when they think the Jews will now certainly fall a prey to them, behold there is a great earthquake, and in the midst of it these two Prophets rise from the dead, and they hear a voice up in the heavens saying—'Come up hither;' and they immediately ascend in the sight of their enemies.

What next? Notwithstanding all this, those nations will be so infatuated, and so determined to persecute the people of God—as much so as Pharaoh and his army in ancient days—that they will say—'Come, now is the time to pitch into the Jews and destroy them.' And they will commence their work of destruction, and they will succeed so far as to take one half the city, and while they are in the very act of destroying Jerusalem, behold the heavens are rent, and the Son of God with all the heavenly hosts appears, and he descends and rests upon the summit of Mount Olives, which is before Jerusalem on the east. And so great will be the power of God that will then be made manifest, that the mountain will divide asunder, half going towards the south, and half towards the north, producing a great valley going east and west, from the walls of Jerusalem eastward.

What next? The Jews that are not taken captive by these nations, will flee to the valleys of the mountains, says the Prophet Zechariah; and when they get into the great valley, where these personages are who have descended, they expect to find the Deliverer which their Prophets have spoken of so long. But they do not for a moment suppose that it is Jesus, oh no, Jesus was an impostor. The personage they have been looking for some eighteen hundred years is the true Messiah, and now, say they—'He has come to deliver us.' But how great will be their astonishment when, while looking at their Deliverer, they see that his hands are marred considerably! Say they, one to another—'There are large scars in his hands; and there is another large scar in his side, and behold his feet, they are scarred also!' And, as the Prophet Zechariah has said, they will begin to enquire of him—'What are these wounds with which thou art wounded?' And he replies—'These are the wounds with which I was wounded in the house of my friends'.

What then? Then they begin to believe, then the Jews are convinced, I mean that portion of them who formerly despised Jesus of Nazareth, and being convinced they begin to mourn, and they mourn every family apart, and their wives apart. The family of the house of Levi apart and their wives apart; the family of the house of David and their wives apart, and all their families that remain will mourn, they and their wives apart, and there will be such mourning in Jerusalem as that city never experienced before. What is the matter? What are they mourning about? They have looked upon him whom their fathers pierced, they behold the wounds, they are now convinced that they and their fathers have been in error some eighteen hundred years, and they repent in dust and ashes.

The next step for them will be baptism for the remission of their sins. They look upon him whom their fathers pierced and they mourn for him as one who mourns for his only son, and, as Zechariah says, they are in bitterness for him. But repentance alone would not be sufficient, they must obey the ordinances of the Gospel; hence there will be a fountain opened at that time on purpose for baptism. Where will it be opened? On the east side of the Temple. A stream will break out from under the threshold of the Temple, says the Prophet, and it will run eastward, and will probably pass directly through the deep valley made by the parting of the Mount of Olives. It will run eastward, and as you go down from the Temple a few thousand cubits it increases so rapidly that it becomes a great river that cannot be forded.

This is the fountain that Zechariah says is open to the inhabitants of Jerusalem and to the house of David for sin and uncleanness. 'How is it that' says one? 'Water for sin and uncleanness?' Why yes, baptism for the remission of sins. Then the Jews will receive the Gospel and they will be cleansed from all their sins by being baptized in water for their remission. Then will be fulfilled the words of the Prophet Isaiah, when speaking of Jerusalem—'For henceforth there shall no more come into thee the uncircumcised and the unclean.' but the name of the city from that day will be—'The Lord is there;' that is, the Lord will be personally there, there with his Apostles and with all his ancient Saints, for Zechariah says that when he comes and stands his feet on the Mount of Olives, all his Saints will come with him.

We have found out the place where Jesus will descend, and we have found out who comes with him. Now we enquire will he remain on the earth after he thus descends? Yes, he will remain on this earth as literally and personally as he went around in ancient times, and taught the people from house to house and synagogue to synagogue. And in that day there shall be one Lord, and his name one. There will not be any heathen gods, for there will be no heathens; no idolatrous worship, but one Lord, and his name one.

And this water which breaks out from the threshold of the Temple, will not only run eastward but westward also, and there will be a great change in the land there, certain portions rising up, others lowered, rough places made smooth and mountains cast down; and half the waters of this spring which will burst forth, will go towards the former sea and half to the other sea; in other words half towards the Dead Sea and half toward the Mediterranean.

From that day forward there shall be written upon the bells of the horses and upon the vessels of the house of the lord,—'Holiness to the Lord;' and thenceforth all the people who are spared from the nations round about, will have to go up to Jerusalem year by year to worship the King, the Lord of Hosts."

Orson Pratt, Journal of Discourses, Vol. 18, p. 178, March 26, 1876.

"Now did all Israel and all Judah know the Lord, from the least of them to the greatest of them? Had they no more need to say, every man to his Jewish neighbor, know ye the Lord? Was that the case anciently, when the Lord offered them the covenant of the everlasting gospel? No; instead of all Israel and all Judah knowing the Lord, from the least to the greatest, they were the very ones that were cut off and lost the privileges of that covenant. But in the latter days when the fullness of the Gentiles is brought in by the proclamation of the Gospel committed by the angel, then is the time that the Lord will renew this covenant, and the same Gospel that he offered to them eighteen hundred years ago, and which they rejected, will be offered to them again, and all Israel will be saved."

Orson Pratt, Journal of Discourses, Vol. 19, p. 21, May 20, 1877.

"The Temple at Jerusalem will undoubtedly be built, by those who believe in the true Messiah. Its construction will be, in some respects different from the Temples now being built. It will contain the throne of the Lord, upon which he will, at times, personally sit, and will reign over the house of Israel for ever. It may also contain twelve other thrones, on which the twelve ancient Apostles will sit, and judge the twelve tribes of Israel. It will, very likely, have an apartment, with a table, on which food and drink will be prepared, such as are suitable to the taste and happiness of immortal resurrected beings, thus fulfilling the words of Jesus—'Ye that have followed me in the regeneration shall eat and drink at my table, and sit upon twelve thrones, judging the twelve tribes of Israel.'"

John Taylor, Journal of Discourses, Vol. 18, p. 199-200, April 6, 1876.

"In looking still forward we find that there are other things ahead of us. One thing is the building of Temples, and that is a very important item, and ought to rest with force upon the minds of all good Saints. I remember, some time ago, having a conversation with Baron Rothschild, a Jew. I was showing him the Temple here, and said he—'Elder Taylor, what do you mean by this Temple? What is the object of it? Why are you building it?' Said I, 'Your fathers had among them Prophets, who revealed to them the mind and will of God; we have among us Prophets who reveal to us the mind and will of God, as they did.' One of your Prophets said—'The Lord whom ye seek shall suddenly come to his Temple, but who may abide the day of his coming? For he shall sit as a refiner's fire and a purifier of silver.' 'Now,' said I, 'Sir, will you point me out a place on the face of the earth where God has a Temple?' Said he, 'I do not know of any.' 'You remember the words of your Prophets that I have quoted?' Said he—'Yes, I know the Prophet said that, but I do not know of any Temple anywhere. Do you consider that this is that Temple?' 'No, sir, it is not.' 'Well, what is this Temple for?' Said I, 'The Lord has told us to build this Temple so that we may administer therein baptisms for our dead (which I explained to him,) and also to perform some of the sacred matrimonial alliances and covenants that we believe in, that are rejected by the world generally, but which are among the purest, most exalting and ennobling principles, that God ever revealed to man.' 'Well, then, this is not our Temple?' 'No, but,' said I, 'You will build a Temple, for the Lord has shown us, among other things, that you Jews have quite a role to perform in the latter days, and that all the things spoken by your old prophets will be fulfilled, that you will be gathered to old Jerusalem, and that you will build a Temple there; and when you build that Temple, and the time has arrived, 'the Lord whom you seek will suddenly come to his Temple.' Do you believe in the Messiah?' 'Yes.' 'Do you remember reading in your old prophets something like this—'They shall look upon him whom they have pierced, and mourn, and be in bitterness for him, as one that is in bitterness for his firstborn. And one shall say, What are these wounds in thine hands and in thy side? And he will say—These with which I was wounded in the house of my friends?' 'Ah! Is that in our Bible?' 'Yes, sir, that is in your Bible.' I spake to him then about the Nephites having left Jerusalem and told him that the Book of Mormon represents them as descendants of their people, and that Jesus came among them, and that they, because of their iniquity and departure from the word and law of God, were stricken with blackness. Said he—'What, as Cain was?' 'Yes, sir, as Cain was.' Said I—'These people, the Lamanites, according to this record,' a French copy of which I given him, he being a Frenchman; 'this people are beginning to feel after these things, that they are coming by hundreds and by thousands and demanding baptism at our hands, just as you find recorded in that book that they would do, and that is given there as a sign that God's work had commenced among all nations'. Said he—'What evidence have you of this?' This conversation took place in the Townsend House, and when the Baron asked me for evidence, said I—'Sir, if you will excuse me a few minutes I will give you some evidence;' and I went to Savage's book stand, in the Townsend Hose, and obtained a photographic copy of David Cannon baptizing Indians, standing in the midst of a great crowd of them. Said I—'Here is the evidence.' 'Well, what shall we do?' Said I—'You can do nothing unless God directs. You as a people are tied hand and foot, and have been for generations, and you can't move a peg unless God strikes off you fetters. When he says the word the things spoken of by the Prophets will be fulfilled; then the measuring line will go forth again in Jerusalem, then your Messiah will come, and all those things spoken of by the Prophets will be fulfilled.'"

Wilford Woodruff, Journal of Discourses, Vol. 2, p. 200, February 25, 1855.

"When the Gentiles reject the Gospel it will be taken from them, and go to the house of Israel, to that long suffering people that are now scattered abroad through all the nations upon the earth, and they will be gathered home by thousands, and by hundreds of thousands, and they will re-build Jerusalem their ancient city, and make it more glorious than at the beginning, and they will have a leader in Israel with them, a man that is full of the power of God and the gift of the Holy Ghost; but they are held now from this work, only because the fulness of the Gentiles has not yet come in. Tens of thousands among the Gentile nations will receive the Gospel, but the majority of them will reject it, and then the Jews will receive it; and it will go to them with all the gifts, blessings, and powers it possessed when it was taken from them."

Wilford Woodruff, Journal of Discourses, Vol. 4, p. 232, February 22, 1857.

"They do not believe in Jesus Christ; there is an unbelief resting upon them, and will until they go home and rebuild Jerusalem and their temple more glorious than at the beginning, and then by and by, after this Church and kingdom has arisen up in its glory, the Saviour will come to them and show the wounds in his hands and side, and they will say to him, 'Where did you get those wounds?' and he will answer, 'In the house of my friends,' and then their eyes will begin to open, and they will repent and mourn, they and their wives apart, and there will be a fountain opened for uncleanness to the house of Judah, and they will for the first time receive Jesus Christ as their Saviour, they will begin to comprehend where they have been wandering for the space of two thousand years.

You cannot convert a Jew, you may as well try to convert this house of solid walls as to convert them into the faith of Christ. They are set in their feelings, and they will be until the time of their redemption. They are looking forward to the time when they will go home and rebuild Jerusalem; they have looked for it many hundreds of years, they are looking for the coming of their king, and they do not suppose for a moment that he has already come, but they are looking for him to come as the Lion of the tribe of Judah, not as a lamb led to the slaughter, and as a sheep that is dumb before his hearers; they are looking for him to come with power and great glory."

Wilford Woodruff, Journal of Discourses, Vol. 22, p. 174-175, June 12, 1881.

"The Lamanites, now a down-trodden people, are a remnant of the house of Israel. The curse of God has followed them as it has done the Jews, though the Jews have not been darkened in their skin as have the Lamanites. The fate of the Jews in this respect is a standing monument to all infidelity. The prediction of Jesus with regard to them has been literally fulfilled. He predicted that they should be led away captive unto all nations, and that Jerusalem should be trodden down of the Gentiles, until the times of the Gentiles be fulfilled. When Pilate was ready to release Jesus because he found no fault in him, the Pharisees and high priests, being filled with prejudice, would not have it. They cried out 'Crucify him, crucify him, and let his blood be upon us and our children.' The prediction of Jesus has been verified, and its fulfillment is before the world today. The Jews have been trampled under the feet of the Gentiles for 1800 years, and they are today being persecuted in European nations. Why? Because that curse of God rests upon them and will rest upon them until Shiloh comes, until they are regathered to Jerusalem and re-build the city in un-belief. You cannot convert a Jew. They will never believe in Jesus Christ until he comes to them in Jerusalem, until these fleeing Jews take back their gold and silver to Jerusalem and re-build their city and temple, and they will do this as the Lord lives. Then the gentiles will say, 'Come let us go up to Jerusalem; let us go up and spoil her. The Jews have taken our gold and silver from the nations of the earth—come let us go up and fight against Jerusalem.' Then will the prophecies that are before you be fulfilled. The Gospel was preached first to the Jews and then to the Gentiles. The Jews rejected the message: the Gentiles received it, and unto them was given all the gifts and blessings of the Gospel. But Paul told them to take heed lest they fell through the same example of unbelief. Yet in time, we Gentiles, departed from the kingdom of God, and the church went into the wilderness. There has not been an organization of the church of Christ on the earth from the days of the ancient Apostles, until the days of Joseph Smith, who came forth in this great and last dispensation, and who by inspiration and power from on high again restored the Gospel."

Wilford Woodruff, Collected Discourses, Vol. 1, March 5, 1889.

"As Brother Cannon has said, God offers the Gospel to a generation, and if they reject that Gospel it will cost them dearly. It is a serious thing for any dispensation to reject the Gospel of Christ and to shed the blood of the prophets. What did it cost to shed the blood of the Savior? He came to His Father's house—the Jews. He brought the Gospel to them, and warned them of the wrath to come. But they rejected the Gospel; they crucified Him and put Him to death. What did it cost them? Jesus told them himself what it would cost them. He said: 'And they shall fall by the edge of the sword, and shall be led away captive into all nations; and Jerusalem shall be trodden down by the Gentiles, until the times of the Gentiles are fulfilled.' That yoke has been upon the Jewish nation until the present day, and it is not broken yet, and will not be until the times of the Gentiles are fulfilled, which is close at our door."

The Discourses of Wilford Woodruff, p. 117-118.

"I thank God that the day is at hand when the Jews will be restored. I have felt to pray for them; I feel interested in their behalf, for they are of the seed of Abraham and a branch of the house of Israel, and the promises of God still remain with them. It is true they fell through unbelief, and the kingdom was taken from them and given to the Gentiles, and when it came from them, it came clothed with all its gifts, powers, and glory, priesthood and ordinances which were necessary for the salvation of men, and to prepare them to dwell in the presence of the Gods; and when the kingdom was given to the Gentiles, they for a while brought forth the natural fruits of the kingdom. But they, like the Jews, have fallen through the same example of unbelief, and now, in the last days, the kingdom of God has to be taken from the Gentiles, and restored back to every branch and tribe of the house of Israel; and when it is restored to them, it must go back with all its gifts, and blessings, and priesthood which it possessed when it was taken from them. But the Lord has said that in restoring these blessings to the children of Abraham, that he would be inquired of by the house of Israel, to do it for them. But from what branch or part of the house of Israel will the Lord look for this petition or request to issue, if not from the Latter-day Saints? For we are out of the tribe of Joseph through the loins of Ephraim, who has been as a mixed cake among the Gentiles, and are the first fruits of the kingdom, and the Lord has given unto us the kingdom and priesthood and keys thereof. Hence the Lord will require us to ask for those blessings which are promised unto Israel, and to labor for their

90

salvation. (JD 4:232-233, February 22, 1857.)"

Franklin D. Richards, A Compendium of the Doctrines of the Gospel, p. 172.

"She (Jerusalem) is yet to take an important part in the great work of the latter days. Like the New Jerusalem of the American continent, this city will descend out of heaven, after the final change of the earth to its celestial condition; (Rev. 21:10–27.)"

Franklin D. Richards, A Compendium of the Doctrines of the Gospel, p. 246.

"The history of the eastern hemisphere for the two thousand years which intervened between the calling of Abraham and the destruction of Jerusalem by the Romans, witnesses that every nation that fought against Israel, or in any way oppressed them, passed away. Time will show the same general result, from the destruction of Jerusalem to the millennium."

Charles W. Penrose, "The Second Advent", Millennial Star, Vol. 21, p. 582-583, Sept. 10, 1859.

"The Jews, still in unbelief that Jesus was the Christ, will separate themselves from among the Gentiles and gather to their fatherland. Events will be so controlled by the God of Israel that they shall possess the land again and build the Temple in its former place: they will increase and multiply in numbers and in riches, and practice the rites of the Mosaic law, looking for the coming of the Messiah to reign over them as king. The bankrupt nations, envying the wealth of the sons of Judah, will seek a pretext to make war upon them, and will invade the `holy land' to `take a prey and a spoil'."

Joseph Fielding Smith, Church History and Modern Revelation, Vol. 2, p. 36.

"The promise is also made to the Jews that they shall be gathered again, after their pain and suffering. They will gather as predicted by Zechariah and by the Lord in a former revelation (Sec. 45) in their unbelief. They will begin to believe in Christ but will not be ready to accept him in his full right as their Deliverer and as the Son of God. (See 2 Nephi 30: 5-8.) In this state they shall gather to Jerusalem and its vicinity. When their enemies come upon them and part of the city is taken, there shall come a great earthquake and the mount of Olives shall cleave in twain forming a valley into which the Jews shall flee for safety. At that time Christ will appear to them and show them his hands and his feet, and they shall fall down and acknowledge him as their King and Redeemer."

Joseph Fielding Smith Jr., The Way to Perfection, p. 119.

"Judah, fourth son of Leah, was honored in one respect above his brethren, for it was through his lineage that the Redeemer of the world came. That, surely, is honor enough for any man. Moreover the blessings of kingly power were conferred upon him. His descendants were given the right to rule and reign in Israel before the division of the kingdom and to continue through David in that capacity in Judah."

Joseph Fielding Smith Jr., The Way to Perfection, p. 133-134.

"It must be admitted that the Jews as a people stand out as one of the greatest evidences in proof of the covenants made by the Lord with Father Abraham. And, then, it is the will of the Lord that they should be kept separate, and so shall they be found at the second coming of our Lord. If these things were not so, and if Jesus were not the Christ, whom the Jews condemned, crying: 'His blood be on us and on our children,' they would have passed out of the picture as a distinct race centuries ago. They are today a standing miracle in their scattered condition, silently testifying to the covenant to Israel and of the divinity of Jesus Christ, yet, themselves, not believing in him."

Joseph Fielding Smith, The Signs of the Times, p. 69.

"So we see that since the armistice in 1918, the Jews have been returning in great numbers, encouraged by both the United States and the nation of Great Britain, the latter taking over the great responsibility in this gathering movement. The prophecies are rapidly being fulfilled. The Jews are returning only partly believing in Jesus Christ. They are willing to accept Him as a great prophet among the prophets of Israel and Judah, but not as their Deliverer, or Messiah. When our Lord shall come to them in the calling of Deliverer, the whole land will be in siege. Jerusalem will be at the mercy of its enemies. There will be a great earthquake and the Mount of Olives will cleave in twain forming a great valley into which the oppressed people will flee from the city for safety. At that time the enemies of the people will be destroyed Christ will appear to the Jews and show them His hands and His feet and then they will accept Him as their Messiah. Then, as Zechariah has predicted, every family will mourn apart, and there will be weeping and wailing because they rejected their King. After those days there will come peace and Israel will come back into his own."

Joseph Fielding Smith, The Signs of the Times, p. 228-229.

"One such story is told by Mr. Arthur H. Michelson in The Jewish Hope published in Los Angeles (September 1950). We give it here and leave it for each reader to draw his own conclusion:

'It is marvelous what God did for the Jews, especially in Jerusalem, during the fighting with Arabs. Though quite a few months had passed since the victory of Israel's army in Israel, they were still telling about what had taken place. Everywhere I went I heard how God had intervened in their behalf, and how He helped them win the battles. One of the officials told me how much the Jews had to suffer. They had hardly anything with which to resist the heavy attacks of the Arabs, who were well organized and equipped with the latest weapons. Besides, they had neither food nor water because all their supplies were cut off.'

'The Arabs who had a great army in strong position, were determined to destroy the Jews, while the Jews were few in number, without any arms and ammunition. The two or three guns they possessed had to be rushed from one point to another, to give the Arabs the impression that they had many of them. The Jews had quite a few tin cans which they beat as they shot the guns, giving the impression of many shots. But as the pressure was too great, they were unable to hold the lines any longer and finally decided to give up the city. At this critical moment God showed them that He was on their side, for He performed one of the greatest miracles that ever happened. The Arabs then suddenly threw down their arms and surrendered. When their delegation appeared with the white flag, they asked, 'Where are the three men that led you, and where are all the troops we saw?' The Jews told them that they did not know anything of the three men, for this group was their entire force. The Arabs said that they saw three persons with long beards and flowing white robes, who warned them not to fight any longer, otherwise they would all be killed. They became so frightened that they decided to give up. What an encouragement this was for the Jews, who realized that God was fighting for them.'

Mr. Michelson relates several other incidents of a similar nature where it appeared that the Lord had intervened in behalf of the Jews when they were at the mercy of their enemies."

Joseph Fielding Smith Jr., Doctrines of Salvation, Vol. 3, p. 8-9.

"Not many of the Jews . . . will believe in Christ before he comes. . . .The Jews today look upon Christ as a great Rabbi. They have accepted him as one of their great teachers; they have said that, 'He is Jew of Jew, the greatest Rabbi of them all,' as one has stated it. When the gospel was restored in 1830, if a Jew had mentioned the name of Christ in one of the synagogues, he would have been rebuked. . . .And so, we see the sentiment has changed. Now I state this on Jewish authority that they are beginning to believe in Christ, and some of them are accepting the gospel.

But in the main they will gather to Jerusalem in their unbelief; the gospel will be preached to them; some of them will believe. . . .The great body of the Jews who are there assembled will not receive Christ as their Redeemer until he comes himself and makes himself manifest unto them."

Teachings of Ezra Taft Benson, p. 98-99.

"There is great conflict yet to come before the millennial reign, before the Christ comes. If you want to get some indication of just what this conflict will be, you may wish to turn to the fourteenth chapter of Zechariah and the eleventh chapter of the book of Revelation, which make it very clear that nations will be pitted against Judah; that there will be great wars, great conflict; that at least two prophets will be raised up among them; that they will make predictions before Christ comes. I have no doubt but what these prophets will be assigned by the leadership of the priesthood, because the Lord's house is a house of order. The gospel will be carried to the Jews and many of them will accept it. ("The Jews Return to Palestine in Fulfillment of Prophecy," Washington D.C. Stake Conference, 3 March 1957.)"

LeGrand Richards, Conference Report, April 1954, p. 55-56.

"In the Jewish Hope, of September 1950, was an article by Arthur U. Michelson. . . .

He told about another case when one man with a white robe and a long beard appeared, and they all saw him, and they gave up their arms. Now I do not know, but the Lord said that he would do something for the Jews in the latter days, and when he permitted the Three Nephites to tarry upon this land, he said:

'And behold they will be among the Gentiles, and the Gentiles shall know them not. They will also be among the Jews, and the Jews shall know them not.

And it shall come to pass, when the lord seeth fit in his wisdom that they shall minister unto all the scattered tribes of Israel, and unto all nations, kindreds, tongues and people, and shall bring out of them unto Jesus many souls, that their desire may be fulfilled, and also because of the convincing power of God which is in them.' (3 Ne. 28:27-29.)

Whoever these persons were, they seemed to have 'convincing power sufficient to cause a whole army to surrender.

In permitting these Three Nephites to tarry upon the earth until he, Jesus, should come in his glory, he must have had in mind some great things for them to accomplish in bringing about a fulfillment of his promises. Whether it was convincing the army of the Arabs to surrender, I do not know, but this I do know: That what is going on in the Holy Land should convince one that the Lord is moving rapidly toward restoring the Jews to the land of their fathers and is giving them that land and redeeming it from its waste condition, as the prophets have foretold."

Bruce R. McConkie, Mormon Doctrine, "Signs of the Times", p. 722.

"'Much of the old Jewish bitterness against Christ has ceased; many now accept him as a great Rabbi, though not the Son of God. A few have accepted him in the full sense . . . the great conversion of the Jews, their return to the truth as a nation, is destined to follow the Second Coming."

Bruce R. McConkie, Mormon Doctrine, "Signs of the Times", p. 723-724.

"Because they rejected the truth and failed to keep the commandments of the Lord, all the curses enumerated by Moses came upon the Jews. 'The Lord shall cause thee to be smitten before thine enemies,' he said, so that thou 'shalt be removed into all the kingdoms of the earth . . . And thou shalt become an astonishment, a proverb, and a byword, among all nations.' (Deut. 28.). . .

They have maintained their distinctive race and will continue to return to Jerusalem. Indeed, their very persecutions have helped cause them to flee unto Jerusalem."

Bruce R. McConkie, The Mortal Messiah, Vol. 4, p. 332.

"Israel the chosen seed; Israel the Lord's people; Israel the only nation since Abraham that had worshipped Jehovah; Israel the children of the prophets; Israel who had been cursed and scattered for her sins; Israel in whose veins believing blood flows—the Israel of God shall be gathered, and fed, and nurtured, and saved, in the last days! Let there be no misunderstanding about this; salvation is of the Jews, and if there are believing Gentiles, they will be adopted into the believing family and inherit with the chosen seed. 'And so all Israel shall be saved: as it is written, There shall come out of Zion the Deliverer, and shall turn away ungodliness from Jacob: For this is my covenant unto them, when I shall take away their sins.' (Rom. 11:26-27.) But sadly: 'They are not all Israel, which a are of Israel' (Rom. 9:6), and only those who turn to their God and accept him as the Promised Messiah shall inherit with the chosen seed either in time or in eternity."

Bruce R. McConkie, The Mortal Messiah, Vol. 4, p. 340-341.

"When the times of the Gentiles are fulfilled, the times of the Jews will commence. The gospel will then go to the Jewish seed of Abraham, and they shall believe; and, except for a limited few, the great day of Jewish conversion will be in the millennial day, after they have seen him whom they crucified and have heard him attest that the wounds in his hands and in his feet are those with which he was wounded in the house of his friends."

Bruce R. McConkie, The Millennial Messiah, p. 221.

"The Jews are not the members of the tribe of Judah as such. . . .Both kingdoms had in them people from all of the tribes. Lehi, who lived in Judah and was a Jew, was of the tribe of Manasseh. The Jews were nationals of the kingdom of Judah without reference to tribal ancestry."

94

See Bruce R. McConkie, The Millennial Messiah, p. 279-280.

"There is only one people who know how to build temples and what to do in them when they are completed. That people is the Latter-day Saints. The temple in Jerusalem will not be built by Jews who have assembled there for political purposes as at present. . . .But it will be built by Jews who have come unto Christ . . . and who have learned anew about temples by The Church of Jesus Christ."

See Bruce R. McConkie, The Millennial Messiah, p. 390.

"Their ministry (two prophets) will take place after the latter-day temple has been built in Old Jerusalem, after some of the Jews who dwell there have been converted, and just before Armageddon and the return of the Lord Jesus. . . .they will hold the holy Melchizedek Priesthood; they will be members of The Church of Jesus Christ of Latter-day Saints. It is reasonable to suppose . . . that they will be two members of the Council of the Twelve or of the First Presidency of the Church."

Also see The Millennial Messiah p. 228-231, 297-299, 462-464.

Bruce R. McConkie, A New Witness for the Articles of Faith, p. 519.

"Judah will gather to old Jerusalem in due course . . .But this gathering will consist of accepting Christ, joining the Church, and receiving anew the Abrahamic covenant as it is administered in holy places. The present assembling of people of Jewish ancestry into the Palestinian nation of Israel is not the scriptural gathering of Israel or of Judah. It may be prelude thereto . . .But a political gathering is not a spiritual gathering, and the Lord's kingdom is not of this world."

Bruce R. McConkie, A New Witness for the Articles of Faith, p. 589.

"The Lord's people will build up Old Jerusalem again; they shall do it in righteousness, including the placing of a holy temple within its walls. Joseph Smith says this temple must be built before the Second Coming."

Bruce R. McConkie, A New Witness for the Articles of Faith, p. 632-633.

"As with the Ten Tribes, so with the Jews—the day of their real gathering is Millennial. Scattered representatives of the Kingdom of Judah and the Kingdom of Israel will be gathered into the true fold of Christ before he comes, but the great day of the gathering of these ancient peoples will be after the King of Israel has taken his place as the ruler of the earth."

SCRIPTURAL REFERENCES

Deuteronomy 30:1

1 And it shall come to pass, when all these things are come upon thee, the blessing and the curse, which I have set before thee, and thou shalt call them to mind among all the nations, whither the LORD thy God hath driven thee,

Isaiah 2:3

3 And many people shall go and say, Come ye, and let us go up to the mountain of the LORD, to the house of the God of Jacob; and he will teach us of his ways, and we will walk in his paths: for out of Zion shall go forth the law, and the word of the LORD from Jerusalem.

Isaiah 11:10-12

10 And in that day there shall be a root of Jesse, which shall stand for an ensign of the people; to it shall the Gentiles seek: and his rest shall be glorious.

11 And it shall come to pass in that day, that the Lord shall set his hand again the second time to recover the remnant of his people, which shall be left, from Assyria, and from Egypt, and from Pathros, and from Cush, and from Elam, and from Shinar, and from Hamath, and from the islands of the sea.

12 And he shall set up an ensign for the nations, and shall assemble the outcasts of Israel, and gather together the dispersed of Judah from the four corners of the earth.

Isaiah 51:17-19

17 Awake, awake, stand up, O Jerusalem, which hast drunk at the hand of the LORD the cup of his fury; thou hast drunken the dregs of the cup of trembling, and wrung them out.

18 There is none to guide her among all the sons whom she hath brought forth; neither is there any that taketh her by the hand of all the sons that she hath brought up.

19 These two things are come unto thee; who shall be sorry for thee? desolation, and destruction, and the famine, and the sword: by whom shall I comfort thee?

Jeremiah 3:18

18 In those days the house of Judah shall walk with the house of Israel, and they shall come together out of the land of the north to the land that I have given for an inheritance unto your fathers.

Jeremiah 4:5-10

5 Declare ye in Judah, and publish in Jerusalem; and say, Blow ye the trumpet in the land: cry, gather together, and say, Assemble yourselves, and let us go into the defenced cities.

6 Set up the standard toward Zion: retire, stay not: for I will bring evil from the north, and a great destruction.

7 The lion is come up from his thicket, and the destroyer of the Gentiles is on his way; he is gone forth from his place to make thy land desolate; and thy cities shall be laid waste, without an inhabitant.

8 For this gird you with sackcloth, lament and howl: for the fierce anger of the LORD is not turned back from us.

9 And it shall come to pass at that day, saith the LORD, that the heart of the king shall perish, and the heart of the princes; and the priests shall be astonished, and the prophets shall wonder.

10 Then said I, Ah, Lord GOD! surely thou hast greatly deceived this people and Jerusalem, saying, Ye shall have peace; whereas the sword reacheth unto the soul.

Ezekiel 37:22-25

22 And I will make them one nation in the land upon the mountains of Israel; and one king shall be king to them all: and they shall be no more two nations, neither shall they be divided into two kingdoms any more at all:

23 Neither shall they defile themselves any more with their idols, nor with their detestable things, nor with any of their transgressions: but I will save them out of all their dwelling places, wherein they have sinned, and will cleanse them: so shall they be my people, and I will be their God.

24 And David my servant shall be king over them; and they all shall have one shepherd: they shall also walk in my judgments, and observe my statutes, and do them.

25 And they shall dwell in the land that I have given unto Jacob my servant, wherein your fathers have dwelt; and they shall dwell therein, even they, and their children, and their children's children for ever: and my servant David shall be their prince for ever.

Ezekiel 39:21-29

21 And I will set my glory among the heathen, and all the heathen shall see my judgment that I have executed, and my hand that I have laid upon them.

22 So the house of Israel shall know that I am the LORD their God from that day and forward.

23 And the heathen shall know that the house of Israel went into captivity for their iniquity: because they trespassed against me, therefore hid I my face from them, and gave them into the hand of their enemies: so fell they all by the sword.

24 According to their uncleanness and according to their transgressions have I done unto them, and hid my face from them.

25 Therefore thus saith the Lord GOD; Now will I bring again the captivity of Jacob, and have mercy upon the whole house of Israel, and will be jealous for my holy name;

26 After that they have borne their shame, and all their trespasses whereby they have trespassed against me, when they dwelt safely in their land, and none made them afraid.

27 When I have brought them again from the people, and gathered them out of their enemies' lands, and am sanctified in them in the sight of many nations;

28 Then shall they know that I am the LORD their God, which cause them to be led into captivity among the heathen: but I have gathered them unto their own land, and have left none of them any more there.

29 Neither will I hide my face any more from them: for I have poured out my spirit upon the house of Israel, saith the Lord GOD.

Ezekiel 44:1-5

1 Then he brought me back the way of the gate of the outward sanctuary which looketh toward the east; and it was shut.

2 Then said the LORD unto me; This gate shall be shut, it shall not be opened, and no man shall enter in by it; because the LORD, the God of Israel, hath entered in by it, therefore it shall be shut.

3 It is for the prince; the prince, he shall sit in it to eat bread before the LORD; he shall enter by the way of the porch of that gate, and shall go out by the way of the same.

4 Then brought he me the way of the north gate before the house: and I looked, and, behold, the glory of the LORD filled the house of the LORD: and I fell upon my face.

5 And the LORD said unto me, Son of man, mark well, and behold with thine eyes, and hear with thine ears all that I say unto thee concerning all the ordinances of the house of the LORD, and all the laws thereof; and mark well the entering in of the house, with every going forth of the sanctuary.

Ezekiel 47:Heading

Waters issue from the house of the Lord and heal the Dead Sea—The Lord shows the borders of the land.

Ezekiel 48:35

35 It was round about eighteen thousand measures: and the name of the city from that day shall be, The LORD is there.

Daniel 9:25-27

25 Know therefore and understand, that from the going forth of the commandment to restore and to build Jerusalem unto the Messiah the Prince shall be seven weeks, and threescore and two weeks: the street shall be built again, and the wall, even in troublous times.

26 And after threescore and two weeks shall Messiah be cut off, but not for himself: and the people of the prince that shall come shall destroy the city and the sanctuary; and the end thereof shall be with a flood, and unto the end of the war desolations are determined.

27 And he shall confirm the covenant with many for one week: and in the midst of the week he shall cause the sacrifice and the oblation to cease, and for the overspreading of abominations he shall make it desolate, even until the consummation, and that determined shall be poured upon the desolate.

Joel 3:16

16 The LORD also shall roar out of Zion, and utter his voice from Jerusalem; and the heavens and the earth shall shake: but the LORD will be the hope of his people, and the strength of the children of Israel.

Zechariah 1:16-7

16 Therefore thus saith the LORD; I am returned to Jerusalem with mercies: my house shall be built in it, saith the LORD of hosts, and a line shall be stretched forth upon Jerusalem.

17 Cry yet, saying, Thus saith the LORD of hosts; My cities through prosperity shall yet be spread abroad; and the LORD shall yet comfort Zion, and shall yet choose Jerusalem.

Zechariah 4:11-14

11 Then answered I, and said unto him, What are these two olive trees upon the right side of the candlestick and upon the left side thereof?

12 And I answered again, and said unto him, What be these two olive branches which through the two golden pipes empty the golden oil out of themselves?

13 And he answered me and said, Knowest thou not what these be? And I said, No, my lord.

14 Then said he, These are the two anointed ones, that stand by the LORD of the whole earth.

Zechariah 8:20-23

20 Thus saith the LORD of hosts; It shall yet come to pass, that there shall come people, and the inhabitants of many cities:

21 And the inhabitants of one city shall go to another, saying, Let us go speedily to pray before the LORD, and to seek the LORD of hosts: I will go also.

22 Yea, many people and strong nations shall come to seek the LORD of hosts in Jerusalem, and to pray before the LORD.

23 Thus saith the LORD of hosts; In those days it shall come to pass, that ten men shall take hold out of all languages of the nations, even shall take hold of the skirt of him that is a Jew, saying, We will go with you: for we have heard that God is with you.

Zechariah 12:10-14

10 And I will pour upon the house of David, and upon the inhabitants of Jerusalem, the spirit of grace and of supplications: and they shall look upon me whom they have pierced, and they shall mourn for him, as one mourneth for his only son, and shall be in bitterness for him, as one that is in bitterness for his firstborn.

11 In that day shall there be a great mourning in Jerusalem, as the mourning of Hadadrimmon in the valley of Megiddon.

12 And the land shall mourn, every family apart; the family of the house of David apart, and their wives apart; the family of the house of Nathan apart, and their wives apart;

13 The family of the house of Levi apart, and their wives apart; the family of Shimei apart, and their wives apart;

14 All the families that remain, every family apart, and their wives apart.

Zechariah 13:6-9

6 And one shall say unto him, What are these wounds in thine hands? Then he shall answer, Those with which I was wounded in the house of my friends.

7 Awake, O sword, against my shepherd, and against the man that is my fellow, saith the LORD of hosts: smite the shepherd, and the sheep shall be scattered: and I will turn mine hand upon the little ones.

8 And it shall come to pass, that in all the land, saith the LORD, two parts therein shall be cut off and die; but the third shall be left therein.

9 And I will bring the third part through the fire, and will refine them as silver is refined, and will try them as gold is tried: they shall call on my name, and I will hear them: I will say, It is my people: and they shall say, The LORD is my God.

Zechariah 14:2-5

2 For I will gather all nations against Jerusalem to battle; and the city shall be taken, and the houses rifled, and the women ravished; and half of the city shall go forth into captivity, and the residue of the people shall not be cut off from the city.

3 Then shall the LORD go forth, and fight against those nations, as when he fought in the day of battle.

4 And his feet shall stand in that day upon the mount of Olives, which is before Jerusalem on the east, and the mount of Olives shall cleave in the midst thereof toward the east and toward the west, and there shall be a very great valley; and half of the mountain shall remove toward the north, and half of it toward the south.

5 And ye shall flee to the valley of the mountains; for the valley of the mountains shall reach unto Azal: yea, ye shall flee, like as ye fled from before the earthquake in the days of Uzziah king of Judah: and the LORD my God shall come, and all the saints with thee.

Zechariah 14:9-17

9 And the LORD shall be king over all the earth: in that day shall there be one LORD, and his name one.

10 All the land shall be turned as a plain from Geba to Rimmon south of Jerusalem: and it shall be lifted up, and inhabited in her place, from Benjamin's gate unto the place of the first gate, unto the corner gate, and from the tower of Hananeel unto the king's winepresses.

11 And men shall dwell in it, and there shall be no more utter destruction; but Jerusalem shall be safely inhabited.

12 And this shall be the plague wherewith the LORD will smite all the people that have fought against Jerusalem; Their flesh shall consume away while they stand upon their feet, and their eyes shall consume away in their holes, and their tongue shall consume away in their mouth.

13 And it shall come to pass in that day, that a great tumult from the LORD shall be among them; and they shall lay hold every one on the hand of his neighbour, and his hand shall rise up against the hand of his neighbour.

14 And Judah also shall fight at Jerusalem; and the wealth of all the heathen round about shall be gathered together, gold, and silver, and apparel, in great abundance.

15 And so shall be the plague of the horse, of the mule, of the camel, and of the ass, and of all the beasts that shall be in these tents, as this plague.

16 And it shall come to pass, that every one that is left of all the nations which came against Jerusalem shall even go up from year to year to worship the King, the LORD of hosts, and to keep the feast of tabernacles.

17 And it shall be, that whoso will not come up of all the families of the earth unto Jerusalem to worship the King, the LORD of hosts, even upon them shall be no rain.

Luke 21:24

24 And they shall fall by the edge of the sword, and shall be led away captive into all nations: and Jerusalem shall be trodden down of the Gentiles, until the times of the Gentiles be fulfilled.

Revelation 11:2-15

2 But the court which is without the temple leave out, and measure it not; for it is given unto the Gentiles: and the holy city shall they tread under foot forty and two months.

3 And I will give power unto my two witnesses, and they shall prophesy a thousand two hundred and threescore days, clothed in sackcloth.

4 These are the two olive trees, and the two candlesticks standing before the God of the earth.

5 And if any man will hurt them, fire proceedeth out of their mouth, and devoureth their enemies: and if any man will hurt them, he must in this manner be killed.

6 These have power to shut heaven, that it rain not in the days of their prophecy: and have power over waters to turn them to blood, and to smite the earth with all plagues, as often as they will.

7 And when they shall have finished their testimony, the beast that ascendeth out of the bottomless pit shall make war against them, and shall overcome them, and kill them.

8 And their dead bodies shall lie in the street of the great city, which spiritually is called Sodom and Egypt, where also our Lord was crucified.

9 And they of the people and kindreds and tongues and nations shall see their dead bodies three days and an half, and shall not suffer their dead bodies to be put in graves.

10 And they that dwell upon the earth shall rejoice over them, and make merry, and shall send gifts one to another; because these two prophets tormented them that dwelt on the earth.

11 And after three days and an half the Spirit of life from God entered into them, and they stood upon their feet; and great fear fell upon them which saw them.

12 And they heard a great voice from heaven saying unto them, Come up hither. And they ascended up to heaven in a cloud; and their enemies beheld them.

13 And the same hour was there a great earthquake, and the tenth part of the city fell, and in the earthquake were slain of men seven thousand: and the remnant were affrighted, and gave glory to the God of heaven.

14 The second woe is past; and, behold, the third woe cometh quickly.

15 And the seventh angel sounded; and there were great voices in heaven, saying, The kingdoms of this world are become the kingdoms of our Lord, and of his Christ; and he shall reign for ever and ever.

1 Nephi 14:17

17 And when the day cometh that the wrath of God is poured out upon the mother of harlots, which is the great and abominable church of all the earth, whose founder is the devil, then, at that day, the work of the Father shall commence, in preparing the way for the fulfilling of his covenants, which he hath made to his people who are of the house of Israel.

1 Nephi 15:13

13 And now, the thing which our father meaneth concerning the grafting in of the natural branches through the fulness of the Gentiles, is, that in the latter days, when our seed shall have dwindled in unbelief, yea, for the space of many years, and many generations after the Messiah shall be manifested in body unto the children of men, then shall the fulness of the gospel of the Messiah come

unto the Gentiles, and from the Gentiles unto the remnant of our seed—

1 Nephi 19:15

15 Nevertheless, when that day cometh, saith the prophet, that they no more turn aside their hearts against the Holy One of Israel, then will he remember the covenants which he made to their fathers.

2 Nephi 6:11

11 Wherefore, after they are driven to and fro, for thus saith the angel, many shall be afflicted in the flesh, and shall not be suffered to perish, because of the prayers of the faithful; they shall be scattered, and smitten, and hated; nevertheless, the Lord will be merciful unto them, that when they shall come to the knowledge of their Redeemer, they shall be gathered together again to the lands of their inheritance.

2 Nephi 6:14-18

14 And behold, according to the words of the prophet, the Messiah will set himself again the second time to recover them; wherefore, he will manifest himself unto them in power and great glory, unto the destruction of their enemies, when that day cometh when they shall believe in him; and none will he destroy that believe in him.

15 And they that believe not in him shall be destroyed, both by fire, and by tempest, and by earthquakes, and by bloodsheds, and by pestilence, and by famine. And they shall know that the Lord is God, the Holy One of Israel.

16 For shall the prey be taken from the mighty, or the lawful captive delivered?

17 But thus saith the Lord: Even the captives of the mighty shall be taken away, and the prey of the terrible shall be delivered; for the Mighty God shall deliver his covenant people. For thus saith the Lord: I will contend with them that contendeth with thee—

18 And I will feed them that oppress thee, with their own flesh; and they shall be drunken with their own blood as with sweet wine; and all flesh shall know that I the Lord am thy Savior and thy Redeemer, the Mighty One of Jacob.

2 Nephi 9:2

2 That he has spoken unto the Jews, by the mouth of his holy prophets, even from the beginning down, from generation to generation, until the time comes that they shall be restored to the true church and fold of God; when they shall be gathered home to the lands of their inheritance, and shall be established in all their lands of promise.

2 Nephi 10:7-9

7 But behold, thus saith the Lord God: When the day cometh that they shall believe in me, that I am Christ, then have I covenanted with their fathers that they shall be restored in the flesh, upon the earth, unto the lands of their inheritance.

8 And it shall come to pass that they shall be gathered in from their long dispersion, from the isles of the sea, and from the four parts of the earth; and the nations of the Gentiles shall be great in the eyes of me, saith God, in carrying them forth to the lands of their inheritance.

9 Yea, the kings of the Gentiles shall be nursing fathers unto them, and their queens shall become nursing mothers; wherefore, the promises of the Lord are great unto the Gentiles, for he hath spoken it, and who can dispute?

2 Nephi 25:16-18

16 And after they have been scattered, and the Lord God hath scourged them by other nations for the space of many generations, yea, even down from generation to generation until they shall be persuaded to believe in Christ, the Son of God, and the atonement, which is infinite for all mankind—and when that day shall come that they shall believe in Christ, and worship the Father in his name, with pure hearts and clean hands, and look not forward any more for another Messiah, then, at that time, the day will come that it must needs be expedient that they should believe these things.

17 And the Lord will set his hand again the second time to restore his people from their lost and fallen state. Wherefore, he will proceed to do a marvelous work and a wonder among the children of men.

18 Wherefore, he shall bring forth his words unto them, which words shall judge them at the last day, for they shall be given them for the purpose of convincing them of the true Messiah, who was rejected by them; and unto the convincing of them that they need not look forward any more for a Messiah to come, for there should not any come, save it should be a false Messiah which should deceive the people; for there is save one Messiah spoken of by the prophets, and that Messiah is he who should be rejected of the Jews.

2 Nephi 30:7-8

7 And it shall come to pass that the Jews which are scattered also shall begin to believe in Christ; and they shall begin to gather in upon the face of the land; and as many as shall believe in Christ shall also become a delightsome people.

8 And it shall come to pass that the Lord God shall commence his work among all nations, kindreds, tongues, and people, to bring about the restoration of his people upon the earth.

3 Nephi 5:24-26

24 And as surely as the Lord liveth, will he gather in from the four quarters of the earth all the remnant of the seed of Jacob, who are scattered abroad upon all the face of the earth.

25 And as he hath covenanted with all the house of Jacob, even so shall the covenant wherewith he hath covenanted with the house of Jacob be fulfilled in his own due time, unto the restoring all the house of Jacob unto the knowledge of the covenant that he hath covenanted with them.

26 And then shall they know their Redeemer, who is Jesus Christ, the Son of God; and then shall they be gathered in from the four quarters of the earth unto their own lands, from whence they have been dispersed; yea, as the Lord liveth so shall it be. Amen.

3 Nephi 16:4-6

4 And I command you that ye shall write these sayings after I am gone, that if it so be that my people at Jerusalem, they who have seen me and been with me in my ministry, do not ask the Father in my name, that they may receive a knowledge of you by the Holy Ghost, and also of the other tribes whom

they know not of, that these sayings which ye shall write shall be kept and shall be manifested unto the Gentiles, that through the fulness of the Gentiles, the remnant of their seed, who shall be scattered forth upon the face of the earth because of their unbelief, may be brought in, or may be brought to a knowledge of me, their Redeemer.

5 And then will I gather them in from the four quarters of the earth; and then will I fulfill the covenant which the Father hath made unto all the people of the house of Israel.

6 And blessed are the Gentiles, because of their belief in me, in and of the Holy Ghost, which witnesses unto them of me and of the Father.

3 Nephi 20:29

29 And I will remember the covenant which I have made with my people; and I have covenanted with them that I would gather them together in mine own due time, that I would give unto them again the land of their fathers for their inheritance, which is the land of Jerusalem, which is the promised land unto them forever, saith the Father.

3 Nephi 21:28-29

28 Yea, and then shall the work commence, with the Father among all nations in preparing the way whereby his people may be gathered home to the land of their inheritance.

29 And they shall go out from all nations; and they shall not go out in haste, nor go by flight, for I will go before them, saith the Father, and I will be their rearward.

Mormon 5:12-14

12 Now these things are written unto the remnant of the house of Jacob; and they are written after this manner, because it is known of God that wickedness will not bring them forth unto them; and they are to be hid up unto the Lord that they may come forth in his own due time.

13 And this is the commandment which I have received; and behold, they shall come forth according to the commandment of the Lord, when he shall see fit, in his wisdom.

14 And behold, they shall go unto the unbelieving of the Jews; and for this intent shall they go—that they may be persuaded that Jesus is the Christ, the Son of the living God; that the Father may bring about, through his most Beloved, his great and eternal purpose, in restoring the Jews, or all the house of Israel, to the land of their inheritance, which the Lord their God hath given them, unto the fulfilling of his covenant;

Ether 13:11

11 And then also cometh the Jerusalem of old; and the inhabitants thereof, blessed are they, for they have been washed in the blood of the Lamb; and they are they who were scattered and gathered in from the four quarters of the earth, and from the north countries, and are partakers of the fulfilling of the covenant which God made with their father, Abraham.

D&C 14:10

10 Wherefore, I must bring forth the fulness of my gospel from the Gentiles unto the house of Israel.

D&C 19:27

27 Which is my word to the Gentile, that soon it may go to the Jew, of whom the Lamanites are a remnant, that they may believe the gospel, and look not for a Messiah to come who has already come.

D&C 45:21

21 And it shall come to pass, that this generation of Jews shall not pass away until every desolation which I have told you concerning them shall come to pass.

D&C 45:24-25

24 And this I have told you concerning Jerusalem; and when that day shall come, shall a remnant be scattered among all nations;
25 But they shall be gathered again; but they shall remain until the times of the Gentiles be fulfilled.

D&C 45:48-53

48 And then shall the Lord set his foot upon this mount, and it shall cleave in twain, and the earth shall tremble, and reel to and fro, and the heavens also shall shake.
49 And the Lord shall utter his voice, and all the ends of the earth shall hear it; and the nations of the earth shall mourn, and they that have laughed shall see their folly.
50 And calamity shall cover the mocker, and the scorner shall be consumed; and they that have watched for iniquity shall be hewn down and cast into the fire.
51 And then shall the Jews look upon me and say: What are these wounds in thine hands and in thy feet?
52 Then shall they know that I am the Lord; for I will say unto them: These wounds are the wounds with which I was wounded in the house of my friends. I am he who was lifted up. I am Jesus that was crucified. I am the Son of God.
53 And then shall they weep because of their iniquities; then shall they lament because they persecuted their king.

D&C 77:15

15 Q. What is to be understood by the two witnesses, in the eleventh chapter of Revelation?
A. They are two prophets that are to be raised up to the Jewish nation in the last days, at the time of the restoration, and to prophesy to the Jews after they are gathered and have built the city of Jerusalem in the land of their fathers.

D&C 90:9

9 That through your administration they may receive the word, and through their administration the word may go forth unto the ends of the earth, unto the Gentiles first, and then, behold, and lo, they shall turn unto the Jews.

D&C 109:64

64 And the children of Judah may begin to return to the lands which thou didst give to Abraham, their father.

D&C 133:18-25

18 When the Lamb shall stand upon Mount Zion, and with him a hundred and forty-four thousand, having his Father's name written on their foreheads.

19 Wherefore, prepare ye for the coming of the Bridegroom; go ye, go ye out to meet him.

20 For behold, he shall stand upon the mount of Olivet, and upon the mighty ocean, even the great deep, and upon the islands of the sea, and upon the land of Zion.

21 And he shall utter his voice out of Zion, and he shall speak from Jerusalem, and his voice shall be heard among all people;

22 And it shall be a voice as the voice of many waters, and as the voice of a great thunder, which shall break down the mountains, and the valleys shall not be found.

23 He shall command the great deep, and it shall be driven back into the north countries, and the islands shall become one land;

24 And the land of Jerusalem and the land of Zion shall be turned back into their own place, and the earth shall be like as it was in the days before it was divided.

25 And the Lord, even the Savior, shall stand in the midst of his people, and shall reign over all flesh.

DESOLATION OF ABOMINATION & ARMAGEDDON

Orson Pratt, Journal of Discourses, Vol. 7, p. 188-189, July 10, 1859.

"After the kingdom of God has spread upon the face of the earth, and every jot and tittle of the prophecies have been fulfilled in relation to the spreading of the Gospel among the nations,—after signs have been shown in the heavens above, and on the earth beneath, blood, fire, and vapour of smoke,—after the sun is turned into darkness, and the moon shall have the appearance of blood, and the stars have apparently been hurled out of their places, and all things have been in commotion, so great will be the darkness resting upon Christendom, and so great the bonds of priestcraft with which they will be bound, that they will not understand, and they will be given up to the hardness of their hearts. Then will be fulfilled that saying, 'That the day shall come when the Lord shall have power over his Saints, and the Devil shall have power over his own dominion.' He will give them up to the power of the Devil, and he will have power over them, and he will carry them about as chaff before a whirlwind. He will gather up millions upon millions of people into the valleys around about Jerusalem in order to destroy the Jews after they have gathered. How will the Devil do this? He will perform miracles to do it. The Bible says the kings of the earth and the great ones will be deceived by these false miracles. It says there shall be three unclean spirits that shall go forth working miracles, and they are spirits of devils. Where do they go? To the kings of the earth; and what will they do? Gather them up to battle unto the great day of God Almighty. Where? Into the valley of Armageddon. And where is that? On the east side of Jerusalem.

When he gets them gathered together, they do not understand any of these things; but they are given up to that power that deceived them, by miracles that had been performed, to get them to go into that valley to be destroyed. Joel, Zephaniah, Zechariah, Isaiah, Ezekiel, and nearly all of the ancient Prophets have predicted that the nations shall be gathered up against Jerusalem, in the valley of Jehoshaphat and the valley of Megiddo,—that there the Lord shall fight for his people, and smite the horse and his rider, and send plagues on these armies, and their flesh shall be consumed from their bones and their eyes from their sockets. They will actually fulfil these prophecies, with all their pretension to Bible and prophetic learning."

Orson Pratt, Journal of Discourses, Vol. 14, p. 352-353, March 10, 1872.

"Now here is the difference between Zion and old Jerusalem. The Jews, or many of them, will gather back to Jerusalem in a state of unbelief in the true Messiah, believing in the prophets but rejecting the New Testament, and looking for the Messiah to come, honest-hearted no doubt, many of them. And they will rebuild Jerusalem after the times of the Gentiles are fulfilled. While in that state of unbelief Gog and Magog, the inhabitants of Russia and all those nations in northern Europe and northern Asia, a great multitude, will gather against the Jews before Jesus comes, and they will fill up the great valley of Armageddon, the great valley of Jehosaphat and all the surrounding valleys; they will be like a cloud covering the land. Horses and chariots and horsemen, a very great army, will gather up there to take a spoil. For you know when the Rothschilds and the great bankers among the Jewish nation shall return back to their own land to rebuild the city of Jerusalem, carrying their capital with them, it will almost ruin some of the nations, and the latter will go up against Jerusalem to take a spoil. And they will succeed in taking half the city captive; and when they are in the act of destroying that city, behold the Lord will come with all his Saints, and he shall stand his feet on the Mount of Olives, 'And in that day' says the Prophet Zachariah 'shall the Lord go forth and fight against all those nations that have fought against Jerusalem, and their flesh shall consume away upon their bones, their eyes in their sockets. This great calamity comes upon the Jewish nation in consequence of their unbelief in the true Messiah."

Joseph Fielding Smith, The Signs of the Times, p. 170.

"Now I have read these passages of Scripture from these various prophets. Here you will find Isaiah saying the Lord will pour out war upon all the world; Jeremiah saying the same thing and speaking of these terrible things; Daniel saying so; Ezekiel saying so. We find Joel, Zephaniah, Zechariah, all proclaiming that in this last day, the day when the sun shall be darkened and the moon turned to blood and the stars fall from heaven, that the nations of the earth would gather against Jerusalem. All of them speak of it; and when that time comes, the Lord is going to come out of His hiding place. You can see what a terrible condition it is going to be; and the Jews besieged, not only in Jerusalem but, of course, throughout Palestine are in the siege; and when they are about to go under, then the Lord comes. There will be the great earthquake. The earthquake will not be only in Palestine. There will not be merely the separation of the Mount of Olives, to form a valley that the Jews may escape, but the whole earth is going to be shaken. There will be some dreadful things take place, and some great changes are going to take place, and that you will find written in the book of Ezekiel (38:17-23), which I did not read to you.

Now, this is very interesting. You can take your Doctrine and Covenants and turn to Section 45 and read what the Lord says about it, confirming what is written here in the book of Zechariah. During this siege, when the nations are gathered and the Lord comes, there will be a great destruction. The armies will become so confused they will fight among themselves. There will be great slaughter. Then the Lord comes to the Jews. He shows Himself. He calls upon them to come and examine His hands and His feet, and they say, 'What are these wounds?' And He answers them, 'These are the wounds with which I was wounded in the house of my friends. I am Jesus Christ.'"

Teachings of Ezra Taft Benson, p. 107.

"The great destructive force which was to be turned loose on the earth and which the prophets for centuries have been calling the 'abomination of desolation' is vividly described by those who saw it in vision. Ours is the first generation to realize how literally these prophecies can be fulfilled now that God, through science, has unlocked the secret to thermonuclear reaction."

Bruce R. McConkie, Mormon Doctrine, "Battle of Armageddon", p. 74.

"Some 60 air miles north of Jerusalem lies the ancient city of Megiddo (now called Tell el-Mutesellim). . . .Megiddo overlooks the great plain of Esdraelon, an area of some 20 by 14 miles in which many great battles took place anciently. Megiddo is the older Hebrew form of Armageddon . . . or the Hill of Battles; it is 'the valley of Megiddon' mentioned in Zechariah. (Zech. 12:11.)

At the very moment of the Second Coming . . . the battle of Armageddon (obviously covering the entire area from Jerusalem to Megiddo, and perhaps more) will be in progress."

Also see The Millennial Messiah 449-451,464-466,472-473, 477-490.

Bruce R. McConkie, The Millennial Messiah, p. 490.

"There are three great things that will grow out of and come because of Armageddon:
1. In the course of this final great conflict the Lord himself shall return, the vineyard shall be burned, and the millennial day will dawn.
2. Out of the defeat of Gog and Magog comes the end of all the nations of the earth and the final triumph of Israel as a people and as a nation.
3. Out of Armageddon comes the destruction of the political kingdom on earth of Lucifer and the fall of the great and abominable church."

Bruce R. McConkie, A New Witness for the Articles of Faith, p. 638-639.

"Holy writ describes the battle of Armageddon as the war of Gog and Magog. These accounts relative to Gog and Magog add to the Armageddon concept the fact that this final war will be religious in nature. Nations bearing the pseudonyms Gog and Magog will attack the Lord's covenant people. These evil forces will be destroyed by fire; the Lord will rain fire and brimstone upon them. That is, they will be burned at his coming. Their destruction will include the overthrow of the political kingdom on earth of Lucifer and the fall of the great and abominable church. The final triumph in this war of wars will bring to pass the triumph of Israel as a people and as a nation.

The destruction of Gog and Magog constitutes the fall of Babylon, the overthrow of the great and abominable church and the destruction of the wicked."

SCRIPTURAL REFERENCES

Ezekiel 38:Heading-12

The battle of Gog and Magog against Israel shall usher in the Second Coming—The Lord will come amid war and pestilence, and all men shall shake at his presence.

1 AND the word of the LORD came unto me, saying,

2 Son of man, set thy face against Gog, the land of Magog, the chief prince of Meshech and Tubal, and prophesy against him,

3 And say, Thus saith the Lord GOD; Behold I am against thee, O Gog, the chief prince of Meshech and Tubal:

4 And I will turn thee back, and put hooks into thy jaws, and I will bring thee forth, and all thine army, horses and horsemen, all of them clothed with all sorts of armour, even a great company with bucklers and shields, all of them handling swords:

5 Persia, Ethiopia, and Libya with them; all of them with shield and helmet:

6 Gomer, and all his bands; the house of Togarmah of the north quarters, and all his bands: and many people with thee.

7 Be thou prepared, and prepare for thyself, thou, and all thy company that are assembled unto thee, and be thou a guard unto them.

8 After many days thou shalt be visited: in the latter years thou shalt come into the land that is brought back from the sword, and is gathered out of many people, against the mountains of Israel, which have been always waste: but it is brought forth out of the nations, and they shall dwell safely all of them.

9 Thou shalt ascend and come like a storm, thou shalt be like a cloud to cover the land, thou, and all thy bands, and many people with thee.

10 Thus saith the Lord GOD; It shall also come to pass, that at the same time shall things come into thy mind, and thou shalt think an evil thought:

11 And thou shalt say, I will go up to the land of unwalled villages; I will go to them that are at rest, that dwell safely, all of them dwelling without walls, and having neither bars nor gates,

12 To take a spoil, and to take a prey; to turn thine hand upon the desolate places that are now inhabited, and upon the people that are gathered out of the nations, which have gotten cattle and goods, that dwell in the midst of the land.

Ezekiel 38:16-23

16 And thou shalt come up against my people of Israel, as a cloud to cover the land; it shall be in the latter days, and I will bring thee against my land, that the heathen may know me, when I shall be sanctified in thee, O Gog, before their eyes.

17 Thus saith the Lord GOD; Art thou he of whom I have spoken in old time by my servants the prophets of Israel, which prophesied in those days many years that I would bring thee against them?

18 And it shall come to pass at the same time when Gog shall come against the land of Israel, saith the Lord GOD, that my fury shall come up in my face.

19 For in my jealousy and in the fire of my wrath have I spoken, Surely in that day there shall be a great shaking in the land of Israel;

20 So that the fishes of the sea, and the fowls of the heaven, and the beasts of the field, and all creeping things that creep upon the earth, and all the men that are upon the face of the earth, shall shake at my presence, and the mountains shall be thrown down, and the steep places shall fall, and every wall shall fall to the ground.

21 And I will call for a sword against him throughout all my mountains, saith the Lord GOD: every man's sword shall be against his brother.

22 And I will plead against him with pestilence and with blood; and I will rain upon him, and upon his bands, and upon the many people that are with him, an overflowing rain, and great hailstones, fire, and brimstone.

23 Thus will I magnify myself, and sanctify myself; and I will be known in the eyes of many nations, and they shall know that I am the LORD.

Ezekiel 39:1-20

1 Therefore, thou son of man, prophesy against Gog, and say, Thus saith the Lord GOD; Behold, I am against thee, O Gog, the chief prince of Meshech and Tubal:

2 And I will turn thee back, and leave but the sixth part of thee, and will cause thee to come up from the north parts, and will bring thee upon the mountains of Israel:

3 And I will smite thy bow out of thy left hand, and will cause thine arrows to fall out of thy right hand.

4 Thou shalt fall upon the mountains of Israel, thou, and all thy bands, and the people that is with thee: I will give thee unto the ravenous birds of every sort, and to the beasts of the field to be devoured.

5 Thou shalt fall upon the open field: for I have spoken it, saith the Lord GOD.

6 And I will send a fire on Magog, and among them that dwell carelessly in the isles: and they shall know that I am the LORD.

7 So will I make my holy name known in the midst of my people Israel; and I will not let them pollute my holy name any more: and the heathen shall know that I am the LORD, the Holy One in Israel.

8 Behold, it is come, and it is done, saith the Lord GOD; this is the day whereof I have spoken.

9 And they that dwell in the cities of Israel shall go forth, and shall set on fire and burn the weapons, both the shields and the bucklers, the bows and the arrows, and the handstaves, and the spears, and they shall burn them with fire seven years:

10 So that they shall take no wood out of the field, neither cut down any out of the forests; for they shall burn the weapons with fire: and they shall spoil those that spoiled them, and rob those that robbed them, saith the Lord GOD.

11 And it shall come to pass in that day, that I will give unto Gog a place there of graves in Israel, the valley of the passengers on the east of the sea: and it shall stop the noses of the passengers: and there shall they bury Gog and all his multitude: and they shall call it The valley of Hamon-gog.

12 And seven months shall the house of Israel be burying of them, that they may cleanse the land.

13 Yea, all the people of the land shall bury them; and it shall be to them a renown the day that I shall be glorified, saith the Lord GOD.

14 And they shall sever out men of continual employment, passing through the land to bury with the

111

passengers those that remain upon the face of the earth, to cleanse it: after the end of seven months shall they search. ˙

15 And the passengers that pass through the land, when any seeth a man's bone, then shall he set up a sign by it, till the buriers have buried it in the valley of Hamon-gog.

16 And also the name of the city shall be Hamonah. Thus shallthey cleanse the land.

17 And, thou son of man, thus saith the Lord GOD; Speak unto every feathered fowl, and to every beast of the field, Assemble yourselves, and come; gather yourselves on every side to my sacrifice that I do sacrifice for you, even a great sacrifice upon the mountains of Israel, that ye may eat flesh, and drink blood.

18 Ye shall eat the flesh of the mighty, and drink the blood of the princes of the earth, of rams, of lambs, and of goats, of bullocks, all of them fatlings of Bashan.

19 And ye shall eat fat till ye be full, and drink blood till ye be drunken, of my sacrifice which I have sacrificed for you.

20 Thus ye shall be filled at my table with horses and chariots, with mighty men, and with all men of war, saith the Lord GOD.

Daniel 9:25-27

25 Know therefore and understand, that from the going forth of the commandment to restore and to build Jerusalem unto the Messiah the Prince shall be seven weeks, and threescore and two weeks: the street shall be built again, and the wall, even in troublous times.

26 And after threescore and two weeks shall Messiah be cut off, but not for himself: and the people of the prince that shall come shall destroy the city and the sanctuary; and the end thereof shall be with a flood, and unto the end of the war desolations are determined.

27 And he shall confirm the covenant with many for one week: and in the midst of the week he shall cause the sacrifice and the oblation to cease, and for the overspreading of abominations he shall make it desolate, even until the consummation, and that determined shall be poured upon the desolate.

Daniel 11:31

31 And arms shall stand on his part, and they shall pollute the sanctuary of strength, and shall take away the daily sacrifice, and they shall place the abomination that maketh desolate.

Daniel 12:11-12

11 And from the time that the daily sacrifice shall be taken away, and the abomination that maketh desolate set up, there shall be a thousand two hundred and ninety days.

12 Blessed is he that waiteth, and cometh to the thousand three hundred and five and thirty days.

Joel 2:1-11

1 Blow ye the trumpet in Zion, and sound an alarm in my holy mountain: let all the inhabitants of the land tremble: for the day of the LORD cometh, for it is nigh at hand;

2 A day of darkness and of gloominess, a day of clouds and of thick darkness, as the morning spread upon the mountains: a great people and a strong; there hath not been ever the like, neither shall be any more after it, even to the years of many generations.

3 A fire devoureth before them; and behind them a flame burneth: the land is as the garden of Eden before them, and behind them a desolate wilderness; yea, and nothing shall escape them.

4 The appearance of them is as the appearance of horses; and as horsemen, so shall they run.

5 Like the noise of chariots on the tops of mountains shall they leap, like the noise of a flame of fire that devoureth the stubble, as a strong people set in battle array.

6 Before their face the people shall be much pained: all faces shall gather blackness.

7 They shall run like mighty men; they shall climb the wall like men of war; and they shall march every one on his ways, and they shall not break their ranks:

8 Neither shall one thrust another; they shall walk every one in his path: and when they fall upon the sword, they shall not be wounded.

9 They shall run to and fro in the city; they shall run upon the wall, they shall climb up upon the houses; they shall enter in at the windows like a thief.

10 The earth shall quake before them; the heavens shall tremble: the sun and the moon shall be dark, and the stars shall withdraw their shining:

11 And the LORD shall utter his voice before his army: for his camp is very great: for he is strong that executeth his word: for the day of the LORD is great and very terrible; and who can abide it?

Joel 2:20

20 But I will remove far off from you the northern army, and will drive him into a land barren and desolate, with his face toward the east sea, and his hinder part toward the utmost sea, and his stink shall come up, and his ill savour shall come up, because he hath done great things.

Joel 3:1-17

1 For, behold, in those days, and in that time, when I shall bring again the captivity of Judah and Jerusalem,

2 I will also gather all nations, and will bring them down into the valley of Jehoshaphat, and will plead with them there for my people and for my heritage Israel, whom they have scattered among the nations, and parted my land.

3 And they have cast lots for my people; and have given a boy for an harlot, and sold a girl for wine, that they might drink.

4 Yea, and what have ye to do with me, O Tyre, and Zidon, and all the coasts of Palestine? will ye render me a recompence? and if ye recompence me, swiftly and speedily will I return your recompence upon your own head;

5 Because ye have taken my silver and my gold, and have carried into your temples my goodly pleasant things:

6 The children also of Judah and the children of Jerusalem have ye sold unto the Grecians, that ye might remove them far from their border.

7 Behold, I will raise them out of the place whither ye have sold them, and will return your recompence upon your own head:

8 And I will sell your sons and your daughters into the hand of the children of Judah, and they shall sell them to the Sabeans, to a people far off: for the LORD hath spoken it.

9 Proclaim ye this among the Gentiles; Prepare war, wake up the mighty men, let all the men of war

draw near; let them come up:

10 Beat your plowshares into swords, and your pruninghooks into spears: let the weak say, I am strong.

11 Assemble yourselves, and come, all ye heathen, and gather yourselves together round about: thither cause thy mighty ones to come down, O LORD.

12 Let the heathen be wakened, and come up to the valley of Jehoshaphat: for there will I sit to judge all the heathen round about.

13 Put ye in the sickle, for the harvest is ripe: come, get you down; for the press is full, the fats overflow; for their wickedness is great.

14 Multitudes, multitudes in the valley of decision: for the day of the LORD is near in the valley of decision.

15 The sun and the moon shall be darkened, and the stars shall withdraw their shining.

16 The LORD also shall roar out of Zion, and utter his voice from Jerusalem; and the heavens and the earth shall shake: but the LORD will be the hope of his people, and the strength of the children of Israel.

17 So shall ye know that I am the LORD your God dwelling in Zion, my holy mountain: then shall Jerusalem be holy, and there shall no strangers pass through her any more.

Zechariah 12:Heading

In the final great war, all nations shall be engaged at Jerusalem but the Lord shall defend his people—Then the Jews shall look upon Jesus whom they crucified, and there shall be great mourning.

Zechariah 12:9

9 And it shall come to pass in that day, that I will seek to destroy all the nations that come against Jerusalem.

Zechariah 14:2-5

2 For I will gather all nations against Jerusalem to battle; and the city shall be taken, and the houses rifled, and the women ravished; and half of the city shall go forth into captivity, and the residue of the people shall not be cut off from the city.

3 Then shall the LORD go forth, and fight against those nations, as when he fought in the day of battle.

4 And his feet shall stand in that day upon the mount of Olives, which is before Jerusalem on the east, and the mount of Olives shall cleave in the midst thereof toward the east and toward the west, and there shall be a very great valley; and half of the mountain shall remove toward the north, and half of it toward the south.

5 And ye shall flee to the valley of the mountains; for the valley of the mountains shall reach unto Azal: yea, ye shall flee, like as ye fled from before the earthquake in the days of Uzziah king of Judah: and the LORD my God shall come, and all the saints with thee.

Zechariah 14:12

12 And this shall be the plague wherewith the LORD will smite all the people that have fought against Jerusalem; Their flesh shall consume away while they stand upon their feet, and their eyes shall consume away in their holes, and their tongue shall consume away in their mouth.

JST Matthew 1:12

12 When you, therefore, shall see the abomination of desolation, spoken of by Daniel the prophet, concerning the destruction of Jerusalem, then you shall stand in the holy place; whoso readeth let him understand.

JST Matthew 1:18-20

18 For then, in those days, shall be great tribulation on the Jews, and upon the inhabitants of Jerusalem, such as was not before sent upon Israel, of God, since the beginning of their kingdom until this time; no, nor ever shall be sent again upon Israel.

19 All things which have befallen them are only the beginning of the sorrows which shall come upon them.

20 And except those days should be shortened, there should none of their flesh be saved; but for the elect's sake, according to the covenant, those days shall be shortened.

JST Matthew 1:31-36

31 And again, this Gospel of the Kingdom shall be preached in all the world, for a witness unto all nations, and then shall the end come, or the destruction of the wicked;

32 And again shall the abomination of desolation, spoken of by Daniel the prophet, be fulfilled.

33 And immediately after the tribulation of those days, the sun shall be darkened, and the moon shall not give her light, and the stars shall fall from heaven, and the powers of heaven shall be shaken.

34 Verily, I say unto you, this generation, in which these things shall be shown forth, shall not pass away until all I have told you shall be fulfilled.

35 Although, the days will come, that heaven and earth shall pass away; yet my words shall not pass away, but all shall be fulfilled.

36 And, as I said before, after the tribulation of those days, and the powers of the heavens shall be shaken, then shall appear the sign of the Son of Man in heaven, and then shall all the tribes of the earth mourn; and they shall see the Son of Man coming in the clouds of heaven, with power and great glory;

Matthew 24:15-22

15 When ye therefore shall see the abomination of desolation, spoken of by Daniel the prophet, stand in the holy place, (whoso readeth, let him understand:)

16 Then let them which be in Judaea flee into the mountains:

17 Let him which is on the housetop not come down to take any thing out of his house:

18 Neither let him which is in the field return back to take his clothes.

19 And woe unto them that are with child, and to them that give suck in those days!

20 But pray ye that your flight be not in the winter, neither on the sabbath day:

21 For then shall be great tribulation, such as was not since the beginning of the world to this time, no, nor ever shall be.

22 And except those days should be shortened, there should no flesh be saved: but for the elect's sake those days shall be shortened.

Revelation 11:2

2 But the court which is without the temple leave out, and measure it not; for it is given unto the Gentiles: and the holy city shall they tread under foot forty and two months.

Revelation 11:12-14

12 And they heard a great voice from heaven saying unto them, Come up hither. And they ascended up to heaven in a cloud; and their enemies beheld them.

13 And the same hour was there a great earthquake, and the tenth part of the city fell, and in the earthquake were slain of men seven thousand: and the remnant were affrighted, and gave glory to the God of heaven.

14 The second woe is past; and, behold, the third woe cometh quickly.

Revelation 16:14-21

14 For they are the spirits of devils, working miracles, which go forth unto the kings of the earth and of the whole world, to gather them to the battle of that great day of God Almighty.

15 Behold, I come as a thief. Blessed is he that watcheth, and keepeth his garments, lest he walk naked, and they see his shame.

16 And he gathered them together into a place called in the Hebrew tongue Armageddon.

17 And the seventh angel poured out his vial into the air; and there came a great voice out of the temple of heaven, from the throne, saying, It is done.

18 And there were voices, and thunders, and lightnings; and there was a great earthquake, such as was not since men were upon the earth, so mighty an earthquake, and so great.

19 And the great city was divided into three parts, and the cities of the nations fell: and great Babylon came in remembrance before God, to give unto her the cup of the wine of the fierceness of his wrath.

20 And every island fled away, and the mountains were not found.

21 And there fell upon men a great hail out of heaven, every stone about the weight of a talent: and men blasphemed God because of the plague of the hail; for the plague thereof was exceeding great.

1 Nephi 22:14

14 And every nation which shall war against thee, O house of Israel, shall be turned one against another, and they shall fall into the pit which they digged to ensnare the people of the Lord. And all that fight against Zion shall be destroyed, and that great whore, who hath perverted the right ways of the Lord, yea, that great and abominable church, shall tumble to the dust and great shall be the fall of it.

D&C 84:117

117 And verily I say unto you, the rest of my servants, go ye forth as your circumstances shall permit, in your several callings, unto the great and notable cities and villages, reproving the world in righteousness of all their unrighteous and ungodly deeds, setting forth clearly and understandingly the desolation of abomination in the last days.

D&C 133:13

13 And let them who be of Judah flee unto Jerusalem, unto the mountains of the Lord's house.

D&C 133:35

35 And they also of the tribe of Judah, after their pain, shall be sanctified in holiness before the Lord, to dwell in his presence day and night, forever and ever.

CHAPTER THREE

REMNANT OF JACOB & THE LAMANITES

"Nephi saw that great promises were made to the Gentiles upon this land, and that the Lord had a marvelous work for them to do in bringing forth the fullness of the Gospel and taking it to the seed of his brethren. The promise was made that after the Gentiles had scattered the Lamanites and had ill-treated them, the time would come when they would become nursing fathers unto them."

(Joseph Fielding Smith, The Way to Perfection, p. 144-145.)

Proclamation of the Twelve, April 6, 1845, p. 9-10.

"The despised and degraded son of the forest, who has wandered in dejection and sorrow, and suffered reproach, shall then drop his disguise, and stand forth in manly dignity, and exclaim to the Gentiles who have envied and sold him: 'Joseph: does my father yet live?' Or, in other words: I am a descendant of that Joseph who was sold into Egypt. You have hated me, and sold me, and thought I was dead. But lo! I live, and am heir to the inheritance, titles, honors, priesthood, sceptre, crown, throne, and eternal life and dignity of my fathers who live for evermore.

He shall then be ordained, washed, anointed with holy oil and arrayed in fine linen, even in the glorious and beautiful garments and royal robes of the high priesthood, which is after the order of the Son of God; and shall enter into the congregation of the Lord, even into the Holy of Holies, there to be crowned with authority and power which shall never end.

The Spirit of the Lord shall then descend upon him, like the dew upon the mountains of Hermon, and like refreshing showers of rain upon the flowers of Paradise.

His heart shall expand with knowledge, wide as eternity; and his mind shall comprehend the vast creations of his God, and His eternal purpose of redemption, glory, and exaltation, which was devised in heaven before the worlds were organized; but made manifest in these last days, for the fulness of the Gentiles, and for the exaltation of Israel.

He shall also behold his Redeemer and be filled with his presence, while the cloud of his glory shall be seen in his temple."

Brigham Young, Journal of Discourses, Vol. 4, p. 346, June 7, 1857.

"Pray that our enemies may have no power over us; pray for the Spirit of the Gospel, that the Lord may strengthen the Elders, and keep them in the spirit of humility, while they are out preaching the Gospel; pray for the anointed of the Lord, for the house of Israel, those poor degraded Lamanites, that light and truth may spring up among them more and more. They begin to improve greatly; pray that it may continue, that they may come to acknowledge of the truth, and help to build up Zion, and they will be a shield to us in the day of trouble."

Orson Pratt, Journal of Discourses, Vol. 3, p. 18-19, May 20, 1855.

"The coming of Christ seems to be near at hand, yet Zion must be redeemed before that day; the temple must be built upon the consecrated spot, the cloud and glory of the Lord rest upon it, and the Lamanites, many of them, brought in, and they must build up the NEW JERUSALEM! It is true, so says the Book of Mormon, that inasmuch as the Gentiles receive the Gospel, they shall assist my people the remnant of Jacob, saith the Lord, to build the New Jerusalem. And when they have got it built, then we are told that they shall assist my people who are of Jacob to be gathered in unto the New Jerusalem."

Orson Pratt, Journal of Discourses, Vol. 14, p. 333-334, February 11, 1872.

"Go to the various islands of the Pacific Ocean, and you find a general resemblance in the characters and countenances of the people. Who are they? According to the Book of Mormon, Israelites were scattered forth from time to time, and colonies planted on these islands of the ocean. In that day the isles will sing with joy; in that day the isles of the sea will wait for the Lord's law; in that day the isles of the sea will rejoice, for they will give up their inhabitants, and they will be wafted in ships to their promised land, and God will show forth his power and gather millions of people from these numerous isles of the ocean, and he will bring them back to the land of their fathers. These poor degraded Lamanites, or American Indians, that are now so far sunk beneath humanity, are to be lifted up by the power of the Almighty when the day shall come for Israel to be restored, for God will not forget them. They are descendants of the tribe of Joseph, and consequently they are numbered with the people of the covenant. God will remember the covenant which he made with our ancient fathers. These Lamanites, these American Indians, will come to the knowledge of the covenant, and they will arise and will build upon the face of this land a magnificent city called Jerusalem, after the pattern and in the same manner that the Jews will build old Jerusalem. That is what the Lamanites will do, and we will go and help them too, for it is predicted in the Book of Mormon that when this work should come forth, when the time fully arrives for the redemption of this small remnant of the house of Joseph, 'As many of the Gentiles as will believe, they shall assist my people, who are a remnant of the house of Israel, that they may build up on the face of this land a city that shall be called the New Jerusalem, and then, behold, the powers of heaven shall come down and be in the midst of this people, and I also will be in your midst.'"

Orson Pratt, Journal of Discourses, Vol. 14, p. 354, March 10, 1872.

"Now let me here remark that this remnant of the house of Israel or Jacob, which we term the American Indians, are eventually to become a righteous branch of the house of Israel; when the times of the Gentiles are fulfilled, they will be numbered among the people of the covenant made with ancient Israel, they will be a branch of the Lord, beautiful and glorious, excellent and comely, and the power of the Lord will be upon them. In that day Jesus will come to them, they being a remnant of the tribe of Joseph."

Orson Pratt, Journal of Discourses, Vol. 16, p. 353, January 25, 1874.

"That is the destiny of our Indian tribes. Many may yet suffer and perish, but when the time of their tribulation is past, when the Lord has rewarded unto them double for all the sins that were committed by their ancient fathers in their apostasy, and when he has visited them in judgment according to the prophecies that are contained in this Book of Mormon, and the times of the Gentiles who now occupy this land are fulfilled, then the Lord will make bare his arm, and he will redeem these remnants of Israel, that they may inherit the blessings promised to their ancient fathers."

Orson Pratt, Journal of Discourses, Vol. 17, p. 300, February 7, 1875.

"There is one thing which I am now about to read which has not yet been fulfilled, and which we must fulfill before Zion is redeemed. I will read it—'Behold, saith the Father, I will bring the fulness of my Gospel from among them, and then I will remember my covenant which I have made unto my people, O house of Israel, and I will bring my Gospel unto them.' Now then, we are here in this land, the house of Israel are scattered all around us, some in the great basin, some in Arizona, some in Idaho, come in Colorado, some in Montana, some in one place, some in another; I refer to the American Indians, all remnants of Joseph and belonging to the house of Israel. They have become very degraded in consequence of the apostasy and wickedness of their ancient fathers. This people—Latter-day Saints, before they can ever return to build up the waste places of Zion and receive their inheritances in Jackson County, Missouri, have got to exert themselves to bring the remnants of Joseph to a knowledge of the truth. We have not made any very great exertions in this direction unto the present time. The Lord has given us time since he brought the fulness of the Gospel from among the Gentiles to lay a foundation so that we could commence this missionary work in behalf of and among the remnants of Joseph."

Orson Pratt, Journal of Discourses, Vol. 17, p. 300-301, February 7, 1875.

"Read the Book of Mormon and you will find what God promised to do for the remnants of Joseph fourteen hundred years ago, about the time that most of them were becoming wicked and corrupt. The Lord said when their record should come forth in the latter days that he would send his messengers to them, and among these messengers he mentioned three persons who lived some eighteen hundred years ago, three of the Twelve who were chosen on this land. The Lord made a promise to these three that they should administer, as holy messengers in the latter days, for and in behalf of the remnants of the house of Israel, which would fall into a low and degraded condition in consequence of the great wickedness and apostasy of their ancient fathers; that they should be instruments in his hands in bringing these remnants to the knowledge of the truth. We hear that these messengers have come, not in one instance alone, but in many instances. Already we have heard of some fourteen hundred Indians, and I do not know but more, who have been baptized. Ask them why they have come so many hundred miles to find Elders of the Church and they will reply—Such a person came to us, he spoke in our language, instructed us and told us what to do, and we have come in order to comply with his requirements.'"

Orson Pratt, Journal of Discourses, Vol. 17, p. 302, February 7, 1875.

"The Latter-day Saints in these mountains never can have the privilege of going back to Jackson County and building that city which is to be called the New Jerusalem, upon the spot that was appointed by revelation through the Prophet Joseph, until quite a large portion of the remnants of Joseph go back with us. . . .

Now, a great many, without reading these things, have flattered themselves that we are the ones who are going to do all this work. It is not so; we have got to be helpers, we have got to be those who co-operate with the remnants of Joseph in accomplishing this great work; for the Lord will have respect unto them, because they are the blood of Israel, and the promises of their fathers extend to them, and they will have the privilege of building that city, according to the pattern that the Lord shall give. Do not misunderstand me, do not think that all the Laminate tribes are going to be converted and receive this great degree of education and civilization before we can return to Jackson County. Do not think this for a moment, it will only be a remnant; for when we have laid the foundation of that city and have built a portion of it, and have built a Temple therein, there is another work which we have got to do in connection with these remnants of Jacob whom we shall assist in building the city. What is it? We have got to be sent forth as missionaries to all parts of this American continent. Not to the Gentiles, for their times will be fulfilled; but we must go to all those tribes that roam through the cold regions of the north—British America, to all the tribes that dwell in the Territories of the United States, also to all those who are scattered through Mexico, and Central and South America, and the object of our going will be to declare the principles of the Gospel unto them, and bring them to a knowledge of the truth. 'Then shall they assist my people who are scattered on all the face of the land, and they may be gathered in to the New Jerusalem.'

Will not this be a great work? It will take a good while to gather all these tribe of South America, for some of them will have to come from five to eight thousand miles in order to reach the New Jerusalem. This will be quite a work, and yet we shall have to perform it after the city is built."

Orson Pratt, Journal of Discourses, Vol. 17, p. 303, February 7, 1875.

"Now who can explain and tell us what this means? Can any of the wise commentators of the day? Can any of those who have studied theology in their life-time, tell us why it is from Joseph that the Shepherd, the Stone of Israel is to be made manifest? Says one—'It cannot have reference to his birth, because Jesus descended from Judah, instead of Joseph, out of the loins of Judah, through the lineage of David. He is the Lion of the tribe of Judah.' Why then this peculiar saying of the old Prophet Jacob, about the tribe of Joseph, that from thence is the Shepherd, the Stone of Israel, if he was not born of Joseph, and did not descend through that tribe? This is a very curious kind of saying. But he will be made manifest in the character of a shepherd, and that shepherd will lead Joseph as a flock and he will stir up his strength and will save the house of Joseph. But it will be in his own time and way. First, a remnant will be converted; second, Zion will be redeemed, and all among the Gentiles who believe will assist this remnant of Jacob in building the New Jerusalem; third, a vast number of missionaries will be sent throughout the length and breadth of this great continent, to gather all the dispersed of his people in unto the New Jerusalem; fourth, the power of heaven will be made manifest in the midst of this people, and the Lord also will be in their midst, in the character of a shepherd, and he will lead Joseph as a flock, and he will instruct and counsel them personally as he did their ancient fathers in the days of their righteousness."

Orson Pratt, Journal of Discourses, Vol. 18, p. 28, April 11, 1875.

"That is the only hope that we Gentiles have. No hope for us whatever, no hope for this great and powerful nation, only by being numbered with these poor, degraded, despised, outcast, dark, and benighted Indians. Are you willing to be numbered with them? In what respect? Not to come down to their customs and habits, their uncleanness, filth, wickedness, darkness and ignorance; but be numbered with them in the inheritance if this great continent, which was given to them by promise, the same as Palestine was given to Abraham and Isaac. God gave it by the mouth of Jacob, who pronounced it upon the head of his son Joseph, it was promised that he should have a separate land from that given to Abraham and Isaac. Read it in the 49th chapter of Genesis. The Lord gave North and South America to the Indians, nearly six hundred years before Christ. And he promised that the Gentiles, in the latter days, who should come upon the face of this land, if they would repent when this Gospel should come forth unto them, they should have the privilege of receiving their inheritance in common with this remnant of Israel—these Indians. But if they did not repent there is another decree. And what is that? 'They shall be utterly cut off from among my people.' Thus it is predicted and you have read it for forty-five years. In another place the Lord says—'If they will not repent, behold I will cut off the cities of their land, I will throw down all their strongholds, and I will cut off their horses out of the midst of them, and I will execute vengeance and fury upon them such as they have not heard of.' In another place, which I have not time to turn to and read, it says—'And it shall come to pass that every soul that will not repent of their sins and come unto my beloved son, will I cut off from among my people, O, house of Israel, and it shall be done unto them even as Moses has said, they shall be cut off from among my people.'"

Wilford Woodruff, Journal of Discourses, Vol. 15, p. 283, January 12, 1873.

"The Lamanites will blossom as the rose on the mountains. I am willing to say here that, though I believe this, when I see the power of the nation destroying them from the face of the earth, the fulfillment of that prophecy is perhaps harder for me to believe than any revelation of God that I ever read. It looks as though there would not be enough left to receive the Gospel; but notwithstanding this dark picture, every word that God has ever said of them will have its fulfillment, and they, by and by, will receive the Gospel. It will be a day of God's power among them, and a nation will be born in a day."

Daniel H. Wells, Millennial Star, Vol. 27, p. 187, March 25, 1865.

"To add to the sufferings and great calamities of the American nation, they will be greatly distressed by the aborigines, who will 'marshall themselves, and become exceeding angry' and vex them 'with a sore vexation'. This event, we believe may not take place in its fullness until the nation has been greatly weakened by the death of millions in their own revolutionary battles. To what extent the Indians will have power over the nation, is not stated in this revelation; but from what Jesus informed their forefathers at the time of his personal ministry among them, as recorded in the Book of Mormon, they will have power in a great measure of the whole nation."

Joseph Fielding Smith, Church History and Modern Revelation, Vol. 2, p. 127.

"The rising up of slaves, it is thought by many, was fulfilled in the Civil War when many of the negroes found their way into the armies of the north and fought against their former masters. Others think this is yet to come. The history of this American continent also gives evidence that the Lamanites have risen up in their anger and vexed the Gentiles. This warfare may not be over. It has been the fault of people in the United States to think that this prophetic saying has reference to the Indians in the United States, but we must remember that there are millions of the 'remnant' in Mexico, Central and South America. It was during our Civil War that the Indians in Mexico rose up and gained their freedom from the tyranny which Napoleon endeavored to inflict upon them contrary to the prediction of Jacob in the Book of Mormon, that there should be no kings among the Gentiles on this land. The independence of Mexico and other nations to the south has been accomplished by the uprising of the 'remnant' upon the land. However, let us not think that this prophecy has completely been fulfilled."

Joseph Fielding Smith, The Way to Perfection, p. 121.

"With the translation of the Book of Mormon many of the descendants of Joseph were made known. Who could have made that great discovery without a revelation from the Lord? The Lamanites are of Israel. Lehi was a descendant of Manasseh. We are informed that Ishmael, whose children joined the family of Lehi, was of Ephraim. In this way children belonging to these two tribes were planted in America. It is true that others also came, and it is just possible that the Lord, remembering his promise to Joseph, sent with the Mulekites others of the tribes of Joseph. At any rate, this land was given to them as their everlasting inheritance. They have inherited it in the past. They will do so more fully in the future."

Joseph Fielding Smith Jr., Doctrines of Salvation, Vol. 2, p. 247-248.

"*Latter-Day Lamanite Work Misunderstood.* My attention has been called to statements in the Book of Mormon which some interpret to mean that the Lamanites will take the lead in building the temple and the New Jerusalem in Missouri. But I fail to find any single passage which indicates that this is to be the order of things when these great events are to be fulfilled. . . .

Remnant Of Israel In All Nations. In these chapters the Lord is speaking throughout of the remnant of Jacob. . . .Most assuredly Jacob is Israel. Then again, when he speaks of the seed of Joseph, who is meant? Those who are descendants of Joseph, son of Israel, and this includes, of course, the Lamanites as well as the Ephraimites who are now being assembled and who are taking their place, according to prophecy, at the head to guide and bless the whole house of Israel. . . .

The remnant of the house of Israel spoken of in First Nephi, chapter 13, and Third Nephi, chapters 16, 20, and 21, does not have reference only to the descendants of Lehi, but to all the house of Israel, the children of Jacob, those upon this land and those in other lands. Reference to the gentiles also is to all the gentiles on this land and in other lands."

Joseph Fielding Smith Jr., Doctrines of Salvation, Vol. 2, p. 249-251.

"Are we justified in applying this merely to the Lamanites and saying that they are to go forth as a young lion pouring out vengeance upon the gentiles? Also does the phrase, 'Ye who are a remnant of the house of Jacob,' in verse 16, have reference just to the Lamanites? . . . it has reference to the remnants of Israel, which had been scattered in all lands. To apply it to the Lamanites in face of the entire theme of this discourse, in my judgment, narrows it too greatly. . . .

Ephraim Presides Over All Israel. I take it we, the members of the Church, most of us of the tribe of Ephraim, are of the remnant of Jacob. We know it to be the fact that the Lord called upon the descendants of Ephraim to commence his work in the earth in these last days. We know further that he has said that he set Ephraim, according to the promises of his birthright, at the head, Ephraim receives the 'richer blessings,' these blessings being those of presidency or direction. The keys are with Ephraim. It is Ephraim who is to be endowed with power to bless and give to the other tribes, including the Lamanites, their blessings. All the other tribes of Jacob, including the Lamanites, are to be crowned with glory in Zion by the hands of Ephraim.

Now do the scriptures teach that Ephraim, after doing all of this is to abdicate, or relinquish his place, and give it to the Lamanites and then receive orders from this branch of the 'remnant of Jacob' in the building of the New Jerusalem? This certainly is inconsistent with the whole plan and with all that the Lord has revealed in the Doctrine and Covenants in relation to the establishment of Zion and the building of the New Jerusalem. . . .

That the remnants of Joseph found among the descendants of Lehi, will have part in this great work is certainly consistent, and the great work of this restoration, the building of the temple and the City of Zion, or New Jerusalem, will fall to the lot of the descendants of Joseph, but it is Ephraim who will stand at the head and direct the work."

The Teachings of Spencer W. Kimball, p. 441.

"The time of Christ's return is affected by our conduct. I've known people who have been promised in their patriarchal blessings that they would live to see the temple built and some of them are dying and haven't seen the temple built. Do you know why? In my estimation, the Lord's timetable is directed a good deal by us. We speed up the clock or we slow the hands down and we turn them back by our activities or our procrastinations. And do you know why I think people who are actually promised that they would live to see the temple built are dying before completion of the temple? Because we haven't converted Indians in large enough numbers; never shall we go to Jackson County until we have converted and brought into this Church great numbers of Lamanites."

The Teachings of Spencer W. Kimball, p. 600.

"Gentiles and Lamanites alike are from Joseph. The Lamanite is a chosen child of God, but he is not the only chosen one. There are many other good people including the Anglos, the French, the German, and the English, who are also of Ephraim and Manasseh. They, with the Lamanites, are also chosen people, and they are a remnant of Jacob. The Lamanite is not wholly and exclusively the remnant of the Jacob which the Book of Mormon talks about. We are all of Israel! We are of Abraham and Isaac and Jacob and Joseph through Ephraim and Manasseh. We are all of us remnants of Jacob."

Spencer W. Kimball, Faith Precedes the Miracle, p. 349.

"The day of the Lamanite is surely here and we are God's instrument in helping to bring to pass the prophecies of renewed vitality, acceptance of the gospel, and resumption of a favored place as part of God's chosen people. The promises of the Lord will all come to pass; we could not thwart them if we would. But we do have it in our power to hasten or delay the process by our energetic or neglectful fulfillment of our responsibilities."

Bruce R. McConkie, The Mortal Messiah, Vol. 1, p. 363-364.

"Jacob gives his son Joseph a coat of many colors; a blood-stained coat remnant is later taken to Jacob with the false tale that its owner has been destroyed by wild beasts; and Jacob, as he handles the part of the garment that 'was preserved and had not decayed,' prophesies: 'Even as this remnant of garment of my son hath been preserved, so shall a remnant of the seed of my son be preserved by the hand of God, and be taken unto himself, while the remainder of the seed of Joseph shall perish, even as the remnant of his garment' (Alma 46:24)—all to the end that whenever the seed of Joseph think upon the coat, upon the sale of their ancestor to the Ishmaelites, and upon the wondrous work he wrought in Egypt, they will rejoice also in the goodness of the Lord to his seed in the latter days."

Bruce R. McConkie, The Mortal Messiah, Vol. 4, p. 334-335.

"And I say unto you, that if the Gentiles do not repent after the blessing which they shall receive, after they have scattered my people—

Then shall ye, who are a remnant of the house of Jacob, go forth among them; and ye shall be in the midst of them who shall be many; and ye shall be among them as a lion among the beasts of the forest, and as a young lion among the flocks of sheep, who, if he goeth through both treadeth down and teareth in pieces, and none can deliver.

Thy hand shall be lifted up upon thine adversaries, and all thine enemies shall be cut off.'

This is millennial; it refers to the Second Coming of Christ. It is not a war that a few Lamanites or any remnant of Israel shall wage against Gentile oppressors; the Lord does not operate in that manner. When he comes the wicked shall be destroyed and the righteous preserved; those who have not hearkened to the prophets shall be cut off from among the people; thus, the 'enemies' of Israel 'shall be cut off.' And it shall be with power, as though a young lion went forth rending and tearing in pieces a helpless flock of sheep. And so, if the Gentiles do not repent and believe in Christ after the gospel is restored among them, then, when the Lord comes, they will be destroyed and the triumph of Israel—because they kept the commandments and did receive the gospel—that triumph will be complete."

Bruce R. McConkie, A New Witness for the Articles of Faith, p. 518-519.

"An occasional whiff of nonsense goes around the Church acclaiming that the Lamanites will build the temple in the New Jerusalem and that Ephraim and others will come to their assistance. . . .The Book of Mormon passages upon which it is thought to rest have reference not to the Lamanites but to the whole house of Israel. The temple in Jackson County will be built by Ephraim, meaning the Church as it is now constituted; this is where the keys of temple building are vested, and it will be to this Ephraim that all the other tribes will come in due course to receive their temple blessings."

SCRIPTURAL REFERENCES

Isaiah 10:20-22

20 And it shall come to pass in that day, that the remnant of Israel, and such as are escaped of the house of Jacob, shall no more again stay upon him that smote them; but shall stay upon the LORD, the Holy One of Israel, in truth.

21 The remnant shall return, even the remnant of Jacob, unto the mighty God.

22 For though thy people Israel be as the sand of the sea, yet a remnant of them shall return: the consumption decreed shall overflow with righteousness.

Micah 5:Heading

Messiah shall be born in Bethlehem—In the last days the remnant of Jacob shall triumph gloriously over the Gentiles.

Micah 5:7-8

7 And the remnant of Jacob shall be in the midst of many people as a dew from the LORD, as the showers upon the grass, that tarrieth not for man, nor waiteth for the sons of men.

8 And the remnant of Jacob shall be among the Gentiles in the midst of many people as a lion among the beasts of the forest, as a young lion among the flocks of sheep: who, if he go through, both treadeth down, and teareth in pieces, and none can deliver.

1 Nephi 22:7-9

7 And it meaneth that the time cometh that after all the house of Israel have been scattered and confounded, that the Lord God will raise up a mighty nation among the Gentiles, yea, even upon the face of this land; and by them shall our seed be scattered.

8 And after our seed is scattered the Lord God will proceed to do a marvelous work among the Gentiles, which shall be of great worth unto our seed; wherefore, it is likened unto their being nourished by the Gentiles and being carried in their arms and upon their shoulders.

9 And it shall also be of worth unto the Gentiles; and not only unto the Gentiles but unto all the house of Israel, unto the making known of the covenants of the Father of heaven unto Abraham, saying: In thy seed shall all the kindreds of the earth be blessed.

2 Nephi 9:53

53 And behold how great the covenants of the Lord, and how great his condescensions unto the children of men; and because of his greatness, and his grace and mercy, he has promised unto us that our seed shall not utterly be destroyed, according to the flesh, but that he would preserve them; and in future generations they shall become a righteous branch unto the house of Israel.

2 Nephi 30:4-6

4 And then shall the remnant of our seed know concerning us, how that we came out from Jerusalem, and that they are descendants of the Jews.

5 And the gospel of Jesus Christ shall be declared among them; wherefore, they shall be restored unto the knowledge of their fathers, and also to the knowledge of Jesus Christ, which was had among their fathers.

6 And then shall they rejoice; for they shall know that it is a blessing unto them from the hand of God; and their scales of darkness shall begin to fall from their eyes; and many generations shall not pass away among them, save they shall be a pure and a delightsome people.

Alma 46:23-24

23 Moroni said unto them: Behold, we are a remnant of the seed of Jacob; yea, we are a remnant of the seed of Joseph, whose coat was rent by his brethren into many pieces; yea, and now behold, let us remember to keep the commandments of God, or our garments shall be rent by our brethren, and we be cast into prison, or be sold, or be slain.

24 Yea, let us preserve our liberty as a remnant of Joseph; yea, let us remember the words of Jacob, before his death, for behold, he saw that a part of the remnant of the coat of Joseph was preserved and had not decayed. And he said—Even as this remnant of garment of my son hath been preserved, so shall a remnant of the seed of my son be preserved by the hand of God, and be taken unto himself, while the remainder of the seed of Joseph shall perish, even as the remnant of his garment.

3 Nephi 5:24-26

24 And as surely as the Lord liveth, will he gather in from the four quarters of the earth all the remnant of the seed of Jacob, who are scattered abroad upon all the face of the earth.

25 And as he hath covenanted with all the house of Jacob, even so shall the covenant wherewith he hath covenanted with the house of Jacob be fulfilled in his own due time, unto the restoring all the house of Jacob unto the knowledge of the covenant that he hath covenanted with them.

26 And then shall they know their Redeemer, who is Jesus Christ, the Son of God; and then shall they be gathered in from the four quarters of the earth unto their own lands, from whence they have been dispersed; yea, as the Lord liveth so shall it be. Amen.

3 Nephi 16:8-16

8 But wo, saith the Father, unto the unbelieving of the Gentiles—for notwithstanding they have come forth upon the face of this land, and have scattered my people who are of the house of Israel; and my people who are of the house of Israel have been cast out from among them, and have been trodden under feet by them;

9 And because of the mercies of the Father unto the Gentiles, and also the judgments of the Father upon my people who are of the house of Israel, verily, verily, I say unto you, that after all this, and I have caused my people who are of the house of Israel to be smitten, and to be afflicted, and to be slain, and to be cast out from among them, and to become hated by them, and to become a hiss and a byword among them—

10 And thus commandeth the Father that I should say unto you: At that day when the Gentiles shall sin against my gospel, and shall reject the fullness of my gospel, and shall be lifted up in the pride of their hearts above all nations, and above all the people of the whole earth, and shall be filled with all manner of lyings, and of deceits, and of mischiefs, and all manner of hypocrisy, and murders, and priestcrafts, and whoredoms, and of secret abominations; and if they shall do all those things, and

shall reject the fullness of my gospel, behold, saith the Father, I will bring the fullness of my gospel from among them.

11 And then will I remember my covenant which I have made unto my people, O house of Israel, and I will bring my gospel unto them.

12 And I will show unto thee, O house of Israel, that the Gentiles shall not have power over you; but I will remember my covenant unto you, O house of Israel, and ye shall come unto the knowledge of the fullness of my gospel.

13 But if the Gentiles will repent and return unto me, saith the Father, behold they shall be numbered among my people, O house of Israel.

14 And I will not suffer my people, who are of the house of Israel, to go through among them, and tread them down, saith the Father.

15 But if they will not turn unto me, and hearken unto my voice, I will suffer them, yea, I will suffer my people, O house of Israel, that they shall go through among them, and shall tread them down, and they shall be as salt that hath lost its savor, which is thenceforth good for nothing but to be cast out, and to be trodden under foot of my people, O house of Israel.

16 Verily, verily, I say unto you, thus hath the Father commanded me—that I should give unto this people this land for their inheritance.

3 Nephi 20:Heading

Jesus provides bread and wine miraculously and again administers the sacrament unto them—The remnant of Jacob shall come to the knowledge of the Lord their God and shall inherit the Americas—Jesus is the prophet like unto Moses, and the Nephites are children of the prophets—Others of the Lord's people shall be gathered to Jerusalem.

3 Nephi 20:12-19

12 And verily, verily, I say unto you, that when they shall be fulfilled then is the fulfilling of the covenant which the Father hath made unto his people, O house of Israel.

13 And then shall the remnants, which shall be scattered abroad upon the face of the earth, be gathered in from the east and from the west, and from the south and from the north; and they shall be brought to the knowledge of the Lord their God, who hath redeemed them.

14 And the Father hath commanded me that I should give unto you this land, for your inheritance.

15 And I say unto you, that if the Gentiles do not repent after the blessing which they shall receive, after they have scattered my people—

16 Then shall ye, who are a remnant of the house of Jacob, go forth among them; and ye shall be in the midst of them who shall be many; and ye shall be among them as a lion among the beasts of the forest, and as a young lion among the flocks of sheep, who, if he goeth through both treadeth down and teareth in pieces, and none can deliver.

17 Thy hand shall be lifted up upon thine adversaries, and all thine enemies shall be cut off.

18 And I will gather my people together as a man gathereth his sheaves into the floor.

19 For I will make my people with whom the Father hath covenanted, yea, I will make thy horn iron, and I will make thy hoofs brass. And thou shalt beat in pieces many people; and I will consecrate their gain unto the Lord, and their substance unto the Lord of the whole earth. And behold, I am he

who doeth it.

3 Nephi 21:2

2 And behold, this is the thing which I will give unto you for a sign—for verily I say unto you that when these things which I declare unto you, and which I shall declare unto you hereafter of myself, and by the power of the Holy Ghost which shall be given unto you of the Father, shall be made known unto the Gentiles that they may know concerning this people who are a remnant of the house of Jacob, and concerning this my people who shall be scattered by them;

3 Nephi 21:12-13

12 And my people who are a remnant of Jacob shall be among the Gentiles, yea, in the midst of them as a lion among the beasts of the forest, as a young lion among the flocks of sheep, who, if he go through both treadeth down and teareth in pieces, and none can deliver.
13 Their hand shall be lifted up upon their adversaries, and all their enemies shall be cut off.

3 Nephi 21:22-28

22 But if they will repent and hearken unto my words, and harden not their hearts, I will establish my church among them, and they shall come in unto the covenant and be numbered among this the remnant of Jacob, unto whom I have given this land for their inheritance;
23 And they shall assist my people, the remnant of Jacob, and also as many of the house of Israel as shall come, that they may build a city, which shall be called the New Jerusalem.
24 And then shall they assist my people that they may be gathered in, who are scattered upon all the face of the land, in unto the New Jerusalem.
25 And then shall the power of heaven come down among them; and I also will be in the midst.
26 And then shall the work of the Father commence at that day, even when this gospel shall be preached among the remnant of this people. Verily I say unto you, at that day shall the work of the Father commence among all the dispersed of my people, yea, even the tribes which have been lost, which the Father hath led away out of Jerusalem.
27 Yea, the work shall commence among all the dispersed of my people, with the Father to prepare the way whereby they may come unto me, that they may call on the Father in my name.
28 Yea, and then shall the work commence, with the Father among all nations in preparing the way whereby his people may be gathered home to the land of their inheritance.

3 Nephi 22:3

3 For thou shalt break forth on the right hand and on the left, and thy seed shall inherit the Gentiles and make the desolate cities to be inhabited.

4 Nephi 1:49

49 And he did hide them up unto the Lord that they might come again unto the remnant of the house of Jacob according to the prophecies and the promises of the Lord. And thus is the end of the record of Ammaron.

Mormon 5:12-24

12 Now these things are written unto the remnant of the house of Jacob; and they are written after this manner, because it is known of God that wickedness will not bring them forth unto them; and they are to be hid up unto the Lord that they may come forth in his own due time.

13 And this is the commandment which I have received; and behold, they shall come forth according to the commandment of the Lord, when he shall see fit, in his wisdom.

14 And behold, they shall go unto the unbelieving of the Jews; and for this intent shall they go—that they may be persuaded that Jesus is the Christ, the Son of the living God; that the Father may bring about, through his most Beloved, his great and eternal purpose, in restoring the Jews, or all the house of Israel, to the land of their inheritance, which the Lord their God hath given them, unto the fulfilling of his covenant;

15 And also that the seed of this people may more fully believe his gospel, which shall go forth unto them from the Gentiles; for this people shall be scattered, and shall become a dark, a filthy, and a loathsome people, beyond the description of that which ever hath been amongst us, yea, even that which hath been among the Lamanites, and this because of their unbelief and idolatry.

16 For behold, the Spirit of the Lord hath already ceased to strive with their fathers; and they are without Christ and God in the world; and they are driven about as chaff before the wind.

17 They were once a delightsome people, and they had Christ for their shepherd; yea, they were led even by God the Father.

18 But now, behold, they are led about by Satan, even as chaff is driven before the wind, or as a vessel is tossed about upon the waves, without sail or anchor, or without anything wherewith to steer her; and even as she is, so are they.

19 And behold, the Lord hath reserved their blessings, which they might have received in the land, for the Gentiles who shall possess the land.

20 But behold, it shall come to pass that they shall be driven and scattered by the Gentiles; and after they have been driven and scattered by the Gentiles, behold, then will the Lord remember the covenant which he made unto Abraham and unto all the house of Israel.

21 And also the Lord will remember the prayers of the righteous, which have been put up unto him for them.

22 And then, O ye Gentiles, how can ye stand before the power of God, except ye shall repent and turn from your evil ways?

23 Know ye not that ye are in the hands of God? Know ye not that he hath all power, and at his great command the earth shall be rolled together as a scroll?

24 Therefore, repent ye, and humble yourselves before him, lest he shall come out in justice against you—lest a remnant of the seed of Jacob shall go forth among you as a lion, and tear you in pieces, and there is none to deliver.

Mormon 7:10

10 And ye will also know that ye are a remnant of the seed of Jacob; therefore ye are numbered among the people of the first covenant; and if it so be that ye believe in Christ, and are baptized, first with water, then with fire and with the Holy Ghost, following the example of our Savior,

according to that which he hath commanded us, it shall be well with you in the day of judgment.

D&C 3:19-20

19 And for this very purpose are these plates preserved, which contain these records—that the promises of the Lord might be fulfilled, which he made to his people;

20 And that the Lamanites might come to the knowledge of their fathers, and that they might know the promises of the Lord, and that they may believe the gospel and rely upon the merits of Jesus Christ, and be glorified through faith in his name, and that through their repentance they might be saved. Amen.

D&C 49:23-25

23 Wherefore, be not deceived, but continue in steadfastness, looking forth for the heavens to be shaken, and the earth to tremble and to reel to and fro as a drunken man, and for the valleys to be exalted, and for the mountains to be made low, and for the rough places to become smooth—and all this when the angel shall sound his trumpet.

24 But before the great day of the Lord shall come, Jacob shall flourish in the wilderness, and the Lamanites shall blossom as the rose.

25 Zion shall flourish upon the hills and rejoice upon the mountains, and shall be assembled together unto the place which I have appointed.

D&C 52:2

2 Saying: I, the Lord, will make known unto you what I will that ye shall do from this time until the next conference, which shall be held in Missouri, upon the land which I will consecrate unto my people, which are a remnant of Jacob, and those who are heirs according to the covenant.

D&C 87:5

5 And it shall come to pass also that the remnants who are left of the land will marshal themselves, and shall become exceedingly angry, and shall vex the Gentiles with a sore vexation.

CHAPTER FOUR

PROPHECIES OF THE UNITED STATES

"But if we and our posterity reject religious instruction and authority, violate the rules of eternal justice, trifle with the injunctions of morality, and recklessly destroy the political constitution which holds us together, no man can tell how sudden the catastrophe may overwhelm us, that shall bury all our glory in profound obscurity."
(Delbert L. Stapley, Conference Report, October 1963, p. 112-113.)

Teachings of the Prophet Joseph Smith, Section One, 1830-34, p. 17.

"And now I am prepared to say by the authority of Jesus Christ, that not many years shall pass away before the United States shall present such a scene of bloodshed as has not a parallel in the history of our nation; pestilence, hail, famine, and earthquake will sweep the wicked of this generation from off the face of the land, to open and prepare the way for the return of the lost tribes of Israel from the north country. The people of the Lord, those who have complied with the requirements of the new covenant, have already commenced gathering together to Zion, which is in the state of Missouri; therefore I declare unto you the warning which the Lord has commanded me to declare unto this generation, remembering that the eyes of my Maker are upon me, and that to Him I am accountable for every word I say, wishing nothing worse to my fellowmen than their eternal salvation; therefore, 'Fear God, and give glory to Him, for the hour of His judgment is come.' Repent ye, repent ye, and embrace the everlasting covenant, and flee to Zion, before the overflowing scourge overtake you, for there are those now living upon the earth whose eyes shall not be closed in death until they see all these things, which I have spoken, fulfilled. Remember these things; call upon the Lord while He is near, and seek Him while He may be found, is the exhortation of your unworthy servant."

Teachings of the Prophet Joseph Smith, Section Six, 1843–44, p. 302.

"I prophesy in the name of the Lord God of Israel, unless the United States redress the wrongs committed upon the Saints in the state of Missouri and punish the crimes committed by her officers that in a few years the government will be utterly overthrown and wasted, and there will not be so much as a potsherd left, for their wickedness in permitting the murder of men, women and children, and the wholesale plunder and extermination of thousands of her citizens to go unpunished, thereby perpetrating a foul and corroding blot upon the fair fame of this great republic, the very thought of which would have caused the high-minded and patriotic framers of the Constitution of the United States to hide their faces with shame."

Brigham Young, Journal of Discourses, Vol. 7, p. 10-11, July 4, 1854.

"When the Supreme Ruler of the universe wishes to destroy a nation, he takes away their wisdom in the first place, and they become insensible to their own interests, and they are filled with wrath; they give way to their anger, and thus lay the foundation of their own destruction. To him who seeks to save, he gives wisdom, which enables any people, nation, or individual to lay the foundation for strength, increase, and power. When we look abroad upon the nations, we can see this truth verified; and when we look at home in our own nation, it is no less verified. We see that wisdom is actually departing from the lawgiver, and the knowledge and the discretion the judge possessed years ago have vanished. We discern that the very policy adopted by the nations to fortify them in strength is calculated to sap their foundations. The axe is laid at the root of the tree, and all nations are filling up the cup of their guilt."

Brigham Young, Journal of Discourses, Vol. 9, p. 5, April 6, 1861.

"I heard Joseph Smith say, nearly thirty years ago, 'They shall have mobbing to their heart's content, if they do not redress the wrongs of the Latter-day Saints.' Mobs will not decrease, but will increase until the whole Government becomes a mob, and eventually it will be State against State, city against city, neighbourhood against neighbourhood, Methodists against Methodists, and so on. Probably you remember reading, not a week ago, an account of a Conference being held in Baltimore, in the course of which they seceded from their fellow churches in the free States. It will be the same with other denominations of professing Christians, and it will be Christian against Christian, and man against man; and those who will not take up the sword against their neighbours must flee to Zion."

Brigham Young, Journal of Discourses, Vol. 10, p. 295, May 15, 1864.

"Joseph said, many and many a time, to us,—'Never be anxious for the Lord to pour out his judgments upon the nation; many of you will see the distress and evils poured out upon this nation till you will weep like children.' Many of us have felt to do so already, and it seems to be coming upon us more and more; it seems as though the fangs of destruction were piercing the very vitals of the nation."

Brigham Young, Journal of Discourses, Vol. 19, p. 96, August 19, 1877.

"Will famine come? Yes! Will plagues come? Yes! Will distress come upon the nations? Yes, and upon this nation, and that, too, before a great while. When they made war upon us some eighteen years ago, how it pleased and tickled the masses who thought that now destruction was to overtake the Latter-day Saints. I told many, and sent word to Congress saying, that it would prove the opening wedge for the struggle of war between the North and South. But some gentlemen took the liberty of saying, time after time, 'No, no, that cannot be.' Said I, 'It will be so, and I tell it to you in the name of Israel's God.' And when the press delight in publishing such falsehoods about the Latter-day Saints as they have done, and the people delight to read them, you will see real trouble crop out in and among themselves. Is there power enough in the Federal Government to put down mobocracy. No! And it is a truth that they whom the Lord makes weak are weak indeed; and those whom the Lord makes strong are strong indeed. Strength was given to the North in the last struggle, and the South suffered extremely. But the time will come when the North will be weaker than the

South was, and they will have no power to muster their forces against the tide of folly that will come upon them, that they bring upon themselves, and they themselves must receive the results."

Heber C. Kimball, Deseret News, May 23, 1931.

"The western boundaries of the state of Missouri will be swept so clean of its inhabitants that as President Young tells us, 'When you return to that place there will not be so much as a yellow dog to wag his tail.' Before that day comes, however, the Saints will be put to tests that will try the integrity of the best of them. The pressure will be so great that the more righteous among them will cry unto the Lord day and night until deliverance comes. Then the Prophet Joseph and others will make their appearance and those who have remained faithful will be selected to return to Jackson County, Missouri and take part in the upbuilding of that beautiful city, the New Jerusalem."

Heber C. Kimball, Journal of Discourses, Vol. 5, p. 275, September 27, 1857.

"When the United States have done their best, then other nations will tackle us, and so things will go on, until every nation is brought into subjection to the kingdom of God. Go and read it in the Bible. I could not say anything else, if I should try."

Heber C. Kimball, Journal of Discourses, Vol. 6, p. 185, December 27, 1857.

"So it will be eventually in the United States. After the truth is all gathered out, you will find that the rest will be destroyed. I do not mean that the land will be destroyed, but I refer to the wicked inhabitants, and the earth will be emptied, according to the words of the Prophet. Why will this be so? Because there are no saving principles there: the saving principles are with this Church, and there is no salvation in the absence of those principles."

Heber C. Kimball, Journal of Discourses, Vol. 9, p. 54-55, April 14, 1861.

"The Almighty through his Prophets foretold that the nation would make war upon this people, and that he would come out of his hiding place, and pour out his judgments upon those that rebel against him, and who persecuted his people, and set themselves against his house. Then it shall go forth like a mighty whirlwind upon the face of the whole earth. In this country the North and the South will exert themselves against each other, and ere long the whole face of the United States will be in commotion, fighting one against another, and they will destroy their nationality. They have never done anything for this people, and I don't believe they ever will. I have never prayed for the destruction of this Government, but I know that dissolution, sorrow, weeping, and distress are in store for the inhabitants of the United States, because of their conduct towards the people of God. Then the judgments will go forth to the nations of the earth."

Orson Hyde , Journal of Discourses, Vol. 7, p. 50.

"Here is a glass that reflects the position and fate of the United States, if they persist in following the Saints with their forces. If the serpent will cast out a flood of waters after the woman who has fled into the wilderness from before his face, the earth may kindly open her mouth in the form of an earthquake, and drink up the flood or army. This would be a mode of warfare upon which their tactics furnish them no information."

Orson Hyde, Journal of Discourses, Vol. 7, p. 110, July 4, 1853.

"If the United States have been guilty of a great dereliction of duty in not making an effort to redress the sufferings and wrongs of the 'Mormons,' and the 'Mormons' have said that this inaction and indifference on the part of the Government in relation to their grievances will draw upon the nation a scourge and chastisement from God, we have no more idea that the great purposes and designs of the Creator will be changed in relation to this nation, in consequence of this merited chastisement, than the purposes and designs of a father to rear up his son in honour, integrity, and truth will become changed by the infliction of chastisement for some transgression or misdemeanour."

Heber C. Kimball, Journal of Discourses, Vol. 9, p. 182, July 7, 1861.

"Our enemies know not what they are doing when they persecute and mob this people. It is true they are doing no more than was done by the wicked Lamanites who once lived upon this continent, and who were a flourishing and prosperous people. They persecuted the people composing the Church of Christ, the Nephites departed from the faith, and the two parties wasted each other away until only a remnant was left, and as such we now see them wandering about in filth, darkness, and the very lowest state of degradation. The Jaredites, who preceded the Israelites upon this continent, did the same things. They fought and contended with each other until the whole people were destroyed, and we are going to live to see similar things befall this nation. Although many may fall away from the truth, and others may embrace it, yet the destruction of this nation is sealed, except they repent, which is not very probable."

Orson Hyde, Journal of Discourses, Vol. 10, p. 375-376, December 18, 1864.

"This country discovered by him (Columbus), is enveloped in war; and if you live a few years longer you will see much of the land that has been blessed with unequalled prosperity from the east to the west, a wilderness and a desolation; and this will be in consequence of the abuse of the blessings bestowed upon it by those who enjoyed them. . . .If the land does not become a wilderness and a desolation, we do not see correctly—we do not understand correctly the revelations which the Almighty has given us. The scripture says, that in the last days His people will go forth and build up the waste places of Zion. But they must first be made desolate, before they can be called 'the waste places of Zion.' Then the hands of the Saints will be required to build them up."

Orson Pratt, Millennial Star, Vol. 28, p. 633-634, October 6, 1866.

"But that great—that powerful nation is destined to an utter overthrow. If it be asked, why is America thus to suffer? The answer is, because they have rejected the kingdom of God, and one of the greatest divine messages ever sent to man; because they have sanctioned the killing of the Saints, and the martyrdom of the Lord's prophets, and have suffered his people to be driven from their midst, and have robbed them of their houses, and homes, and land, and millions of property, and have refused to redress their wrongs. For these great evils, they must suffer, the decrees of Jehovah have gone forth against them; the sword of the Lord has been unsheathed, and will fall with pain upon their devoted heads. Their great and magnificent cities are to be cut off. New York, Boston, Albany, and numerous other cities will be left desolate. Party will be arrayed in deadly strife against party;

State against State; and the whole nation will be broken up; the sanguinary weapons of the dreadful revolution will devour the land. Then shall there be a fleeing from one city to another, from one State to another, from one part of the continent to another, seeking refuge from the devastations of bandits and armies; then shall their dead be left unburied, and the fowls of heaven shall summer upon them, and the beasts of the earth shall winter upon them. Moreover, the Lord will visit them with the deadly pestilence which shall sweep away many millions by its ravages; for their eyes shall fall from their sockets, an their flesh from their bones, and their tongues shall be stayed in their mouths, that they shall not be able to blaspheme against their Maker. And it will come to pass, that the heavens will withhold their rains, and their fruitful fields be turned into barrenness, and the waters of their rivers will be dried up, and left in standing pools, and the fish therein will die; and the Lord will send forth a grievous plague to destroy the horses and cattle from the land. Thus by sword, and by pestilence, and by famine, and by the strong arm of the Almighty, shall the inhabitants of that wicked nation be destroyed."

Orson Pratt, Journal of Discourses, Vol. 12, p. 344, December 27, 1868.

"This great war is only a small degree of chastisement, just the beginning; nothing compared to that which God has spoken concerning this nation, if they will not repent. For the Lord has said in this book, (the Book of Mormon) which has been published for thirty eight years, that if they will not repent He will throw down all their strongholds and cut off the cities of the land, and will execute vengeance and fury on the nation, even as upon the heathen, such as they have not heard. That He will send a desolating scourge on the land; that He will leave their cities desolate, without inhabitants. For instance the great, powerful and populous city of New York, that may be considered one of the greatest cities of the world, will in a few years become a mass of ruins. The people will wonder while gazing on the ruins that cost hundreds of millions to build, what has become of inhabitants. Their houses will be there, but they will be left desolate.

So saith the Lord God. That will be only a sample of numerous other towns and cities on the face of this continent.

Now I am aware that it is almost impossible for even some of the Latter-day Saints to get that confidence and that strong faith in the events which God intends to accomplish on this land in the future to believe in such a thing, to say nothing about outsiders, that do not believe a word of it. Outsiders do not believe it any more than they believed me when I was a boy and took that revelation which was given in 1832, and carried it forth among many towns and cities and told them there was to be a great and terrible war between the North and the South, and read to them the revelation. Did they believe it? Would they consider that there was any truth in it? Not in the least, 'that is a Mormon humbug' they would say. 'What! this great and powerful nation of ours to be divided one part against the other and many hundreds of thousands of souls to be destroyed by civil wars!' Not a word of it would they believe. They do not believe what is still in the future. But there are some in this congregation who will live, to behold the fulfillment of these other things, and will visit the ruins of mighty towns and cities scattered over the face of this land destitute and desolate of inhabitants. If inquiry shall then be made, why such great destruction? the answer will be, wickedness has destroyed them. Wickedness and corruption have brought about the fulfillment of the ancient decrees of Heaven concerning this land. Wickedness and corruption have brought desolation into their towns and cities. The time will come when there will be no safety in carrying on the peaceable pursuits of farming or agriculture. But these will be neglected, and the people will think themselves well off if they can flee from city to city, from town to town and escape with their lives. Thus will the Lord visit the people, if they will not repent. Thus will He pour out His wrath and indignation upon them and make manifest to the people that that which he has spoken must be fulfilled.

But what shall become of this people? Shall we be swept off in the general ruin? Shall desolation come upon us? Shall we feel the chastening hand of the Almighty like those who will not repent? That will depend altogether upon our conduct. We have it within our power; God has granted it to us, to save ourselves from the desolation and calamities that will come upon the nation. How? By doing that which is right; by living honest before God and all men; by seeking after that righteousness that comes through the Gospel of the Son of God; by following after the law of Heaven; by doing unto others as we would have others do unto us; by putting away all the evils and abominations that are practiced by the wicked. If we do this prosperity will be upon the inhabitants of Utah; prosperity will be upon the towns and cities erected by this people, the hand of the Lord will be over us to sustain us, and we will spread forth. He will multiply us in the land; He will make us a great people, and strengthen our borders, and send forth the missionaries of this people to the four quarters of the earth to publish peace and glad tidings of great joy, and proclaim that there is still a place left in the heart of the American continent where there are peace and safety and refuge from the storms, desolations and tribulations coming upon the wicked. But on the other hand, Latter-day Saints, how great are the responsibilities resting upon us and upon our rising generations. If we will not keep the commandments of God, and if our rising generations will not give heed to the law of God and to the great light which has shone from Heaven in these latter days, but turn their hearts from the Lord their God and from the counsels of His priesthood, then we shall be visited like the wicked, then we shall have the hand of the Lord upon us in judgment; then that saying that the Lord has delivered in the Book of Doctrines and Covenants will be fulfilled upon us, 'that I will visit Zion, if she does not do right, with sore afflictions, with pestilence, with sword, with famine and with the flame of devouring fire.' Now here we have the choice."

Orson Pratt, Journal of Discourses, Vol. 15, p. 48-49, April 7, 1872.

"In the eighteenth chapter of the prophecies of Isaiah we have a prediction about a time when the Lord should make a great destruction upon a certain portion of the earth. The Prophet begins the chapter by saying, 'woe to the land shadowing with wings, which is beyond the rivers of Ethiopia. Recollect where the Prophet dwelt when he uttered this prophecy—in Palestine, east of the Mediterranean Sea. Where was Ethiopia? South-west from Palestine. Where was there a land located beyond the rivers of Ethiopia. Every person acquainted with the geography of our globe knows that this American continent was beyond the rivers of Ethiopia from the land of Palestine, where the prophecy was uttered. A woe was pronounced upon that land, and that woe is this: 'For afore the harvest, when the bud is perfect and the sour grape is ripening in the flower, he shall both cut off the sprigs with pruning-hooks, and take away and cut down the branches. They shall be left together unto the fowls of the mountains, and to the beasts of the earth. And the fowls shall summer upon them, and all the beasts of the earth shall winter upon them.' But first, before this destruction, there is a remarkable prophecy. Says the Prophet: 'All ye inhabitants of the world, and dwellers on the earth, see ye when he lifteth up an ensign on the mountains, and when he bloweth a trumpet, hear ye.' From this we learn that, before this great destruction, there is to be an ensign lifted up on the mountains, and this, too, beyond the rivers of Ethiopia, from Palestine. This is the reason why Zion in the latter days goes up into the mountains, in order that an ensign might be lifted up on the mountains. This prophecy was uttered some twenty-five hundred years ago, and has been fulfilled before the eyes of the people in our day."

Orson Pratt, Journal of Discourses, Vol. 15, p. 72-73, February 4, 1872.

"This prophecy of Daniel will give a true understanding of the matter to our wise men and statesmen, and all who desire to know the future destiny of the American government, the European governments, and all the kingdoms of the earth. Their destiny is total destruction from our earth, no matter how great or powerful they may become. Though our nation may grasp on the right hand and on the left; though it may annex the British possessions, and extend its dominions to the south and grasp the whole of this great western hemisphere, and although our nation shall become as powerful in population as in extent of territory, its destiny is foretold in the saying of the Prophet Daniel, 'They shall become like the chaff of the summer threshing floor, the wind shall carry them away and no place shall be found for them.' So with the kingdoms of Europe, so with the kingdoms of Western Asia and Eastern Europe."

Orson Pratt, Journal of Discourses, Vol. 17, p. 320-321, February 28, 1875.

"The harvest is said to be the end of the wicked world; and if it is so, 'afore the harvest,' that is, before the final end comes he will visit the inhabitants of the land shadowing with wings, beyond the rivers of Ethiopia with judgments that are terribly severe, that will cause them to lie by hundreds and thousands unburied, from one end of the land to the other, to be meat for the fowls of the air and the beasts of the earth. Why? Because the judgments will be swift, giving no time for burial."

Orson Pratt, Journal of Discourses, Vol. 18, p. 181-182, March 26, 1876.

"Read the 18th chapter of Isaiah. Isaiah, when standing in Palestine delivering his prophecy, looked off to the south-west and saw the rivers of Ethiopia, or Africa; and after having seen these rivers in vision he also sees a land shadowing with wings away beyond the rivers of Ethiopia. What kind of a land was that, away beyond the rivers of Ethiopia, from where Isaiah stood in Palestine? Why it is a land that had the appearance of wings. You have been struck doubtless, with the great resemblance that North and South America have to the two great wings of a bird. While Isaiah was thus gazing upon a land away beyond the rivers of Ethiopia, it looked so much like the wings of a bird that he says—A land shadowing with wings, away, beyond the rivers of Ethiopia.' Well, Isaiah, what have you to say about that land? Why, says he, there is a proclamation to be had there. How extensive, Isaiah? To all people. Hear the words of Isaiah. Says he 'All ye inhabitants of the world and dwellers on the earth, see ye when he lifts up an ensign on the mountains.' Not on the low places of that land shadowing with wings, next to the seashore, but in the mountains. What is the nature of this ensign? It is characteristic of a standard, often spoken of by the Prophets, and called by the name of standard. Isaiah speak of it as an ensign in a number of places. What would naturally be a

139

standard? The kingdom of God is a standard to which the people rally and gather together. Does it affect all people, Isaiah? Yes. 'All ye inhabitants of the world.' What could be more extensive than that? 'And dwellers on the earth, see ye when he lifts up an ensign on the mountains, and when he bloweth a trumpet hear ye.' What else is to take place, Isaiah? He says that a severe judgment is to take place on that land shadowing with wings. What kind of a judgment, one that is to be very severe, Isaiah? Yes, for he says—'Afore the harvest, when the bud is perfect, and the sour grape is ripening in the flower, he shall both cut off the sprigs with pruning hooks, and take away and cut down the branches. They shall be left together unto the fowls of the mountains and to the beasts of the earth; and the fowls shall summer upon them, and all the beasts of the earth shall winter upon them.' When will this be, Isaiah? After this proclamation, after all the nations of the world have heard it, after the people have heard the sound of the warning message; then the first among all the nations where the extremities of the image have sent forth one of its governments, there will be the commencement of a most terrible judgment, so much so that the people on that land will not have time to bury their dead, and the fowls shall summer upon them. Why is all this? Because they will not hearken when that sound goes to all people; they will not repent of their sins; they will not receive the message that God has sent by his angel, he therefore visits them first, because they are the first to hear those glad tidings. No wonder, then, that Zion, that brings good tidings, was commanded by the ancient Prophet to get up into the high mountain."

Orson Pratt, Journal of Discourses, Vol. 18, p. 338, February 25, 1877.
"For instance, this great republic must pass away in the manner indicated unless the people repent. There is only one condition by which they can be preserved as a nation, and the Lord himself has decreed it. We can read it in the various revelations which God has given, respecting this land. The Book of Mormon, for instance, speaks in many places, of the overthrow of the government that should exist on this land if they should reject the divine message contained therein. Inasmuch as they repent not, the Lord has said that he would visit them in his anger, and that he would throw down all their strongholds. And he further says, that he will cut off their horses out of their midst. This will doubtless be done through some great calamity or disease. He also says the he will cut off the cities of our land, that all manner of lying, deceits, hypocrisy, murders, priestcrafts, whoredoms and secret abominations shall be done away, having reference particularly to this nation. He says, too, 'I will execute vengeance and fury upon them, even as upon the heathen, such as they have not heard.' We are told, too, that the nature of these judgments is to be swift and terrible, coming upon them like a fierce wind, when they expect it not; when they are crying peace and safety, behold sudden destruction is at their doors."

Orson Pratt, Journal of Discourses, Vol. 18, p. 340, February 25, 1877.
"For instance, this great republic must pass away in the manner indicated unless the people repent. There is only one condition by which they can be preserved as a nation, and the Lord himself has decreed it. We can read it in the various revelations which God has given, respecting this land. The Book of Mormon, for instance, speaks in many places, of the overthrow of the government that should exist on this land if they should reject the divine message contained therein. Inasmuch as they repent not, the Lord has said that he would visit them in his anger, and that he would throw down all

their strongholds. And he further says, that he will cut off their horses out of their midst. This will doubtless be done through some great calamity or disease. He also says the he will cut off the cities of our land, that all manner of lying, deceits, hypocrisy, murders, priestcrafts, whoredoms and secret abominations shall be done away, having reference particularly to this nation. He says, too, 'I will execute vengeance and fury upon them, even as upon the heathen, such as they have not heard.' We are told, too, that the nature of these judgments is to be swift and terrible, coming upon them like a fierce wind, when they expect it not; when they are crying peace and safety, behold sudden destruction is at their doors."

Orson Pratt, Journal of Discourses, Vol. 18, p. 340-341, February 25, 1877.

"It has been revealed that the time will come in the history of our nations, that one State will rise against another, one city against another, even every man's hand shall be against his neighbor, until the whole Republic will be in general commotion and warfare. How and when this will take place, the Lord, in his wisdom, has not told us; but it is sufficient for us to say, that he has told us of the facts that such and such will be the case.

For aught we know, the fulfillment of this prophecy may grow out of politics. If the people are very nearly equally divided in politics, this feeling may run so high, in years to come, as to be the direct cause of war. And if this should be the case, it would very naturally spread to every neighborhood in the Union. One class of political opponents would rise up against the other class in the same city and country, and thus would arise a war of mobocracy.

If a war of this description should take place, who would carry on his business in safety? Who would feel safe to put his crops in the ground or to carry on any enterprise? There would be fleeing from one State to another, and general confusion would exist throughout the whole Republic. Such eventually is to be the condition of this whole nation, if the people do not repent of their wickedness; and such a state of affairs means no more or less than the complete overthrow of the nation, and not only of this nation, but the nations of Europe, which form the feet and toes of that great image. They are the powers to be first broken; it is not the nation representing the head of gold, the remnant of the Babylonish Empire that still exists in Asia, that will be attacked first, neither is it the Persians and Medes, whose descendants still live; but the Lord will first break up those kingdoms which represent the feet and toes of the image of which I have been speaking. After that, he will proceed to break in pieces the kingdoms that represent the brass, the silver, and the gold. Some are to be spared for a little season."

Orson Pratt, Journal of Discourses, Vol. 20, p. 150-151, March 9, 1879.

"But what about the American nation. That war that destroyed the lives of some fifteen or sixteen hundred thousand people was nothing, compared to that which will eventually devastate that country. The time is not very far distant in the future, when the Lord God will lay his hand heavily upon that nations. 'How do you know this? inquires one.' I know from the revelations which God has given upon this subject. I read these revelations, when they were first given. I waited over twenty-eight years and saw their fulfillment to the very letter. Should I not, then, expect that the balance of them should be fulfilled? That same God who gave the revelations to his servant Joseph Smith in regard to these matters, will fulfil every jot and every tittle that has been spoken, concerning that nation. What then will be the condition of that people, when this great and terrible war shall come? It will be very different from the war between the North and the South. Do you wish me to describe it? I will do so. It will be a war of neighborhood against neighborhood, city against city, town against town, county against county, state against state, and they will go forth destroying and being destroyed and manufacturing will, in a great measure, cease, for a time, among the American nation. Why? Because in these terrible wars, they will not be privileged to manufacture, there will be too much bloodshed—too much mobocracy—too much going forth in bands and destroying and pillaging the land to suffer people to pursue any local vocation with any degree of safety. What will become of millions of the farmers upon that land? They will leave their farms and they will remain uncultivated, and they will flee before the ravaging armies from place to place; and thus will they go forth burning and pillaging the whole country; and that great and powerful nation, now consisting of some forty millions of people, will be wasted away, unless they repent.

Now these are predictions you may record. You may let them sink down into your hearts. And if the Lord your God shall permit you to live, you will see my words fulfilled to the very letter. They are not my words, but the words of inspiration—the words of the everlasting God who has sent forth his servants with this message to warn the nations of the earth. The Book of Mormon contains many of these predictions."

Orson Pratt, Journal of Discourses, Vol. 20, p. 152, March 9, 1879.
"And the Lord also made a similar decree, recorded, too, in the same book, in regard to the present great populous nations called the people of the United States. They must perish, unless they repent. They will be wasted away, and the fullness of the wrath of Almighty God will be poured out upon them, unless they repent. Their cities will be left desolate. A time is coming when the great and populous city of New York—the greatest city of the American Republic, will be left without inhabitants. The houses will stand, some of them, not all. They will stand there, but unoccupied, no people to inherit them. It will be the same in regard to numerous other cities, or, in the words of the Lord, 'I will throw down all their strongholds, and I will execute vengeance and fury upon them, even as upon the heathen, such as they have not heard.' It will all be fulfilled. But there will be a remnant who will be spared. It will be those who repent of their sins; it will be those who believe in the Lord Jesus Christ, and are willing to obey his commandments, willing to hearken to his voice, willing to be baptized for the remission of their sins, willing to be born of the spirit, or receive the Holy Ghost, by the laying on of hands, willing to walk uprightly and honestly with all men, and justly one with another."

Orson Pratt, Journal of Discourses, Vol. 24, p. 31-32, October 26, 1879.
"Now, there are a great many cities in the United States that will not be totally destroyed when the inhabitants are swept off the surface of the earth. Their houses, their desolate cities will still remain unoccupied until Zion in her glory and strength shall enlarge the place of her tents, and stretch forth the curtains of her habitations. That is the destiny of this nation, and the destiny of the Latter-day Saints."

John Taylor, Journal of Discourses, Vol. 9, p. 234, April 28, 1861.

"The people of this nation are evidently bent upon their own destruction, and they are full of enmity, hatred, war, and bloodshed. To all human appearance, it would seem that they will not stop short of the entire destruction of this great nation. In the language of one of old who uttered this singular prophetic declaration I will say, 'They are drunken, but not with wine; they stagger, but not with strong drink.' They have neglected righteousness, justice, and truth for years that are past and gone; they have allowed the honest, the virtuous, the just, and the true-hearted to be abused and afflicted, and they have winked and mocked at their sufferings; and not only so, but they have unblushingly used their force and strength to bring about the destruction of God's people. They have, however, failed in all their attempts to crush out the kingdom of God, because the Almighty has protected his people; but they will not fail when they make their attacks upon one another. When the potsherds of the earth strive with the potsherds of the earth, and God does not interfere, they will be more likely to accomplish the destruction of each other. They have been using their energies against the Saints of the Most High; they have cast us out, sought to destroy and root us out from the earth; but there was a God who was watching over the interests of his people. There was a Being that their philosophy and theology knew nothing about, a Being whose eyes were open to see, and whose ears listened to the cries of his people. When the full time for deliverance arrives, he stretches forth his hand and we are preserved, and we come out from the difficulties and trials unscathed. This we have done, supported by the hand of Jehovah; and this will be done again should we be placed in circumstances to require it."

John Taylor, Journal of Discourses, Vol. 20, p. 318-319, October 6, 1879.

"But I tell you today the end is not yet. You will see worse things than that, for God will lay his hand upon this nation, and they will feel it more terribly than ever they have done before; there will be more bloodshed, more ruin, more devastation than never they have seen before. Write it down! You will see it come to pass; it is only just starting in. And would you feel to rejoice? No; I would feel sorry. I knew very well myself when this last war was commencing, and could have wept and did weep, over this nation; but there is yet to come a sound of war, trouble and distress, in which brother will be arrayed against brother, father against son, son against father, a scene of desolation and destruction that will permeate our land until it will be a vexation to hear the report thereof. Would you help to bring it about? No, I would not; I would stop it if I could."

Wilford Woodruff, Deseret News, Vol. 33, p. 678, November 12, 1884.

"You are to become men and women, fathers and mothers; yea, the day will come, after your fathers, and these prophets and apostles are dead, you will have the privilege of going into the towers of a glorious Temple built unto the name of the Most High east of us upon the Logan bench; and while you stand in the towers of the Temple and your eyes survey this glorious valley filled with cities and villages, occupied by tens of thousands of Latter-day Saints, you will then call to mind this visitation of President Young and his company. You will say: 'That was in the days when Presidents Benson and Maughan presided over us; that was before New York was destroyed by an earthquake; it was before Boston was swept into the sea, by the sea heaving itself beyond its bounds; it was before Albany was destroyed by fire; yea, at that time you will remember the scenes of this day. Treasure them up and forget them not.'

President Young followed and said: 'What Brother Woodruff has said is revelation and will be fulfilled.'"

Wilford Woodruff's Journal, Vol. 7, p. 419-423, Salt Lake City, UT, night of December 16, 1877.

"I went to bed at my usual hour, half past nine o'clock. I had been reading the Revelations in the French language. My mind was calm, more so than usual if possible to be so. I composed myself for sleep, but could not sleep. I felt a strange stupor come over me and apparently become partially unconscious. Still I was not asleep nor awake, but had a strange far-away dreaming feeling.

The first thing I recognized was that I was in the Tabernacle at Ogden, Utah, sitting on the back seat in the corner for fear they would call on me to preach, which after singing the second time, they did by calling me to the stand.

I arose to speak and said I did not know that I had anything special to say except to bear my testimony of the truth of the latter-day work, when all at once it seemed as though I was lifted out of myself. I said, `Yes, I have something to say, it is this—Some of my brethren present have been asking me what is coming to pass, what the wind is blowing up. I will answer you right here what is coming to pass shortly.

I was immediately in Salt Lake City wandering about the streets. In all parts of the city and on the door of every house, I found a badge of mourning, and I could not find a house but what was in mourning. I passed by my own house and saw the same sign there, and asked, `Is that me that is dead?' Something gave me (the) answer, `No, you'll live through it all.'

It seemed strange to me that I saw no person on the street in my wandering about through the city. They seemed to be in their houses with their sick and dead. I saw no funeral procession, or anything of that kind, but the city looked very still and quiet as though the people were praying and had control of the disease, whatever it was.

I then looked in all directions over the territory,—east, west, north and south, and found the same mourning in every place throughout the land. The next I knew I was just this side of Omaha. It seemed as though I was above the earth, looking down to it as I passed along on my way east. I saw the roads full of people, principally women, with just what they could carry in bundles on their backs, traveling to the mountains on foot. And I wondered how they could get there with nothing but a small pack upon their backs. It was remarkable to me that there were so few men among them. It did not seem as though the trains were running. The rails looked rusty, and the road abandoned. And I have no conception how I traveled myself.

As I looked down upon the people, I continued eastward through Omaha and Council Bluffs, which were full of disease, and women everywhere. The states of Missouri and Illinois were in turmoil and strife, men killing each another, and women joining in the fight, family against family cutting each other to pieces in the most horrid manner.

The next I saw was Washington, D.C., and found the city a desolation. The White House empty, the Halls of Congress the same, everything in ruins. The people seemed to have fled from the city and left it to take care of itself.

I was next in the city of Baltimore, and in the square where the Monument of 1812 stands, in front of St. Charles and other hotels I saw the dead piled up so high as to fill the square. I saw mothers cut the throats of their own children for the sake of their blood, which they drank from their veins, to quench their thirst, and then lie down and die. The waters of the Chesapeake Bay and of the

144

city were so stagnant, and such a stench arose from them on account of the putrefaction of the dead bodies that the very smell caused death. Singularly again, I saw no men except they were dead, lying in the streets, and very few women, and they were crazy mad, and in a dying condition. Everywhere I went I beheld the same all over the city. It was horrible beyond description to look at.

I thought this must be the end. But no, I was seemingly in Philadelphia and there everything was still. No living soul was to be seen to greet me. It seemed as though the whole city was without an inhabitant. In Arch and Chestnut streets, in fact, everywhere I went the putrefaction of the dead bodies created such a stench that it was impossible for any creature to exist alive, nor did I see any living thing in the city.

I next found myself on Broadway in New York. Here it seemed the people had done their best to overcome the disease. But in wandering down Broadway, I saw the bodies of beautiful women lying stone dead, and others in a dying condition on the sidewalk. I saw men crawl out of the cellers (basements) and rob the dead bodies of the valuables they had on, and before they could return to their coverts in the cellers they themselves would roll over a time or two and die in agony. On some of the back streets I saw mothers kill their own children and eat raw flesh, and then in a few minutes die themselves. Wherever I went, I saw the same scenes of horror and desolation, rapine and death. No busses or streetcars, nothing but death and destruction everywhere.

I then went to Central Park and looking back, I saw a fire start and just at that moment a mighty east wind sprang up and carried the flames west over the city. And it burned until there was not a single building left standing whole, even down to the wharfs. The shipping all seemed to be burned and swallowed up in common destruction, and left nothing but a desolation where the great city was a short time before. The stench from the bodies that were burning was so great that it was carried a great distance across the Hudson River and bay, and thus spread disease and death wherever the flames penetrated.   I cannot paint in words the horror that seemed to encompass me around. It was beyond description or thought of man to conceive.

I supposed this was the end, but I was given to understand to understand that the same horror was being enacted were all over the country, north, south, east, and west, that few were left alive. Still there were some.

Immediately after I seemed to be standing on the west bank of the Missouri River, opposite the city of Independence, but I saw no city. I saw the whole states of Illinois and Missouri and part of Iowa were a complete wilderness with no living human being in them. I then saw a short distance from the river twelve men dressed in the robes of the Temple, standing in a square, or nearly so. I understood it represented the twelve gates of the New Jerusalem. And they were with hands uplifted consecrating the ground and laying the cornerstones. I saw myriads of angels hovering over them and around them, and also an immense pillar of a cloud over them. And I heard the singing of the most beautiful music. The words: `Now is established the Kingdom of our God and His Christ, and He shall reign forever and ever! And the Kingdom shall never be thrown down, for the Saints have overcome!' I saw people coming from the river and different places a long way off to help build the Temple. It seemed that the hosts of the angels also helped to get the material to build the Temple. And I saw some come who wore their Temple robes to help build the Temple and the city. And all the time I saw the great pillar of cloud hovering over the place.

Instantly I found I was in the Ogden Tabernacle, yet I could see the building going on and got quite animated in calling to the people in the Tabernacle to listen to the beautiful music that the angels were making. I called to them to look at the Angels, as the house seemed to be full of them, and they were singing the same words that I heard before: `Now is the Kingdom of our God established forever and ever!' And then a voice said 'Now shall come to pass that which was spoken by Isaiah the prophet `that seven women shall take hold of one man saying, etc.''

. . .I rolled over in my bed and heard the clock strike twelve." [1]

Wilford Woodruff, Journal of Discourses, Vol. 5, p. 268-269, September 27, 1857.

"If the United States make war upon this people, the Lord will hold them responsible for it, and the measure they mete will be measured unto them again; and if they are ripe and the cup of their iniquity full, they will be shattered to pieces—their union broken up and destroyed. They will be visited with thunder and lightning and hail and the judgments of God; and every man that will not draw his sword against his neighbour will be obliged to flee to Zion."

---

[1]There has been some controversy surrounding this journal entry. In the book "Victims" by Richard E. Turley, Jr. it says, "On June 15, 1878, asst. church historian Wilford Woodruff (who later became the church's fourth president) spent most of the day in the church Historian's Office. Later, he recorded in his journal that while he was in the office, he "had a very strange vision copied". In the same journal entry, Woodruff transcribed a copy of the peculiar vision. . . .Because the copy Woodruff made in his journal was written in the first person, some later readers attributed the vision to Woodruff. Several factors, however, suggested Woodruff had not authored the vision but had simply made a copy of a curious but anonymous document that had been circulating. His journal entry introducing the vision explained that he had the vision copied but did not say he had experienced the vision himself. Although he made the journal copy in mid-1878, the vision itself was dated December 16, 1877, and nowhere in his journal for December 1877 did Woodruff, a meticulous journal keeper, record receiving such a vision. Morover, even though Woodruff's journal copy of the vision began in the first person with the words "I went to bed at the usual hour," Woodruff left a large blank between the words "I" and "went", showing an intention to fill in the name of the vision's author when he learned it. Similarly, the church Historian's Office clerk whom Woodruff had copy the vision added a filing notation to the document that included a large blank after the words "Vision had by." Finally, the text of the purported vision claimed its recipient was "reading the Revelations in the French language" when the vision occurred, and Woodruff did not know French." (p. 16-17.)

It was later attributed to Joseph F. Smith who disclaimed the vision as a fraud in a letter in the Deseret News on November 17, 1880. John Taylor has been suggested as the author of the vision, but his French was limited. Also his close associates in the church leadership denounced the vision as a fraud.

The vision does bear some similarity to another vision told by George Albert Smith in 1946 to his family, and recorded by David Hughes Horne who was present. His grandmother was a cousin to George Albert Smith.

Wilford Woodruff, Journal of Discourses, Vol. 10, p. 15, July 27, 1862.

"When the United States sent an army to this land for our destruction, the Lord had his eye upon us for good and he delivered us from all our enemies. The wicked have designed our destruction from the first organization of this Church and kingdom, but our leaders have been inspired by the gift and power of God. Who frustrated that army in their design? The Lord our God; and now the judgments that have come upon the nation in consequence of their treatment to this people, are a sore vexation to them, but it is the hand-dealing of the Almighty and we cannot help it. Every Elder in this Church who lives his religion knows that this which is now transpiring is according to the mind and foreshadowings of the Holy Spirit, and those out of the Church may know if they will. If persons will believe the Bible, the Book of Doctrines and Covenants, and the Book of Mormon, they can therein learn the fate of the world, for it is there pointed out in great plainness. Who can stay this war that is devastating the whole nation both North and South? No human hand; it is out of the power of man, excepting by the repentance of the whole nation, for they have shed the blood of the Prophets, driven this Church and people from their midst, yes, the very people that hold the keys of salvation for the world they have banished from their midst, they have turned those keys that will seal their condemnation, and for this the Lord our God has taken peace out of their midst. Will there ever be any more peace among them? No, not until the earth is drenched with the blood of the inhabitants thereof. When the spirit of the Gospel leaves any people it leaves them in a worse condition than it found them, the spirit of ferocity, darkness and war will take hold of that people, and the time will come when every man that does not take his sword against his neighbor will have to go to Zion for safety."

Wilford Woodruff, Journal of Discourses, Vol. 21, p. 301, August 1st, 1880.

"When I contemplate the condition of our nation, and see that wickedness and abominations are increasing, so much so that the whole heavens groan and weep over the abominations of this nation and the nations of the earth, I ask myself the question, can the American nation escape? The answer comes, No; its destruction, as well as the destruction of the world, is sure; just as sure as the Lord cut off and destroyed the two great and prosperous nations that once inhabited this continent of North and South America, because of their wickedness, so will he them destroy, and sooner or later they will reap the fruits of their own wicked acts, and be numbered among the past."

Wilford Woodruff, Journal of Discourses, Vol. 22, p. 235-236, June 26, 1881.

"Joseph went to God, and he opened his mind by vision, in which he saw the destruction of our nation; he saw that famine and pestilence and war would lay waste our land, until it became so terrible that he prayed God to close the vision. Well may we say, 'Father, forgive them.' Well may we pray for them, and feel in our hearts not to envy them, but leave them in the hands of God."

Wilford Woodruff, Journal of Discourses, Vol. 25, p. 11, January 6, 1884.

"Have we any warfare with our Government? Have we any reproach to offer them? Not at all. I feel sorry that this nation should sow seeds which when ripe will bring destruction; for I know as God lives that if this or any other government departs from the principles of truth, becomes ripened in iniquity, forsakes the Lord, forsakes the principles of life and liberty, the God of heaven will hold it responsible. Judgments will come upon the wicked. When men depart from the principles of truth and cleave unto darkness and wickedness, they reap the whirlwind; they lay the foundation for desolation."

George Q. Cannon, Journal of Discourses, Vol. 25, p. 243-244, June 22, 1884.

"The day will come when our own nation will be convulsed with intestine strife. The civil war that is past is not the only war that will take place in this land. It is a matter of regret to think it should be otherwise. But God has spoken. There will be intestine strife in our own nation. Already we can see, as it were, the seeds of this germinating and sprouting in the midst of neighborhoods and of communities, and it will break out after a while, and men will flee to Zion. The prediction was made 52 years ago by Joseph Smith, that the time would come when those that would not take up their sword to fight against their neighbor in this blessed land, (the most favored of any land under the heavens, so favored in government, so favored in climate, so favored in every element of wealth, and in all its surroundings) they would be compelled to come here for protection, for we will be the only people that will be at peace on the continent. That prediction was made 52 years ago. It will be fulfilled just as sure as God has spoken it."

George Q. Cannon, Journal of Discourses, Vol. 25, p. 273-275, August 31, 1884.

"I know just as well as I know that I stand here, and that I am speaking to you, that the Latter-day Saints, this Church, or what we call the Zion of our God, will be delivered, and it will roll forth in mighty power, and it will accomplish all that has been predicted concerning it. For the day will come, and it is not far distant, when in our own nation, there will be civil strife, there will be domestic broils, there will be a withdrawal of peace, and men will yet have to come to the Latter-day Saints for that peace and that freedom from civil strife that cannot be found elsewhere. God revealed this and predicted it, upwards of fifty years ago, and it will, just as sure as He predicted it, be fulfilled to the letter. All we have to do is to take the course that He has pointed out to us, to keep His commandments, leaving the results with Him, and He will control all things for the glory of His name. We have been taught to believe that the time will come when constitutional government will be overthrown upon this land, and that it will be the province of the Latter-day to uphold those principles which God inspired the founders of this government to embody in the Constitution; and it seems to be fast approaching. When assassination can be justified, assassination of men peaceably worshipping their God, offending no one, committing no violation of law or of good order; when they can be shot down cruelly and inhumanly, and their murderers be justified for the deed, it seems as though the time when constitutional principle so would fail, is near at hand. But this is not all. When we who have built up this country, and made it that which it is by the sacrifices we have made—living here in peace, men and women industriously pursuing their various avocations, molesting no one, observing every law that promotes good order—when such a people as we, I say, are legislated against and considered unworthy of the rights of citizenship, almost every right being taken from us, that free men value, and for which the fathers of many of this people have suffered and died—when we see these acts justified and the men who do them think they are committing acts which will be applauded by their constituents, what are we to conclude? Shall we not say, Surely the predictions are coming to pass, and the time is drawing near when constitutional government will have to be maintained by some other hands than those who now profess to be its upholders?"

George Q. Cannon, Gospel Truth, Vol. 1, p. 307-308.

"Not only have these religious reformers been inspired to do a work in preparing for the advent of the Kingdom of God upon the earth; but others have been raised up for the same purpose. Columbus was inspired to penetrate the ocean and discover this Western continent . . . and the consequences which God desired to follow its discovery have taken place—a free government has been established on it. The men who established that government were inspired of God . . .We believe it was a preparatory work for the establishment of the Kingdom of God.

This Church and Kingdom could not have been established on the earth if their work had not been performed or a work of a similar character. The Kingdom of God could not have been established in Asia amid the despotisms there, nor in Africa amid the darkness there; it could not have been built up in Europe amid the monarchies which crowd every inch of its surface. It had to be built up on this land; hence, this land had to be discovered. It was not discovered too soon; if it had been, it would have been overrun by the nations of the earth, and no place would have been found even here for the Kingdom of God. It was discovered at the right time and by the right man, inspired of God not to waver or shrink; but, undaunted by the difficulty with which he was surrounded and contending with a mutinous crew, he persevered and continued his journey westward until he discovered this land, the existence of which God had inspired him to demonstrate.

. . .Because God had in view the restoration of the everlasting Gospel to the earth again, and in addition to this the set time had come for Him to build up His Kingdom and to accomplish the fulfilment of His long deferred purposes."

George Q. Cannon, Journal of Discourses, Vol. 19, p. 202-203, July 21, 1867.

"But God, our Heavenly Father, reserved this—the land of promise—for the especial purpose of building up his kingdom in the latter days. As the 'Book of Mormon' informs us, it has been hid from the eyes of the generations of men for this purpose. If it had not been thus hidden the nations of the earth would have overrun the land until there would have been no foothold found for the establishment of the kingdom of God upon it. But the Lord concealed it, from the days of the flood, from the eyes of men, excepting those whom he led hither; as we are informed by the 'Book of Mormon' that no nation after the flood, knew anything about this land; although I believe it is said in the Norwegian Antiquarian researches, that this land was visited by the Icelanders in the eleventh century. But there is nothing authentic in this. But be that as it may, this land was kept secret until Columbus was moved upon by the Spirit of God, to go forth and penetrate the western ocean. Then the land was settled and a government was formed under the protecting aegis of liberty, and a place was found for the establishment of the kingdom of God, to which the Saints from every nation under Heaven could gather together. Hence we are surrounded by many more favorable circumstances than they who preceded us in the work of God in the days of Jesus and the Apostles. They did not possess the advantages that we enjoy; but we have them, and our Heavenly Father intends that we shall possess them, and that we shall build up his kingdom on the earth, establish righteousness."

Harold B. Lee, Conference Report, April 1942, p. 87

"We talk of security in this day, and yet we fail to understand that here on this Temple Block we have standing the holy temple wherein we may find the symbols by which power might be generated that will save this nation from destruction."

Harold B. Lee, Conference Report, October 1965, p. 128.

"President Heber C. Kimball, shortly after the Saints had arrived here in the mountains—and some, I suppose, were somewhat gloating over the fact that they had triumphed for a temporary period over their enemies—had this to say: '. . . we think we are secure here in the chambers of the everlasting hills where we can close those few doors of the canyons against mobs and persecutors, the wicked and the vile, who have always beset us with violence and robbery, but I want to say to you, my brethren, the time is coming when we will be mixed up in these now peaceful valleys to that extent that it will be difficult to tell the face of a Saint from the face of an enemy to the people of God. Then, brethren, look out for the great sieve, for there will be a great sifting time, and many will fall—for I say unto you there is a test, a TEST, a TEST coming, and who will be able to stand? . . ."

Harold B. Lee, Church News, November 3, 1973, p. 7-8.

"The United States will stand despite whatever trials and crisis it may have to pass through. Men may fail in this country. Earthquakes may come; seas may heave themselves beyond their bounds; there may be great drought and disaster and hardship, but this nation, founded as it was on a foundation of principle laid down by men whom God raised up, will never fail. . . .

This is a great nation, it is a great country. This is the most favored of all lands. While it is true there are dangers and difficulties that lie ahead of us, we must not assume that we are going to lie down and watch the country go to ruin.

We should not be heard to predict ills and calamities for the nation. On the contrary, we should be providing optimistic support of the nation.

You must remember that this church is one of the most powerful agencies for progress in the world, and we must all sound with one voice. We must tell the world how we feel about this land and this nation, and should bear our testimonies about the great mission and destiny that it has.

If we do this we will help turn the tide of this country. We must be careful that we do not say or do anything that will further weaken the country.

There's no agency that has as powerful a voice as the church and kingdom of God and the holy priesthood that speaks to the world.

We who carry these sacred responsibilities must preach the gospel of peace, and peace can only come by overcoming the things of the world. We must be the dynamic force that will help turn the tide of fear and pessimism. . . .

We should not be so concerned about finding out what's wrong with America, but we should be finding out what's right about America. . . .

I have faith in America. You and I must have faith in America if we understand the gospel of Jesus Christ."

Harold B. Lee, Ye Are the Light of the World, p. 350-351, 1974.

"Men may fail in this country, earthquakes may come, seas may heave beyond their bounds, there may be great drought, disaster, and hardship, but this nation, founded on principles laid down by men whom God raised up, will never fail. This is the cradle of humanity, where life on this earth began in the Garden of Eden. This is the place of the new Jerusalem. This is the place that the Lord said is favored above all other nations in all the world. This is the place where the Savior will come to His temple. This is the favored land in all the world. Yes, I repeat, men may fail, but this nation won't fail. I have faith in America; you and I must have faith in America, if we understand the teachings of the gospel of Jesus Christ. We are living in a day when we must pay heed to these challenges.

I plead with you not to preach pessimism. Preach that this is the greatest country in all the world. This is the favored land. This is the land of our forefathers. It is the nation that will stand despite whatever trials or crises it may yet have to pass through."

Ezra Taft Benson, Conference Report, April 1960, p. 99.

"Nations that truly love freedom love God. History is replete with examples of once powerful nations that have forgotten God. No nation ripened in iniquity can long endure. 'Righteousness exalteth a nation: but sin is a reproach to any people.' (Proverbs 14:34)."

Ezra Taft Benson, Conference Report, April 1962, p. 104.

"Now God will not permit his base of operations—America—to be destroyed. He has promised protection to this land if we will but serve the God of the land. He has also promised protection to the righteous even, if necessary, to send fire from heaven to destroy their enemies. (Ether 2:12, 1 Nephi 22:17.)

No, God's base of operations will not be destroyed. But it may be weakened and made less effective. One of the first rules of war strategy—and we are at war with the adversary and his agents—is to protect the base of operations. This we must do if we are to build up the kingdom throughout the world and safeguard our God-given freedom. . . .

We must protect this base from complacency—from the dangerous feeling that all is well—from being lulled away into a false security. We must protect this American base from the brainwashing, increasingly administered to our youth in many educational institutions across the land, by some misinformed instructors and some wolves in sheep's clothing. Their false indoctrination, often perpetrated behind the front of so-called academic freedom, is leaving behind many faithless students, socialist-oriented, who are easy subjects for state tyranny.

'At what point, then, is the approach of danger to be expected?' asked Abraham Lincoln, and answered, '. . . If it ever reaches us, it must spring up among us. It cannot come from abroad. If destruction be our lot, we must ourselves be its author and finisher. As a nation of freemen, we must live through all time or die by suicide.' (Springfield, Ill., Jan. 27, 1837.) . . .

Lenin said, 'The soundest strategy in war is to postpone operations until the moral disintegration of the enemy renders the mortal blow possible and easy.' Commenting on Lenin's statement the Indianapolis Star adds: 'Where then does the real danger lie? It lies with us—the American people. . . . Other great civilizations have died by suicide. The first free people, the Greeks, died thus. And why did Greece fall: 'A slackness and softness finally came over them to their ruin. In the end more than they wanted freedom they wanted security, a comfortable life, and they lost all—security, comfort and freedom.' "

Teachings of Ezra Taft Benson, p. 571.

"When this nation was established, the Church was restored and from here the message of the restored gospel has gone forth—all according to divine plan. This then becomes the Lord's base of operations in these latter days. And this base—the land of America—will not be shifted out of its place. This nation will, in a measure at least, fulfill its mission even though it may face serious and troublesome days. The degree to which it achieves its full mission depends upon the righteousness of its people. God, through His power, has established a free people in this land as a means of helping to carry forward His purposes."

Teachings of Ezra Taft Benson, p. 571.

"It was here under a free government and a strong nation that protection was provided for His restored Church. Now God will not permit America, His base of operations, to be destroyed. He has promised protection to this land if we will but serve the God of the land (see Ether 2:12). He has also promised protection to the righteous even, if necessary, to send fire from heaven to destroy their enemies (1 Nephi 22:17)."

Teachings of Ezra Taft Benson, p. 621.

"Two great American Christian civilizations—the Jaredites and the Nephites—were swept off because they did not 'serve the God of the land, who is Jesus Christ' (Ether 2:12). What will become of our civilization?"

Ezra Taft Benson, An Enemy Hath Done This, p. 109.

"The Soviets would not attempt military conquest of so powerful and so extensive a country as the United States without availing themselves of a sufficiently strong fifth column in our midst, a fifth column which would provide the sabotage, the false leadership, and the sudden seizures of power and of means of communication, needed to convert the struggle, from the very beginning, into a civil war rather than a clear-cut war with an external enemy."

Delbert L. Stapley, Conference Report, October 1963, p. 112-113.

"But if we and our posterity reject religious instruction and authority, violate the rules of eternal justice, trifle with the injunctions of morality, and recklessly destroy the political constitution which holds us together, no man can tell how sudden the catastrophe may overwhelm us, that shall bury all our glory in profound obscurity."

Gordon B. Hinckley, Conference Report, Ensign, May 1992, p. 71.

"What a treasured privilege to have citizenship in this holy nation. Never belittle the rights, privileges, and responsibilities that flow therefrom."

SCRIPTURAL REFERENCES

Isaiah 18:1-7

1 Woe to the land shadowing with wings, which [is] beyond the rivers of Ethiopia:

2 That sendeth ambassadors by the sea, even in vessels of bulrushes upon the waters, [saying], Go, ye swift messengers, to a nation scattered and peeled, to a people terrible from their beginning hitherto; a nation meted out and trodden down, whose land the rivers have spoiled!

3 All ye inhabitants of the world, and dwellers on the earth, see ye, when he lifteth up an ensign on the mountains; and when he bloweth a trumpet, hear ye.

4 For so the LORD said unto me, I will take my rest, and I will consider in my dwelling place like a clear heat upon herbs, [and] like a cloud of dew in the heat of harvest.

5 For afore the harvest, when the bud is perfect, and the sour grape is ripening in the flower, he shall both cut off the sprigs with pruning hooks, and take away [and] cut down the branches.

6 They shall be left together unto the fowls of the mountains, and to the beasts of the earth: and the fowls shall summer upon them, and all the beasts of the earth shall winter upon them.

7 In that time shall the present be brought unto the LORD of hosts of a people scattered and peeled, and from a people terrible from their beginning hitherto; a nation meted out and trodden under foot, whose land the rivers have spoiled, to the place of the name of the LORD of hosts, the mount Zion.

D&C 84:114-117

114 Nevertheless, let the bishop go unto the city of New York, also to the city of Albany, and also to the city of Boston, and warn the people of those cities with the sound of the gospel, with a loud voice, of the desolation and utter abolishment which await them if they do reject these things.

115 For if they do reject these things the hour of their judgment is nigh, and their house shall be left unto them desolate.

116 Let him trust in me and he shall not be confounded; and a hair of his head shall not fall to the ground unnoticed.

117 And verily I say unto you, the rest of my servants, go ye forth as your circumstances shall permit, in your several callings, unto the great and notable cities and villages, reproving the world in righteousness of all their unrighteous and ungodly deeds, setting forth clearly and understandingly the desolation of abomination in the last days.

D&C 87:3-7

3 For behold, the Southern States shall be divided against the Northern States, and the Southern States will call on other nations, even the nation of Great Britain, as it is called, and they shall also call upon other nations, in order to defend themselves against other nations; and then war shall be poured out upon all nations.

4 And it shall come to pass, after many days, slaves shall rise up against their masters, who shall be marshaled and disciplined for war.

5 And it shall come to pass also that the remnants who are left of the land will marshal themselves, and shall become exceedingly angry, and shall vex the Gentiles with a sore vexation.

6 And thus, with the sword and by bloodshed the inhabitants of the earth shall mourn; and with

famine, and plague, and earthquake, and the thunder of heaven, and the fierce and vivid lightning also, shall the inhabitants of the earth be made to feel the wrath, and indignation, and chastening hand of an Almighty God, until the consumption decreed hath made a full end of all nations;

7 That the cry of the saints, and of the blood of the saints, shall cease to come up into the ears of the Lord of Sabaoth, from the earth, to be avenged of their enemies.

D&C 101:76-80

76 And again I say unto you, those who have been scattered by their enemies, it is my will that they should continue to importune for redress, and redemption, by the hands of those who are placed as rulers and are in authority over you—

77 According to the laws and constitution of the people, which I have suffered to be established, and should be maintained for the rights and protection of all flesh, according to just and holy principles;

78 That every man may act in doctrine and principle pertaining to futurity, according to the moral agency which I have given unto him, that every man may be accountable for his own sins in the day of judgment.

79 Therefore, it is not right that any man should be in bondage one to another.

80 And for this purpose have I established the Constitution of this land, by the hands of wise men whom I have raised up unto this very purpose, and redeemed the land by the shedding of blood.

D&C 101:85-92

85 Thus will I liken the children of Zion.

86 Let them importune at the feet of the judge;

87 And if he heed them not, let them importune at the feet of the governor;

88 And if the governor heed them not, let them importune at the feet of the president;

89 And if the president heed them not, then will the Lord arise and come forth out of his hiding place, and in his fury vex the nation;

90 And in his hot displeasure, and in his fierce anger, in his time, will cut off those wicked, unfaithful, and unjust stewards, and appoint them their portion among hypocrites, and unbelievers;

91 Even in outer darkness, where there is weeping, and wailing, and gnashing of teeth.

92 Pray ye, therefore, that their ears may be opened unto your cries, that I may be merciful unto them, that these things may not come upon them.

CHAPTER FIVE

PERSECUTION & ENEMIES

"The Lord never had a people who were received with open arms by the world, admired, cherished and respected; on the contrary they have been persecuted or totally destroyed from off the earth. . . .The Latter-day Saints have had the same experience to pass through . . .There will come a time, however, in the history of the Saints, when they will be tried with peace, prosperity, popularity and riches." (Daniel H. Wells, Journal of Discourses, Vol. 19, p. 369, June 1, 1878.)

Joseph Smith, Lectures on Faith, Lecture 4, p. 43-44.

"It is also of equal importance that men should have the idea of the existence of the attribute judgment in God, in order that they may exercise faith in Him for life and salvation; for without the idea of the existence of this attribute in the Deity, it would be impossible for men to exercise faith in Him for life and salvation, seeing that it is through the exercise of this attribute that the faithful in Christ Jesus are delivered out of the hands of those who seek their destruction; for if God were not to come out in swift judgment against the workers of iniquity and the powers of darkness, His saints could not be saved; for it is by judgment that the Lord delivers His saints out of the hands of all their enemies, and those who reject the gospel of our Lord Jesus Christ. But no sooner is the idea of the existence of this attribute planted in the minds of men, than it gives power to the mind for the exercise of faith and confidence in God, and they are enabled by faith to lay hold on the promises which are set before them, and wade through all the tribulations and afflictions to which they are subjected by reason of the persecution from those who know not God, and obey not the gospel of our Lord Jesus Christ, believing that in due time the Lord will come out in swift judgment against their enemies, and they shall be cut off from before Him, and that in His own due time He will bear them off conquerors, and more than conquerors, in all things."

Joseph Smith, Lectures on Faith, Lecture 4, p. 44.

"And again, it is equally important that men should have the idea of the existence of the attribute mercy in the Deity, in order to exercise faith in Him for life and salvation; for without the idea of the existence of this attribute in the Deity, the spirits of the saints would faint in the midst of the tribulations, afflictions, and persecutions which they have to endure for righteousness' sake. But when the idea of the existence of this attribute is once established in the mind it gives life and energy to the spirits of the saints, believing that the mercy of God will be poured out upon them in the midst of their afflictions, and that He will compassionate them in their sufferings, and that the mercy of God will lay hold of them and secure them in the arms of His love, so that they will receive a full reward for all their sufferings."

Joseph Smith, Lectures on Faith, Lecture 4, p. 45.

"Let the mind once reflect sincerely and candidly upon the ideas of the existence of the before-mentioned attributes in the Deity, and it will be seen that as far as His attributes are concerned, there is a sure foundation laid for the exercise of faith in Him for life and salvation. For inasmuch as God possesses the attribute knowledge, He can make all things known to His saints necessary for their salvation, and as He possesses the attribute power, He is able thereby to deliver them from the power of all enemies; and seeing, also, that justice is an attribute of the Deity, He will deal with them upon the principles of righteousness and equity, and a just reward will be granted unto them for all their afflictions and sufferings for the truth's sake. And as judgment is an attribute of the Deity also, His saints can have the most unshaken confidence that they will, in due time, obtain a perfect deliverance out of the hands of their enemies, and a complete victory over all those who have sought their hurt and destruction. And as mercy is also an attribute of the Deity, His saints can have confidence that it will be exercised towards them, and through the exercise of that attribute towards them comfort and consolation will be administered unto them abundantly, amid all their afflictions and tribulations. And, lastly, realizing that truth is an attribute of the Deity, the mind is led to rejoice amid all its trials and temptations, in hope of that glory which is to be brought at the revelation of Jesus Christ, and in view of that crown which is to be placed upon the heads of the saints in the day when the Lord shall distribute rewards unto them, and in prospect of that eternal weight of glory which the Lord has promised to bestow upon them, when He shall bring them in the midst of His throne to dwell in His presence eternally."

Joseph Smith, Lectures on Faith, Lecture 6, p. 57-58.

"An actual knowledge to any person, that the course of life which he pursues is according to the will of God, is essentially necessary to enable him to have that confidence in God without which no person can obtain eternal life. It was this that enabled the ancient saints to endure all their afflictions and persecutions, and to take joyfully the spoiling of their goods, knowing (not believing merely) that they had a more enduring substance. (Hebrews 10:34.)

3. Having the assurance that they were pursuing a course which was agreeable to the will of God, they were enabled to take, not only the spoiling of their goods, and the wasting of their substance, joyfully, but also to suffer death in its most horrid forms; knowing (not merely believing) that when this earthly house of their tabernacle was dissolved, they had a building of God, a house not made with hands, eternal in the heavens. (2 Corinthians 5:1.)

4. Such was, and always will be, the situation of the saints of God, that unless they have an actual knowledge that the course they are pursuing is according to the will of God they will grow weary in their minds, and faint; for such has been, and always will be, the opposition in the hearts of unbelievers and those that know not God against the pure and unadulterated religion of heaven (the only thing which insures eternal life), that they will persecute to the uttermost all that worship God according to His revelations, receive the truth in the love of it, and submit themselves to be guided and directed by His will; and drive them to such extremities that nothing short of an actual knowledge of their being the favorites of heaven, and of their having embraced the order of things which God has established for the redemption of man, will enable them to exercise that confidence in Him necessary for them to overcome the world, and obtain that crown of glory which is laid up for them

156

that fear God."

Joseph Smith, History of the Church, Vol. 1, p. 449.

"This one thing is sure, that they who will live godly in Christ Jesus, shall suffer persecution; and before their robes are made white in the blood of the Lamb, it is to be expected, according to John the Revelator, they will pass through great tribulation."

Teachings of the Prophet Joseph Smith, Section One, 1830-34, p. 42.

"We have all been children, and are too much so at the present time; but we hope in the Lord that we may grow in grace and be prepared for all things which the bosom of futurity may disclose unto us. Time is rapidly rolling on, and the prophecies must be fulfilled. The days of tribulation are fast approaching, and the time to test the fidelity of the Saints has come. Rumor with her ten thousand tongues is diffusing her uncertain sounds in almost every ear; but in these times of sore trial, let the Saints be patient and see the salvation of God. Those who cannot endure persecution, and stand in the day of affliction, cannot stand in the day when the Son of God shall burst the veil, and appear in all the glory of His Father, with all the holy angels."

Teachings of the Prophet Joseph Smith, Section Two, 1834-37, p. 66.

"From apostates the faithful have received the severest persecutions . . . Where is one like Christ? He cannot be found on earth. Then why should His followers complain, if from those whom they once called brethren, and considered as standing in the nearest relation in the everlasting covenant they should receive persecution? From what source emanated the principle which has ever been manifest by apostates from the true Church to persecute with double diligence, and seek with double perseverance, to destroy those whom they once professed to love, with whom they once communed, and with whom they once covenanted to strive with every power in righteousness to obtain the rest of God? Perhaps our brethren will say the same that caused Satan to seek to overthrow the kingdom of God, because he himself was evil, and God's kingdom is holy."

Teachings of the Prophet Joseph Smith, Section Three, 1838-39, p. 123.

"Dear brethren, do not think that our hearts faint, as though some strange thing had happened unto us, for we have seen and been assured of all these things beforehand, and have an assurance of a better hope than that of our persecutors. Therefore God hath made broad our shoulders for the burden. We glory in our tribulation, because we know that God is with us, that He is our friend, and that He will save our souls. We do not care for them that can kill the body; they cannot harm our souls. We ask no favors at the hands of mobs, nor of the world, nor of the devil, nor of his emissaries the dissenters, and those who love, and make, and swear falsehoods, to take away our lives. We have never dissembled, nor will we for the sake of our lives."

Teachings of the Prophet Joseph Smith, Section Five, 1842-43, p. 259.

"The enemies of this people will never get weary of their persecution against the Church, until they are overcome. I expect they will array everything against me that is in their power to control, and that we shall have a long and tremendous warfare. He that will war the true Christian warfare against the corruptions of these last days will have wicked men and angels of devils, and all the infernal powers of darkness continually arrayed against him. When wicked and corrupt men oppose, it is a criterion to judge if a man is warring the Christian warfare. When all men speak evil of you falsely, blessed are ye. Shall a man be considered bad, when men speak evil of him? No. If a man stands and opposes the world of sin, he may expect to have all wicked and corrupt spirits arrayed against him. But it will be but a little season, and all these afflictions will be turned away from us, inasmuch as we are faithful, and are not overcome by these evils. By seeing the blessings of the endowment rolling on, and the kingdom increasing and spreading from sea to sea, we shall rejoice that we were not overcome by these foolish things."

Teachings of the Prophet Joseph Smith, Section Six, 1843–44, p.309.

"Many men will say, 'I will never forsake you, but will stand by you at all times.' But the moment you teach them some of the mysteries of the kingdom of God that are retained in the heavens and are to be revealed to the children of men when they are prepared for them they will be the first to stone you and put you to death. It was this same principle that crucified the Lord Jesus Christ, and will cause the people to kill the prophets in this generation."

Teachings of the Prophet Joseph Smith, Section Six, 1843-44, p. 392.

"Said Joseph, 'Our lives have already become jeopardized by revealing the wicked and bloodthirsty purposes of our enemies; and for the future we must cease to do so. All we have said about them is truth, but it is not always wise to relate all the truth. Even Jesus, the Son of God, had to refrain from doing so, and had to restrain His feelings many times for the safety of Himself and His followers, and had to conceal the righteous purposes of His heart in relation to many things pertaining to His Father's kingdom. When still a boy He had all the intelligence necessary to enable Him to rule and govern the kingdom of the Jews, and could reason with the wisest and most profound doctors of law and divinity, and make their theories and practice to appear like folly compared with the wisdom He possessed; but He was a boy only, and lacked physical strength even to defend His own person; and was subject to cold, to hunger and to death. So it is with the Church of Jesus Christ of Latter-day Saints; we have the revelation of Jesus, and the knowledge within us is sufficient to organize a righteous government upon the earth, and to give universal peace to all mankind, if they would receive it, but we lack the physical strength, as did our Savior when a child, to defend our principles, and we have a necessity to be afflicted, persecuted and smitten, and to bear it patiently until Jacob is of age, then he will take care of himself.'"

Brigham Young, Messages of the First Presidency, Vol. 2, April 7, 1851, p. 73.

"Amid all the revolutions that are taking place among the nations, the elders will ever pursue an undeviating course in being subject to the government wherever they may be, and sustain the same by all their precepts to the Saints, having nothing to do with political questions which engender strife, remembering that the weapons of their warfare are not carnal but spiritual, and that the Gospel which they preach is not of man but from heaven; and if they persecute you beyond measure in one city, country, or kingdom, leave the testimony which Jesus has given for a witness unto your father in heaven, that you are free from their blood, and flee to other cities, countries, or kingdoms where they will receive you and believe your testimony."

Brigham Young, Messages of the First Presidency, Vol. 2, p. 184-185, October 29, 1855.

"It is easy to bear persecution, to contend for the faith, and even to die for it; the hardest of all is to live it, to be always actuated by its holy influences and practice it in all the walks of life. It is not a plaything or mere toy to believe, amuse ourselves with at our convenience, and then lay aside, but a tangible, every day experience and solid fact, entering into every avenue of business, of pastime and repose, as well as into the spiritually religious exercises of the mind."

Brigham Young, Journal of Discourses, Vol. 1, p. 202-203, April 6, 1852.

"The kingdom will continue to increase, to grow, to spread and prosper more and more. Every time its enemies undertake to overthrow it, it will become more extensive and powerful; instead of its decreasing, it will continue to increase, it will spread the more, become more wonderful and conspicuous to the nations, until it fills the whole earth."

Brigham Young, Journal of Discourses, Vol. 2, p. 7-8, October 23, 1853.

"Joseph could not have been perfected, though he had lived a thousand years, if he had received no persecution. If he had lived a thousand years, and led this people, and preached the Gospel without persecution, he would not have been perfected as well as he was at the age of thirty-nine years. You may calculate when this people are called to go through scenes of affliction and suffering, are driven from their homes, and cast down, and scattered, and smitten, and peeled, the Almighty is rolling on His work with greater rapidity."

Brigham Young, Journal of Discourses, Vol. 2, p. 177, February 18, 1855.

"Why should we have enemies? 'Why is it,' say our objectors, 'that you cannot mingle and mix in society like other religious denominations?' It has been seen that the people would not permit us to dwell in their midst in peace. We have been universally driven by illegal force, by mobs, murderers, and assassins, as unworthy of having a place amongst the abodes of civilized man, until, as a last resort, we found peace in these distant valleys. It is because our religion is the only true one. It is because we have the only true authority, upon the face of the whole earth, to administer in the ordinances of the Gospel. It is because the keys of this dispensation were committed by messengers sent from the Celestial world unto Joseph Smith, and are now held on the earth by this people. It is because Christ and Lucifer are enemies, and cannot be made friends; and Lucifer, knowing that we have this Priesthood, this power, this authority, seeks our overthrow."

Brigham Young, Journal of Discourses, Vol. 2, p. 319-320, June 17, 1855.

"Christ and Belial cannot be made friends; the devil is at war with the Kingdom of God on the earth, and always has been, and will continue to be, until he is bound. They do not personally hate you, nor me, any more than they did Joseph Smith, whom they have slain; they do not hate the Latter-day Saints any more now than they did twenty years ago. The same deadly hatred was then in the heart of every one who had the privilege of hearing the doctrines of this Church and refused to embrace them, that we see exhibited at this day. If they had had the power twenty or twenty-five years ago, they would have slain the Prophet Joseph as readily and with as much rejoicing as they did when they massacred him in Carthage Jail, in the State of Illinois. It is not any particular doctrine or men and women that they are opposed to, but they are opposed to Christ and to the Kingdom of God on the earth. I observed here last Sabbath, 'Let the wicked rage and the people mock on, for now is their day, and it will soon be over.' Let them do all they can, and if they have power to destroy any more of this people, Amen to it; what will it do? It will only augment the cause of Zion, spread the Gospel of Salvation, and increase the Kingdom of God on the earth. Their persecutions will never destroy this people, or the everlasting Gospel. Every time they have killed any of this people and opposed the Gospel, both have increased ten fold, and the work has spread still the more; yes, more than it would have done had they let it alone, and not have come against the Saints to drive them from their possessions. If it is wisdom that the Saints should be driven again, it would be the greatest blessing that could come to this people, for it would give greater permanency to the Kingdom of God on the earth."

Brigham Young, Journal of Discourses, Vol. 6, p. 322, April 7, 1852.

"There is a class of person that persecution will not drive from the Church of Christ, but prosperity will; and again, there is another class that prosperity will not drive, but persecution will. The Lord must and will have a company of Saints who will follow him to the cross, if it be necessary; and these he will crown. They are the ones who will wear a celestial crown and have dominion, rule, and government. These are thy who will receive honour of the Father, with glory, exaltation, and eternal lives. They shall reign over kingdoms, and have power to be Gods, even the sons of God."

Brigham Young, Journal of Discourses, Vol. 6, p. 77, November 22, 1857.

"We are a blessed people, and we shall be preserved from our enemies, if we continue to do right, and the Lord will sustain us. And I can tell you that this people will do right and God will sustain us. Ere long Zion will triumph and the glory and knowledge of God will cover the earth, and we will still be in the old ship Zion and ride all wicked opposition down to destruction."

Brigham Young, Journal of Discourses, Vol. 8, p. 152, August 26, 1860.

"Marvel not that we have what are called troubles: marvel not that our enemies seek to destroy us and the kingdom of God from the earth. These persecutions are to prepare the humble and faithful to dwell in the presence of God the Father and his Son, while the vast multitudes of the earth must dwell in the kingdoms prepared for them, but cannot dwell in his presence. If you expect to gain the glory you anticipate, never grieve, nor sorrow, nor mourn at the providences of God when they cause you to suffer, or to part with every earthly object you have. If they cause fathers and mothers to separate from their children, and husbands from their wives, it matters not: God is our Father, and the offspring of Adam are our brothers and sisters. Who is my father, mother, sister, and brother? Those who do the will of the my Father in heaven."

Brigham Young, Journal of Discourses, Vol. 8, p. 204-205, October 8, 1860.

"There is a great difference between persecuting this people and the people of other sects. God will make persecutors pay every debt they contract with this people. This is the Priesthood of the Almighty. God has set his hand the second time to gather the people. It will not do to trifle with this people. 'Touch not mine anointed,' saith the Lord. O ye inhabitants of the earth, be careful how you infringe upon the Latter-day Saints. They are the anointed of the Lord, and are like the apple of his eye, and he will bring you into judgment for every act and move you make against them . . . The time is nigh when every man that will not take up his sword against his neighbour must needs flee to Zion. Where is Zion? Where the organization of the Church of God is. And may it dwell spiritually in every heart; and may we so live as to always enjoy the Spirit of Zion! Amen."

Brigham Young, Journal of Discourses, Vol.8, p.225-226, October 21, 1860.

"Every time they persecute and try to overcome this people, they elevate us, weaken their own hands, and strengthen the hands and the arms of this people. And every time they undertake to lessen our number, they increase it. And when they try to destroy the faith and virtue of this people, the Lord strengthens the feeble knees, and confirms the wavering in faith and power in God, in light, and intelligence. Righteousness and power with God increase in this people in proportion as the Devil struggles to destroy it."

Brigham Young, Journal of Discourses, Vol. 10, p. 32, April 8, 1862.

"As the kingdom of God rises and advances upon the earth, so will the power of Satan increase to impede its progress until God shall purge that power from the earth, and so give the Saints the victory, that they can bear off his kingdom triumphantly in spite of the powers of Satan and wicked men. But so far as the power of Satan extends, just so far will be seen his operations to overthrow all righteousness. There is nothing that would so soon weaken my hope and discourage me as to see this people in full fellowship with the world, and receive no more persecution from them because they are one with them. In such an event, we might bid farewell to the Holy Priesthood with all its blessings, privileges and aids to exaltations, principalities and powers in the eternities of the Gods."

Brigham Young, Journal of Discourses, Vol.11, p.274, December 23, 1866.

"You inquire if we shall stay in these mountains. I answer yes, as long as we please to do the will of God, our Father in heaven. If we are pleased to turn away from the holy commandments of the Lord Jesus Christ, as ancient Israel did, every man turning to his own way, we shall be scattered and peeled, driven before our enemies and persecuted, until we learn to remember the Lord our God and are willing to walk in his ways."

Brigham Young, Journal of Discourses, Vol. 11, p. 280-281, December 23, 1866.

"The Latter-day Saints will never again pull up stakes and give their possessions to their enemies. You think that you can get the Government to help you to do this. It will never be done worlds without end."

Brigham Young, Journal of Discourses, Vol. 12, p. 308-309, November 29, 1868.

"When we look at the Latter-day Saints we ask, is there any necessity of their being persecuted? Yes, if they are disobedient. Is there any necessity of chastening a son or a daughter?

Yes, if they are disobedient. But suppose they are perfectly obedient to every requirement of their parents, is there any necessity of chastening them then? If there is, I do not understand the principle of it. I have not yet been able to see the necessity of chastening an obedient child, neither have I been able to see the necessity of chastisement from the Lord upon a people who are perfectly obedient. Have this people been chastened? Yes, they have."

Brigham Young, Journal of Discourses, Vol. 13, p. 61-62, July 18, 1869.

"I will say, now, to the Latter day Saints, sometimes you know, if a word be dropped unguardedly, we are threatened with an army; if we speak a word out of the wrong side of the mouth we are threatened with a legalized mob just as we were in the States. Hence, we must be careful of what we say, for our enemies are ready to 'make a man an offender for a word, and to lay a snare for him that reproveth in the gate.' I will say, however, that if you, Latter-day Saints, will live your religion there will be no necessity whatever to fear all the powers of earth and hell, for God will sustain you. Jesus is king of this earth and he will sustain those who walk humbly before him, loving and serving him and keeping his commandments. I pray the Latter-day Saints to be faithful; love and serve the Lord, keep His commandments, refrain from evil and walk humbly before him."

Brigham Young, Journal of Discourses, Vol.14, p.97, April 8, 1871.

"We have been persecuted, driven, smitten, cast out, robbed and hated; and I may say it was for our coldness and neglect of duty; and if we did not exactly deserve it, there have been times when we did deserve it. If we did not deserve it at the time, it was good for and gave us an experience, though I must say that one of the hardest lessons for me to learn on earth is to love a man who hates me and would put me to death if he had the power. I do not think I have got this lesson by heart, and I do not know how long I shall have to live to learn it. I am trying."

Brigham Young, Journal of Discourses, Vol. 18, p. 359, May 6, 1877.

"If I were to tell you one half of the things that I know in many particulars it would astonish the half hearted who have but little or no faith, and who do not understand the workings of the providences of God among the children of men. But as to the persecution, it is nothing at all, neither one way nor another, only to purify the Saints and prepare the nations for the good or evil, for the Lord Almighty to send forth his judgments to cleanse the earth, to sanctify it, and to justify the righteous and condemn the guilty, and to prepare the way for the coming of the Son of Man. I wish to say to you, to those who are in the truth, as well as to those who are out of the truth, if we did not have to bear the iron hand of persecution, the principles we believe in which attract the attention of the good and the evil upon the earth and which occupy so many tongues and circumscribe their philosophy, would be embraced by thousands who are now indifferent to them."

Brigham Young, Journal of Discourses, Vol. 25, p. 192, June 22, 1884.

"Persecution has done us no harm. In fact it seems to me that we need about so much persecution—that we need to carry great loads to make us remember our God. If all was prosperity and peace, I presume we would lose our faith, just as the ancient Christians did when they became popular. But I pray that the time may never come that we may be popular with a people who foster such institutions as are found in Christendom today.”

Discourses of Brigham Young, p. 346.

"Purpose of Persecution—Let any people enjoy peace and quiet, unmolested, undisturbed, — never be persecuted for their religion, and they are very likely to neglect their duty, to become cold and indifferent, and lose their faith.”

Discourses of Brigham Young, p. 348-349.

"Do you know that that very principle caused the death of all the Prophets, from the days of Adam until now? Let a Prophet arise upon the earth, and never reveal the evils of men, and do you suppose that the wicked would desire to kill him? No, for he would cease to be a Prophet of the Lord, and they would invite him to their feasts, and hail him as a friend and brother. Why? Because it would be impossible for him to be anything but one of them. It is impossible for a Prophet of Christ to live in an adulterous generation without speaking of the wickedness of the people, without revealing their faults and their failings, and there is nothing short of death that will stay him from it, for a Prophet of God will do as he pleases.

The false religion that is in the world, is what raises this 'hue and cry,' misguides the people, and opposes itself against the Kingdom of God on the earth. Now if we would only fall in with the wicked all would be right, and then no person would wish to persecute us.”

Discourses of Brigham Young, p. 351-352.

"Let us alone, and we will send Elders to the uttermost parts of the earth, and gather out Israel, wherever they are; and if you persecute us, we will do it the quicker, because we are naturally dull when let alone, and are disposed to take a little sleep, a little slumber, and a little rest. If you let us alone, we will do it a little more leisurely; but if you persecute us, we will sit up nights to preach the Gospel.

Moses was not to blame because Pharaoh's heart became more and more hard. He was not to blame because an overwhelming destruction came upon that devoted army. Neither is God, Jesus Christ, Joseph Smith, myself, or the Apostles and Prophets of this last dispensation to blame for the unbelief of this nation, and for the dark and lowering tempest that now threatens to overthrow them with a terrible destruction. Still, as Pharaoh's heart became harder and harder, so will it be with the persecutors of God's people and purposes in the latter times, until they are utterly destroyed.”

Discourses of Brigham Young, p. 353.

"The sufferings that have come upon the Latter-day Saints, through persecution, will not compare in severity with the sufferings which have come upon the wicked in our own day.”

Heber C. Kimball, Deseret News, May 23, 1931.

"After a while the Gentiles will gather to this place by the thousands and Salt Lake City will be classed among the wicked cities of the world. A spirit of speculation and extravagance will take possession of the Saints and the result will be financial bondage. Persecution comes next and all true Latter-day Saints will be tested to the limit; many will apostatize and others will stand still, not

163

knowing what to do. Darkness will cover the earth and gross darkness the minds of the people. The judgments of God will be poured out upon the wicked to the extent that our elders from far and near will be called home."

Life of Heber C. Kimball, p. 442, 1856.
"The time would come when the government would stop the Saints from holding meetings. When this was done the Lord would pour out His judgments."

Life of Heber C. Kimball, p. 449-450, 1867.
"There are many within hearing who had often wished that they could have been associated with the Prophet Joseph. You imagine that you would have stood by him when persecution raged, and he was assailed by foes from within and without. You would have defended him and been true to him in the midst of every trial. You think you would have been delighted to have shown your integrity in the days of mobs and traitors.

Let me say to you, that many of you will see the time when you will have all the trouble, trials, and persecution that you can stand and plenty of opportunities to show that you are true to God and his work. This Church has before it many close places through which it will have to pass before the work of God is crowned with victory. To meet the difficulties that are coming, it will be necessary for you to have a knowledge of the truth of this work for yourselves. The difficulties will be of such a character that the man or woman who does not possess this personal knowledge or witness will fall. If you have not got the testimony, live right and call upon the Lord, and cease not until you obtain it. If you do not, you will not stand.

Remember these things, for many of you will live to see them fulfilled. The time will come when no man or woman will be able to endure on borrowed light. Each of you will have to be guided with the light within himself. If you do not have it, how can you stand?. . .

You will have all the persecution you want and more too, and all the opportunity to show your integrity to God and truth that you could desire."

Orson Pratt, Journal of Discourses, Vol. 6, p. 204, January 24, 1859.
"If we are dilatory, we shall have to suffer as in days gone by, and our enemies will come in here and bring in their whoredoms and abominations that they have been accustomed to from their youth up. This will be the case, if we do not save ourselves by our diligence and obedience. But if we show to God that we are willing to stand up in behalf of his kingdom and of the truth, even unto death, then, notwithstanding our enemies may be two hundred to our one, we shall feel strong in the Lord, and he will fight our battles. Then we shall accomplish that which has been promised by the Prophets; and not only the United States will have to suffer, but as the Prophet Isaiah says—'The multitude of the nations that fight against Zion shall become like the dream of a night vision, as when a man who is hungry dreameth that he is satisfied with food, and he awaketh and behold he is faint.' So will be all nations who fight against this people: they will pass away before the power of the servants of God. His servants will be clothed with wisdom and with the power of the Most High to prevail against all their enemies."

Orson Pratt, Journal of Discourses, Vol. 7, p. 313, September 18, 1859.

"I recollect reading of Enoch's having gathered his people, and that their enemies came up against them to battle. What kind of weapons did Enoch use to destroy his enemies? It says, 'And he (Enoch) spake the word of the Lord, and the earth trembled, and the mountains fled, according to his command; and the rivers of water were turned out of their course, and the roar of the lions was heard out of the wilderness, and all nations feared greatly, so powerful was the word of Enoch, and so great was the power of language which God had given him.'"

Orson Pratt, Journal of Discourses, Vol. 13, p. 362, May 5, 1870.

"It will depend upon the conduct of the Latter-day Saints whether we suffer more tribulation. We may suffer tribulation although we are righteous in every respect, though there were no sin found in the midst of the people. Why? Because the wicked always did persecute the righteous, they always did hate the principles and plan of salvation; still we have greater claim upon the arm of Jehovah for protection and assistance when we keep His commandments and love and serve Him."

Orson Pratt, Journal of Discourses, Vol. 17, p. 111-112, June 14, 1874.

"Now, why is it, Latter-day Saints, that we have been tossed to and fro and smitten and persecuted for these many years? It is because we have disobeyed the law of heaven, we have not kept the commandments of the Most High God, we have not fulfilled his law; we have disobeyed the word which he gave through his servant Joseph, and hence the Lord has suffered us to be smitten and afflicted under the hands of our enemies."

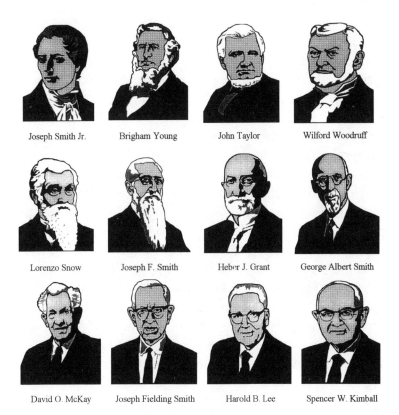

Joseph Smith Jr.   Brigham Young   John Taylor   Wilford Woodruff

Lorenzo Snow   Joseph F. Smith   Heber J. Grant   George Albert Smith

David O. McKay   Joseph Fielding Smith   Harold B. Lee   Spencer W. Kimball

John Taylor, Messages of the First Presidency, Vol. 3, p. 4-5, April 4, 1885.

"For a wise purpose in His providence He permits the wicked, in the exercise of their agency, from time to time to afflict His followers. Since the days of our father Adam this has always been the case, and it will continue to be, so long as Satan has any power over the hearts of the children of men. We are all children of the same Great Parent, and each one has the opportunity and privilege granted to him or her to exercise his or her agency. We have chosen to serve the God of Israel. We have submitted to His laws, have obeyed His Gospel, and have chosen the path which He assures us will bring us into His presence. Others of His children prefer a different course. They yield to a different influence, and under its power, they seek to destroy the work of God and all who are connected with it. This they can do in the exercise of the agency which the Father has given unto them. Not only in times past, but in our own day, the wicked have persecuted, tormented and murdered the Saints of God. But, while in so doing, they bring upon themselves everlasting condemnation, their acts are overruled for the glory and exaltation of His faithful people, and the accomplishment of His purposes in the redemption of the earth."

John Taylor, Messages of the First Presidency, Vol. 3, p. 20, July 24, 1885.

"Time after time it has seemed to all human vision that our destruction was inevitable, and our enemies have rejoiced at the prospects. But God has not forgotten Zion nor the promises He has made. He permits the wicked to exercise their agency, and their acts are the means of testing and proving His people. But there are limits beyond which they cannot go. They cannot interfere with His designs, nor destroy His work. He controls all their acts for His glory, and out of seeming evil He brings forth abundant salvation."

John Taylor, Messages of the First Presidency, Vol. 3, p. 48-49, March 1886.

"We scarcely need remind you that if you live godly in Christ Jesus, while Satan has power, you will suffer persecution. In the providence of the Almighty persecution serves a most useful purpose. Every faithful Saint must perceive and acknowledge this. Each one feels its effect upon himself; he sees its effect upon his friends and neighbors. Persecution develops character. Under its influence we all know ourselves better than we did before we felt its pressure; and we discover traits in our brethren and sisters of the existence of which, perhaps, we were in entire ignorance. The persecution from which we have been suffering . . . though very painful, has not been without profit to the Latter-day Saints. It has strengthened and infused new zeal, courage and determination into the faithful. It has also caused many who were careless and indifferent to arouse themselves from their lethargy and to renew their diligence in the work of God. It has also brought to light the hypocrisy of many, and caused them to throw off the mask of friendship and fellowship which they wore, and to exhibit themselves in their true lineaments. But it is upon the young of our community that the effect of this persecution has been most marked. Many of the young of both sexes, when all was peace and no war was made upon their parents and friends seemed to be of the opinion that they could, without any danger to themselves or their faith, be in full fellowship with the world. . . .

We need not say to you . . . how fallacious are these hopes of our present persecutors. Instead of crushing the truth they are advertising it; instead of showing the world how unworthy and contemptible we are, they are, unwittingly, furnishing us with opportunities to exhibit the heroic qualities we possess; instead of weakening or unsettling the minds of true Latter-day Saints, they are stimulating their faith and supplying them with additional proofs of the divinity of their religion."

John Taylor, Messages of the First Presidency, Vol. 3, p. 99-100, October 26, 1886.

"If we meet with no persecution in our day, we shall hardly feel at home when we go into the spirit world and meet with the ancient prophets and with Christ and the Apostles, who passed through much persecution and tribulation."

John Taylor, Messages of the First Presidency, Vol. 3, p. 127-128.

"If we are persecuted for our religion, it is no more than we have been taught to expect. . . We need not, therefore, be surprised nor disappointed when persecution comes."

John Taylor, Journal of Discourses, Vol. 17, p. 372, April 8, 1875.

"Jesus preached the Gospel. Was it right? Yes. Why did it not continue? I do not know, but it did not continue, and the Prophets said it would not, and one of them prophesied that a certain power would seek to make war with the Saints of God, and that it would prevail against them, and that they would be given into his hands until a time, and times, and the dividing of a time."

John Taylor, Journal of Discourses, Vol. 23, p. 33-36, March 5, 1882.

"Our course is onward; and are we going to stop? No. Zion must be built up, God has decreed it and no power can stay its progress. Do you hear that? I prophecy that in the name of the Lord Jesus Christ. For Zion must and will be built up despite all opposition, the kingdom of God established upon the earth in accordance with the designs and purposes of God. That is true, and you will find it to be true if you live long enough, and if you die you will find it to be true; it will make no difference. 'But shall we not be persecuted?' Yes, and does not Jesus say, Blessed are ye when men revile you and persecute you, etc.,—would you be deprived of that blessing. 'But we have had enough of it.' O, have you? no matter, you will have to put up with it. 'But,' say you, 'have we not certain constitutional rights?' Yes, on paper, but when you get through with them, the paper does not amount to much; it is like pie-crust, easily broken. We do not pay much attention to these things. Honorable men will be governed by constitutions, and laws, and principles, but dishonorable persons will not. Therefore, we have to do the best we can, taking a righteous course that we may be entitled to the blessings of God."

John Taylor, Journal of Discourses, Vol. 25, p. 95-96, February 10, 1884.

"Let us maintain the Constitution of this government. It was ordained of God, and if wicked and corrupt men do wrong, and administer improperly and unrighteously, God will deal with them. We need not rail and rant and get up a commotion about them. We do not cherish any ill-will or ill-feelings, but they would not like it to be said that they are doing the works of their father, the devil: but that is what Jesus said about people of the same kind in His day. We need not be angry with them. Jesus, at the very last, even when hanging on the cross and expiring, said, as it were with His last breath, 'Father, forgive them, for they know not what they do.' Neither do they in this day. But we are the children of the light. Let us walk in the light, and be governed by the principles of truth and righteousness, virtue and honor, and seek to cleave to God in our bodies and in our spirits, which are His. If the Latter-day Saints throughout the land of Zion, would only fear God and work righteousness, there is not a power on this side of hell, or the other side either, that could harm them; for God will carry out His work and His purposes, and if He suffers us, at any time to be chastened, it will be for our good; but Zion will triumph, and the Kingdom of God will roll forth, and no man shall stop its progress from this time, henceforth and forever, in the name of Jesus. Amen."

John Taylor, Journal of Discourses, Vol. 25, p. 215-217, June 29, 1884.

"We need not trouble our heads about any of these matters; there is an overruling Providence that controls the affairs of men and nations. So you can rest perfectly easy, you Latter-day Saints. We shall continue to do right. We will continue to sustain good principle. And what will you do? Just what Jesus said. We will do good for evil. What else? We will pray for them that despitefully use us and evilly treat us. Why? That we may be the children of our Heavenly Father, and act on the same principle that He does towards the human family. Does He act in that way? Yes. For he maketh His sun to rise on the evil and on the good, and sendeth His rain on the just and on the unjust. He has introduced certain laws into the system of His government that regulates all things pertaining to these matters. He does not make those little divisions that the United States are trying to make today. He is more philantropic. He treats all alike, and places all on the same basis. Then, we will try and operate with Him and for Him, and in the interests of humanity, and in the protection of human rights, and we will try by every legal and constitutional method to maintain and sustain the principles of human rights in behalf of ourselves, in behalf of our children, and in behalf of thousands and tens of thousands of honorable men that live in these United States. We can very well afford to abide by the Constitution of the United States, and to sustain it, and we can afford to believe in the Bible and to obey its ordinances, and practice them, which they cannot do, and do not do. As I have said, we can afford to treat all men well, and to pray for those which despitefully use us and persecute us."

John Taylor, The Government of God, Chapter 9.

"Where has God ever had a people but they have been persecuted? The testimony of God has always been rejected, and his people trodden under foot. Paul tells us that they 'were tempted, tried, sawn asunder, that they wandered about in sheep skins, and goat skins, being destitute, afflicted, and tormented.' (Heb. 11:37.) And to such an extent had this prevailed among the ancient Jews, that Stephen gravely asks the question, 'Which of the prophets have not your fathers persecuted? and they have slain them, which shewed before, the coming of the Just One, of whom ye have been now the betrayers and murderers.' (Acts 7:52.) What did they do with Jesus! and what with his followers! We may here ask, Is it right, is it proper, is it just, for this state of things to continue? It is true that the saints have had a hope of joys to come, and this state of trial has been permitted for their ultimate good; but although this is the case, it does not make the thing the more just. 'It must needs be,' says Jesus, 'that offenses come, but woe to that man by whom the offence cometh'."

Wilford Woodruff, Journal of Discourses, Vol. 7, p. 105, January 10, 1858.

"The more I look at the words which the Lord has spoken concerning our enemies, and especially those of this nation, the more I become satisfied that they will not escape the judgments of the Almighty, any more than the Nephites of old did, or any of the other nations who have rejected the message sent unto them by the God of heaven."

Wilford Woodruff, Journal of Discourses, Vol. 18, p. 115-116, September 12, 1875.

"But what do we see today? What do the Gods, the heavens and all eternity see? They see a generation of men and women making war against God and his Christ, making war against Prophets and Apostles, and laboring night and day to overpower and annihilate every principle of salvation and eternal life which God has restored to the world. And I will here say, in the ears of this congregation, that were this not the dispensation of the fullness of times, and were it not for the decrees which the Lord has made in relation to it, one of which is that he will set up a kingdom which shall stand for ever, there is not an Apostle or Latter-day Saint on the face of the earth but would have to seal his testimony with his blood, as has almost every other Apostle that ever breathed the breath of life. I say that were it not for these things, we should all have to follow our leaders, Joseph and Hyrum Smith, who laid down their lives for the word of God, and the testimony of Jesus Christ. But hear it ye Gentile nations and all ye nations of the earth, the Lord Almighty has set to his hand to build up his kingdom on the earth, and he will not be thwarted. The Lord is going to make a short work in the earth, and he will defend his anointed, his Prophets, his Zion and his people. This is the decree of Almighty God."

Wilford Woodruff, Journal of Discourses, Vol. 21, p. 192-193, July 3, 1880.

"And who are these Latter-day Saints? They are the people whom the God of heaven has raised up in fulfillment of promise and revelation. He has carefully gathered them together by the power of the Gospel, by the power of revelation, and placed them here in the valleys of the mountains. Has there ever been any power formed against this people that has been successful? Nay; and this people will never see the day when our enemies shall prevail, for the very reason that God had decreed that Zion shall be built up; the kingdom that Daniel saw shall roll forth, until the little stone cut out of the mountain without hands shall fill the whole earth. The people of God shall be prepared in the Latter-days to carry out the great programme of the Almighty, and all the powers of the earth and hell combined cannot prevent them. When I see the view that the world take in regard to this great latter-day work; when I hear it questioned as to whether God has anything to do with it; when I see the feeling of hatred that is manifested towards us, to me it is the strongest evidence that this is the work of God. Why? Because we have been chosen out of the world and therefore the world hate us. This is a testimony that Jew and Gentile and the whole world look at. Then if this is the work of God what is the world going to do about it? What can this nation or the combined nations of the earth do about it? Can any power beneath the heavens stay the progress of the work of God? I tell you nay, it cannot be done. I do not boast of these things as the work of man; it is the work of the Almighty; it is not the work of man."

Wilford Woodruff, Journal of Discourses, Vol. 23, p. 130, May 14, 1882.

"The Lord Almighty has set His hand to gather His people, and to build up his Zion and to establish his Church in these the last days; and the world do not like the doctrine we teach, as it lays the axe at the root of the tree, and consequently we have been persecuted from the time that this Church was organized until today; and the persecution will continue more or less until He reigns whose right it is to reign, until the Lord Jesus Christ comes in the clouds of heaven to reward every man according to the deeds done in the body."

Wilford Woodruff, Journal of Discourses, Vol. 23, p. 326-328, December 10, 1882.
"And while we sometimes feel and have felt in days that are past and gone, to complain because we meet with oppression, persecution and affliction, yet I wish to say to my brethren and sisters that these things are the heritage of the Saints of God. Any people whom God calls will meet with opposition from those who will not receive the Gospel of Jesus Christ. This has been the legacy of the Saints of God in every age from Father Adam down to our own day. Those that live godly in Christ Jesus must suffer persecution. I believe myself, from the reading of the revelations of God, that it is necessary for a people who are destined to inherit the celestial kingdom to be a tried people."

Wilford Woodruff, Collected Discourses, Vol. 2, April 6, 1890.
"As to persecution, all men who live godly in Christ Jesus suffer persecution. Why this combination by priest and people against Joseph Smith, an illiterate boy, as soon as he was administered to by the angels of God? Why did he wade in deep waters up to the day of his death? Why did he pass through forty or fifty vexatious lawsuits? Because he was a servant of God and warned the inhabitants of the earth of the judgments that were to come. So it has been with all who have followed him. If this people were not the people of God, you would not see a combination of the inhabitants of the earth for our destruction. Are these Latter-day Saints all the sinners there are in the world? If they are, I tell you the inhabitants of the earth are in a good condition. But it is not so. We sin enough, it is true; perhaps too much; we are guilty of a good many things, probably, that we ought to repent of; I have no doubt there should be a reformation among us in some things; we do not pray as much as we ought to; but we are not so bad as the world call us by any means."

The Discourses of Wilford Woodruff, p. 101-102.
"It is true that the elders who are called to bear record of the gospel of Christ to the nations of the earth are many times called to pass through persecution for the gospel's sake, and in some instances to lay down their lives, as did the ancient Saints, and quite a number in our day, for Christ's sake. But there seems to be a special crown of glory, laid up for every man who is martyred for Christ's sake and the gospel's. No matter in what age of the world he lays down his life for Christ's sake, he will find it again, and eternal life in the world to come."

Teachings of Lorenzo Snow, p. 176.
"The Church does not fight its enemies. It is not our business to fight our enemies. There is no man or woman on the face of the earth, but is our brother or our sister. They are the children of God and we are here to bear and forbear with them in their interest and for the glory of God. It is not our business to destroy life. It is not our business to make war upon our enemies. They should let us alone. I would not say that I could govern and control my passions if a man were to try to take my life. That is another thing altogether. But it is not our business to fight them. They are our brethren

170

and sisters and God have mercy upon them. That should be our prayer. (CR, October 7, 1899, p. 28-29.)"

Erastus Snow, Journal of Discourses, Vol. 23, p. 187-188, May 6, 1882.

"Understanding this as we understand them, we do not wonder at this class of persons combining with the powers of earth to throw stumbling blocks in the way of this community. But will the Lord suffer them to bring persecution upon us? Peradventure he may; and he will if it is necessary to prune the vineyard, to cleanse his people from sin, to purge out evil and frighten away the hypocrites in Zion; for it has been decreed that fearfulness shall surprise the hypocrites in Zion; and if he suffers the wicked to combine against us, he will overrule it for the salvation of the righteous."

Franklin D. Richards, Journal of Discourses, Vol. 26, p. 255, April 6, 1885.

"I want to have us consider these things; and instead of being anxious and worried, troubled and filled with fear, learn to rely upon the arm of the Lord and trust Him for His goodness; cultivate the peace of heaven and let the love of God dwell in our hearts. Though our enemies may harass, trouble, and disturb us; the trouble that they will bring upon us will be but as a drop in the bucket compared with what will come upon them by and by. They cannot stop the work of God. His decree has established it. We have the promise that it never shall be overthrown or given to another people."

Franklin D. Richards, Collected Discourses, Vol. 1, April 7, 1886.

"The great boon to the human family is peace. Notwithstanding they want us to become like them, they cannot give us peace. And although we may be harassed, persecuted and deprived of our rights and liberties as citizens of this great nation, let me tell you that we all have a peace of mind such as they know nothing at all about—the peace of God that passeth understanding, which is the Comforter, the Holy Ghost."

Daniel H. Wells, Journal of Discourses, Vol. 19, p. 369, June 1, 1878.

"There is an opposition to the Lord having on the earth a people, called by his name and doing his will. It has been so from the beginning. The Lord never had a people who were received with open arms by the world, admired, cherished and respected; on the contrary they have been persecuted or totally destroyed from off the earth. The wicked have invariably prevailed over the good; it might almost be said that the first bad man killed the first good man. The Latter-day Saints have had the same experience to pass through, and when a time of comparative peace has come around, as it has sometimes, they are apt to ask, 'What is the matter? Have we lost our faith, that the Adversary should thus let us alone?' There will come a time, however, in the history of the Saints, when they will be tried with peace, prosperity, popularity and riches."

George Q. Cannon, Journal of Discourses, Vol. 11, p. 230-231, May 6, 1866.

"In suggesting to men to shed the blood of Jesus Christ, and the blood of innocence in every dispensation and age when God has had a people on the earth the devil has shown great ignorance and blindness, and God has, through his superior wisdom and power, overruled all these acts for his own glory, and for the accomplishment of his own purposes and the salvation of man upon the earth.

171

We shall have his hatred to meet, and no man need suppose for a moment that Latter-day Saints can avoid it, for in so doing he deceives himself. As long as there is any power on the earth that can be wielded by Satan we shall have to encounter these things and contend with them; and any man not connected with us who imagines that this continued and unceasing warfare is going to discourage us, or cause our determination to roll forth the kingdom of God to slacken in the least, deceives himself. He knows not the men who are engaged in this work, and the power which God has bestowed, and the light and intelligence he has imparted to us respecting this conflict in which we are engaged. God has reserved spirits for this dispensation who have the courage and determination to face the world, and all the powers of the evil one, visible and invisible to proclaim the Gospel, and maintain the truth, and establish and build up the Zion of our God, fearless of all consequences. He has sent these spirits in this generation to lay the foundation of Zion never more to be overthrown, and to raise up a seed that will be righteous, and that will honor God, and honor him supremely, and be obedient to him under all circumstances. The experience that we have gained in this respect in the past is only a foretaste of that which is in the future. Those who started in this Work with an understanding of its nature, made their calculations that, if it were necessary to lay down their lives and sacrifice everything that is near and dear to them, they with the Lord's help, would do so to break the yoke of Satan and free mankind from the thraldom of sin that has so long oppressed them. There is no doubt that many have had their lives shortened through the cruelty of their enemies; many have been spoiled of their goods and have been called upon to make sacrifices, if we may term them such, but in our view they are not sacrifices, yet we cannot express the idea better than by using this word. The difficulties which we have encountered in the past in this respect we shall doubtless meet in the future, with this difference, that the kingdom of God is gaining power and strength; the people are gaining faith and experience, which enable them to endure far more than in former days."

George Q. Cannon, Journal of Discourses, Vol. 23, p. 99-100, November 20, 1881.
"In this way God has built up this Church. It did not, as we have often heard, depend upon one man. Men thought if they killed Joseph Smith they would destroy the keystone; that his existence was the means of upholding the work and giving it solidity. But he was killed, and still the work prospered, and it will prosper if every man that is now in position in the Church should be killed or should die. The testimony of Jesus is in the hearts of the people. You travel throughout the Territory, and call the people together and ask them: 'What influence brought you here?' Every one who is an adult, and has retained the faith, will tell you that it was the Spirit and power of God. No other influence nor power could have done this but that. Well, now, men will fight it, men are fighting it. It is strange today to see people who call themselves religious, advocating all manner of means to be brought against this people to destroy them. To shed their blood is thought to be justifiable; the killing of people in order to destroy an organization that they think is so full of menace; and yet we are told in the Bible—and we have been taught it from childhood, that the righteous never persecute the wicked, but it has always been the case that the wicked persecute the righteous; and we are told by the Savior himself that his followers should be hated of all men, and that men in seeking to kill them would think they were doing God's service. It was not the Apostles of Jesus who persecuted the wicked, it was not the righteous who hated them and who sought their destruction. There were no petitions went out from the humble followers of Christ against the Pharisees and against the

religious sects of that day to have them destroyed, to have governmental aid to assist them in extirpating their heresies; nothing of this kind has ever been witnessed, but here we find today the professedly righteous, the ministers, advocating the most dreadful measures."

George Q. Cannon, Journal of Discourses, Vol. 23, p. 273-274, October 8, 1882.

"A great many of our brethren and sisters have thought, and may still think, that we are likely to see very hard times, as the result of the attacks now being made upon us. The hearts of some may almost fail them in looking forward to the future, anticipating that there will be such intense hatred and such active exertions made against us that it will be very difficult for us to sustain ourselves. No doubt we shall have all we can endure. No doubt the Lord will require us to pass through and endure ordeals that will test our faith to the uttermost, and it will seem at times as though we were about to be overwhelmed. The powers of darkness will gather around us and everything will look so threatening, so black and so impenetrable, that except to those who look at these things with the eye of faith, it will seem almost impossible for us to escape. There will be, doubtless, many such hours and many such times in our history in the future as there have been in the past. But what of that? As the trial may be, so will be the strength to endure it. There is a wise desire of the Lord our God in permitting these tests to our faith, to see whether in the midst of gloomy and threatening surroundings we shall falter, shall shrink and become timid and be overcome, or whether in the midst of this gloom, in the midst of these forbidding appearances, our faith will still be strong in our God, and in the promises, the precious promises, which He has made to us."

George Q. Cannon, Journal of Discourses, Vol. 24, p. 362-365, December 2, 1883.

"As a servant of God I am willing to stake my reputation in making this statement, that if you will listen to the voice of God as manifested through His servant who stands at our head, you never will, from this time forward until eternity dawns upon you, you never will be overcome by your enemies or by the enemies of God's Kingdom."

George Q. Cannon, Journal of Discourses, Vol. 25, p. 26-27, January 6, 1884.

"Every kind of opposition will be brought against this work. There is nothing that you can conceive of that will be kept back, and it will come upon us as fast as we are able to bear it. It is only the power of God that restrains our enemies from overwhelming us. If it were not that God has said this shall not be, and has told us that He will establish this work never more to be thrown down, we would not be able to stand. But victory will perch upon our banners, and will do so until the end. But it will not be without a mighty warfare, the hostility against this work will be continuous. No man need calculate on anything else. Why, just think of the results that are to be wrought out. Just think of what depends upon our labors and upon this contest? . . .

Every power that is conceivable is brought to bear against us. We are maligned. We are represented as everything that is vile. Men think that in killing us they will be doing God service; not because of our wickedness, but because they believe we were wicked, because the adversary has had such power through falsehood and misrepresentation, that men believe that they will be doing God Service in exterminating us from the face of the earth. And what is it that restrains the efforts of our enemies? It is the power of God only. We should be overwhelmed if it were not for this invisible agency—invisible to us. There are legions of angels around us. Their power is exerted in our behalf, and the results we can see in the deliverances which are wrought out so miraculously for our good. It is a cause of amazement how we are delivered from time to time, so few in numbers, and so hated as we are. Our friends are filled with astonishment. Every few days, every few weeks, or every few months, they think that something is going to occur, that will cause our destruction—I mean friends who have not the faith and the knowledge that we have. But this work of our God will go forth, despite all the opposition that will be brought against it. It will win, because it is true. As we have been told by Brother Woodruff, the eternal principles of truth are on the earth now in an organized form, and you cannot kill them unless you kill the people themselves. There is no way to stop this work, except by the extermination of the 'Mormons,' or Latter-day Saints, root and branch! No other method can destroy them but that, and God will not permit it. His Priesthood is on the earth, and it will remain on the earth. You may kill off a few, still the Priesthood will remain, and it will exercise power in the earth. It will unite the people, an the power of God will attend its administration in the midst of the people. The honest will receive the Holy Ghost, they will have a knowledge of this work for themselves, and they will be ready to endure all the consequences that may attend the espousal of the truth, just as their predecessors have done in times that are past and in our own age. God will bless us if we seek to do His will. Remember, my brethren and sisters, that that which obeys law is preserved and sanctified by law. If you want to escape evils, obey the law that God has revealed. Keep His commandments. There is safety in this. It is a great work we are engaged in."

George Q. Cannon, Journal of Discourses, Vol. 25, p. 276, August 24, 1884.

"It is not a new thing in the history of the work of the last days for the blood of innocence to be shed; but the frequency of these occurrences does not take away from the anguish and the sorrow, and those poignant feelings that are created by such atrocious acts. We cannot become reconciled to these things sufficiently, fortify ourselves as we may, to escape feeling upon occasions of this character that we are all liable at any time to be called to lay down our lives for the truth's sake. Whenever our brethren are thus called as sacrifices for the truth, it requires the comforting influence and strength which God alone can give to reconcile us, so that we can bear these blows with equanimity and with the resignation which should characterize people of our profession."

George Q. Cannon, Journal of Discourses, Vol. 26, p. 283-284, November 23, 1884.

"My brethren and sisters: we can rejoice exceedingly in the prospects before us. We may be hated as our brethren have described; we may be maligned and calumniated and called all manner of evil names; but with all these things we can rejoice, because it is the legacy that was left to us and left to every follower of Jesus Christ by himself when he was upon the earth. He that lives godly in Christ Jesus, Paul says, shall suffer persecution. He did not say that they might suffer it—He did not put it in a doubtful manner—but He said they should suffer—'they shall suffer persecution.' We have proved the truth of that saying of the Apostle's. But notwithstanding all this, we can look around us, and see what God is doing for us. We have the most abundant causes for thanksgiving and praise. He is blessing us as no other people today upon the face of the earth are being blessed."

George Q. Cannon, Collected Discourses, Vol. 1, April 8, 1889.

"Satan intends or has intended persecution to destroy the work of God. But instead of that it becomes a means of developing His work. It has the effect of purifying the people; it has the effect of giving them a knowledge concerning the work in which they are engaged. It tests them and develops their character, and gives them opportunities of exhibiting unto the Lord and to their fellow men the kind of characters they are. . .It is most important, indeed, that we should know ourselves, that we should become familiar with the peculiarities of our own natures, that we may see our weaknesses, and so be able by the help of the Lord to correct them. I therefore feel gratified that the Lord has permitted these things. I do not know what would become of us if we had nothing but prosperity. Suppose Satan did not persecute us—that there was no opposition to us—would we be tested? Would we be the people that we are today if we had no afflictions, no persecutions, no ordeals to endure, no temptations to resist. Certainly not. Prosperity would not develop us."

George Q. Cannon, Collected Discourses, Vol. 1, October 6, 1889.

"I know that notwithstanding all our trials, notwithstanding all that we have to contend with, there is no enemy of ours, there is no combination of enemies of ours, whose happiness compares in the least degree with the joy and with the happiness that the Latter-day Saints have in their possession. "

George Q. Cannon, Collected Discourses, Vol. 2, February 23, 1890.

"The reason we are hated today is because of these very things. If we would be like the rest of the world we would have no opposition from the world. Jesus said to His disciples, 'If ye were of the world, the world would love his own: but because ye are not of the world, but I have chosen you out of the world, therefore the world hateth you.' It is just the same today. If we were like the world the world would love us; but because God has chosen us out of the world, therefore the world hates us; and we shall be hated as long as we preserve these virtues and contend for them, as long as we refuse to partake of the cup of fornications which the mother of abominations holds out to us; as long as we refuse to have the mark of the beast upon us, so long shall we have this opposition to contend with, until Babylon is overthrown and destroyed from the face of the earth—a consummation that is not very far distant. If we would drink of that cup which that great mother of abominations holds in her hands opposition would cease, for we would then be like them, we would be of them. But while we stand firm and steadfast ... you may depend upon it, the world will have no love for us."

Joseph F. Smith, Messages of the First Presidency, Vol. 4, p. 169.

"To emphasize this we feel justified in saying that the time has been in our experience as a Church and is now, we very much regret to say, when certain secret societies have used, and are using their influence against us; and we have no assurance whatever that the time will never come when they will not combine their influence against us, and thereby bring home, and make plain that most significant saying of our Lord and Master, He who is not for us, is against us; for without doubt the time will ultimately come when every man-made institution will be arrayed against the Church and Kingdom of God—the only institution of divine origin on the earth, and the only institution that will stand and remain unmoved, while all others will fall, disintegrate and decay."

Joseph F. Smith, Journal of Discourses, Vol. 18, p. 89-90, October 6, 1875.

"At no time in the history of this Church has the hand of the Lord been withdrawn from this people, his power shortened, or his eye slept, but his eye has been upon us, his hand has been over us, and his providences have been in our favor. Circumstances have been over-ruled for good, the hand of the enemy has been turned away paralyzed, the efforts of the wicked to destroy us have resulted in our good and in their own discomfiture. The greater the efforts on the part of our enemies to destroy us, the greater the growth of the Church and kingdom of God, and the closer has our union been, the better have we been able to see the hand of the Lord over us, and the inspiration of the Almighty in the counsels of his servants, and the more have we been inclined to respect and abide by the counsels given. The very fact that the spirit of bitterness in the hearts of the wicked toward us at the present time is as virulent as it ever was, and is every way similar to that manifested against the former-day Saints, against the Savior when he was upon the earth, and against his disciples, or the people of God in any former age of the world, is an unmistakable evidence that the Lord God Almighty is with us today as much as he ever was since the organization of the Church, or as much as he ever was with any people he ever acknowledged as his since the world began. I do not believe there ever was a people who were guided by revelation, or acknowledged of the Lord as his people, that were not hated and persecuted by the wicked and the corrupt, and perhaps no people were ever more persecuted than this people would be, if it were in the power of the enemy today to persecute us, as it was in the power of Nero and the Romans to persecute the Saints in their day. There never was a time when it was more fixed and determined in the heart of the wicked to fight against, and destroy the kingdom from the earth, than now, and their failure will be due only to the impossibility of the task they have undertaken. And this is an evidence to every one that possesses the least spark of the light of the Holy Spirit—and should be to all mankind—that the kingdom of God is established, that his Priesthood is here, and that the Saints, or many of them, are magnifying their calling and honoring the Priesthood, and also the Lord, both with their lives and with their substance, which are his.

For my part I do not fear the influence of our enemies from without, as I fear that of those from within. An open and avowed enemy, whom we may see and meet in an open field, is far less to be feared than a lurking, deceitful, treacherous enemy hidden within us, such as are many of the weaknesses of our fallen human nature, which are too often allowed to go unchecked, beclouding our minds, leading away our affections from God and his truth, until they sap the very foundation of our faith and debase us beyond the possibility or hope of redemption either in this world or that to come. These are the enemies that we all have to battle with, they are the greatest that we have to contend with in the world, and the most difficult to conquer. They are the fruits of ignorance, generally arising out of unrebuked sin and evil in our own hearts. The labor that is upon us, is to subdue our passions, conquer our inward foes, and see that our hearts are right in the sight of the Lord, that there is nothing calculated to grieve his Spirit and lead us away from the path of duty."

Joseph F. Smith, Journal of Discourses, Vol. 19, p. 26-27, April 2, 1877.

"It is a consolation therefore to know, that, notwithstanding our many shortcomings, frailties, and imperfections, the Evil one, with the world at his back, considers us of sufficient importance to oppose and persecute us with such bitter hatred as he does. Yes, I say it is encouraging to know, that, as a people we are sufficiently faithful and worthy before the Lord, notwithstanding our opportunities for improvement, to arouse the indignation and hatred of the wicked, and to entitle us to the chastisement of God, through his servants, for our improprieties, for 'whomsoever the Lord loveth he chasteneth.' But we should not provoke the displeasure or incur the chastisement of the Almighty—presuming upon his forbearance and mercy by neglecting to perform those duties and responsibilities so justly required of us—but we should be most diligent, putting forth every energy in our power to correct our ways, and thus increase our faith that we may become more worthy of the blessings and protection of God, than hitherto."

Joseph F. Smith, Journal of Discourses, Vol. 23, p. 283-285, October 7, 1882.

"Jesus taught the doctrine that we should pray for those that despitefully use us; that we should love our enemies; that we should do good to them that do evil to us; that we should not return evil for evil, but good for evil. There is no particular credit due to any person who returns good for good. Even the publicans and sinners did this, but it is somewhat difficult to return good for evil. Nevertheless to do so was enjoined by the commandments of the Lord Jesus. We are to love our enemies; do good to them that hate and persecute us; and when we are persecuted, persecute not again; when we are derided, deride not in return; if we are injured, seek not to injure those who injure us; that which is required at our hands is to establish peace on earth and good will to man. Hence, when we forget the object of our calling and step out of the path of duty to return blow for blow, to inflict evil for evil, to persecute because we may be persecuted, we forget the injunction of the Lord and the covenants we have made with God, to keep His commandments. It is a difficult matter, I am aware, for human nature to become subject to these scriptural injunctions. It is difficult for men to curb their passions, to restrain their feelings, and to resist the temptation to rebel and administer measure for measure, but it is enjoined upon us. We have been actually commanded in the revelations given to us in this dispensation to forgive our enemies, without their asking forgiveness. It is laid down that if your enemies come up against you to destroy you, the first time, if the Lord delivers you out of their hands, you shall forgive them; and if they come the second time, you shall forgive them; and if they come the third time against you, the Lord has said they are then in your hands to do with them whatsoever you will; but it will redound to your honor, credit and glory if you forgive them the third time, even if they have not repented and have not asked forgiveness. Now this may seem to be rather a difficult requirement; nevertheless it is so written and is so required of the Latter-day Saints. But how often shall we forgive them if they repent of their sins and ask forgiveness? Jesus has laid down the law that we should forgive them as often as they will repent and ask forgiveness. I am speaking now of individual trespasses; of people who offend me or you or trespass against us; I am not speaking of those who trespass against the immutable, the righteous and the holy laws of God; they come under another law, and God and His servants will reckon with them. It is for us to obtain the spirit of forgiveness, to feel to love those that are so ignorant as to do evil to their fellow-creatures without a cause; we should feel as Christ felt, when upon the cross. He said, 'Father, forgive them, for they know not what they do.' It was urged yesterday by one of the brethren, that we could scarcely claim this for many of those who were engaged in persecuting the Saints today, for they do know what they are doing, and they are not ignorant of the course that they are pursuing. They are in a position to learn the truth, if they would, and to comprehend the fact that they are lying about us. Yet how do we feel towards them for this offence? Do we feel that we should retaliate? Do we feel that we should execute vengeance upon them because we know that they are telling falsehoods, and are misrepresenting and slandering the people of this Church? No. For years and years we have sat quietly down and listened to their abuse, insults, slanders, misrepresentations and falsehoods, which they have spread broadcast throughout the land to the utmost of their power, and no man has so much as said, 'Why do you so?' They enjoy the utmost liberty to lie and slander and go to the fullest extent of their power to accomplish their wicked and nefarious desires and purposes, and we are willing to risk the judgment of God in these matters in His own due time. We do not propose to keep ourselves eternally in hot water, wrangling, contending and snarling with our enemies; if we did we should soon become as sour, as vicious, as foul, as low and as contemptible as they are themselves. Well, do you love them? Now here is the rub! Do you love these slanderers, these liars, these defamers, these persecutors of the innocent and of the unoffending—do you love them? [several voices, No, no.] I can scarcely blame you. [Laughter.] But that is not according to the law of God. I want to tell you how I feel towards them. I love them so much that if I had it in my power to annihilate them from the earth I would not harm a hair of their heads—not one hair of their heads. I love them so well that if I could possibly make them better men, convert them from the error of their ways I would do it, God being my helper. I love them so much that I would not throw a straw in their way to prosperity and happiness, but so far as possible I would hedge up their headlong and downward course to destruction, and yet I detest and abominate their infamous actions and their wicked course. That is how I feel towards them, and that is how much I love them, and if this is not the love that Jesus desired us to have for our enemies, tell me what kind of love we should have for them? I do not love them so that I would take them into my bosom, or invite them to associate with my family, or that I would give my daughters to their embraces, nor my sons to their counsels. I do not love them so well that I would invite them to the councils of the Priesthood, and the ordinances of the House of God, to scoff and jeer at sacred things which they do not understand, nor would I share with them the inheritance that God, my Father, has given me in Zion; I do not love them well enough for this, and I do not believe that God ever designed that I should; but I love them so much that I would not hurt them, I would do them good, I would tell the truth about them, I would benefit them if it was in my power, and I would keep them to the utmost of my ability from doing harm to themselves and to their neighbors. I love them that much; but I do not love them with that affection with which I love my wife, my brother, my sister or my friend. There is a difference between the love we should bear towards our enemies and that we should bear towards our friends. Do not say that it is hatred of our enemies when we would keep them from hurting themselves and their neighbors, do not call that hatred, that is love for them. If it were possible to find one of this class of people who had been deceived, and who had slandered the Saints of God ignorantly, as Paul did, and we could prevail upon him to repent of his sins, to turn away from wickedness, and to acknowledge God and His laws, then we should love him as a brother, as a friend, and as a neighbor. That would be the difference. But we do not love to associate with our enemies, and I do not think the Lord requires us to do it. If He does He will have to reveal it, for I cannot find it anywhere revealed. I have never read it in any of the books, I have never heard it taught that we are to love our enemies so much as to become like them, or condescend to their vile and contemptible

178

ways, or as to share the inheritance God has given us with them, or as to suppose for a moment that the wicked and the ungodly will ever inherit the kingdom of God, or enter into His presence, or enjoy the society, blessing and award of the faithful; they never will, they cannot, for they are not worthy; they have not obeyed the law and therefore cannot receive the blessing thereof."

Moses Thatcher, Journal of Discourses, Vol. 25, p. 280-282, August 24, 1884.
"As for the dead all is well with them—that is, with the brethren who have sealed their testimony with their blood. You have heard what will be their glory, and to that testimony I will add mine. When we clearly understand, by the light of the Spirit of God, what martyrs for the truth will receive, death fails to create fear in our minds. . . .

I remember distinctly the impressions that were made upon the minds of some of our people when they first learned of the organization of certain secret societies in the east, organized with the intention, no doubt, of taking life; and it is my strong belief and my firm opinion that the body which lies before us today, lifeless, is the result of the operations of the secret societies which, we have been forewarned, would be organized in the latter times. It may be that others will be called to wear the crowns of martyrs. Certainly that passage of Scripture which was read in our hearing today, would lead us so to think. But what matters it to us? We have received the testimony of Jesus. We have received the light of the everlasting Gospel. We have received that which will give us influence and power and dominion and glory and endless happiness. Why, then, should we care for the lengthening or shortening of our days here in this mortal condition."

Rudger Clawson, Collected Discourses, Vol. 5, April 6, 1888.
"If the Gospel of Christ is worth anything to us it is worth everything, and there is no sacrifice we can make that will compensate for the loss of the glorious promises which have been made unto this people. Ought we to be willing to suffer persecution? Certainly. Ought we to be willing to go to prison for the truth? Most assuredly. By going to prison for a time we may lose our liberty, lose the privilege of citizenship, lose the association of our family and friends; but the truth for which we are suffering will, in the end, not only restore these privileges, but exalt us in the Kingdom of God. Ought we to be willing to suffer death for the Gospel of Christ if necessary? Yes, without hesitation. We should be willing at all times to meet every emergency that presents itself, and if these sentiments do not prevail in our souls we are not fit subjects for the Kingdom of God."

Hyrum M. Smith , Doctrine and Covenants Commentary, Sec. 120, p. 752.
"The repeated mobbings and drivings of the Latter-day Saints were a severe discipline, but they served a great purpose in God's plan. While the Saints were prosperous, many hypocrites joined the Church. They were the chaff. The blasts of adversity blew these to the four winds, and only the good wheat remained. The Church was purified by persecution."

George Albert Smith, Journal of Discourses, Vol. 6, p. 364, July 4, 1854.
"Persons present to-day may consider that no other country in the world would have allowed the persecutions and oppressions that have fallen upon the work of God in this land, of which many of you have been partakers. But in this you are mistaken; for there is no nation under heaven among

whom the kingdom of God could have been established and rolled forth with as little opposition as it has received in the United States. Every species of oppression and opposition, which has aimed at the destruction of the lives and liberties of the members of this Church, has been in open violation of the laws of the country; while, among other nations, the links of the chain of government are so formed that the very constitution and laws of the country would oppose the government of God. This is the case almost without an exception."

David O. McKay, Gospel Ideals, p. 308-309.

"The Church is little if at all injured by persecution and calumnies from ignorant, misinformed, or malicious enemies; a greater hindrance to its progress comes from faultfinders, shirkers, commandment breakers, and apostate cliques within its own ecclesiastical and quorum groups."

Orson F. Whitney, Collected Discourses, Vol. 5, May 8, 1898.

"The Prophet then told him, 'You yourself will yet see the day when you will pity these very men who are inflicting these injuries upon you. God has shown to me in vision the sufferings of the ungodly, and I had to pray to Him to close the vision when I saw the terrible judgments that would come upon the wicked.' The Prophet taught the principle of patient submission to wrong. And it is this that lifts men up above other men. When men injure us they put themselves in our debt, and that debt remains until we cancel it by an act of retaliation.

But men will say, as I have heard them say, 'Why, if I should return good for evil to this or that person, he would not appreciate my motive; he would think I was soft, foolish, that I was truckling, and that I meant it as an acknowledgement that he was right and I was wrong and had deserved all that he had done.' What if he should think so? What if some men's souls are so limited that they cannot appreciate a magnanimous act? It is not for the effect upon them alone that you are taught to practice the golden rule; it is for the effect upon yourself. You cannot grow if you hate mankind. You cannot increase and expand, at least as rapidly as you might, if you cherish feelings of anger, jealousy and strife. It is because God wants you to grow, to become like Him, that He asks you to keep your hearts free from these things. Therefore what matters it whether your motives are understood or not? You are not the first to have your motives misunderstood. The effect upon you and upon me cannot be otherwise than good, if we forgive those who have injured us, and strive to love our enemies; for I believe that even this is possible, if we stand upon a plane high enough. If we remember who and what we are; that we were sent into this world to teach and exemplify the truth; that we came to be saviors of men, bearing the Holy Priesthood, having the Gospel of peace and goodwill to administer; if we remember that we have been chosen to follow the Lamb of God whithersoever He goeth, can we not advocate and practice the principles that He preached and that He died for? If we cannot, what right have we to call ourselves His disciples? Follow me, he said. He that would be my disciple, let him take up his cross and follow me; 'Father forgive them, for they know not what they do.' This was one reason why He could practice the principle; He recognized that it was ignorance, to a great extent, that prevented men from doing right. They did not know fully the results of a wicked course. Even the men who murdered him did not know to the full extent what they were doing. He could pity their ignorance; and he lifted himself so high above them by a righteous life that He could say, and not only say but feel, 'Father, forgive them; for they know not what they do.' He came to suffer for their sakes, and He was willing to suffer. And He has said to us in these latter times, 'I, the Lord, will forgive whom I will forgive, but of you it is required that you forgive all men.' Why? Because God wants us to grow and expand and become godlike. We cannot do this with hatred in our hearts. We can only do it to the best of our advantage with love in our hearts, with feelings of kindness, generosity, mercy, forbearance and forgiveness. That is why we are required to practice these virtues."

Joseph Fielding Smith, Church History and Modern Revelation, Vol. 4, p. 176.
    "I (Joseph Smith) am exposed to far greater danger from traitors among ourselves than from enemies without, although my life has been sought for many years by the civil and military authorities, priests, and people of Missouri; and if I can escape from the ungrateful treachery of assassins, I can live as Caesar might have lived were it not for a right-hand Brutus. I have had pretended friends betray me. All the enemies upon the face of the earth may roar and exert all their power to bring about my death, but they can accomplish nothing, unless some who are among us and enjoy our society, have been with us in our councils, participated in our confidence, taken us by the hand, called us brother, saluted us with a kiss, join with our enemies, turn our virtues into faults, and, by falsehood and deceit, stir up their wrath and indignation against us, and bring their united vengeance upon our heads. All the hue-and-cry of the chief priests and elders against the Savior, could not bring down the wrath of the Jewish nation upon His head, and thereby cause the crucifixion of the Son of God, until Judas said unto him, 'Whomsoever I shall kiss, he is the man; hold him fast.' Judas was one of the Twelve Apostles, even their treasurer, and dipped with their Master in the dish, and through his treachery the crucifixion was brought about; and we have a Judas in our midst.' (D.H.C. 6:152.)"

James E. Talmage, The Articles of Faith, p. 423-424.
    "It is not required of them to suffer without protest imposition by lawless persecutors, or through the operation of unjust laws; but their protests should be offered in legal and proper order. The saints have practically demonstrated their acceptance of the doctrine that it is better to suffer evil than to do wrong by purely human opposition to unjust authority. And if by thus submitting themselves to the laws of the land, in the event of such laws being unjust and subversive of human freedom, the people be prevented from doing the work appointed them of God, they are not to be held accountable for the failure to act under the higher law. The word of the Lord has defined the position and duty of the people in such a contingency: 'Verily, verily, I say unto you, that when I give a commandment to any of the sons of men to do a work unto my name, and those sons of men go with all their might and with all they have to perform that work, and cease not their diligence, and their enemies come upon them and hinder them from performing that work, behold, it behooveth me to require that work no more at the hands of those sons of men, but to accept of their offerings. And the iniquity and transgression of my holy laws and commandments I will visit upon the heads of those who hindered my work, unto the third and fourth generation, so long as they repent not, and hate me, saith the Lord God.'"

James E. Talmage, The Great Apostasy, p. 157-158.
    "The thoughtful student cannot fail to see in the progress of the great apostasy and its results

the existence of an overruling power, operating toward eventual good, however mysterious its methods. The heart-rending persecutions to which the saints were subjected in the early centuries of our era, the anguish, the torture, the bloodshed, incurred in defense of the testimony of Christ, the rise of an apostate church, blighting the intellect and leading captive the souls of men—all these dread scenes were foreknown to the Lord. While we cannot say or believe that such exhibitions of human depravity and blasphemy of heart were in accordance with the divine will, certainly God willed to permit full scope to the free agency of man, in the exercise of which agency some won the martyr's crown, and others filled the measure of their iniquity to overflowing."

James E. Talmage, The Great Apostasy, Notes, Chapter 4, Note 1.

"It may be argued that, judging from the history of the re-established Church in the present dispensation, persecution may tend to strengthen rather than to weaken the Church, and that therefore violent opposition in earlier times cannot be considered a true cause leading to final disruption. In reply it may be said that the present is the dispensation of the fullness of times,—a period in which the Church shall triumph, and during which the powers of evil are limited and restrained in their opposition; whereas the period of the apostasy was one of temporary victory for Satan. Our belief in the eventual triumph of good over evil must not blind us to the fact that evil is frequently allowed a short-lived success, and a seeming victory. The permanency of the Latter-day Church has been not less surely predicted than was the temporary duration of the Primitive Church. Satan was given power to overcome the saints in former days, and the persecutions he waged against them and the officers of the Church contributed to his passing success. It has been decreed that he shall not have power to destroy the Church in the last dispensation, and his persecution of the saints today will be futile as a means of bringing about a general apostasy in these latter times."

James E. Talmage, The Great Apostasy, Notes, Chapter 4, Note 2.

"The idea that the right is always victorious in this world, that truth is always triumphant and innocence always divinely protected, are old, fond fables with which well-meaning men have amused credulous multitudes; but the stern facts of history and actual experience in life correct the pleasing delusion. Do not mis-understand me. I believe in the ultimate victory of the right, the ultimate triumph of truth, the final immunity of innocence from violence. These—innocence, truth and the right—will be at the last more than conquerors; they will be successful in the war, but that does not prevent them from losing some battles. It should be remembered always that God has given to man his agency; and that fact implies that one man is as free to act wickedly as another is to do righteousness. Cain was as free to murder his brother as that brother was to worship God; and so the pagans and Jews were as free to persecute and murder the Christians as the Christians were to live virtuously and worship Christ as God. The agency of man would not be worth the name if it did not grant liberty to the wicked to fill the cup of their iniquity, as well as liberty to the virtuous to round out the measure of their righteousness. Such perfect liberty or agency God has given man; and it is only so variously modified as not to thwart his general purposes. (B. H. Roberts, 'A New Witness for God,' p. 47-48.)"

J. Reuben Clark, Jr., Conference Report, April 1944, p. 116.

"Brethren, let us think about that, because I say unto you with all the soberness I can, that we stand in danger of losing our liberties, and that once lost, only blood will bring them back; and once lost, we of this Church will, in order to keep the Church going forward, have more sacrifices to make and more persecutions to endure than we have yet known, heavy as our sacrifices and grievous as our persecutions of the past have been."

J. Reuben Clark, Jr., Conference Report, October 1959, p. 46.
"I cannot bring too strongly that here in the last days, paganism is under one head, and that head is guided by Satan himself. Please, brethren and sisters of the Church, keep the home fires of testimony and knowledge of the gospel and of God and of Jesus Christ, keep the home fires burning in your homes, in your priesthood quorums, and all the rest, for I am sure, one way or another, we shall have to face dire persecution."

Ezra Taft Benson, Conference Report, April 1955, p. 47.
"I am grateful that we have our free agency which to me is an eternal blessing, an eternal principle. I recognize that today Satan, the adversary, is still alert. He is not using the means of persecution towards this people which he once used, but he is still the enemy of truth, and he is using other methods today. He is probably using the method of encouraging complacency. He is probably making an effort to lull us away into a false security because things seem well in Zion."

Ezra Taft Benson, "Our Immediate Responsibility", BYU, October 25, 1966.
"Often the Lord has to send persecutions in order to rebuke and try to purge the unfaithful. He has done it in the past and he can do it again. If we deserve it—we will get it."

Teachings of Ezra Taft Benson, p. 166.
"The Church has survived exile from four states, the harassment and persecution of its members, an extermination order from a governor, the execution of its prophet, disenfranchisement by the government, and continuous persecution of its leaders and people. That is what this Church endured and survived in the first sixty years of its history—and it was through such adversity, persecution, and impoverishment that the Church gained strength and matured. (CR, April 1980, Ensign, May 1980, p. 32.)"

Teachings of Ezra Taft Benson, p. 292-293.
"We are far removed from the days of our forefathers who were persecuted for their peculiar beliefs. Some of us seem to want to share their reward but are ofttimes afraid to stand up for principles that are controversial in our generation. We need not solicit persecution, but neither should we remain silent in the presence of overwhelming evils, for this makes cowards of men. We should not go out of the path of duty to pick up a cross there is no need to bear, but neither should we sidestep a cross that clearly lies within the path of duty. (CR, October 1964, Improvement Era, December 1964, p. 1067.)"

Teachings of Ezra Taft Benson, p. 393.
"Some of our members have become disturbed because of derogatory things said about the

Church and its leaders, or because of misrepresentations about our doctrines or our practices. But opposition is not new to the Church. We have had opposition in the past, and we shall continue to have opposition in the future. Do not become discouraged by what others say or do. Stay on the strait and narrow path. You do this by holding fast to the iron rod—the words of God as contained in the scriptures and as given by His living servants on this earth (see 1 Nephi 8:19). (CR, April 1984, Ensign, May 1984, p. 8.)"

Teachings of Ezra Taft Benson, p. 398.

"There may come persecution; there may come opposition; there may come reverses; there may come criticism and misrepresentation. Your motives may be questioned. You may be attacked. But if we place our trust in the Almighty and do that which is right, there will come an inner assurance, an inner calm, a peace that will bring joy and happiness to our souls. (CR, April 1954, Improvement Era, June 1954, p. 407.)"

Bruce R. McConkie, Mormon Doctrine, "Persecution", p. 569.

"When one group of professing worshipers has poured out the bitter draughts of persecution upon another, the source of direction and guidance has been Lucifer. As the author and father of persecution, Satan has been able to bend mortal men to his will proportionately as they have been willing to serve him. . . . the severest and most wicked persecutions of all the ages have been fostered, promoted, and carried out by those who have the closest ties with the devil. Indeed, it is of the church of the devil which the revelation speaks when it says, she is 'the great persecutor of the church'."

Bruce R. McConkie, Mormon Doctrine, "Signs of the Times", p. 723.

"Where the gospel is, there will be opposition and persecution, for Lucifer will not stand idly by while the work of God rolls forward. . . . Persecution is the heritage of the faithful; when men join the Church, it commences; when they leave the truth, their persecutors become their friends."

Bruce R. McConkie, Doctrinal New Testament Commentary, Vol. 2, p. 130-131.

"Why is it that unbelievers stir themselves and others up to persecute the saints? Why should one person feel so strongly about what others believe as to seek to imprison and slay them? From a purely rational standpoint there is no sensible explanation. But religion involves feelings and emotions; prejudices become deep seated; passions consume the whole being; and Satan takes control of his persecuting agent. When emotions, passions, and man's innate religious feelings become so distorted and perverted as to place the human soul under Satan's control, these feelings then find expression in persecution."

Bruce R. McConkie, The Promised Messiah, p. 34.

"Nephi saw in vision 'a church which is most abominable above all other churches, which slayeth the saints of God, yea, and tortureth them and bindeth them down, and yoketh them with a yoke of iron, and bringeth them down into captivity.' (1 Ne. 13:5.) From this vision we learn two of the saddest truths of all history: (1) prophets are persecuted by religiously inclined people, and (2) the fact that there are false churches is itself the very reason why the Lord's saints suffer at the hands of evil and ungodly men.""

Bruce R. McConkie, The Mortal Messiah, Vol. 4, p. 355.

"Those who do not believe the restored gospel; who reject the messengers of salvation who are sent to them; and who continue to live after the manner of the world—they shall be cut off from among the people who are of the covenant. This we have already noted. It refers to the return of the Son of Man; to the day when every corruptible thing shall be destroyed; to the day when the wicked shall be burned as stubble; to the day when the vineyard shall be burned and none shall remain except those who are able to abide the day. It is then, and, in this way, that the Lord's people will triumph over their enemies."

Bruce R. McConkie, The Millennial Messiah, p. 313.

"Of course, Satan will slay some of the righteous that their blood—with the blood of all the martyrs of all the ages—may cry from the ground as a witness against those who fight against God."

Boyd K. Packer, BYU Speeches, April 12, 1966, p. 10.

"If you seriously expect to be the only generation ever born upon the earth in any dispensation to have the gospel without any challenge, without any opposition or resistance, without persecution from the world, you expect that which will never be."

David B. Haight, Conference Report, Ensign, November 1992, p. 74.

"Michael Hirsley, who writes for the Chicago Tribune, recently observed that predicting America's religious future is risky business—that `the nation's most widely accepted prejudice is anti-Christian'."

Neal A. Maxwell, All These Things Shall Give Thee Experience, p. 17.

"Though His plans are known to Him, there is no premature exposure of the Lord's plans. This could bring unnecessary persecution upon an unready Lord's people. Further, a premature showing of His power and strength in support of His Saints could cut short the trial of our faith."

Neal A. Maxwell, All These Things Shall Give Thee Experience, p. 126.

"We should not even be dismayed either if, in the winding-up scenes, the enemies of God attack the very foundation of the Church. Their assaults will include derision of the Prophet Joseph Smith, the Book of Mormon, and the reality of continuing revelation. These efforts will surely fail, but not before damaging some unsteady members—those who have unnecessary difficulty in following the Brethren."

Neal A. Maxwell, But for a Small Moment, p. 113.

"Even with and perhaps because of such vistas, the revelations given to jailed Joseph counseled him to be patient. This included being patient about the manner and the season in which the Lord will bring judgment upon those who are the sworn enemies of his work; he will bring his 'swift judgment in the season thereof' (D&C 121:24), that season not being always according to the timetable we might desire."

Neal A. Maxwell, Things As They Really Are, p. 90.

"Just how fashionable it can be in some seasons to persecute the saints of God is seen in the words of Nephi when he says some of the churches of the world and some of the gentile nations that 'slayeth the saints of God' actually do it 'for the praise of the world . . . and bring them down into captivity.' (1 Nephi 13:9.) Even today, those who turn against the Church do so to play to their own private gallery, but when, one day, the applause has died down and the cheering has stopped, they will face a smaller audience, the judgment bar of God."

Neal A. Maxwell, We Will Prove Them Herewith, p. 118.

"Properly responded to, temptation, persecution, and tribulation can do wonderful things to refine our lives. Perhaps it is only when the things that do not matter are made to fall away that we see, at last, 'things as they really are'! Then the worries of the world soon disappear from one's 'radarscope'."

Neal A. Maxwell, Wherefore Ye Must Press Forward, p. 81.

"Recall how a young Joseph Smith was puzzled as to why he, in his youth and obscurity and poverty, 'should be thought a character of sufficient importance to attract the attention of the great ones of the most popular sects of the day, and in a manner to create in them a spirit of the most bitter persecution and reviling.' (Joseph Smith 2:23.) Well, so it is (and will be) with us, collectively, especially as the Church is brought forth out of obscurity. If the Church were not true, our enemies would be bored rather than threatened, and acquiescent rather than anxious. Hell is moved only when things move heavenward."

SCRIPTURAL REFERENCES

Daniel 7:21-22
21 I beheld, and the same horn made war with the saints, and prevailed against them;
22 Until the Ancient of days came, and judgment was given to the saints of the most High; and the time came that the saints possessed the kingdom.

Matthew 5:10-12
10 Blessed are they which are persecuted for righteousness' sake: for theirs is the kingdom of heaven.
11 Blessed are ye, when men shall revile you, and persecute you, and shall say all manner of evil against you falsely, for my sake.
12 Rejoice, and be exceeding glad: for great is your reward in heaven: for so persecuted they the prophets which were before you.

Matthew 5:44-45
44 But I say unto you, Love your enemies, bless them that curse you, do good to them that hate you, and pray for them which despitefully use you, and persecute you;
45 That ye may be the children of your Father which is in heaven: for he maketh his sun to rise on the evil and on the good, and sendeth rain on the just and on the unjust.

Matthew 10:22-23
22 And ye shall be hated of all men for my name's sake: but he that endureth to the end shall be saved.
23 But when they persecute you in this city, flee ye into another: for verily I say unto you, Ye shall not have gone over the cities of Israel, till the Son of man be come.

Matthew 10:28
28 And fear not them which kill the body, but are not able to kill the soul: but rather fear him which is able to destroy both soul and body in hell.

Matthew 13:18-22
18 Hear ye therefore the parable of the sower.
19 When any one heareth the word of the kingdom, and understandeth it not, then cometh the wicked one, and catcheth away that which was sown in his heart. This is he which received seed by the way side.
20 But he that received the seed into stony places, the same is he that heareth the word, and anon with joy receiveth it;
21 Yet hath he not root in himself, but dureth for a while: for when tribulation or persecution ariseth because of the word, by and by he is offended.
22 He also that received seed among the thorns is he that heareth the word; and the care of this world, and the deceitfulness of riches, choke the word, and he becometh unfruitful.

187

Matthew 24:9-10

9 Then shall they deliver you up to be afflicted, and shall kill you: and ye shall be hated of all nations for my name's sake.

10 And then shall many be offended, and shall betray one another, and shall hate one another.

Mark 4:17

17 And have no root in themselves, and so endure but for a time: afterward, when affliction or persecution ariseth for the word's sake, immediately they are offended.

Mark 13:9-10

9 But take heed to yourselves: for they shall deliver you up to councils; and in the synagogues ye shall be beaten: and ye shall be brought before rulers and kings for my sake, for a testimony against them.

10 And the gospel must first be published among all nations.

JST Luke 6:28

28 Bless them who curse you, and pray for them who despitefully use you and persecute you.

John 15:18-19

18 If the world hate you, ye know that it hated me before [it hated] you.

19 If ye were of the world, the world would love his own: but because ye are not of the world, but I have chosen you out of the world, therefore the world hateth you.

Romans 8:35-39

35 Who shall separate us from the love of Christ? shall tribulation, or distress, or persecution, or famine, or nakedness, or peril, or sword?

36 As it is written, For thy sake we are killed all the day long; we are accounted as sheep for the slaughter.

37 Nay, in all these things we are more than conquerors through him that loved us.

38 For I am persuaded, that neither death, nor life, nor angels, nor principalities, nor powers, nor things present, nor things to come,

39 Nor height, nor depth, nor any other creature, shall be able to separate us from the love of God, which is in Christ Jesus our Lord.

2 Timothy 3:11-13

11 Persecutions, afflictions, which came unto me at Antioch, at Iconium, at Lystra; what persecutions I endured: but out of them all the Lord delivered me.

12 Yea, and all that will live godly in Christ Jesus shall suffer persecution.

13 But evil men and seducers shall wax worse and worse, deceiving, and being deceived.

1 Nephi 13:9

9 And also for the praise of the world do they destroy the saints of God, and bring them down into captivity.

1 Nephi 22:13-19

13 And the blood of that great and abominable church, which is the whore of all the earth, shall turn upon their own heads; for they shall war among themselves, and the sword of their own hands shall fall upon their own heads, and they shall be drunken with their own blood.

14 And every nation which shall war against thee, O house of Israel, shall be turned one against another, and they shall fall into the pit which they digged to ensnare the people of the Lord. And all that fight against Zion shall be destroyed, and that great whore, who hath perverted the right ways of the Lord, yea, that great and abominable church, shall tumble to the dust and great shall be the fall of it.

15 For behold, saith the prophet, the time cometh speedily that Satan shall have no more power over the hearts of the children of men; for the day soon cometh that all the proud and they who do wickedly shall be as stubble; and the day cometh that they must be burned.

16 For the time soon cometh that the fulness of the wrath of God shall be poured out upon all the children of men; for he will not suffer that the wicked shall destroy the righteous.

17 Wherefore, he will preserve the righteous by his power, even if it so be that the fulness of his wrath must come, and the righteous be preserved, even unto the destruction of their enemies by fire. Wherefore, the righteous need not fear; for thus saith the prophet, they shall be saved, even if it so be as by fire.

18 Behold, my brethren, I say unto you, that these things must shortly come; yea, even blood, and fire, and vapor of smoke must come; and it must needs be upon the face of this earth; and it cometh unto men according to the flesh if it so be that they will harden their hearts against the Holy One of Israel.

19 For behold, the righteous shall not perish; for the time surely must come that all they who fight against Zion shall be cut off.

2 Nephi 6:17-18

17 But thus saith the Lord: Even the captives of the mighty shall be taken away, and the prey of the terrible shall be delivered; for the Mighty God shall deliver his covenant people. For thus saith the Lord: I will contend with them that contendeth with thee—

18 And I will feed them that oppress thee, with their own flesh; and they shall be drunken with their own blood as with sweet wine; and all flesh shall know that I the Lord am thy Savior and thy Redeemer, the Mighty One of Jacob.

2 Nephi 26:5-6

5 And they that kill the prophets, and the saints, the depths of the earth shall swallow them up, saith the Lord of Hosts; and mountains shall cover them, and whirlwinds shall carry them away, and buildings shall fall upon them and crush them to pieces and grind them to powder.

6 And they shall be visited with thunderings, and lightnings, and earthquakes, and all manner of destructions, for the fire of the anger of the Lord shall be kindled against them, and they shall be as stubble, and the day that cometh shall consume them, saith the Lord of Hosts.

Desolation & Destruction in the Last Days

2 Nephi 28:16

16 Wo unto them that turn aside the just for a thing of naught and revile against that which is good, and say that it is of no worth! For the day shall come that the Lord God will speedily visit the inhabitants of the earth; and in that day that they are fully ripe in iniquity they shall perish.

2 Nephi 28:20

20 For behold, at that day shall he rage in the hearts of the children of men, and stir them up to anger against that which is good.

Alma 10:22-23

22 Yea, and I say unto you that if it were not for the prayers of the righteous, who are now in the land, that ye would even now be visited with utter destruction; yet it would not be by flood, as were the people in the days of Noah, but it would be by famine, and by pestilence, and the sword.
23 But it is by the prayers of the righteous that ye are spared; now therefore, if ye will cast out the righteous from among you then will not the Lord stay his hand; but in his fierce anger he will come out against you; then ye shall be smitten by famine, and by pestilence, and by the sword; and the time is soon at hand except ye repent.

Helaman 3:34-35

34 And they were lifted up in pride, even to the persecution of many of their brethren. Now this was a great evil, which did cause the more humble part of the people to suffer great persecutions, and to wade through much affliction.
35 Nevertheless they did fast and pray oft, and did wax stronger and stronger in their humility, and firmer and firmer in the faith of Christ, unto the filling their souls with joy and consolation, yea, even to the purifying and the sanctification of their hearts, which sanctification cometh because of their yielding their hearts unto God.

Helaman 13:12-14

12 Yea, wo unto this great city of Zarahemla; for behold, it is because of those who are righteous that it is saved; yea, wo unto this great city, for I perceive, saith the Lord, that there are many, yea, even the more part of this great city, that will harden their hearts against me, saith the Lord.
13 But blessed are they who will repent, for them will I spare. But behold, if it were not for the righteous who are in this great city, behold, I would cause that fire should come down out of heaven and destroy it.
14 But behold, it is for the righteous' sake that it is spared. But behold, the time cometh, saith the Lord, that when ye shall cast out the righteous from among you, then shall ye be ripe for destruction; yea, wo be unto this great city, because of the wickedness and abominations which are in her.

3 Nephi 6:13

13 Some were lifted up in pride, and others were exceedingly humble; some did return railing for railing, while others would receive railing and persecution and all manner of afflictions, and would not turn and revile again, but were humble and penitent before God.

3 Nephi 12:10-12

10 And blessed are all they who are persecuted for my name's sake, for theirs is the kingdom of heaven.

11 And blessed are ye when men shall revile you and persecute, and shall say all manner of evil against you falsely, for my sake;

12 For ye shall have great joy and be exceedingly glad, for great shall be your reward in heaven; for so persecuted they the prophets who were before you.

Mormon 8:26-27

26 And no one need say they shall not come, for they surely shall, for the Lord hath spoken it; for out of the earth shall they come, by the hand of the Lord, and none can stay it; and it shall come in a day when it shall be said that miracles are done away; and it shall come even as if one should speak from the dead.

27 And it shall come in a day when the blood of saints shall cry unto the Lord, because of secret combinations and the works of darkness.

Mormon 8:41

41 Behold, the sword of vengeance hangeth over you; and the time soon cometh that he avengeth the blood of the saints upon you, for he will not suffer their cries any longer.

D&C 38:9

9 Wherefore, gird up your loins and be prepared. Behold, the kingdom is yours, and the enemy shall not overcome.

D&C 40:2

2 And he received the word with gladness, but straightway Satan tempted him; and the fear of persecution and the cares of the world caused him to reject the word.

D&C 45:49-50

49 And the Lord shall utter his voice, and all the ends of the earth shall hear it; and the nations of the earth shall mourn, and they that have laughed shall see their folly.

50 And calamity shall cover the mocker, and the scorner shall be consumed; and they that have watched for iniquity shall be hewn down and cast into the fire.

D&C 87:6-7

6 And thus, with the sword and by bloodshed the inhabitants of the earth shall mourn; and with famine, and plague, and earthquake, and the thunder of heaven, and the fierce and vivid lightning also, shall the inhabitants of the earth be made to feel the wrath, and indignation, and chastening hand of an Almighty God, until the consumption decreed hath made a full end of all nations;

7 That the cry of the saints, and of the blood of the saints, shall cease to come up into the ears of the Lord of Sabaoth, from the earth, to be avenged of their enemies.

D&C 98:14-15

14 Therefore, be not afraid of your enemies, for I have decreed in my heart, saith the Lord, that I will prove you in all things, whether you will abide in my covenant, even unto death, that you may be found worthy.

15 For if ye will not abide in my covenant ye are not worthy of me.

D&C 101:35-38

35 And all they who suffer persecution for my name, and endure in faith, though they are called to lay down their lives for my sake yet shall they partake of all this glory.

36 Wherefore, fear not even unto death; for in this world your joy is not full, but in me your joy is full.

37 Therefore, care not for the body, neither the life of the body; but care for the soul, and for the life of the soul.

38 And seek the face of the Lord always, that in patience ye may possess your souls, and ye shall have eternal life.

D&C 101:81-94

81 Now, unto what shall I liken the children of Zion? I will liken them unto the parable of the woman and the unjust judge, for men ought always to pray and not to faint, which saith—

82 There was in a city a judge which feared not God, neither regarded man.

83 And there was a widow in that city, and she came unto him saying: Avenge me of mine adversary.

84 And he would not for a while, but afterward he said within himself: Though I fear not God, nor regard man, yet because this widow troubleth me I will avenge her, lest by her continual coming she weary me.

85 Thus will I liken the children of Zion.

86 Let them importune at the feet of the judge;

87 And if he heed them not, let them importune at the feet of the governor;

88 And if the governor heed them not, let them importune at the feet of the president;

89 And if the president heed them not, then will the Lord arise and come forth out of his hiding place, and in his fury vex the nation;

90 And in his hot displeasure, and in his fierce anger, in his time, will cut off those wicked, unfaithful, and unjust stewards, and appoint them their portion among hypocrites, and unbelievers;

91 Even in outer darkness, where there is weeping, and wailing, and gnashing of teeth.

92 Pray ye, therefore, that their ears may be opened unto your cries, that I may be merciful unto them, that these things may not come upon them.

93 What I have said unto you must needs be, that all men may be left without excuse;

94 That wise men and rulers may hear and know that which they have never considered;

D&C 103:24-28

24 And inasmuch as mine enemies come against you to drive you from my goodly land, which I have consecrated to be the land of Zion, even from your own lands after these testimonies, which ye

have brought before me against them, ye shall curse them;

25 And whomsoever ye curse, I will curse, and ye shall avenge me of mine enemies.

26 And my presence shall be with you even in avenging me of mine enemies, unto the third and fourth generation of them that hate me.

27 Let no man be afraid to lay down his life for my sake; for whoso layeth down his life for my sake shall find it again.

28 And whoso is not willing to lay down his life for my sake is not my disciple.

D&C 121:7-8

7 My son, peace be unto thy soul; thine adversity and thine afflictions shall be but a small moment;

8 And then, if thou endure it well, God shall exalt thee on high; thou shalt triumph over all thy foes.

D&C 134:11

11 We believe that men should appeal to the civil law for redress of all wrongs and grievances, where personal abuse is inflicted or the right of property or character infringed, where such laws exist as will protect the same; but we believe that all men are justified in defending themselves, their friends, and property, and the government, from the unlawful assaults and encroachments of all persons in times of exigency, where immediate appeal cannot be made to the laws, and relief afforded.

CHAPTER SIX

FALSE MESSIAHS & PROPHETS/ANTI-CHRISTS

"False prophets always arise to oppose the true prophets and they will prophesy so very near the truth that they will deceive almost the very chosen ones. . . .In relation to the kingdom of God, the devil always sets up his kingdom at the very same time in opposition to God." (Joseph Smith, History of the Church, Vol. 6, p. 364.)

Joseph Smith, History of the Church, Vol. 4, p. 608.

"The keys are certain signs and words by which false spirits and personages may be detected from true, which cannot be revealed to the Elders till the Temple is completed. The rich can only get them in the Temple, the poor may get them on the mountain top as did Moses. . . .There are signs in heaven, earth and hell; the Elders must know them all, to be endowed with power, to finish their work and prevent imposition. The devil knows many signs, but does not know the sign of the Son of Man, or Jesus. No one can truly say he knows God until he has handled something and this can only be in the holiest of holies."

Joseph Smith, History of the Church, Vol. 5, p. 215.

"If any person should ask me if I were a prophet, I should not deny it, as that would give me the lie; for, according to John, the testimony of Jesus is the spirit of prophecy; therefore if I profess to be a witness or teacher, and have not the spirit of prophecy, which is the testimony of Jesus, I must be a false witness; but if I be a true teacher and witness, I must possess the spirit of prophecy, and that constitutes a prophet; and any man who says he is a teacher or preacher of righteousness, and denies the spirit of prophecy, is a liar, and the truth is not in him; and by this key false teachers and imposters may be detected."

Joseph Smith, History of the Church, Vol. 6, p. 364.

"My enemies say that I have been a true prophet. Why, I had rather be a fallen true prophet than a false prophet. When a man goes about prophesying, and commands men to obey his teachings, he must either be a true or false prophet. False prophets always arise to oppose the true prophets and they will prophesy so very near the truth that they will deceive almost the very chosen ones.

The doctrine of eternal judgments belongs to the first principles of the Gospel, in the last days. In relation to the kingdom of God, the devil always sets up his kingdom at the very same time in opposition to God."

Teachings of the Prophet Joseph Smith, Section One, 1830-34, p. 9.

"Until we have perfect love we are liable to fall and when we have a testimony that our names are sealed in the Lamb's book of life we have perfect love and then it is impossible for false Christs to deceive us."

Teachings of the Prophet Joseph Smith, Section One, 1830-34, p. 21.

"I will inform you that it is contrary to the economy of God for any member of the Church, or any one, to receive instruction for those in authority, higher than themselves; therefore you will see the impropriety of giving heed to them; but if any person have a vision or a visitation from a heavenly messenger, it must be for his own benefit and instruction; for the fundamental principles, government, and doctrine of the Church are vested in the keys of the kingdom."

Teachings of the Prophet Joseph Smith, Section Four, 1839–42, p. 205.

"As we have noticed before, the great difficulty lies in the ignorance of the nature of spirits, of the laws by which they are governed, and the signs by which they may be known; if it requires the Spirit of God to know the things of God; and the spirit of the devil can only be unmasked through that medium, then it follows as a natural consequence that unless some person or persons have a communication, or revelation from God, unfolding to them the operation of the spirit, they must eternally remain ignorant of these principles; for I contend that if one man cannot understand these things but by the Spirit of God, ten thousand men cannot; it is alike out of the reach of the wisdom of the learned, the tongue of the eloquent, the power of the mighty. And we shall at last have to come to this conclusion, whatever we may think of revelation, that without it we can neither know nor understand anything of God, or the devil; and however unwilling the world may be to acknowledge this principle, it is evident from the multifarious creeds and notions concerning this matter that they understand nothing of this principle, and it is equally as plain that without a divine communication they must remain in ignorance. The world always mistook false prophets for true ones, and those that were sent of God, they considered to be false prophets and hence they killed, stoned, punished and imprisoned the true prophets, and these had to hide themselves "in deserts and dens, and caves of the earth," and though the most honorable men of the earth, they banished them from their society as vagabonds, whilst they cherished, honored and supported knaves, vagabonds, hypocrites, impostors, and the basest of men."

Teachings of the Prophet Joseph Smith, Section Five, 1842–43, p. 278.

"This morning I read German and visited with a brother and sister from Michigan, who thought that "a prophet is always a prophet;" but I told them that a prophet was a prophet only when he was acting as such. (DHC 5:265.)"

Teachings of the Prophet Joseph Smith, Section Six, 1843–44, p. 341.

"Jesus Christ never did reveal to any man the precise time that He would come. Go and read the Scriptures, and you cannot find anything that specifies the exact hour He would come; and all that say so are false teachers."

Orson Hyde, Millennial Star, May 15, 1846, p. 157.

"In my meditations, this morning, the Spirit of the Lord came upon me, and I was moved to write: and being grieved in my spirit on account of false pretenses by evil designing persons to gain power, and lead away the flock of God; It whispered (to) me and said:

Evil men, ambitious of power, must needs arise among you, and they shall be led by their own self-will and not by me. Yet they are instruments in my hands, and are permitted to try my people, and to collect from among them those who are not the elect, and such as are unworthy of eternal life. Grieve not after them, neither mourn nor be alarmed. My people know my voice and also the voice of my spirit, and a stranger they will not follow; therefore such as follow strangers are not my people."

Orson Pratt, Journal of Discourses, Vol. 13, p. 65, December 19, 1869.

"A succession of wonderful manifestations of the power of God was made through Moses, and in all, save two or three instances, the magicians did likewise. What would naturally be the conclusion at which wicked men would arrive under such circumstances? They would naturally say, 'Here is Moses, who has been brought up in all the learning of the Egyptians and he is more advanced than our magicians; he has learned lessons that they have not yet acquired,' consequently men of that stamp would decide that it was all by the same spirit, and they would not acknowledge the finger of God in it.

That may be a sample to all people in future generations in the manifestations of these powers. The wicked cannot discern and comprehend the difference between these two powers. If we believe that there is a God and a heavenly host standing in His presence, ready to do His behests, we must believe in the manifestations of divine power; and if we believe that there are fallen spirits who have been cast down to this earth, we must also believe that they will manifest their power just as far as they are suffered or permitted."

George Q. Cannon, Collected Discourses, Vol. 3, October 8, 1893.

"But I heard Joseph Smith predict that the day would come when there would be false spirits go forth among the children of men, and that they would deceive them. I remember on one occasion his speaking about the false prophet that should call down fire from heaven, and he warned the people in the most impressive and solemn manner against being deceived by these works that should be wrought to deceive the children of men."

George Q. Cannon, Collected Discourses, Vol. 4, April 8, 1894.

"Of course, there are many other things that we need to be warned about. We need to be warned about these false spirits that are going abroad. I do not suppose there ever was a time when there were so many delusive spirits going abroad among the people as at the present time—false Christs, false prophets, and all sorts of things to lead away the people of God. Everything, it is said, will be shaken that can be shaken. God is going to have a pure people. Those who commit sin and persist in it will lose the Spirit of God and be removed from among the people of God. We may expect that sinners will leave us, and that we shall have men and women falling into the dark because of transgression; but it is our duty, as watchmen upon the walls of Zion, and as the shepherds of the flock of Christ, to lift up our voices and warn the people of the dangers there are around them, and to point out the path of safety, that they may not stray away from the flock and be devoured. We therefore feel to warn the Latter-day Saints in regard to these delusive spirits. We warn you to be on your guard, to watch carefully, to pray earnestly, to live in purity, so that you shall have constantly the light of the Spirit of God to be with you. Do not be carried away by every wind of doctrine, nor by deceivers; but listen to the voice of the Spirit of God, which bears testimony to you in your hearts concerning the truths which you hear. You ought to be able to tell the voice of the true Shepherd from all other voices, so that no one assuming sheep's clothing and professing to be what he is not can deceive you. It is your privilege to recognize the voice of the true Shepherd, and to know by the testimony of Jesus whether that which you are taught is true or not."

Joseph F. Smith, Gospel Doctrine, p. 36.

"And I know this, that God has organized his Church in the earth, and I know that when he designs or purposes to make any change in the matter of governing or controlling or presiding over the affairs of his Church, that he will make the change, and he will make it in such a way that the whole people of the Church, who are doing right, will understand and accept it. I know that the Lord will not raise up 'Tom, Dick, or Harry,' here, there and everywhere, claiming to be Christ, or 'one mighty and strong,' claiming to be inspired and called to do some wonderful thing. The Lord will not deal with men in that way; that while the organization of the Church exists, while quorums and councils of the Priesthood are intact in the Church, the Lord will reveal his purposes through them, and not through 'Tom, Dick, or Harry.' Put that in your little note books now, and remember it; it is true. (Apr. C. R., 1912, p. 10.)"

George Teasdale, Collected Discourses, Vol. 5, June 26, 1898.

"The doctrine of Christ never was popular, and never will be until we all see eye to eye, and there is a separation of the wheat from the tares. As long as they grow together there always will be opposition against the truth. What does the history of the world teach us? That there has always been anti-Christ; and anti-Christ is everything that is opposed to Christ and regards the doctrine of Christ as non-essential. Those who are for Christ believe in His doctrine and in living it. But those who love the world and the things of the world do not have the love of God in their hearts. If we loved the world, the love of God would not be with us. Our ambition should be to please God, to keep His commandments, and to see His righteousness established upon the face of the earth, because it brings happiness. The love of the world does not bring happiness."

Joseph Fielding Smith, Conference Report, April 1962, p. 45.

"We have people who go out of the Church from time to time and set up organizations of their own, claiming that the kingdom of God has failed, that they have something better. I am sorry for these people. I cannot believe that any of them are sincere. If they are, then they are to be pitied, but I think that they are malicious deceivers, trying to destroy the kingdom of God."

Joseph Fielding Smith, Church History and Modern Revelation, Vol. 1, p. 127-128.

"Let the members of the Church remember that the Lord has said that when a man is called to any position of responsibility, and especially to preside over the Church, he will 'come in at the gate and be ordained as I have told you before, to teach those revelations which you have received and shall receive through him whom I have appointed.' (D&C 43:7.) This counsel and commandment was given that the Saints should know how to be edified and instructed and how to direct the Church in all holiness before the Lord. For many years our communities have been troubled with impostors claiming to be called of God to lead the Church as the 'one mighty and strong, holding the scepter of power,' and to set in order the inheritances. Some of these impostors have passed away, but others come, and at times are able to lead away unwise members who lack the understanding and knowledge by which the Church is governed. These revelations given in 1830 and 1831, are for our benefit and guidance in all such matters. The Lord would have us know that he does all things in order, and whenever he calls one to lead the Church that one will come in at the gate and be ordained by those who hold authority. It has been so from the beginning and will continue so to the end."

Joseph Fielding Smith, Church History and Modern Revelation, Vol. 2, p. 114.

"One would think in such a matter as this that sufficient native modesty would assert itself to restrain a man from announcing himself as the one upon whom such high honors are to be conferred, and who is to exercise such great powers in establishing the Saints in their inheritances; and that even if one suspected, for any reason, that such a position, and such exceptional powers were to be conferred upon him, he would wait until the Lord would clearly indicate to the Church, as well as to himself, that he had been indeed sent of God to do the work of so noble a ministry, as is described in the passage under question. Those, however, who have so far proclaimed themselves as being the 'one mighty and strong,' have manifested the utmost ignorance of the things of God and the order of the Church. Indeed their insufferable ignorance and egotism have been at the bottom of all their pretensions, and the cause of all the trouble into which they have fallen. They seem not to have been aware of the fact that the Church of Christ and of the saints is completely organized, and that when the man who shall be called upon to divide unto the Saints their inheritances comes, he will be designated by the inspiration of the Lord to the proper authorities of the Church, appointed and provided for in the government of the Church."

Joseph Fielding Smith Jr., Doctrines of Salvation, Vol. 1, p. 284-285.

"The Lord will never ignore the presiding officer and quorum of the Church, for he respects authority, as he requires us to respect authority. And it will always be a key to us, if we will bear it in mind, that whenever he has a revelation or commandment to give to his people that it will come through the presiding officer of the Church. This is plainly taught in the revelations. . . .

We have a key given us by revelation by which false spirits may be known, by which false revelation may be known. There is only one man in this Church, at a time, who has the right to receive revelation for the Church. The Lord has said that his house is a house of order, not a house of confusion, and therefore one is appointed to speak One has the right to receive the word of the Lord and give it to the Church.

We all have the right to receive revelation for our own guidance. A president of a stake has the right of revelation for the guidance of his stake. But no man has the right to receive revelation for this Church, except the one whom the Lord has called.

If he receives a revelation it will be declared without question, if it is intended for the Church, in a manner by which we may all know the source from whence it comes. And when we find people secretly distributing to the Church what are said to be revelations, or visions, or manifestations, that have not come from nor received the approval of the authorities of the Church, we may put it down that such things are not of God."

James E. Talmage, Jesus the Christ, p. 152.

"The Savior's promise in a former day (Mark 16:17-18), as in the present dispensation (D&C 84:65-73), is definite, to the effect that specified gifts of the Spirit are to follow the believer as signs of divine favor. The possession and exercise of such gifts may be taken therefore as essential features of the Church of Christ. Nevertheless we are not justified in regarding the evidence of miracles as infallible testimony of authority from heaven; on the other hand, the scriptures furnish abundant proof that spiritual powers of the baser sort have wrought miracles, and will continue so to do, to the deceiving of many who lack discernment. If miracles be accepted as infallible evidence of godly power, the magicians of Egypt, through the wonders which they accomplished in opposition to the ordained plan for Israel's deliverance, have as good a claim to our respect as has Moses (Ex. 7:11). John the Revelator saw in vision a wicked power working miracles, and thereby deceiving many; doing great wonders, even bringing fire from heaven (Rev. 13:11-18). Again he saw three unclean spirits, whom he knew to be 'the spirits of devils working miracles' (Rev. 16:13-14). Consider, in connection with this, the prediction made by the Savior: —'There shall arise false Christs, and false prophets, and shall show great signs and wonders, insomuch that, if it were possible, they shall deceive the very elect' (Matt. 24:24). The invalidity of miracles as a proof of righteousness is indicated in an utterance of Jesus Christ regarding the events of the great judgment:—'Many will say to me in that day, Lord, Lord, have we not prophesied in thy name? and in thy name have we not cast out devils? and in thy name done many wonderful works? And then will I profess unto them, I never knew you; depart from me, ye that work iniquity' (Matt. 7:22-23). The Jews, to whom these teachings were addressed, knew that wonders could be wrought by evil powers; for they charged Christ with working miracles by the authority of Beelzebub the prince of devils (Matt. 12:22-30; Mark 3:22; Luke 11:15)."

Ezra Taft Benson, Conference Report, October 1963, p. 19.

"We all should know by now what President McKay has said about liberty-loving peoples' greatest responsibility. We've heard him tell of our drift toward socialism and communism. We know of his feelings regarding recent tragic decisions of the Supreme Court. We know the Church's position supporting right to work laws and the Church's opposition to programs of federal aid to education. These and many more things has President McKay told us that involve the great struggle against state slavery and the anti-Christ."

Ezra Taft Benson, BYU Speeches, December 10, 1963, p. 17.

"These are the three main keys—apply them and you will avoid pitfalls and traps which even members of the Church and some teachers may set for you. President Joseph F. Smith said that one of the three things that plagued the Church within was false educational ideas—and I am sure you will be introduced to some of these ideas somewhere along your path. Using the scriptures and the prophets and the spirit as a guide, we can eliminate a lot of the deceptions and false philosophies and cure-alls of men and discern between the wheat and the chaff."

Ezra Taft Benson, Conference Report, April 1966, p. 97.

"But whenever the God of heaven reveals His gospel to mankind, Satan, the archenemy to Christ, introduces a counterfeit."

Ezra Taft Benson, Conference Report, October 1966, p. 122.

"As members of the Church we have some close quarters to pass through if we are going to get home safely. We will be given a chance to choose between conflicting counsel given by some. That's why we must learn—and the sooner we learn, the better—to keep our eye on the Prophet, the President of the Church."

Ezra Taft Benson, An Enemy Hath Done This, p. 290.

"A natural question that might arise would be that if the Lord knew in advance that these men would fall, as he undoubted did, why did he have his prophet call them to such high office? The answer is, to fill the Lord's purposes. For even the Master followed the will of the Father by selecting Judas. President George Q. Cannon suggested an explanation, too, when he stated, 'Perhaps it is his own design that faults and weaknesses should appear in high places in order that his saints may learn to trust in him and not in any man or men."

Marion G. Romney, Conference Report, October 1960, p. 74.

"Now we know he is not going to drive the Priesthood from the earth in this dispensation because the Lord has said it is here to stay until the Savior comes. But there is no guarantee that he will not deceive a lot of men who hold the Priesthood. The Savior, talking about these days in which we live, said, 'For in those days there shall also arise false Christs, and false prophets, and shall show great signs and wonders, insomuch, that, if possible, they shall deceive the very elect, who are the elect according to the covenant (the covenant of the gospel and the Priesthood).' (Joseph Smith 1:22.)

So far as Satan's war against the Priesthood is concerned, he is making no exception in this last dispensation. His objective is still to deceive every one of us he can and to drive the Priesthood from the earth. Satan is very real. His power is very real. His influence is felt everywhere. He literally stalks the earth. 'The powers of darkness prevail upon the earth . . . and, behold, the enemy is combined.' (D&C 38: 11-12.)"

Marion G. Romney, Ensign, September 1979, p. 5.

"In distinguishing communism from the United Order, Pres. David O. McKay said that communism is Satan's counterfeit for the gospel plan, and that it is an avowed enemy of the God of the land. Communism is the greatest anti-Christ power in the world today and therefore the greatest menace not only to our peace but to our preservation as a free people. By the extent to which we tolerateit, accommodate ourselves to it, permit ourselves to be encircled by its tentacles and drawn to it, to that extent we forfeit the protection of the God of this land."

N. Eldon Tanner, Conference Report, October 1966, p. 98.

"The Prophet spoke out clearly on Friday morning, telling us what our responsibilities are. He mentioned and spoke emphatically of liquor by the drink. A man said to me after that 'You know,

201

there are people in our state who believe in following the Prophet in everything they think is right, but when it is something they think isn't right, and it doesn't appeal to them, then that's different.' He said, 'Then they become their own prophet. They decide what the Lord wants and what the Lord doesn't want.'

I thought how true, and how serious when we begin to choose which of the covenants, which of the commandments we will keep and follow. When we decide that there are some of them that we will not keep or follow, we are taking the law of the Lord into our own hands and become our own prophets, and believe me, we will be led astray, because we are false prophets to ourselves when we do not follow the Prophet of God. No, we should never discriminate between these commandments, as to those we should and should not keep."

Bruce R. McConkie, Mormon Doctrine, "Tribes of Israel", p. 809.
"Scholars speculate that 'the tribe of Dan is not mentioned (Revelation 7), perhaps because of a Jewish tradition that Antichrist was to come from the tribe.' (Dummelow, The One Volume Bible Commentary, p. 1079.)"

Bruce R. McConkie, The Promised Messiah, p. 324.
"It is not difficult to envision that there will be false prophets and false teachers in the last days. But what of the promise that there will be false Christs? In our age of enlightenment and sophistication, as we suppose, is it to be assumed that there will be those come who will profess to be Christ? As a prelude to finding answer to these questions, let us note these words of Jesus, spoken along with the others on the Mount of Olives: 'If they shall say unto you: Behold, he is in the desert; go not forth; Behold, he is in the secret chambers; believe it not; For as the light of the morning cometh out of the east, and shineth even unto the west, and covereth the whole earth, so shall also the coming of the Son of Man be.' (JS-H 25-26.)

There are, of course, those deluded souls who announce, from time to time, that they are Christ or God or the Holy Ghost, or one mighty and strong, or whatever Satan or the workings of a deranged mind places in their thoughts. But in a larger and more realistic sense, false Christs are false systems of religion that use his name and profess to present his teachings to the world. The cries, 'Lo, here,' and 'Lo, there,' which went forth in Joseph Smith's day, when 'some were contending for the Methodist faith, some for the Presbyterian, and some for the Baptist' (JS-H 5), meant that each group of gospel expounders was saying, 'Lo, here is Christ; we have his system of salvation; ours is the true church; we know the way; come, Join with us.'"

Bruce R. McConkie, The Mortal Messiah, Vol. 2, p. 170-171.
"'Ye shall know them by their fruits,' Jesus said. By their fruits—their words, their acts, the wonders that they do—these things shall separate true prophets and teachers frown false ones. Do they receive revelations and see visions? Does the Holy Ghost speak by their mouth? Are they legal administrators who have power to bind and seal on earth and in heaven? Is their doctrine true and sound and in harmony with all that is found in Holy Writ? Do they enjoy the gifts of the Spirit, so that the sick are healed under their hands? And does the Lord God give his Holy Spirit to attest the truth of their words and to approve the acts that they do? Without true prophets there is no salvation; false

prophets lead people astray; men choose, at the peril of their salvation, the prophets whom they follow."

Bruce R. McConkie, The Mortal Messiah, Vol. 3, p. 437-438.

"In the day preceding our Lord's return, false religions will cover the earth. Each will be, as it were, a false Christ, inviting men to this or that system of salvation; each will have its own ministers and evangelists who, as false prophets, will propound its doctrines and extol its wonders. So great and wondrous will be these false systems that men will think, How could a church be false that builds such cathedrals as these? How could a church be false that crowns kings and emperors; that sends forth armies into battle; that commands the services of artists and sculptors; that has, as it seems, all the gold and power of earth? With such 'signs' and 'wonders' as these, will not all but the very elect be deceived?"

Also see Bruce R. McConkie, The Millennial Messiah, p. 72-84.

Boyd K. Packer, Conference Report, Ensign, November 1992, p. 73.

"There are some among us now who have not been regularly ordained by the heads of the Church who tell of impending political and economic chaos, the end of the world—something of the `sky is falling, chicken licken' of the fables. They are misleading members to gather to colonies or cults.

Those deceivers say that the Brethren do not know what is going on in the world or that the Brethren approve of their teaching but do not wish to speak of it over the pulpit. Neither is true. The Brethren, by virtue of traveling constantly everywhere on earth, certainly know what is going on, and by virtue of prophetic insight are able to read the signs of the times.

Do not be deceived by them—those deceivers. If there is to be any gathering, it will be announced by those who have been regularly ordained and who are known to the Church to have authority. Come away from any others. Follow your leaders who have been duly ordained and have been publicly sustained, and you will not be led astray."

Neal A. Maxwell, All These Things Shall Give Thee Experience, p. 115.

"Following the Brethren can be more difficult when in some settings wolves are sent among the flock. False prophets will arise, enticing some to follow them, and by their evil works they deceive careless observers into discounting any and all who claim to be prophets. Satan's order of battle is such that if it is necessary to encourage a hundred false prophets in order to obscure the validity of one true prophet, he will gladly do so."

Neal A. Maxwell, Things As They Really Are, p. 79.

"Believers must not stereotype false prophets either, thereby failing to recognize them in their many forms. Just as the living prophets are consistent in their doctrines and objectives, so false prophets follow certain patterns. Peter warned us of false prophets who would 'bring in damnable heresies, even denying the Lord that bought them.' (2 Peter 2:1.) The denial of the divinity and the atonement of Christ is such a constant characteristic. We see it not only in the Sherems and Korihors of yesteryear but, today, among those leaders who espouse and promote a Christianity without a divine Christ. John the Beloved said, '. . . for the testimony of Jesus is the spirit of prophecy.' (Revelation 19:10.) The living prophets will always testify of the reality and the livingness of Jesus Christ. . . .

Living prophets will likewise be concerned with telling us the truth and will not flatter us or give us the messages we want to hear."

M. Russell Ballard, Ensign, December 1996, p. 57.

"Some Latter-day Saints may not be aware of it, but there are 'false prophets' rising within and without the Church. They believe they have had revelations, that they know something the First Presidency and the Twelve Apostles don't know. We need to be very careful of such people. The Savior said that in the last days even the very elect could be pulled away from the truth by such false prophets."

SCRIPTURAL REFERENCES

Amos 3:7
7 Surely the Lord GOD will do nothing, but he revealeth his secret unto his servants the prophets.

JST-Matthew 1:6-11
6 For many shall come in my name, saying—I am Christ—and shall deceive many;
7 Then shall they deliver you up to be afflicted, and shall kill you, and ye shall be hated of all nations, for my name's sake;
8 And then shall many be offended, and shall betray one another, and shall hate one another;
9 And many false prophets shall arise, and shall deceive many;
10 And because iniquity shall abound, the love of many shall wax cold;
11 But he that remaineth steadfast and is not overcome, the same shall be saved.

JST-Matthew 1:21-26
21 Behold, these things I have spoken unto you concerning the Jews; and again, after the tribulation of those days which shall come upon Jerusalem, if any man shall say unto you, Lo, here is Christ, or there, believe him not;
22 For in those days there shall also arise false Christs, and false prophets, and shall show great signs and wonders, insomuch, that, if possible, they shall deceive the very elect, who are the elect according to the covenant.
23 Behold, I speak these things unto you for the elect's sake; and you also shall hear of wars, and rumors of wars; see that ye be not troubled, for all I have told you must come to pass; but the end is not yet.
24 Behold, I have told you before;
25 Wherefore, if they shall say unto you: Behold, he is in the desert; go not forth: Behold, he is in the secret chambers; believe it not;
26 For as the light of the morning cometh out of the east, and shineth even unto the west, and covereth the whole earth, so shall also the coming of the Son of Man be.

Matthew 7:15-20
15 Beware of false prophets, which come to you in sheep's clothing, but inwardly they are ravening wolves.
16 Ye shall know them by their fruits. Do men gather grapes of thorns, or figs of thistles?
17 Even so every good tree bringeth forth good fruit; but a corrupt tree bringeth forth evil fruit.
18 A good tree cannot bring forth evil fruit, neither can a corrupt tree bring forth good fruit.
19 Every tree that bringeth not forth good fruit is hewn down, and cast into the fire.
20 Wherefore by their fruits ye shall know them.

Mark 13:5-6
5 And Jesus answering them began to say, Take heed lest any man deceive you:
6 For many shall come in my name, saying, I am Christ; and shall deceive many.

Luke 6:26

26 Woe unto you, when all men shall speak well of you! for so did their fathers to the false prophets.

Luke 21:8

8 And he said, Take heed that ye be not deceived: for many shall come in my name, saying, I am Christ; and the time draweth near: go ye not therefore after them.

2 Thessalonians 2:3-12

3 Let no man deceive you by any means: for that day shall not come, except there come a falling away first, and that man of sin be revealed, the son of perdition;

4 Who opposeth and exalteth himself above all that is called God, or that is worshipped; so that he as God sitteth in the temple of God, shewing himself that he is God.

5 Remember ye not, that, when I was yet with you, I told you these things?

6 And now ye know what withholdeth that he might be revealed in his time.

7 For the mystery of iniquity doth already work: only he who now letteth will let, until he be taken out of the way.

8 And then shall that Wicked be revealed, whom the Lord shall consume with the spirit of his mouth, and shall destroy with the brightness of his coming:

9 Even him, whose coming is after the working of Satan with all power and signs and lying wonders,

10 And with all deceivableness of unrighteousness in them that perish; because they received not the love of the truth, that they might be saved.

11 And for this cause God shall send them strong delusion, that they should believe a lie:

12 That they all might be damned who believed not the truth, but had pleasure in unrighteousness.

2 Timothy 3:13

13 But evil men and seducers shall wax worse and worse, deceiving, and being deceived.

2 Peter 2:1

1 But there were false prophets also among the people, even as there shall be false teachers among you, who privily shall bring in damnable heresies, even denying the Lord that bought them, and bring upon themselves swift destruction.

1 John 2:18-23

18 Little children, it is the last time: and as ye have heard that antichrist shall come, even now are there many antichrists; whereby we know that it is the last time.

19 They went out from us, but they were not of us; for if they had been of us, they would no doubt have continued with us: but they went out, that they might be made manifest that they were not all of us.

20 But ye have an unction from the Holy One, and ye know all things.

21 I have not written unto you because ye know not the truth, but because ye know it, and that no lie is of the truth.

22 Who is a liar but he that denieth that Jesus is the Christ? He is antichrist, that denieth the Father

and the Son.

23 Whosoever denieth the Son, the same hath not the Father: (but) he that acknowledgeth the Son hath the Father also.

1 John 4:1-3

1 Beloved, believe not every spirit, but try the spirits whether they are of God: because many false prophets are gone out into the world.

2 Hereby know ye the Spirit of God: Every spirit that confesseth that Jesus Christ is come in the flesh is of God:

3 And every spirit that confesseth not that Jesus Christ is come in the flesh is not of God: and this is that spirit of antichrist, whereof ye have heard that it should come; and even now already is it in the world.

2 John 1:7

7 For many deceivers are entered into the world, who confess not that Jesus Christ is come in the flesh. This is a deceiver and an antichrist.

Revelation 16:13-14

13 And I saw three unclean spirits like frogs come out of the mouth of the dragon, and out of the mouth of the beast, and out of the mouth of the false prophet.

14 For they are the spirits of devils, working miracles, which go forth unto the kings of the earth and of the whole world, to gather them to the battle of that great day of God Almighty.

Revelation 19:20-21

20 And the beast was taken, and with him the false prophet that wrought miracles before him, with which he deceived them that had received the mark of the beast, and them that worshipped his image. These both were cast alive into a lake of fire burning with brimstone.

21 And the remnant were slain with the sword of him that sat upon the horse, which sword proceeded out of his mouth: and all the fowls were filled with their flesh.

Revelation 20:10

10 And the devil that deceived them was cast into the lake of fire and brimstone, where the beast and the false prophet are, and shall be tormented day and night for ever and ever.

2 Nephi 25:18

18 Wherefore, he shall bring forth his words unto them, which words shall judge them at the last day, for they shall be given them for the purpose of convincing them of the true Messiah, who was rejected by them; and unto the convincing of them that they need not look forward any more for a Messiah to come, for there should not any come, save it should be a false Messiah which should deceive the people; for there is save one Messiah spoken of by the prophets, and that Messiah is he who should be rejected of the Jews.

Alma 30:6

6 But it came to pass in the latter end of the seventeenth year, there came a man into the land of Zarahemla, and he was Anti-Christ, for he began to preach unto the people against the prophecies which had been spoken by the prophets, concerning the coming of Christ.

Alma 30:12-18

12 And this Anti-Christ, whose name was Korihor, (and the law could have no hold upon him) began to preach unto the people that there should be no Christ. And after this manner did he preach, saying:

13 O ye that are bound down under a foolish and a vain hope, why do ye yoke yourselves with such foolish things? Why do ye look for a Christ? For no man can know of anything which is to come.

14 Behold, these things which ye call prophecies, which ye say are handed down by holy prophets, behold, they are foolish traditions of your fathers.

15 How do ye know of their surety? Behold, ye cannot know of things which ye do not see; therefore ye cannot know that there shall be a Christ.

16 Ye look forward and say that ye see a remission of your sins. But behold, it is the effect of a frenzied mind; and this derangement of your minds comes because of the traditions of your fathers, which lead you away into a belief of things which are not so.

17 And many more such things did he say unto them, telling them that there could be no atonement made for the sins of men, but every man fared in this life according to the management of the creature; therefore every man prospered according to his genius, and that every man conquered according to his strength; and whatsoever a man did was no crime.

18 And thus he did preach unto them, leading away the hearts of many, causing them to lift up their heads in their wickedness, yea, leading away many women, and also men, to commit whoredoms—telling them that when a man was dead, that was the end thereof.

3 Nephi 14:15-17

15 Beware of false prophets, who come to you in sheep's clothing, but inwardly they are ravening wolves.

16 Ye shall know them by their fruits. Do men gather grapes of thorns, or figs of thistles?

17 Even so every good tree bringeth forth good fruit; but a corrupt tree bringeth forth evil fruit.

Moroni 7:15-19

15 For behold, my brethren, it is given unto you to judge, that ye may know good from evil; and the way to judge is as plain, that ye may know with a perfect knowledge, as the daylight is from the dark night.

16 For behold, the Spirit of Christ is given to every man, that he may know good from evil; wherefore, I show unto you the way to judge; for every thing which inviteth to do good, and to persuade to believe in Christ, is sent forth by the power and gift of Christ; wherefore ye may know with a perfect knowledge it is of God.

17 But whatsoever thing persuadeth men to do evil, and believe not in Christ, and deny him, and serve not God, then ye may know with a perfect knowledge it is of the devil; for after this manner doth the devil work, for he persuadeth no man to do good, no, not one; neither do his angels; neither

do they who subject themselves unto him.

18 And now, my brethren, seeing that ye know the light by which ye may judge, which light is the light of Christ, see that ye do not judge wrongfully; for with that same judgment which ye judge ye shall also be judged.

19 Wherefore, I beseech of you, brethren, that ye should search diligently in the light of Christ that ye may know good from evil; and if ye will lay hold upon every good thing, and condemn it not, ye certainly will be a child of Christ.

D&C 46:7-8

7 But ye are commanded in all things to ask of God, who giveth liberally; and that which the Spirit testifies unto you even so I would that ye should do in all holiness of heart, walking uprightly before me, considering the end of your salvation, doing all things with prayer and thanksgiving, that ye may not be seduced by evil spirits, or doctrines of devils, or the commandments of men; for some are of men, and others of devils.

8 Wherefore, beware lest ye are deceived; and that ye may not be deceived seek ye earnestly the best gifts, always remembering for what they are given;

D&C 49:22-23

22 And again, verily I say unto you, that the Son of Man cometh not in the form of a woman, neither of a man traveling on the earth.

23 Wherefore, be not deceived, but continue in steadfastness, looking forth for the heavens to be shaken, and the earth to tremble and to reel to and fro as a drunken man, and for the valleys to be exalted, and for the mountains to be made low, and for the rough places to become smooth--and all this when the angel shall sound his trumpet.

D&C 50:2-3

2 Behold, verily I say unto you, that there are many spirits which are false spirits, which have gone forth in the earth, deceiving the world.

3 And also Satan hath sought to deceive you, that he might overthrow you.

D&C 64:37-39

37 Behold, I, the Lord, have made my church in these last days like unto a judge sitting on a hill, or in a high place, to judge the nations.

38 For it shall come to pass that the inhabitants of Zion shall judge all things pertaining to Zion.

39 And liars and hypocrites shall be proved by them, and they who are not apostles and prophets shall be known.

CHAPTER SEVEN

APOSTASY

"That man who rises up to condemn other, finding fault with the Church, saying that they are out of the way, while he himself is righteous, then know assuredly, that that man is in the high road to apostasy; and if he does not repent, will apostatize, as God lives." (Teachings of the Prophet Joseph Smith, Section Four, 1839-42, p.156.)

Joseph Smith, History of the Church, Vol. 2, Introduction, p. 32.

"Such rebellions and apostasies as occurred in this Kirtland period of the Church's history but test and exhibit the strength of the fabric. Such circumstances force a review of the work as far as accomplished. The whole is re-examined to see if in it there is any flaw or defect; if any worthless material is being worked into its structure. Hence periods usually considered calamitous are accompanied by corrections of what may be wrong; and the body religious is purified by the expulsion of those whose rebellion and apostasy but prove them unworthy of the Lord's work. Let me be rightly understood here. I am not contending that adverse circumstances, rebellions and apostasies are in themselves good. Whatever may be the over-ruled results to the body religious, rebellion and apostasy spell condemnation and the destruction of spiritual life for the individuals overtaken by such calamities. . . .

The first step in the process of correcting human nature is to discover its defects. It may not always follow that when the defects are made known they will be corrected. But it is true that no correction will be made until the necessity of correction is manifest, until the defects are pointed out. Hence God has said: 'If men will come unto me, I will show unto them their weaknesses.' But, unhappily, it sometimes is the case that men resist God, they love their sins, they become hardened in their iniquity, they resist the Spirit, and prove themselves unworthy of the Father's kingdom. What then? Shall they pollute that kingdom, or shall they be cast out as material unfitted for the Master's use, and of their own volition choose to remain so? There can be but one reasonable answer to the question. They refuse to go peaceably, however. They are boisterous, they accuse the innocent, they justify their own course, they seek to wreck the Church, to bring to pass chaos; and in the midst of this disorder they are cast out; and although this may not always end their power to work mischief, or create annoyance for the body-religious—for the power to work evil is still with them—yet the Church is rid of them, and in no way can be regarded as responsible for their wickedness. It is our custom to enumerate such scenes as among the calamitous events of the Church; and they are so, in some aspects of the case. As already remarked it is a calamitous time for those who are cast out, for they are overcome of the evil one; and as the heavens wept when the Son of the Morning and his following were cast out of heaven, so it is to be expected that the Saints will be sad, and sorrow over those who are overcome of the adversary. But for the Church herself it is well that this intractable material is gotten rid of; that the body religious is purged of those who can only be a source of weakness and of shame to her. She is helped by the event; purified by it; strengthened; made more acceptable with God and pleasing to reasonable men."

Joseph Smith, History of the Church, Vol. 6, p. 299.

"If you hear of any one in high authority, that he is rather inclined to apostasy, don't let prejudice arise, but pray for him. God may feel after him, and he may return. Never speak reproachfully nor disrespectfully; he is in the hands of God."

Teachings of the Prophet Joseph Smith, Section Two, 1834-37, p. 66-67.

"Strange as it may appear at first thought, yet it is no less strange than true, that notwithstanding all the professed determination to live godly, apostates after turning from the faith of Christ, unless they have speedily repented, have sooner or later fallen into the snares of the wicked one, and have been left destitute of the Spirit of God, to manifest their wickedness in the eyes of multitudes. From apostates the faithful have received the severest persecutions. Judas was rebuked and immediately betrayed his Lord into the hands of His enemies, because Satan entered into him. There is a superior intelligence bestowed upon such as obey the Gospel with full purpose of heart, which, if sinned against, the apostate is left naked and destitute of the Spirit of God, and he is, in truth, nigh unto cursing, and his end is to be burned. When once that light which was in them is taken from them, they become as much darkened as they were previously enlightened, and then, no marvel, if all their power should be enlisted against the truth, and they, Judas like, seek the destruction of those who were their greatest benefactors. What nearer friend on earth, or in heaven, had Judas than the Savior? And his first object was to destroy Him."

Teachings of the Prophet Joseph Smith, Section Four, 1839-42, p.156.

"I will give you one of the Keys of the mysteries of the Kingdom. It is an eternal principle, that has existed with God from all eternity: That man who rises up to condemn other, finding fault with the Church, saying that they are out of the way, while he himself is righteous, then know assuredly, that that man is in the high road to apostasy; and if he does not repent, will apostatize, as God lives. The principle is as correct as the one that Jesus put forth in saying that he who seeketh a sign is an adulterous person; and that principle is eternal, undeviating, and firm as the pillars of heaven; for whenever you see a man seeking after a sign, you may set it down that he is an adulterous man."

Teachings of the Prophet Joseph Smith, Section Six, 1843–44, p. 358.

"All sins shall be forgiven, except the sin against the Holy Ghost; for Jesus will save all except the sons of perdition. What must a man do to commit the unpardonable sin? He must receive the Holy Ghost, have the heavens opened unto him, and know God, and then sin against Him. After a man has sinned against the Holy Ghost, there is no repentance for him. He has got to say that the sun does not shine while he sees it; he has got to deny Jesus Christ when the heavens have been opened unto him, and to deny the plan of salvation with his eyes open to the truth of it; and from that time he begins to be an enemy. This is the case with many apostates of the Church of Jesus Christ of Latter-day Saints."

Brigham Young, Messages of the First Presidency, Vol. 2, p. 204, December 10, 1856.

"Notwithstanding these and many other good qualities which characterize this people, still we find too prevalent a disposition to murmur, find fault and complain at the dispensations of an All-wise Providence; a disposition of careless indifference to His counsels, and a dull lethargy which lulls the people into a false security; all of which gives Satan the advantage, darkens counsel, and leads many into a spirit of apostacy. We must remember that we live in a world of sin, wickedness and sorrow, and that the enemy of all righteousness is ever on the alert to destroy the Saints and lead them into temptation, darkness, sin and transgression."

Brigham Young, Journal of Discourses, Vol. 10, p. 300, June 4, 1864.

"Whether we are poor or rich, if we neglect our prayers and our sacrament meetings, we neglect the spirit of the Lord, and a spirit of darkness comes over us. If we lust for gold, for the riches of the world, and spare no pains to obtain and retain them, and feel 'these are mine,' then the spirit of anti-Christ comes upon us. This is the danger the Latter-day Saints are in, consequently it is better for us to live in the absence of what is called the riches of this world, than to possess them and with them inherit the spirit of anti-Christ and be lost."

Discourses of Brigham Young, p. 82.

"It was said here this morning that no person ever apostatized, without actual transgression. Omission of duty leads to commission."

Discourses of Brigham Young, p. 82-83.

"Let a man or woman who has received much of the power of God, visions and revelations, turn away from the holy commandments of the Lord, and it seems that their senses are taken from them, their understanding and judgment in righteousness are taken away, they go into darkness, and become like a blind person who gropes by the wall."

Discourses of Brigham Young, p. 83.

"Whenever there is a disposition manifested in any of the members of this Church to question the right of the President of the whole Church to direct in all things, you see manifested evidences of apostasy—of a spirit which, if encouraged, will lead to a separation from the Church and to final destruction; wherever there is a disposition to operate against any legally appointed officer of this Kingdom, no matter in what capacity he is called to act, if persisted in, it will be followed by the same results; they will "walk after the flesh in the lust of uncleanness, and despise government. Presumptuous are they, self-willed; they are not afraid to speak evil of dignities.""

Discourses of Brigham Young, p. 83-84.

"When men lose the spirit of the work in which we are engaged, they become infidel in their feelings. They say that they do not know whether the Bible is true, whether the Book of Mormon is true, nor about new revelations, nor whether there is a God or not. When they lose the spirit of this work, they lose the knowledge of the things of God in time and in eternity; all is lost to them."

Discourses of Brigham Young, p. 84.

"You hear many say, 'I am a Latter-day Saint, and I never will apostatize;' 'I am a Latter-day Saint, and shall be to the day of my death.' I never make such declarations, and never shall. I think I have learned that of myself I have no power, but my system is organized to increase in wisdom, knowledge, and power, getting a little here and a little there. But when I am left to myself, I have no power, and my wisdom is foolishness; then I cling close to the Lord, and I have power in his name. I think I have learned the Gospel so as to know, that in and of myself I am nothing."

Discourses of Brigham Young, p. 84.

"Men begin to apostatize by taking to themselves strength, by hearkening to the whisperings of the enemy who leads them astray little by little, until they gather to themselves that which they call the wisdom of man; then they begin to depart from God, and their minds become confused."

Discourses of Brigham Young, p. 84.

"You have known men who, while in the Church, were active, quick and full of intelligence; but after they have left the Church, they have become contracted in their understandings, they have become darkened in their minds and everything has become a mystery to them, and in regard to the things of God, they have become like the rest of the world, who think, hope and pray that such and such things may be so, but they do not know the least about it This is precisely the position of those who leave this Church; they go into the dark, they are not able to judge, conceive or comprehend things as they are. They are like the drunken man—he thinks that everybody is the worse for liquor but himself, and he is the only sober man in the neighborhood, The apostates think that everybody is wrong but themselves."

Discourses of Brigham Young, p. 85.

"People do, however, leave this Church, but they leave it because they get into darkness, and the very day they conclude that there should be a democratic vote, or in other words, that we should have two candidates for the presiding Priesthood in the midst of the Latter-day Saints, they conclude to be apostates. There is no such thing as confusion, division, strife, animosity, hatred, malice, or two sides to the question in the house of God; there is but one side to the question there."

Discourses of Brigham Young, p. 86.

"Many receive the Gospel because they know it is true; they are convinced in their judgment that it is true; strong argument overpowers them, and they are rationally compelled to admit the Gospel to be true upon fair reasoning. They yield to it, and obey its first principles, but never seek to be enlightened by the power of the Holy Ghost; such ones frequently step out of the way."

John W. Taylor, Collected Discourses, Vol. 1, April 6, 1888.

"Whenever you see a man beginning to apostatize from the Church the first thing you will notice is that he neglects his prayers. Therefore I exhort you all, my brethren and sisters, that if your are in the habit of neglecting this duty, repent and return unto the Lord, supplicate Him for His Holy Spirit, express your gratitude, day after day, in simple, plain language, for the blessings which have been bestowed upon you."

John Taylor, The Gospel Kingdom, p. 334-335.

"We have met on the road a great many apostates. I do not want to say much about them. If they can be happy, all right. But they do not exhibit it. When a man deserts from the gospel, from the ordinances, from the priesthood and its authority, from the revelations of the Spirit of God, from the spirit of prophecy, from that sweet, calm influence that broods over the upright man in all his acts, he loses the blessing of God and falls back into error; and, as the scripture says, the last state of that man is worse than the first. (Compare Matthew 12:45.)"

John Taylor, Mediation and Atonement, Appendix.

"Men have been ever prone to apostasy; our fallen nature is at enmity with a godly life; sometimes in one way, sometimes in another, Satan led men from the right path and under the influences of a false or diabolic inspiration many errors were introduced; as well as through the natural corrupt ambition of men who sought to obtain power over their fellows by promulgating new theories in the name of God and under the auspices of religion."

Wilford Woodruff, Journal of Discourses, Vol. 21, p. 190-191.

"He gave Joseph to understand that he held the priesthood, which priesthood was after the order of God, after the order of Melchizedek, the same priesthood by which God himself performed all his works in the heavens and in the earth, and any man who bore that priesthood had the same power. That priesthood had communication with the heavens, power to move the heavens, power to perform the work of the heavens, and wherever any man magnified that calling, God gave his angels charge concerning him and his ministrations were of power and force both in this world and the world to come; but let that man use that priesthood for any other purpose than the building up of the kingdom of God, for which purpose it was given, and the heavens withdraw themselves, the power of the priesthood departs, and he is left to walk in darkness and not in light, and this is the key to apostasy of all men whether in this generation or any other."

Wilford Woodruff, Journal of Discourses, Vol. 21, p. 284, July 4, 1880.

"Well, we have got the kingdom, and we must bear it off. It won't pay you nor me to apostatize. But then there is this danger, you know. Brother Joseph used to counsel us in this wise: 'The moment you permit yourselves to lay aside any duty that God calls you to perform, to gratify your own desires; the moment you permit yourselves to become careless, you lay a foundation for apostasy. Be careful; understand you are called to a work, and when God requires you to do that work do it.' Another thing he said: 'In all your trials, tribulations and sickness, in all your sufferings, even unto death, be careful you don't betray God, be careful you don't betray the priesthood, be careful you don't apostatize; because if you do, you will be sorry for it.'"

Wilford Woodruff, Journal of Discourses, Vol. 23, p. 331, December 10, 1882.

"We are under great responsibility. It won't pay to apostatize; 'there is no money in it.' Any man who receives this Priesthood and tastes of the word of God, and of the powers of the world to come—any man that turns away from these things, apostatizes, and turns away from the Church of God, shall not, in accordance with the revelations of the Lord to Joseph Smith, 'have forgiveness of sins in this world nor in the world to come.'"

Teachings of Lorenzo Snow, p. 52.

"Everyone's faith will be tested. Those persons who received this work without religious motives, and without an honest conviction of its divine requirements, but solely for the 'loaves and fishes,' cannot possibly abide the test to which everyone's faith, sooner or later, must be brought; but will have his dishonesty and hypocrisy exposed, and will sooner or later apostatize. (6 March 1886, Journal of Discourses, 26:374-75.)"

George Q. Cannon, Gospel Truth, Vol. 1, p. 278.

"There is one thing that the Lord has warned us about from the beginning and that is not to speak evil of the Lord's anointed. He has told us that any member of the Church who indulged in this is liable to lose the Spirit of God and go into darkness. The Prophet Joseph said time and again that it was one of the first and strongest symptoms of apostasy."

George Q. Cannon, Collected Discourses, Vol. 4, September 7, 1895.

"There must be on the part of the Latter-Saints a determination not to listen to Satan, not to be governed by him, not to allow him to lead them into sin, because it is sin that causes apostasy. No man ever apostatized from this Church who had not committed sin. God does not desert those who are faithful and keep His commandments. But when they commit sin, when they transgress the commandments of God, when they defile themselves, then they have no claim upon the promises of God. Do we want apostasy to cease? If we do, then we must break away from sin, and we must teach our children to do the same and not commit sin in any form, or if they do not, they will apostatize and be destroyed; for God is going to cleanse the earth of the wicked, until there will be but few men left."

Joseph F. Smith, Gospel Doctrine, p. 48.

"I think that in the realms of liberty, and the exercise of human judgment, all men should exercise extreme caution, that they do not change nor abolish those things which God has willed and has inspired to be done. It has been in this realm of freedom, and the exercise of human judgment that most of the evils that have occurred in the world have been done—the martyrdom of Saints, the crucifixion of the Son of God himself, and much of the apostasy and departure from the work of righteousness, and from the laws of God, have occurred in this realm of freedom and the exercise of human judgment. God in his boundless wisdom and gracious mercy has provided means, and has shown the way to the children of men whereby, even in the realms of freedom and the exercise of their own judgment, they may individually go unto God in faith and prayer, and find out what should guide and direct their human judgment and wisdom; and I do not want the Latter-day Saints to forget that this is their privilege. I would rather that they should seek God for a counselor and guide, than to follow the wild harangues of political leaders, or leaders of any other cult. (CR., Oct. 1912, p. 41-42.)"

Joseph F. Smith, Gospel Doctrine, p. 224.

"And I cannot emphasize too strongly the importance of Latter-day Saints honoring and sustaining in truth and in deed the authority of the Holy Priesthood which is called to preside. The moment a spirit enters the heart of a member to refrain from sustaining the constituted authorities of the Church, that moment he becomes possessed of a spirit which inclines to rebellion or dissension; and if he permits that spirit to take a firm root in his mind, it will eventually lead him into darkness and apostasy. It makes no difference how much we may profess to love the gospel and prize our standing in the Church, if we allow the spirit of darkness to take possession of our minds, the light and love within us will go out, and bitterness and enmity will take possession of our souls. Then, oh how dark, how bitter and wicked we may become! (Salt Lake Stake, CR., June 12, 1898.)"

Joseph F. Smith, Gospel Doctrine, p. 254.

"One fruitful source of apostasy from the Church comes from an inclination on the part of those who apostatize to consider the small, mostly unintentionally committed errors of its officers, rather than the broader and more important labors which enter into their experience. Young men so inclined turn from the infinite truth of the gospel, and the mighty plan of salvation, the eternal purposes of God, to carp and cavil upon the insignificant actions and the imperfect achievements of men, judging the inspiring magnitude of the former by the disagreeable and tiresome detail of the latter. Many of the serious annoyances of communal life among the Saints would be obliterated entirely, if men would search for the great and noble aspirations actuating their neighbors, rather than for the imperfect sidelights that lay bare their puny shortcomings. Those who wish to advance in the world will avoid soul-destroying, mind-narrowing thoughts, and devote the days allotted to them, which it will be found are none too numerous, in studying the greater, nobler, and grander subjects that tend to build character, provide happiness, and create harmony with the mighty purposes of the Church and its founder, the Lord Jesus Christ."

Francis M. Lyman, Collected Discourses, Vol. 1, January 13, 1889.

"The greatest apostasies we have ever had have been when the people were in peace and when let alone; not in times of great trouble and serious difficulty. Trials seem to draw the people together, to make them seek after the Lord, and become better acquainted with Him and the workings of His Holy Spirit, than is the case in times of peace. I have heard a great many express themselves as though they thought the Latter-day Saints were in rather a perilous condition—that is, at home in the Wards and in the Stakes; that they were growing cold, neglecting their duties, etc. Now, there may be an appearance of this, and there may be some truth in it for a foundation; but let me testify to you that the Latter-day Saints are not going to apostatize, they are not going to desert the Kingdom; for the Lord has made no mistake, and He has chosen the very spirits that He wanted. He has sent them at the time He wanted them on the earth, and He sent the Gospel at the time He wanted it on the earth, for them to receive. . . .God's Kingdom . . . is established in the earth, and it will endure. Men may fail, but there will be plenty remain; plenty that will endure faithfully to the end."

Anthon H. Lund, Collected Discourses, Vol. 2, April 4, 1890.

"It is true that men have apostatized, that men high in authority have fallen, but that is no proof that this work is not of God. Some of those men who followed the Prophet Joseph Smith and were called to assist him did not remain faithful; but one thing is evident to all those who study the matter, that those witnesses to the Book of Mormon, those who published their names to the world, all adhered to their testimony; they never recanted or took it back. They did not dare to deny; and although cut off from the Church, we find that they would still give their testimony to the world that they had seen the plates from which this work was translated. Some persons may ask, 'How is it possible that men who had seen angels and had such a testimony could fall away from the Church, as these men did?' Men may see angels and have revelations, and as long as they obey the whisperings of the Holy Spirit they will not apostatize; but when they begin to feel that they have strength enough in themselves, and fail to acknowledge God as their Helper, then they cannot stand."

Francis M. Lyman, Collected Discourses, Vol. 3, April 5, 1892.

"I tell you that everything that comes along will try some of the people. But I say that we are today a tried and proven people so far that there will not be the apostasy, in proportion to our numbers, that was witnessed in the beginning of the Church. Some will apostatize, no doubt, and lose the faith, and die in that condition. But I tell you the very best and choicest, the most independent spirits that could be found in the earth, have been gathered. . .And the Lord has tried and proven us. Not only this, but the strength of the trials that we have endured, and the faith and power that we have, tinctures our children, and they will walk measurably in our footsteps, though some of them may be lost."

Heber J. Grant, Gospel Standards, p. 31.

"Next to the committing of sin there is no more fruitful cause of apostasy among the Latter-day Saints than when we put our trust in the arm of flesh. I firmly believe that no man who honestly bows down every day of his life and supplicates God in sincerity for the light of His Holy Spirit to guide him will ever become proud and haughty. On the contrary, his heart will become filled with meekness, humility, and childlike simplicity."

Joseph Fielding Smith, Church History and Modern Revelation, Vol. 3, p. 150.

"How does apostasy come about? By neglect of duty, failing to keep in our souls the spirit of prayer, of obedience to the principles of the Gospel; by failure to pay an honest tithing, or to observe the word of wisdom, and to absent one's self from sacrament meetings where we have been commanded to go and renew our covenants. Apostasy comes through the sins of omission as well as through the sins of commission. Immorality is a deadly sin and those who are guilty, if they do not repent, will lose the spirit and deny the faith. Apostasy does not come upon an individual suddenly, but it is a gradual growth in which darkness through sin crowds out the spirit of light from the soul. When a man who was once enlightened loses the Spirit of truth, the darkness which takes its place is overwhelming. Alma gives us a good example of this in teaching Zeezrom. (Alma 12:9-11.)"

Joseph Fielding Smith Jr., Doctrines of Salvation, Vol. 1, p. 244.

"But so far as the Latter-day Saints are concerned, the majority of them will not turn from the faith of their fathers. It is not destined that such should be the case, for when this gospel was restored, the Lord declared through his servants who came from the heavens with the message of salvation, that the gospel was restored for the last time, and that it must grow and increase and the knowledge grow and spread until it shall fill the whole earth."

Joseph Fielding Smith Jr., Doctrines of Salvation, Vol. 1, p. 285-286.

"If we will follow the spirit of light, the spirit of truth, the spirit that is set forth in the revelations of the Lord; if we will, through the spirit of prayer and humility, seek for the guidance of the Holy Ghost, the Lord will increase our light and our understanding so that we shall have the spirit of discernment; we shall understand the truth; we shall know falsehood when we see it, and we shall not be deceived.

Who is it that is deceived in this Church? Not the man who has been faithful in the discharge of duty; not the man who has made himself acquainted with the word of the Lord; not the man who has practiced the commandments given in these revelations; but the man who is not acquainted with the truth, the man who is in spiritual darkness, the man who does not comprehend and understand the principles of the gospel. Such a man will be deceived, and when these false spirits come among us, he may not understand or be able to distinguish between light and darkness."

Joseph Fielding Smith Jr., Doctrines of Salvation, Vol. 1, p. 287.

"There is no reason in the world why each member of the Church should not have a thorough understanding of the principles of the gospel, of the order of the Church, and the government of the Church, so that none need be led astray by any wind of doctrine, or notion that prevails among the children of men, which may come to his attention."

Joseph Fielding Smith Jr., Doctrines of Salvation, Vol. 3, p. 295.

"The man who receives the light of truth and then turns away, loses the light which he had, and if he continues in that course, eventually he will be bound by the chains of spiritual darkness. Darkness will take the place of truth, as the truth becomes gradually dimmed, until he has lost knowledge of spiritual things. He who walks in the light of truth receives more truth."

Joseph Fielding Smith Jr., Doctrines of Salvation, Vol. 3, p. 298-299.

"We hear so much in these days about being tolerant and broad-minded. . .Satan is very broad-minded, extremely so as long as he can get people to do evil and avoid the truth. He will teach any kind of theory, or principle, or doctrine, if it doesn't conform to the fundamental things of life—the gospel of Jesus Christ. He is even willing to teach some truth, if he can join that truth with error, and by teaching the error with the truth lead men astray. This is how broad-minded he is, and that is how the apostasy came about in the primitive Church."

Joseph Fielding Smith Jr., Doctrines of Salvation, Vol. 3, p. 309.

"Almost without exception when a person leaves the Church, it is due to transgression. The

Spirit of the Lord will not dwell in unclean tabernacles, and when the Spirit is withdrawn, darkness supersedes the light, and apostasy will follow. This is one of the greatest evidences of the divinity of this latter-day work. In other organizations men may commit all manner of sin and still retain their membership, because they have no companionship with the Holy Ghost to lose; but in the Church when a man sins and continues without repentance, the Spirit is withdrawn, and when he is left to himself the adversary takes possession of his mind and he denies the faith."

James. E. Talmage, Jesus the Christ, p. 745.

"Among the disintegrating forces acting from without, the most effective was the persistent persecution to which the saints were subjected, incident to both Judaistic and pagan opposition. Vast numbers who had professed membership and many who had been officers in the ministry deserted the Church; while a few were stimulated to greater zeal under the scourge of persecution. The general effect of opposition from the outside—of external causes of decline in faith and works considered as a whole—was the defection of individuals, resulting in a widespread apostasy from the Church. But immeasurably more serious was the result of internal dissension, schism and disruption, whereby an absolute apostasy of the Church from the way and word of God was brought about."

James. E. Talmage, Jesus the Christ, p. 748-749.

"The most important of the internal causes by which the apostasy of the Primitive Church was brought about may be thus summarized: (1) The corrupting of the simple doctrines of the gospel of Christ by admixture with so-called philosophic systems. (2) Unauthorized additions to the prescribed rites of the Church and the introduction of vital alterations in essential ordinances. (3) Unauthorized changes in Church organization and government."

James. E. Talmage, The Great Apostasy, p. 49.

"The Book of Mormon record is definite in its specifications of the immediate reasons for, or causes of the great apostasy on the western hemisphere. While the members of the Church remained faithful to their covenants and obligations, they as individuals and the Church as an organization prospered; and their enemies were unable to prevail against them. With prosperity, however, came pride and class distinctions, the rich dominated the poor, and earthly gain became the object of life. Secret organizations of evil purpose flourished; the people were divided into two opposing factions . . .With the growth of pride and its attendant sins, the Nephites became as wicked as the non-professing Lamanites; and in their wickedness these people sought each other's destruction."

John A. Widtsoe, Evidences and Reconciliations, p. 39-40.

"A testimony, being a living thing, may die. Sorrowfully, all of us may have seen such a passing. Witness the life of any apostate. Refuse to do the things that lead to a testimony, and, gradually, it will starve, wither, and perish. It does not matter how strong it may have been. It must be fed to be kept alive."

Harold B. Lee, Improvement Era, December 1970, p. 126.

"We have some tight places to go before the Lord is through with this church and the world in this dispensation, which is the last dispensation, which shall usher in the coming of the Lord. The gospel was restored to prepare a people ready to receive him. The power of Satan will increase; we see it in evidence on every hand. There will be inroads within the Church. There will be, as President Tanner has said, 'Hypocrites, those professing, but secretly are full of dead men's bones. We will see those who profess membership but secretly are plotting and trying to lead people not to follow the leadership that the Lord has set up to preside in this church."

Harold B. Lee, Stand Ye In Holy Places, p. 18.

"One of the greatest threats to the work of the Lord today comes from false educational ideas. There is a growing tendency of teachers within and without the Church to make academic interpretations of gospel teachings—to read, as a prophet-leader has said, 'by the lamp of their own conceit.' Unfortunately, much in the sciences, the arts, politics, and the entertainment field, as has been well said by an eminent scholar, is 'all dominated by this humanistic approach which ignores God and His word as revealed through the prophets.' This kind of worldly system apparently hopes to draw men away from God by making man the 'measure of all things,' as some worldly philosophers have said."

The Teachings of Spencer W. Kimball, p. 112.

"Remembering covenants prevents apostasy. That is the real purpose of the sacrament, to keep us from forgetting, to help us to remember. I suppose there would never be an apostate, there would never be a crime, if people remembered, really remembered, the things they had covenanted at the water's edge or at the sacrament table and in the temple. I suppose that is the reason the Lord asked Adam to offer sacrifices, for no other reason than that he and his posterity would remember —remember the basic things that they had been taught. I guess we as humans are prone to forget. It is easy to forget. Our sorrows, our joys, our concerns, our great problems seem to wane to some extent as time goes on, and there are many lessons that we learn which have a tendency to slip from us."

The Teachings of Spencer W. Kimball, p. 425.

"Philosophy replaced revelation. In the early centuries of the Christian era, the apostasy came not through persecution, but by relinquishment of faith caused by the superimposing of a man-made structure upon and over the divine program. Many men with no pretense nor claim to revelation, speaking without divine authority or revelation, depending only upon their own brilliant minds, but representing as they claim the congregations of the Christians and in long conference and erudite councils, sought the creation process to make a God which all could accept."

The Teachings of Spencer W. Kimball, p. 462.

"Apostasy often begins with criticism of current leaders. Apostasy usually begins with question and doubt and criticism. It is a retrograding and devolutionary process. The seeds of doubt are planted by unscrupulous or misguided people, and seldom directed against the doctrine at first,

221

but more often against the leaders."

Spencer W. Kimball, Faith Precedes the Miracle, p. 306.

"To satisfy his own egotism, to feed his pride, to justify vain ambition, a man took a stand against the authorities of the Church. He followed the usual pattern—no apostasy at first, only superiority of knowledge with mild criticism of the brethren. He loved the brethren, he said, but they had failed to see things he saw. He was sure his interpretation was correct. He would still love the Church, he maintained, but his criticism grew and developed into ever-widening areas. He could not yield in good conscience; he had his pride. He spoke of it among his associates; he talked of it at home. His children did not accept his philosophy wholly, but their confidence was shaken in the brethren and the Church. They were frustrated and became inactive. They married out of the Church and he lost them. He later realized the folly of his position and returned to humbleness and activity, but he had lost his children."

Spencer W. Kimball, The Miracle of Forgiveness, p. 132.

"Similarly the wise Church member will not take the first step in separating himself from the Church, as many do through apostasy. He will pray frequently and regularly, read the scriptures, and generally stay close to the Lord. He will diligently fulfil his Church and family duties and will follow the counsel of his spiritual leaders. By so doing he will always be able to repent of his sins as he pursues the upward road; he will never approach the unforgivable sin; he will never get anywhere near the point of no return."

Ezra Taft Benson, BYU Speeches, May 10, 1966, p. 6-7.

"Now these false educational ideas—set forth in many textbooks today—are prevalent in the prevalent in the world, and we have not entirely escaped them among teachers in our own system. There are a few teachers within the Church who, while courting apostasy, still want to remain members of the Church, for being members makes them more effective in misleading the Saints. But their day of judgment is coming, and when it does come, for some of them it would have been better, as the Savior said, that a millstone had been put around their necks and they had drowned in the depths of the sea, than to have led away any of the youth of the Church.

The Lord has stated that His Church will never again be taken from the earth because of apostasy. But He has also stated that some members of His Church will fall away. There has been individual apostasy in the past, it is going on now, and there will be an even increasing amount in the future. While we cannot save all the flock from being deceived, we should, without compromising our doctrine, strive to save as many as we can. For, as President J. Reuben Clark said, 'We are in the midst of the greatest exhibition of propaganda that the world has ever seen.' Do not believe all you hear. . . .

Don't let the philosophies and falsehoods of men throw you. Hold on to the iron rod. Learn to sift. Learn to discern error through the promptings of the Spirit and your study of the truth."

Ezra Taft Benson, Conference Report, April 1969, p. 10.

"One of the grand promises which the Lord made when he restored his Church in these latter days was that the Church should never again be taken from the earth nor given to another people. This is reassuring, for no matter how much individual apostasy we may see occur among Church members, the Church itself shall endure and remain intact. Our task, then, is to see that we personally endure to the end in faithful fellowship with the Church."

Ezra Taft Benson, Conference Report, April 1969, p. 11.

"Yes, within the Church today there are tares among the wheat and wolves within the flock. As President Clark stated, 'The ravening wolves are amongst us, from our own membership, and they, more than any others, are clothed in sheep's clothing because they wear the habiliments of the priesthood. . . . We should be careful of them. . . .' (Era, May 1949, p. 268. See also Conference Report, April 1949, p. 163.)

The wolves amongst our flock are more numerous and devious today than when President Clark made this statement."

Ezra Taft Benson, Conference Report, April 1969, p. 12.

"'A friend . . . wished to know whether we . . . considered an honest difference of opinion between a member of the Church and the Authorities of the Church was apostasy. . . . We replied that we had not stated that an honest difference of opinion between a member of the Church and the Authorities constituted apostasy, for we could conceive of a man honestly differing in opinion from the Authorities of the Church and yet not be an apostate; but we could not conceive of a man publishing those differences of opinion and seeking by arguments, sophistry and special pleading to enforce them upon the people to produce division and strife and to place the acts and counsels of the Authorities of the Church, if possible, in a wrong light and not be an apostate, for such conduct was apostasy as we understood the term.' (Deseret News, November 3, 1869.)"

Ezra Taft Benson, Conference Report, Ensign, May 1986, p. 79.

"'We live in a day of great challenge. We live in that time of which the Lord spoke when he said, 'Peace shall be taken from the earth, and the devil shall have power over his own dominion.' (D&C 1:35) We live in that day which John the Revelator foresaw when 'the dragon was wroth with the woman, and went to make war with the remnant of her seed, which keep the commandments of God, and have the testimony of Jesus Christ.' (Rev. 12:17) The dragon is Satan; the woman represents the Church of Jesus Christ. Satan is waging war against the members of the Church who have testimonies and are trying to keep the commandments. And while many of our members are remaining faithful and strong, some are wavering. Some are falling. Some are fulfilling John's prophecy that in the war with Satan, some Saints would be overcome. (see Rev. 13:7)'"

Teachings of Ezra Taft Benson, p. 56.

"The Book of Mormon brings men to Christ through two basic means. First, it tells in a plain manner of Christ and His gospel. It testifies of His divinity and of the necessity for a Redeemer and the need of our putting trust in Him. It bears witness of the Fall and the Atonement and the first principles of the gospel, including our need of a broken heart and a contrite spirit and a spiritual rebirth. It proclaims we must endure to the end in righteousness and live the moral life of a Saint.

Second, the Book of Mormon exposes the enemies of Christ. It confounds false doctrines and lays down contention (see I Nephi 3:12). It fortifies the humble followers of Christ against the evil designs, strategies, and doctrines of the devil in our day. The type of apostates in the Book of Mormon are similar to the type we have today. God, with His infinite foreknowledge, so molded the Book of Mormon that we might see the error and know how to combat false educational, political, religious, and philosophical concepts of our time. ('The Book of Mormon Is the Word of God,' Regional Representatives Seminar, Salt Lake City, Utah, 4 April 1986.)"

Teachings of Ezra Taft Benson, p. 82.

"Because God has given men their agency, there will always be those who will misuse it. The gospel net draws in the good and the bad, the best and the worst. The worst because the devil, before the final cleansing, will put some of his followers within the kingdom in order to try and destroy it. We have some of them within the kingdom today, and in due course their number shall be known. Time has a way of taking care of all things, of elevating the good and bringing down the bad. If we see things going on within the kingdom that disturb us, we might first resolve, if the matter falls within our stewardship, to go to the person or people involved. If it is of such a nature that we think it should be called to the attention of higher authority, then we can, in a kindly and quiet manner, take the necessary steps at the proper level. ("Jesus Christ—Gifts and Expectations," New Era, May 1975, p. 18.)"

Teachings of Ezra Taft Benson, p. 88.

"Sometimes we hear someone refer to a division in the Church. In reality, the Church is not divided. It simply means that there are some who, for the time being at least, are members of the Church but not in harmony with it. These people have a temporary membership and influence in the Church; but unless they repent, they will be missing when the final membership records are recorded. (God, Family, Country, p. 253-254.)"

Teachings of Ezra Taft Benson, p. 90.

"Not only are there apostates within our midst, but there are also apostate doctrines that are sometimes taught in our classes and from our pulpits and that appear in our publications. And these apostate precepts of men cause our people to stumble. As the Book of Mormon, speaking of our day, states: 'They have all gone astray save it be a few, who are the humble followers of Christ; nevertheless, they are led, that in many instances they do err because they are taught by the precepts of men' (2 Nephi 28:14). (God, Family, Country, p. 255.)

Certain individuals within the Church may go astray and even fall away. This may happen even to a person in the Church who is in a position of some influence and authority. It has happened in the past. It will happen in the future. If our faith is in Jesus Christ and not in the arm of flesh, then we will know that we are members of the Church of Jesus Christ and not the church of men. ('Jesus Christ—Gifts and Expectations,' New Era, May 1975, p. 17.)"

Teachings of Ezra Taft Benson, p. 172.

"This is the dispensation of the fullness of times. Every other gospel dispensation from the days of Adam through the ancient Apostles has drifted into apostasy. But our dispensation is different. We have been assured by the Lord that the kingdom of God, The Church of Jesus Christ of Latter-day Saints, will remain on earth to prepare the way and meet the kingdom of heaven when the Lord comes again. ('Our Obligation and Challenge,' Regional Representatives Seminar, Salt Lake City, Utah, September 30, 1977.)"

Teachings of Ezra Taft Benson, p. 467.

"Not to be valiant in one's testimony is a tragedy of eternal consequences. There are members who know this latter-day work is true, but who fail to endure to the end. One who rationalizes that he or she has a testimony of Jesus Christ but cannot accept direction and counsel from the leadership of His Church is in a fundamentally unsound position and is in jeopardy of losing exaltation. ('Valiant in the Testimony of Jesus,' Ensign, February 1987, p. 2.)"

Ezra Taft Benson, An Enemy Hath Done This, p. 282-283.

"Some things are changeless, priceless. We must anchor ourselves to the eternal verities of life, for life is eternal. The honors of men, more often than not, are fleeting. Anxious to run after the honors of office or succumb to the pressures of public glamour and worldly acclaim, some of us are no longer willing to stand up for all the principles of the gospel. We seek to justify our unrighteousness by claiming that, if only we can get title or position, then think of the good we can do. Hence we lose our salvation en route to those honors. We sometimes look among our numbers to find one to whom we can point who agrees with us, so we can have company to justify our apostasy. We rationalize by saying that someday the Church doctrine will catch up with our way of thinking. Truth is not established by Gallup polls.

Seeking the applause of the world, we like to be honored by the men the world honors. But therein lies real danger, for ofttimes in order to receive these honors, we must join forces with and follow those same devilish influences and policies which brought some of those men to positions of prominence.

More and more the honors of this world are being promoted by the wicked for the wicked. We see this in publicity and awards that are given to movies, literature, art, journalism, etc. We see in our own newspapers widely-read columnists carried who advocate one-world socialism, who have been consistently caught in falsehoods, and who continually parrot the communist line. Less and less we see the virtuous rewarded by the world, and when they are, ofttimes it almost seems to be done insidiously in order to get us to swallow the many evils for which the wicked are even more profusely honored."

Hugh B. Brown, Conference Report, October 1959, p. 108.

"However, the Church must not condone evil or wrongdoing in the name of tolerance. It must not acquiesce or become an accessory, even by silence, when error and sin are arrayed against truth and righteousness. We must be on guard against alien ideologies and subtle, subversive concepts, leading to immoral conduct and apostasy. Whenever symptoms of apostasy appear in propaganda or conduct, remedial measures are applied. But when counsel, admonition, and instruction fail, the Church has a duty to its members to take positive action and either heal or amputate malignant growths."

Bruce R. McConkie, The Mortal Messiah, Vol. 1, p. 229.

"Apostasy consists of two things: 1. Believing false doctrine. 'And all those who preach false doctrines, . . . wo be unto them, saith the Lord God Almighty, for they shall be thrust down to hell!'

2. Living after the manner of the world. 'And all those who commit whoredoms, and pervert the right way of the Lord, wo, wo, wo be unto them, saith the Lord God Almighty, for they shall be thrust down to hell!' (2 Ne. 28:15.)

And so, from the very beginning, 'Satan came among them, . . . and he commanded them, saying: Believe it not; and they believed it not, and they loved Satan more than God. And men began from that time forth to be carnal, sensual, and devilish.' (Moses 5:11-13.) Thus apostasy began; men fell away from the truth even in the day of righteous Adam; men turned to carnal and ungodly practices even in the day when there were living witnesses to tell them of Eden's beauty, of the fall and promised redemption, and of angelic ministrations and heavenly revelations of the mind and will of Him whose they and we are."

Bruce R. McConkie, The Mortal Messiah, Vol. 1, p. 230.

"Apostasy has been and is the prevailing social and religious state of most men in all ages from Adam's to ours. The devil is not dead: Lucifer lives as surely as God does; he slays others but has not himself been slain. His influence covers the earth and has done so since the fall of man. He seeks to damn men, and 'wide is the gate, and broad is the way, that leadeth to destruction.' (Matt. 7:13.) Of our own day it is written: 'Darkness covereth the earth, and gross darkness the minds of the people, and all flesh has become corrupt before my face.' (D&C 112:23.) Also: 'The whole world lieth in sin, and groaneth under darkness and under the bondage of sin.' (D&C 84:49.) The war that began in heaven is continuing here among mortals, and up to this point most of the victories have been won by the enemy of all righteousness."

Bruce R. McConkie, The Mortal Messiah, Vol. 1, p. 237-238.

"Apostasy is the result of unrighteousness. No one ever forsakes or rejects the truth who is guided by the power of the Holy Ghost, and the Spirit will not dwell in an unclean tabernacle."

Bruce R. McConkie, The Mortal Messiah, Vol. 3, p. 242.

"It is the age-old answer to the age-old heresy. Apostate peoples always look back to their fathers; always suppose they are treading where the saints have trod; always reject new prophets who seem to them to teach a new doctrine that differs from their traditions. And the answer always is: The old prophets foretold the coming of the new ones, and if men believe the ancient scriptures they would accept the new revelations that come in their day."

Bruce R. McConkie, The Mortal Messiah, Vol. 3, p. 398.

"One of the marks of personal or universal apostasy is to center on religious trifles to the exclusion of eternal principles. Abstain from the use of tea, coffee, and tobacco, but indulge in lustful acts or forsake standards of business integrity; refrain from picking an olive or shucking an ear of maize on the Sabbath, but ignore the command to worship the Father in spirit and in truth on his holy day; pay tithing on the leaves and stalks of herbs grown in pots on the windowsill, but give no heed to judgment, mercy, and faith—such are the marks of apostate fanaticism. By such a course it is easy to have a form of godliness and a zeal for religion without doing the basic things that require the whole heart and the whole soul."

SCRIPTURAL REFERENCES

Isaiah 24:5-6

5 The earth also is defiled under the inhabitants thereof; because they have transgressed the laws, changed the ordinance, broken the everlasting covenant.

6 Therefore hath the curse devoured the earth, and they that dwell therein are desolate: therefore the inhabitants of the earth are burned, and few men left.

Isaiah 30:Heading

Israel scattered for rejecting her seers and prophets—She shall be gathered and blessed temporally and spiritually—The Lord shall come in a day of apostasy to judge and destroy the wicked.

Isaiah 33:Heading

Apostasy and wickedness precede the Second Coming—The Lord shall come with devouring fire—Zion and her stakes shall be perfected—The Lord is our Judge, Lawgiver, and King.

JST Matthew 1:37

37 And whoso treasureth up my word, shall not be deceived, for the Son of Man shall come, and he shall send his angels before him with the great sound of a trumpet, and they shall gather together the remainder of his elect from the four winds, from one end of heaven to the other.

2 Thessalonians 2:3-12

3 Let no man deceive you by any means: for that day shall not come, except there come a falling away first, and that man of sin be revealed, the son of perdition;

4 Who opposeth and exalteth himself above all that is called God, or that is worshipped; so that he as God sitteth in the temple of God, shewing himself that he is God.

5 Remember ye not, that, when I was yet with you, I told you these things?

6 And now ye know what withholdeth that he might be revealed in his time.

7 For the mystery of iniquity doth already work: only he who now letteth will let, until he be taken out of the way.

8 And then shall that Wicked be revealed, whom the Lord shall consume with the spirit of his mouth, and shall destroy with the brightness of his coming:

9 Even him, whose coming is after the working of Satan with all power and signs and lying wonders,

10 And with all deceivableness of unrighteousness in them that perish; because they received not the love of the truth, that they might be saved.

11 And for this cause God shall send them strong delusion, that they should believe a lie:

12 That they all might be damned who believed not the truth, but had pleasure in unrighteousness.

2 Nephi 27:5

5 For behold, the Lord hath poured out upon you the spirit of deep sleep. For behold, ye have closed your eyes, and ye have rejected the prophets; and your rulers, and the seers hath he covered because of your iniquity.

2 Nephi 28:19-32

19 For the kingdom of the devil must shake, and they which belong to it must needs be stirred up unto repentance, or the devil will grasp them with his everlasting chains, and they be stirred up to anger, and perish;

20 For behold, at that day shall he rage in the hearts of the children of men, and stir them up to anger against that which is good.

21 And others will he pacify, and lull them away into carnal security, that they will say: All is well in Zion; yea, Zion prospereth, all is well—and thus the devil cheateth their souls, and leadeth them away carefully down to hell.

22 And behold, others he flattereth away, and telleth them there is no hell; and he saith unto them: I am no devil, for there is none—and thus he whispereth in their ears, until he grasps them with his awful chains, from whence there is no deliverance.

23 Yea, they are grasped with death, and hell; and death, and hell, and the devil, and all that have been seized therewith must stand before the throne of God, and be judged according to their works, from whence they must go into the place prepared for them, even a lake of fire and brimstone, which is endless torment.

24 Therefore, wo be unto him that is at ease in Zion!

25 Wo be unto him that crieth: All is well!

26 Yea, wo be unto him that hearkeneth unto the precepts of men, and denieth the power of God, and the gift of the Holy Ghost!

27 Yea, wo be unto him that saith: We have received, and we need no more!

28 And in fine, wo unto all those who tremble, and are angry because of the truth of God! For behold, he that is built upon the rock receiveth it with gladness; and he that is built upon a sandy foundation trembleth lest he shall fall.

29 Wo be unto him that shall say: We have received the word of God, and we need no more of the word of God, for we have enough!

30 For behold, thus saith the Lord God: I will give unto the children of men line upon line, precept upon precept, here a little and there a little; and blessed are those who hearken unto my precepts, and lend an ear unto my counsel, for they shall learn wisdom; for unto him that receiveth I will give more; and from them that shall say, We have enough, from them shall be taken away even that which they have.

31 Cursed is he that putteth his trust in man, or maketh flesh his arm, or shall hearken unto the precepts of men, save their precepts shall be given by the power of the Holy Ghost.

32 Wo be unto the Gentiles, saith the Lord God of Hosts! For notwithstanding I shall lengthen out mine arm unto them from day to day, they will deny me; nevertheless, I will be merciful unto them, saith the Lord God, if they will repent and come unto me; for mine arm is lengthened out all the day long, saith the Lord God of Hosts.

3 Nephi 2:1-2

1 And it came to pass that thus passed away the ninety and fifth year also, and the people began to forget those signs and wonders which they had heard, and began to be less and less astonished at a sign or a wonder from heaven, insomuch that they began to be hard in their hearts, and blind in their

minds, and began to disbelieve all which they had heard and seen—

2 Imagining up some vain thing in their hearts, that it was wrought by men and by the power of the devil, to lead away and deceive the hearts of the people; and thus did Satan get possession of the hearts of the people again, insomuch that he did blind their eyes and lead them away to believe that the doctrine of Christ was a foolish and a vain thing.

Mormon 8:35-41

35 Behold, I speak unto you as if ye were present, and yet ye are not. But behold, Jesus Christ hath shown you unto me, and I know your doing.

36 And I know that ye do walk in the pride of your hearts; and there are none save a few only who do not lift themselves up in the pride of their hearts, unto the wearing of very fine apparel, unto envying, and strifes, and malice, and persecutions, and all manner of iniquities; and your churches, yea, even every one, have become polluted because of the pride of your hearts.

37 For behold, ye do love money, and your substance, and your fine apparel, and the adorning of your churches, more than ye love the poor and the needy, the sick and the afflicted.

38 O ye pollutions, ye hypocrites, ye teachers, who sell yourselves for that which will canker, why have ye polluted the holy church of God? Why are ye ashamed to take upon you the name of Christ? Why do ye not think that greater is the value of an endless happiness than that misery which never dies—because of the praise of the world?

39 Why do ye adorn yourselves with that which hath no life, and yet suffer the hungry, and the needy, and the naked, and the sick and the afflicted to pass by you, and notice them not?

40 Yea, why do ye build up your secret abominations to get gain, and cause that widows should mourn before the Lord, and also orphans to mourn before the Lord, and also the blood of their fathers and their husbands to cry unto the Lord from the ground, for vengeance upon your heads?

41 Behold, the sword of vengeance hangeth over you; and the time soon cometh that he avengeth the blood of the saints upon you, for he will not suffer their cries any longer.

D&C:1:14-16

14 And the arm of the Lord shall be revealed; and the day cometh that they who will not hear the voice of the Lord, neither the voice of his servants, neither give heed to the words of the prophets and apostles, shall be cut off from among the people;

15 For they have strayed from mine ordinances, and have broken mine everlasting covenant;

16 They seek not the Lord to establish his righteousness, but every man walketh in his own way, and after the image of his own God, whose image is in the likeness of the world, and whose substance is that of an idol, which waxeth old and shall perish in Babylon, even Babylon the great, which shall fall.

D&C 13:1

1 Upon you my fellow servants, in the name of Messiah I confer the Priesthood of Aaron, which holds the keys of the ministering of angels, and of the gospel of repentance, and of baptism by immersion for the remission of sins; and this shall never be taken again from the earth, until the sons of Levi do offer again an offering unto the Lord in righteousness.

D&C: 45:56-57

56 And at that day, when I shall come in my glory, shall the parable be fulfilled which I spake concerning the ten virgins.

57 For they that are wise and have received the truth, and have taken the Holy Spirit for their guide, and have not been deceived—verily I say unto you, they shall not be hewn down and cast into the fire, but shall abide the day.

D&C 85:11

11 And they who are of the High Priesthood, whose names are not found written in the book of the law, or that are found to have apostatized, or to have been cut off from the church, as well as the lesser priesthood, or the members, in that day shall not find an inheritance among the saints of the Most High;

D&C 86:4-7

4 But behold, in the last days, even now while the Lord is beginning to bring forth the word, and the blade is springing up and is yet tender—

5 Behold, verily I say unto you, the angels are crying unto the Lord day and night, who are ready and waiting to be sent forth to reap down the fields;

6 But the Lord saith unto them, pluck not up the tares while the blade is yet tender (for verily your faith is weak), lest you destroy the wheat also.

7 Therefore, let the wheat and the tares grow together until the harvest is fully ripe; then ye shall first gather out the wheat from among the tares, and after the gathering of the wheat, behold and lo, the tares are bound in bundles, and the field remaineth to be burned.

D&C 112:25-26

25 And upon my house shall it begin, and from my house shall it go forth, saith the Lord;

26 First among those among you, saith the Lord, who have professed to know my name and have not known me, and have blasphemed against me in the midst of my house, saith the Lord.

CHAPTER EIGHT

THE GREAT & ABOMINABLE CHURCH

"The titles church of the devil and great and abominable church are used to identify all churches or organizations of whatever name or nature—whether political, philosophical, educational, economic social, fraternal, civic, or religious—which are designed to take men on a course that leads away from God and his laws and thus from salvation in the kingdom of God. (Bruce R. McConkie, Mormon Doctrine, p. 137.)

Orson Hyde, Journal of Discourses, Vol. 5, p. 141.

"In view of the sentiment contained in the foregoing quotation, I am led to believe that whatever branch of the great and abominable church shall lead the way to fight against the Lamb of God, will have a greater task to perform than they are aware of. It is not merely a little handful of Latter-day Saints that they have to contend with; but, it is with all the celestial powers. This, however, they do not believe; and, consequently, like the unthinking horse, they rush to the onset."

Orson Pratt, Journal of Discourses, Vol. 7, p. 181, July 10, 1859.

"He (Nephi) saw that after the Gospel should be preached by the Twelve Apostles of the Lamb to the Jews and to the Gentiles, there would arise a great and abominable church, the most corrupt of all churches upon the face of all the earth, and that that great and abominable church should have power given unto them over the Saints of the Lamb to destroy them, etc., and that they should corrupt the Jewish Scriptures which should issue from the mouth of the Twelve Apostles of the Lamb, and take away from them many parts that were plain, and precious, and easy to the understanding of all men; and by reason of this great stumblingblock, the scriptures being in such a state, there should be many among the nations of the Gentiles in the latter times that should exceedingly stumble and build up numerous churches after the forms of different doctrines, and they should deny miracles and the power of God, saying, 'They are done away.'"

Orson Pratt, Journal of Discourses, Vol. 7, p. 184, July 10, 1859.

"Again: Although the great 'mother of abominations' has not gathered together in multitudes upon the face of the earth among all the nations and kingdoms of the Gentiles to fight against the Lamb of god and his Saints, yet there has been enough fulfilled to show that the balance will be accomplished. Has this great and abominable power, under the name of 'the mother of harlots,' popularly called Christendom, fought against the Saints in this country? Let the history of this Church answer that question; let the scenes we have passed through in the land of Missouri testify; let the tribulation this people had to endure in the state of Illinois bear witness. We will not refer to persecutions in Utah, for here we have had but little, compared with scenes we have past through in former years. Suffice it to say multitudes have been gathered together—under the influence of what? Under the influence of that great and abominable church or system called 'the mother of harlots.'

When we come to search to the bottom of this matter, we find that has been the great influence which has produced all the persecutions that have come upon the Latter-day Saints since the organization of this Church. How many preachers were gathered together in the western part of Missouri at the time we were driven from the State to give their advice in a pretended court martial to have some fifteen or twenty of the leaders of this people taken out and shot on the public square the next morning? There were not less than seventeen priests who advised the measure.

When we come to hunt for the great influence that has existed on the multitudes that gathered to persecute the Saints of the Lamb of God, we find it proceeding from the pulpit. Through the falsehoods of priests and the publishing of false principles, they have endeavoured to set on the frenzied multitude to put to death the Latter-day Saints and deprive them of citizenship."

Orson Pratt, Journal of Discourses, Vol. 18, p. 172, March 26, 1876.

"But there has been a long apostasy, during which the nations have been cursed with apostate churches in great abundance, and they are represented in the revelations of St. John as a woman sitting upon a scarlet colored beast, having a golden cup in her hand, full of filthiness and abominations, full of the wine of the wrath of her fornication; that in her forehead there was a name written—'Mystery, Babylon the Great, the mother of harlots.' This kind of a church has existed in great abundance, for as John the Revelator says, she was to have her dominion upon many waters, and she was to make all nations drunken with the wine of the wrath of her fornication."

Hyrum M. Smith, Doctrine and Covenants Commentary, Sec. 18, p. 85–86.

"The church of the adversary may be known by its fundamental principle of government. In the beginning he declared himself in favor of salvation by compulsion, and although he was cast out of heaven for refusing to submit to the divine Council, he has continued his agitation for that plan among the children of men ever since. His church consists of those who adopt his plan and seek to destroy the free agency of man by brute force. In the Church of the Lamb of God the 'law of liberty,' which is the law of 'common consent,' prevails. The church of the adversary may also be known by contention and strife, by false doctrines, and by all manner of iniquity. A minister of the Lord makes war upon the domain of the adversary by the sword of the Spirit; not by persecution."

Joseph Fielding Smith, Church History and Modern Revelation, Vol. 1, p. 78.

"When we are commanded to 'contend against no church save it be the church of the devil,' we must understand that this is instruction to us to contend against all evil, that which is opposed to righteousness and truth. James declares, that 'every good gift and every perfect gift is from above, and cometh down from the Father of lights, with whom is no variableness, neither shadow of turning,' and the scriptures also teach 'for there is nothing which is good save it comes from the Lord; and that which is evil cometh from the devil.' (Omni 25.) All who go forth to teach should do so in wisdom and not contend with the churches or engage in profitless debates, but teach in the spirit of kindness and try to persuade people to receive the truth."

Bruce R. McConkie, Mormon Doctrine, "Communism", p. 151.

"Communism is a form of false religion; one of the major divisions of the church of the devil."

Bruce R. McConkie, Doctrinal New Testament Commentary, Vol. 3, p. 548.

"There has always been a church of the devil on earth. Speaking of the Church as the kingdom of God on earth, the Prophet Joseph Smith said: 'In relation to the kingdom of God, the devil always sets up his kingdom at the very same time in opposition to God.' (Teachings, p. 365.) Thus when Adam and Eve taught the gospel to their children, 'Satan came among them, saying: I am also a son of God; and he commanded them, saying: Believe it not; and they believed it not, and they loved Satan more than God. And men began from that time forth to be carnal, sensual, and devilish.' As a consequence, Cain said: 'Who is the Lord that I should know him?. . . And Cain loved Satan more than God. And Satan commanded him, saying: Make an offering unto the Lord.' (Moses 5:13-18.)"

Bruce R. McConkie, Doctrinal New Testament Commentary, Vol. 3, p. 550-551.

"Thereupon Nephi saw—and we are following a chronological series of events!—the formation of that church of the devil which grew out of the apostasy in the Old World. (1 Ne. 13:1-3.) And as it was with the apostasy on the American continent, there were many churches comprising Lucifer's earthly kingdom, one of which churches was more abominable than all the rest. Indeed, the mere fact that there are more churches than one in the kingdom of the enemy of all righteousness is of itself sufficient proof that all are not equal and that some are better, some worse, than others."

Bruce R. McConkie, Doctrinal New Testament Commentary, Vol. 3, p. 552.

"Truly Nephi saw and described 'that great and abominable church, which is the mother of abominations, whose foundation is the devil,' as that organization existed during the dark ages. (1 Ne. 14:9.) But now the scene changes. He views our day; the restoration is past; the great day is at hand for the restored gospel to be preached in all the world for a witness unto all nations. Now the entire concept of the church of the devil changes; now the great and abominable church is not one among many, but it is all the forces of evil linked together; as the scene is set for the final warfare between the saints and the world, we find 'there are save two churches only'—the Lord's and the devil's. All men are in one camp or the other; those who are not for the Lord are against him.

In other words, the church of the devil is the world; it is all the carnality and evil to which fallen man is heir; it is every unholy and wicked practice; it is every false religion, every supposed system of salvation which does not actually save and exalt man in the highest heaven of the celestial world. It is every church except the true church, whether parading under a Christian or a pagan banner. As Moroni will say in a later era of Nephite history, and as we shall ascertain in our evaluation of Rev. 18:1-24, it is 'secret combinations,' oath-bound societies, and the great world force of Godless communism. (Ether 8:14-26.)"

Bruce R. McConkie, Doctrinal New Testament Commentary, Vol. 3, p. 555.

"It seems clear that if the great whore, which is the church of the devil, has daughters who are harlots, the interpretation of this expression is that false churches beget false churches, that the sponsor of one set of abominations begets sponsors of others."

Bruce R. McConkie, Doctrinal New Testament Commentary, Vol. 3, p. 559.
    "In effect, John is describing the fall of a particular part of the devil's earthly kingdom and is illustrating the fall of that whole realm, as our analysis of the whole chapter will show. In this setting, note the Lord's interpretation of the parable of the wheat and the tares: 'Behold, verily I say, the field was the world, and the apostles were the sowers of the seed; And after they have fallen asleep, the great persecutor of the church, the apostate, the whore, even Babylon, that maketh all nations to drink of her cup, in whose hearts the enemy, even Satan, sitteth to reign—behold he soweth the tares; wherefore, the tares choke the wheat and drive the church into the wilderness.' (D&C 86:2-3.)"

Bruce R. McConkie, The Promised Messiah, p. 34.
    "Nephi saw in vision 'a church which is most abominable above all other churches, which slayeth the saints of God, yea, and tortureth them and bindeth them down, and yoketh them with a yoke of iron, and bringeth them down into captivity.' (1 Ne. 13:5.) From this vision we learn two of the saddest truths of all history: (1) prophets are persecuted by religiously inclined people, and (2) the fact that there are false churches is itself the very reason why the Lord's saints suffer at the hands of evil an ungodly men."

The Mortal Messiah, Vol. 1, p. 272-273.
    "It was of these ancient scriptures, in their original form and before they fell into evil hands, that an angel said to Nephi: 'The book that thou beholdest is a record of the Jews, which contains the covenants of the Lord, which he hath made unto the house of Israel.' Then the angel, speaking more particularly of the New Testament, continued: 'Thou hast beheld that the book proceeded forth from the mouth of a Jew; and when it proceeded forth from the mouth of a Jew it contained the plainness of the gospel of the Lord, of whom the twelve apostles bear record.' After these scriptures went forth 'in purity,' they came into the hands of 'a great and abominable church, which is most abominable above all other churches.' Of this ill-spawned and devil-built perverter of true religion, the angel said: 'They have taken away from the gospel of the Lamb many parts which are plain and most precious; and also many covenants of the Lord have they taken away.' (1 Ne. 13:23-26.) That is to say, both the Old and the New Testaments found among men in our day have been subject to the deletions, perversions, and alterations of persons whose interests were not compatible with those of the prophets and apostles whose words they dared to twist."

Also see Bruce R. McConkie, The Millennial Messiah, p. 53-56, 493-494.

SCRIPTURAL REFERENCES

Revelation 17:6
6 And I saw the woman drunken with the blood of the saints, and with the blood of the martyrs of Jesus: and when I saw her, I wondered with great admiration.

Revelation 17:9
9 And here is the mind which hath wisdom. The seven heads are seven mountains, on which the woman sitteth.

Revelation 17:16
16 And the ten horns which thou sawest upon the beast, these shall hate the whore, and shall make her desolate and naked, and shall eat her flesh, and burn her with fire.

Revelation 17:18
18 And the woman which thou sawest is that great city, which reigneth over the kings of the earth.

1 Nephi 13:4-9
4 And it came to pass that I saw among the nations of the Gentiles the formation of a great church.
5 And the angel said unto me: Behold the formation of a church which is most abominable above all other churches, which slayeth the saints of God, yea, and tortureth them and bindeth them down, and yoketh them with a yoke of iron, and bringeth them down into captivity.
6 And it came to pass that I beheld this great and abominable church; and I saw the devil that he was the founder of it.
7 And I also saw gold, and silver, and silks, and scarlets, and fine-twined linen, and all manner of precious clothing; and I saw many harlots.
8 And the angel spake unto me, saying: Behold the gold, and the silver, and the silks, and the scarlets, and the fine-twined linen, and the precious clothing, and the harlots, are the desires of this great and abominable church.
9 And also for the praise of the world do they destroy the saints of God, and bring them down into captivity.

1 Nephi 13:26-29
26 And after they (scriptures) go forth by the hand of the twelve apostles of the Lamb, from the Jews unto the Gentiles, thou seest the formation of a great and abominable church, which is most abominable above all other churches; for behold, they have taken away from the gospel of the Lamb many parts which are plain and most precious; and also many covenants of the Lord have they taken away.
27 And all this have they done that they might pervert the right ways of the Lord, that they might blind the eyes and harden the hearts of the children of men.
28 Wherefore, thou seest that after the book hath gone forth through the hands of the great and abominable church, that there are many plain and precious things taken away from the book, which

is the book of the Lamb of God.

29 And after these plain and precious things were taken away it goeth forth unto all the nations of the Gentiles; and after it goeth forth unto all the nations of the Gentiles, yea, even across the many waters which thou hast seen with the Gentiles which have gone forth out of captivity, thou seest—because of the many plain and precious things which have been taken out of the book, which were plain unto the understanding of the children of men, according to the plainness which is in the Lamb of God—because of these things which are taken away out of the gospel of the Lamb, an exceedingly great many do stumble, yea, insomuch that Satan hath great power over them.

1 Nephi 13:32-34

32 Neither will the Lord God suffer that the Gentiles shall forever remain in that awful state of blindness, which thou beholdest they are in, because of the plain and most precious parts of the gospel of the Lamb which have been kept back by that abominable church, whose formation thou hast seen.

33 Wherefore saith the Lamb of God: I will be merciful unto the Gentiles, unto the visiting of the remnant of the house of Israel in great judgment.

34 And it came to pass that the angel of the Lord spake unto me, saying: Behold, saith the Lamb of God, after I have visited the remnant of the house of Israel—and this remnant of whom I speak is the seed of thy father—wherefore, after I have visited them in judgment, and smitten them by the hand of the Gentiles, and after the Gentiles do stumble exceedingly, because of the most plain and precious parts of the gospel of the Lamb which have been kept back by that abominable church, which is the mother of harlots, saith the Lamb—I will be merciful unto the Gentiles in that day, insomuch that I will bring forth unto them, in mine own power, much of my gospel, which shall be plain and precious, saith the Lamb.

1 Nephi 14:3

3 And that great pit, which hath been digged for them by that great and abominable church, which was founded by the devil and his children, that he might lead away the souls of men down to hell—yea, that great pit which hath been digged for the destruction of men shall be filled by those who digged it, unto their utter destruction, saith the Lamb of God; not the destruction of the soul, save it be the casting of it into that hell which hath no end.

1 Nephi 14:9-17

9 And it came to pass that he said unto me: Look, and behold that great and abominable church, which is the mother of abominations, whose founder is the devil.

10 And he said unto me: Behold there are save two churches only; the one is the church of the Lamb of God, and the other is the church of the devil; wherefore, whoso belongeth not to the church of the Lamb of God belongeth to that great church, which is the mother of abominations; and she is the whore of all the earth.

11 And it came to pass that I looked and beheld the whore of all the earth, and she sat upon many waters; and she had dominion over all the earth, among all nations, kindreds, tongues, and people.

12 And it came to pass that I beheld the church of the Lamb of God, and its numbers were few,

because of the wickedness and abominations of the whore who sat upon many waters; nevertheless, I beheld that the church of the Lamb, who were the saints of God, were also upon all the face of the earth; and their dominions upon the face of the earth were small, because of the wickedness of the great whore whom I saw.

13 And it came to pass that I beheld that the great mother of abominations did gather together multitudes upon the face of all the earth, among all the nations of the Gentiles, to fight against the Lamb of God.

14 And it came to pass that I, Nephi, beheld the power of the Lamb of God, that it descended upon the saints of the church of the Lamb, and upon the covenant people of the Lord, who were scattered upon all the face of the earth; and they were armed with righteousness and with the power of God in great glory.

15 And it came to pass that I beheld that the wrath of God was poured out upon that great and abominable church, insomuch that there were wars and rumors of wars among all the nations and kindreds of the earth.

16 And as there began to be wars and rumors of wars among all the nations which belonged to the mother of abominations, the angel spake unto me, saying: Behold, the wrath of God is upon the mother of harlots; and behold, thou seest all these things—

17 And when the day cometh that the wrath of God is poured out upon the mother of harlots, which is the great and abominable church of all the earth, whose founder is the devil, then, at that day, the work of the Father shall commence, in preparing the way for the fulfilling of his covenants, which he hath made to his people who are of the house of Israel.

1 Nephi 22:11-14

11 Wherefore, the Lord God will proceed to make bare his arm in the eyes of all the nations, in bringing about his covenants and his gospel unto those who are of the house of Israel.

12 Wherefore, he will bring them again out of captivity, and they shall be gathered together to the lands of their inheritance; and they shall be brought out of obscurity and out of darkness; and they shall know that the Lord is their Savior and their Redeemer, the Mighty One of Israel.

13 And the blood of that great and abominable church, which is the whore of all the earth, shall turn upon their own heads; for they shall war among themselves, and the sword of their own hands shall fall upon their own heads, and they shall be drunken with their own blood.

14 And every nation which shall war against thee, O house of Israel, shall be turned one against another, and they shall fall into the pit which they digged to ensnare the people of the Lord. And all that fight against Zion shall be destroyed, and that great whore, who hath perverted the right ways of the Lord, yea, that great and abominable church, shall tumble to the dust and great shall be the fall of it.

1 Nephi 22:23

23 For the time speedily shall come that all churches which are built up to get gain, and all those who are built up to get power over the flesh, and those who are built up to become popular in the eyes of the world, and those who seek the lusts of the flesh and the things of the world, and to do all manner of iniquity; yea, in fine, all those who belong to the kingdom of the devil are they who need fear, and

tremble, and quake; they are those who must be brought low in the dust; they are those who must be consumed as stubble; and this is according to the words of the prophet.

2 Nephi 6:12

12 And blessed are the Gentiles, they of whom the prophet has written; for behold, if it so be that they shall repent and fight not against Zion, and do not unite themselves to that great and abominable church, they shall be saved; for the Lord God will fulfil his covenants which he has made unto his children; and for this cause the prophet has written these things.

2 Nephi 28:18-19

18 But behold, that great and abominable church, the whore of all the earth, must tumble to the earth, and great must be the fall thereof.

19 For the kingdom of the devil must shake, and they which belong to it must needs be stirred up unto repentance, or the devil will grasp them with his everlasting chains, and they be stirred up to anger, and perish;

Alma 5:39-40

39 And now if ye are not the sheep of the good shepherd, of what fold are ye? Behold, I say unto you, that the devil is your shepherd, and ye are of his fold; and now, who can deny this? Behold, I say unto you, whosoever denieth this is a liar and a child of the devil.

40 For I say unto you that whatsoever is good cometh from God, and whatsoever is evil cometh from the devil.

3 Nephi 27:8-12

8 And how be it my church save it be called in my name? For if a church be called in Moses' name then it be Moses' church; or if it be called in the name of a man then it be the church of a man; but if it be called in my name then it is my church, if it so be that they are built upon my gospel.

9 Verily I say unto you, that ye are built upon my gospel; therefore ye shall call whatsoever things ye do call, in my name; therefore if ye call upon the Father, for the church, if it be in my name the Father will hear you;

10 And if it so be that the church is built upon my gospel then will the Father show forth his own works in it.

11 But if it be not built upon my gospel, and is built upon the works of men, or upon the works of the devil, verily I say unto you they have joy in their works for a season, and by and by the end cometh, and they are hewn down and cast into the fire, from whence there is no return.

12 For their works do follow them, for it is because of their works that they are hewn down; therefore remember the things that I have told you.

Mormon 8:28

28 Yea, it shall come in a day when the power of God shall be denied, and churches become defiled and be lifted up in the pride of their hearts; yea, even in a day when leaders of churches and teachers shall rise in the pride of their hearts, even to the envying of them who belong to their churches.

D&C 18:20

20 Contend against no church, save it be the church of the devil.

D&C 29:21

21 And the great and abominable church, which is the whore of all the earth, shall be cast down by devouring fire, according as it is spoken by the mouth of Ezekiel the prophet, who spoke of these things, which have not come to pass but surely must, as I live, for abominations shall not reign.

D&C 88:94

94 And another angel shall sound his trump, saying: That great church, the mother of abominations, that made all nations drink of the wine of the wrath of her fornication, that persecuteth the saints of God, that shed their blood—she who sitteth upon many waters, and upon the islands of the sea—behold, she is the tares of the earth; she is bound in bundles; her bands are made strong, no man can loose them; therefore, she is ready to be burned. And he shall sound his trump both long and loud, and all nations shall hear it.

Joseph Smith History 1:18-19

18 My object in going to inquire of the Lord was to know which of all the sects was right, that I might know which to join. No sooner, therefore, did I get possession of myself, so as to be able to speak, than I asked the Personages who stood above me in the light, which of all the sects was right (for at this time it had never entered into my heart that all were wrong)—and which I should join.

19 I was answered that I must join none of them, for they were all wrong; and the Personage who addressed me said that all their creeds were an abomination in his sight; that those professors were all corrupt; that: 'they draw near to me with their lips, but their hearts are far from me, they teach for doctrines the commandments of men, having a form of godliness, but they deny the power thereof.'

CHAPTER NINE

BABYLON

"The fall of Babylon and the hour of God's judgment were to follow upon the heels of the restoration of the Gospel. Hence God's people were warned to 'come out of her,' to partake not of her sins that they might not receive of her plagues. . . We must come out of Babylon in spirit, in feeling, in faith, in practice, forsaking the ways and customs of the wicked." (Orson F. Whitney, Collected Discourses, Vol. 4.)

Joseph Smith, History of the Church, Vol. 6, p. 26.

"Though Babylon says, 'I sit as a queen, and am no widow, and shall see no sorrow,' the Revelator says, 'Therefore shall her plagues come in one day, death and mourning and famine; and she shall be utterly burned with fire, for strong is the Lord God who judgeth her.'"

Brigham Young, Journal of Discourses, Vol. 16, p. 26, April 6, 1873.

"Elders of Israel, High Priests, Seventies, High Councilors, Presidents, brethren and sisters, no matter who, if you have an idea that you are going to take Babylon—I use this term, because it is well understood that Babylon means confusion, discord, strife, folly and all the vanities the world possesses—if you have the idea that you are going to take Babylon in one hand, and with the other cling to the Savior and drag yourselves into his presence, you will find yourselves mistaken, for he will drop you, and you will sink. You may just as well believe this today, and shape your lives accordingly, as to betray yourselves."

Orson Pratt, Journal of Discourses, Vol. 14, p. 256, December 10, 1871.

"This was the first message; but John says, 'I saw another angel follow him.' There were two angels then, the first one with a message of the gospel of peace, proclaiming peace to the inhabitants of the earth, and then judgment immediately to follow. The second angel had no message of peace, but this was his proclamation; 'Behold, Babylon the great is fallen, is fallen, because she made all nations drink of the wine of the wrath of her fornication.' We learn that a certain power, under the name of Great Babylon, is to meet with a total downfall after the gospel had been preached, that was to be brought by an angel. A third angel followed, and declared that all who would not receive the message of truth should be cast down, and should be punished, and the smoke of their torment should rise up for ever and for ever. After having predicted the coming of these three angels he then proclaims the coming of the Son of God sitting on a cloud, of which I have spoken."

Orson Pratt, Journal of Discourses, Vol. 14, p. 346, March 10, 1872.

"How long has this order of things existed, this dreadful apostasy, this class of people that pronounced themselves Zion, or Christians, without any of the characteristics of Zion? It has existed for some sixteen or seventeen centuries. It has spread itself and grown and gone into the four quarters of the earth. It is the great ecclesiastical power that is spoken of by the revelator John, and called by him the most corrupt and most wicked of all the powers of the earth, under the name of spiritual Babylon, or in other words Babel, which signifies confusion. This great and corrupt power is also represented by John as presenting a golden cup to the nations, full of all manner of filthiness and abominations."

Orson Pratt, Journal of Discourses, Vol. 18, p. 60-61, July 25, 1875.

"The description of this fall of Babylon is given in various places in John's revelations. Awful and most terrible judgments will fall upon Mystery Babylon the Great. She is to be punished with plagues of various kinds; a grievous sore will fall upon her people, so much so that they will blaspheme God, but they will not repent of their sins. They are to be punished with having the fountains and rivers turned into blood, and the waters of the great ocean are to become as the blood of a dead man, and every living thing that is therein will die; and one of the last plagues and judgments that will be poured out upon her will be devouring fire, and she will sink as a millstone, and her name will be blotted from under heaven and all that are connected with her."

Orson Pratt, Journal of Discourses, Vol. 18, p. 178-179, March 26, 1876.

"Who is Babylon? I have already explained that Babylon is a great power that should be in the earth under the name of a church, a woman—that generally represents a church—full of blasphemy. She had the inscription of her name upon her forehead—'Mystery Babylon, the mother of harlots and abominations of the earth.' What is to become of her? Where does she sit? Upon many waters, says John; and to interpret this to the understanding of the people, the waters are many people nations, kindreds and tongues where the woman hath her seat. These churches are scattered over the wide face of the earth, and this is called Babylon. Another angel is to follow the one that brings the Gospel, after it has been sufficiently preached, and proclaim the downfall of this great and corrupt power in the earth. Well, will all the Christians that are there perish, or will they be gathered out? Hear what John says—'I heard a great voice from heaven, saying, 'Come out of her, oh my people, that you partake not of her sins, that you receive not of her plagues, for her sins have reached to the heavens, and God hath remembered her iniquities." Then there is only one way to escape, is there? We can't stay in Babylon and be spared from these judgments, can we? Not at all. Why not? Because her sins have reached to the very heavens. Look at her abominations, her whoredoms, her murders, her priestcraft, her false doctrines, her forms of godliness without any power; look at them, all the nations are following after and consider it popular to follow and embrace these doctrines. 'Come out of her, oh, my people.' What people? God had no people in Babylon until the Church was organized, he could not have; he sent his servants to organize his Church, that there might be a people called his people. But when that Church is organized among these nations, kindreds, tongues and people, its members are not permitted to remain where they are. This is not an invention of a learned company of divines, saying it will be a good thing for us to gather in one; it is not something invented by human wisdom; but the Revelator John says—'I heard a voice from heaven.' What, a new revelation, John? Yes, a voice from heaven. God was again to speak, before the downfall of Babylon; and this should be the voice—'Come out of her, O my people.'"

John Taylor, The Gospel Kingdom, p. 261.

"Now then, in regard to our temporal affairs, these are the things which seem to perplex us more or less. We have been brought up in Babylon, and have inherited Babylonish ideas and systems of business. We have introduced, too, among us, all kinds of chicanery, deception, and fraud. It is time that these things were stopped, and that matters assumed another shape. It is time that we commenced to place ourselves under the guidance and direction of the Almighty."

George Q. Cannon, Millennial Star Vol. 23, p. 612, Sept. 21, 1861.

"Babylon must fall; no power can avert her destruction. Machines of warfare, machines of offense and defense of every description will be needed in great abundance to complete her destruction; and it must be confessed that the nations of which she is composed are doing all in their power to furnish them for the occasion. . . .Until Babylon meets with her long-promised fate, the manufacture of machines and weapons of war will be continued and peace may be looked for in vain among the nations of the earth."

George Q. Cannon, Journal of Discourses, Vol. 22, p. 356-357, July 24, 1881.

"The sixth verse of the 14th chapter of the same book (Revelation) says: 'And I saw another angel fly in the midst of heaven, having the everlasting Gospel to preach unto them that dwell on the earth, and to every nation, and kindred, and tongue, and people, saying with a loud voice, Fear God, and give glory to Him, for the hour of His judgment is come: and worship Him that made heaven, and earth, and the sea, and the fountains of water.' The next verse says—'And there followed another angel saying, Babylon is fallen, is fallen, that great city, because she made all nations drink of the wine of the wrath of her fornication.' We would infer from this that one consequence of the preaching of the Gospel, or the declaration of it by this angel that should fly through the midst of heaven, would be the downfall of Babylon. We are not left in doubt, as Latter-day Saints, respecting the application of this name Babylon. Commentators have been puzzled to explain what this meant, or to what city or people it applied, but in the records that have come to us this is made so plain that I suppose there is no Latter-day Saint who entertains any doubt respecting this matter. One consequence which should follow the preaching of the Gospel, as I have said, should be the downfall of Babylon; but in the first verses that I have read it appears there should be a cry go forth before Babylon should fall. 'And I heard another voice from heaven saying, Come out of her, my people, that ye be not partakers of her sins and that ye receive not of her plagues.' There should be, it appears from these passages that I have read in your hearing, several events connected with the preaching of the declaration of the Gospel by this angel that should fly through the midst of heaven—there should be a cry go forth among the people to come out of Babylon, out of this system which had made all nations drunk with her fornications, and no doubt this would be done in a manner that would be so remarkable that all the inhabitants of the earth would have the testimony concerning it."

Joseph F. Smith, Gospel Doctrine, p. 192.

"The Gentiles among whom the Priesthood had been established and the gospel preached, fell away also after the example of unbelief and the manner of the Jews, or children of Israel. God who spared not the natural branches, also cut off engrafted ones, and 'Mystery, Babylon the Great, the mother of harlots and abominations of the earth,' was set up as foretold by the Prophet Daniel and the Apostle John. This power made war with the Saints, and overcame them, changed time and laws, 'wore out the Saints of the Most High,' was drunken with their blood and with the blood of the martyrs of Jesus, and destroyed the holy people. But this mystical power, in turn, is to be overcome and, in the due time of the Lord, utterly destroyed.

Before this great event shall occur must come to pass the restoration of the gospel of Christ, and the establishment of the kingdom of God again on the earth, with all the powers and blessings of the Holy Priesthood, concerning which we have the most positive assurances."

Abraham H. Cannon, Collected Discourses, Vol. 2, March 2, 1890.
"We are following in a measure the sins of the world; we are bringing Babylon into our midst. There are strings leading from us to this great harlot Babylon and if she were to fall, many of us would fall with her. The only course for us to pursue as Latter-day Saints is to cut these bands which bind us to Babylon and when she falls we will not go with her."

Orson F. Whitney, Collected Discourses, Vol. 4.
"The fall of Babylon and the hour of God's judgment were to follow upon the heels of the restoration of the Gospel. Hence God's people were warned to 'come out of her,' to partake not of her sins that they might not receive of her plagues. This is one of the reasons for the gathering—the migration of the Saints to America—the Zion. And yet to come out of Babylon does not merely mean to come from Liverpool to Salt Lake City. Satan could do that, and doubtless has done it in more than one instance. That is merely a physical act, and will not stand alone. We must come out of Babylon in spirit, in feeling, in faith, in practice, forsaking the ways and customs of the wicked. Not that we are required to hate our fellow creatures. On the contrary, we are commanded to love them and labor to save them. But we must first save ourselves, first plant our feet upon the rock of safety, and then extend the helping hand to others. We are not a perfect people. We are full of faults. But our religion is perfect, and will make us and all who embrace it wise unto salvation."

Joseph Fielding Smith, Church History and Modern Revelation, Vol 2, p. 11.
"We are all commanded to labor 'while it is called today.' None shall be spared from this burning who 'remain in Babylon.' Babylon is the world, those who remain in Babylon are those who follow the practices of the world, and who do not accept in their hearts the word of the Lord. He has said that he will send his angels in that day and they 'shall gather out of his kingdom all things that offend, and them which do iniquity.' Matt. 13:41."

The Teachings of Spencer W. Kimball, p. 362.
"Unfortunately we live in a world that largely rejects the values of Zion. Babylon has not and never will comprehend Zion."

Bruce R. McConkie, Mormon Doctrine, "Babylon", p. 68.
"Anciently Babylon was the chief and capital city of the Babylonian empire. . . .As the seat of world empire, Babylon was the persistent persecutor and enemy of the Lord's people. . . .To the

Lord's people anciently, Babylon was known as the center of iniquity, carnality, and worldliness."

Bruce R. McConkie, Doctrinal New Testament Commentary, Vol. 3, p. 559.

" As we have seen in Rev. 17:1-18, Babylon the great is the church of the devil; it is the world with all its evil and carnality; it is every organization of every kind, sort and form—whether religious, civic, political, fraternal, or otherwise—which espouses a philosophy or promotes a cause which leads men away from salvation and toward the kingdoms of lesser glory in the eternal world."

Also see Bruce R. McConkie, The Millennial Messiah, p. 424-430, 439-440.

Bruce R. McConkie, A New Witness for the Articles of Faith, p. 638-639.

"The destruction of Gog and Magog constitutes the fall of Babylon, the overthrow of the great and abominable church and the destruction of the wicked."

Neal A. Maxwell, A Wonderful Flood of Light, p. 48.

"Furthermore, Babylon does not give exit permits gladly— an ironic implementation of that ancient boast, 'one soul shall not be lost' (Moses 4:1). Babylon is also a noisy, distracting place. No wonder some therein are 'called many times and . . . would not hear' (Alma 10:6). No wonder Jesus' open invitation to leave Babylon's slums and to join Him in the stunning, spiritual highlands goes largely unheeded. There, however, redeeming Jesus waits 'with open arms to receive [us]' (Mormon 6:17)."

SCRIPTURAL REFERENCES

Isaiah 13:Heading
Destruction of Babylon is a type of destruction at Second Coming—It shall be a day of wrath and vengeance—Babylon (the world) shall fall forever—Compare 2 Nephi 23.

Isaiah 13:13-22
13 Therefore I will shake the heavens, and the earth shall remove out of her place, in the wrath of the LORD of hosts, and in the day of his fierce anger.
14 And it shall be as the chased roe, and as a sheep that no man taketh up: they shall every man turn to his own people, and flee every one into his own land.
15 Every one that is found shall be thrust through; and every one that is joined unto them shall fall by the sword.
16 Their children also shall be dashed to pieces before their eyes; their houses shall be spoiled, and their wives ravished.
17 Behold, I will stir up the Medes against them, which shall not regard silver; and as for gold, they shall not delight in it.
18 Their bows also shall dash the young men to pieces; and they shall have no pity on the fruit of the womb; their eye shall not spare children.
19 And Babylon, the glory of kingdoms, the beauty of the Chaldees' excellency, shall be as when God overthrew Sodom and Gomorrah.
20 It shall never be inhabited, neither shall it be dwelt in from generation to generation: neither shall the Arabian pitch tent there; neither shall the shepherds make their fold there.

Isaiah 14:Heading
Israel shall be gathered and enjoy Millennial rest—Lucifer cast out of heaven for rebellion—Israel shall triumph over Babylon (the world)—Compare 2 Nephi 24.

Isaiah 21:Heading
Babylon is fallen, is fallen!—Other nations also are destroyed.

Isaiah 21:9
9 And, behold, here cometh a chariot of men, with a couple of horsemen. And he answered and said, Babylon is fallen, is fallen; and all the graven images of her gods he hath broken unto the ground.

Jeremiah 32:36
36 And now therefore thus saith the LORD, the God of Israel, concerning this city, whereof ye say, It shall be delivered into the hand of the king of Babylon by the sword, and by the famine, and by the pestilence;

Jeremiah 50:8-9

8 Remove out of the midst of Babylon, and go forth out of the land of the Chaldeans, and be as the he goats before the flocks.

9 For, lo, I will raise and cause to come up against Babylon an assembly of great nations from the north country: and they shall set themselves in array against her; from thence she shall be taken: their arrows shall be as of a mighty expert man; none shall return in vain.

Jeremiah 50:13

13 Because of the wrath of the LORD it shall not be inhabited, but it shall be wholly desolate: every one that goeth by Babylon shall be astonished, and hiss at all her plagues.

Jeremiah 50:22-32

22 A sound of battle is in the land, and of great destruction.

23 How is the hammer of the whole earth cut asunder and broken! how is Babylon become a desolation among the nations!

24 I have laid a snare for thee, and thou art also taken, O Babylon, and thou wast not aware: thou art found, and also caught, because thou hast striven against the LORD.

25 The LORD hath opened his armoury, and hath brought forth the weapons of his indignation: for this [is] the work of the Lord GOD of hosts in the land of the Chaldeans.

26 Come against her from the utmost border, open her storehouses: cast her up as heaps, and destroy her utterly: let nothing of her be left.

27 Slay all her bullocks; let them go down to the slaughter: woe unto them! for their day is come, the time of their visitation.

28 The voice of them that flee and escape out of the land of Babylon, to declare in Zion the vengeance of the LORD our God, the vengeance of his temple.

29 Call together the archers against Babylon: all ye that bend the bow, camp against it round about; let none thereof escape: recompense her according to her work; according to all that she hath done, do unto her: for she hath been proud against the LORD, against the Holy One of Israel.

30 Therefore shall her young men fall in the streets, and all her men of war shall be cut off in that day, saith the LORD.

31 Behold, I am against thee, O thou most proud, saith the Lord GOD of hosts: for thy day is come, the time that I will visit thee.

32 And the most proud shall stumble and fall, and none shall raise him up: and I will kindle a fire in his cities, and it shall devour all round about him.

Jeremiah 50:46

46 At the noise of the taking of Babylon the earth is moved, and the cry is heard among the nations.

Jeremiah 51:1

1 Thus saith the LORD; Behold, I will raise up against Babylon, and against them that dwell in the midst of them that rise up against me, a destroying wind;

Jeremiah 51:6-9

6 Flee out of the midst of Babylon, and deliver every man his soul: be not cut off in her iniquity; for this is the time of the LORD's vengeance; he will render unto her a recompence.

7 Babylon hath been a golden cup in the LORD's hand, that made all the earth drunken: the nations have drunken of her wine; therefore the nations are mad.

8 Babylon is suddenly fallen and destroyed: howl for her; take balm for her pain, if so she may be healed.

9 We would have healed Babylon, but she is not healed: forsake her, and let us go every one into his own country: for her judgment reacheth unto heaven, and is lifted up even to the skies.

Jeremiah 51:29-37

29 And the land shall tremble and sorrow: for every purpose of the LORD shall be performed against Babylon, to make the land of Babylon a desolation without an inhabitant.

30 The mighty men of Babylon have forborn to fight, they have remained in their holds: their might hath failed; they became as women: they have burned her dwellingplaces; her bars are broken.

31 One post shall run to meet another, and one messenger to meet another, to shew the king of Babylon that his city is taken at one end,

32 And that the passages are stopped, and the reeds they have burned with fire, and the men of war are affrighted.

33 For thus saith the LORD of hosts, the God of Israel; The daughter of Babylon is like a threshingfloor, it is time to thresh her: yet a little while, and the time of her harvest shall come.

34 Nebuchadrezzar the king of Babylon hath devoured me, he hath crushed me, he hath made me an empty vessel, he hath swallowed me up like a dragon, he hath filled his belly with my delicates, he hath cast me out.

35 The violence done to me and to my flesh be upon Babylon, shall the inhabitant of Zion say; and my blood upon the inhabitants of Chaldea, shall Jerusalem say.

36 Therefore thus saith the LORD; Behold, I will plead thy cause, and take vengeance for thee; and I will dry up her sea, and make her springs dry.

37 And Babylon shall become heaps, a dwellingplace for dragons, an astonishment, and an hissing, without an inhabitant.

Jeremiah 51:42-58

42 The sea is come up upon Babylon: she is covered with the multitude of the waves thereof.

43 Her cities are a desolation, a dry land, and a wilderness, a land wherein no man dwelleth, neither doth any son of man pass thereby.

44 And I will punish Bel in Babylon, and I will bring forth out of his mouth that which he hath swallowed up: and the nations shall not flow together any more unto him: yea, the wall of Babylon shall fall.

45 My people, go ye out of the midst of her, and deliver ye every man his soul from the fierce anger of the LORD.

46 And lest your heart faint, and ye fear for the rumour that shall be heard in the land; a rumour shall both come one year, and after that in another year shall come a rumour, and violence in the land, ruler

against ruler.

47 Therefore, behold, the days come, that I will do judgment upon the graven images of Babylon: and her whole land shall be confounded, and all her slain shall fall in the midst of her.

48 Then the heaven and the earth, and all that is therein, shall sing for Babylon: for the spoilers shall come unto her from the north, saith the LORD.

49 As Babylon hath caused the slain of Israel to fall, so at Babylon shall fall the slain of all the earth.

50 Ye that have escaped the sword, go away, stand not still: remember the LORD afar off, and let Jerusalem come into your mind.

51 We are confounded, because we have heard reproach: shame hath covered our faces: for strangers are come into the sanctuaries of the LORD's house.

52 Wherefore, behold, the days come, saith the LORD, that I will do judgment upon her graven images: and through all her land the wounded shall groan.

53 Though Babylon should mount up to heaven, and though she should fortify the height of her strength, yet from me shall spoilers come unto her, saith the LORD.

54 A sound of a cry cometh from Babylon, and great destruction from the land of the Chaldeans:

55 Because the LORD hath spoiled Babylon, and destroyed out of her the great voice; when her waves do roar like great waters, a noise of their voice is uttered:

56 Because the spoiler is come upon her, even upon Babylon, and her mighty men are taken, every one of their bows is broken: for the LORD God of recompences shall surely requite.

57 And I will make drunk her princes, and her wise men, her captains, and her rulers, and her mighty men: and they shall sleep a perpetual sleep, and not wake, saith the King, whose name is the LORD of hosts.

58 Thus saith the LORD of hosts; The broad walls of Babylon shall be utterly broken, and her high gates shall be burned with fire; and the people shall labour in vain, and the folk in the fire, and they shall be weary.

Revelation 14:8

8 And there followed another angel, saying, Babylon is fallen, is fallen, that great city, because she made all nations drink of the wine of the wrath of her fornication.

Revelation 16:19

19 And the great city was divided into three parts, and the cities of the nations fell: and great Babylon came in remembrance before God, to give unto her the cup of the wine of the fierceness of his wrath.

Revelation 17:Heading-18

John is shown that Babylon the great, the mother of harlots and abominations, has become established throughout the earth.

1 And there came one of the seven angels which had the seven vials, and talked with me, saying unto me, Come hither; I will shew unto thee the judgment of the great whore that sitteth upon many waters:

2 With whom the kings of the earth have committed fornication, and the inhabitants of the earth have

been made drunk with the wine of her fornication.

3 So he carried me away in the spirit into the wilderness: and I saw a woman sit upon a scarlet coloured beast, full of names of blasphemy, having seven heads and ten horns.

4 And the woman was arrayed in purple and scarlet colour, and decked with gold and precious stones and pearls, having a golden cup in her hand full of abominations and filthiness of her fornication:

5 And upon her forehead was a name written, MYSTERY, BABYLON THE GREAT, THE MOTHER OF HARLOTS AND ABOMINATIONS OF THE EARTH.

6 And I saw the woman drunken with the blood of the saints, and with the blood of the martyrs of Jesus: and when I saw her, I wondered with great admiration.

7 And the angel said unto me, Wherefore didst thou marvel? I will tell thee the mystery of the woman, and of the beast that carrieth her, which hath the seven heads and ten horns.

8 The beast that thou sawest was, and is not; and shall ascend out of the bottomless pit, and go into perdition: and they that dwell on the earth shall wonder, whose names were not written in the book of life from the foundation of the world, when they behold the beast that was, and is not, and yet is.

9 And here is the mind which hath wisdom. The seven heads are seven mountains, on which the woman sitteth.

10 And there are seven kings: five are fallen, and one is, and the other is not yet come; and when he cometh, he must continue a short space.

11 And the beast that was, and is not, even he is the eighth, and is of the seven, and goeth into perdition.

12 And the ten horns which thou sawest are ten kings, which have received no kingdom as yet; but receive power as kings one hour with the beast.

13 These have one mind, and shall give their power and strength unto the beast.

14 These shall make war with the Lamb, and the Lamb shall overcome them: for he is Lord of lords, and King of kings: and they that are with him are called, and chosen, and faithful.

15 And he saith unto me, The waters which thou sawest, where the whore sitteth, are peoples, and multitudes, and nations, and tongues.

16 And the ten horns which thou sawest upon the beast, these shall hate the whore, and shall make her desolate and naked, and shall eat her flesh, and burn her with fire.

17 For God hath put in their hearts to fulfil his will, and to agree, and give their kingdom unto the beast, until the words of God shall be fulfilled.

18 And the woman which thou sawest is that great city, which reigneth over the kings of the earth.

Revelation 18:1-24

1 And after these things I saw another angel come down from heaven, having great power; and the earth was lightened with his glory.

2 And he cried mightily with a strong voice, saying, Babylon the great is fallen, is fallen, and is become the habitation of devils, and the hold of every foul spirit, and a cage of every unclean and hateful bird.

3 For all nations have drunk of the wine of the wrath of her fornication, and the kings of the earth have committed fornication with her, and the merchants of the earth are waxed rich through the abundance of her delicacies.

4 And I heard another voice from heaven, saying, Come out of her, my people, that ye be not partakers of her sins, and that ye receive not of her plagues.

5 For her sins have reached unto heaven, and God hath remembered her iniquities.

6 Reward her even as she rewarded you, and double unto her double according to her works: in the cup which she hath filled fill to her double.

7 How much she hath glorified herself, and lived deliciously, so much torment and sorrow give her: for she saith in her heart, I sit a queen, and am no widow, and shall see no sorrow.

8 Therefore shall her plagues come in one day, death, and mourning, and famine; and she shall be utterly burned with fire: for strong is the Lord God who judgeth her.

9 And the kings of the earth, who have committed fornication and lived deliciously with her, shall bewail her, and lament for her, when they shall see the smoke of her burning,

10 Standing afar off for the fear of her torment, saying, Alas, alas, that great city Babylon, that mighty city! for in one hour is thy judgment come.

11 And the merchants of the earth shall weep and mourn over her; for no man buyeth their merchandise any more:

12 The merchandise of gold, and silver, and precious stones, and of pearls, and fine linen, and purple, and silk, and scarlet, and all thyine wood, and all manner vessels of ivory, and all manner vessels of most precious wood, and of brass, and iron, and marble,

13 And cinnamon, and odours, and ointments, and frankincense, and wine, and oil, and fine flour, and wheat, and beasts, and sheep, and horses, and chariots, and slaves, and souls of men.

14 And the fruits that thy soul lusted after are departed from thee, and all things which were dainty and goodly are departed from thee, and thou shalt find them no more at all.

15 The merchants of these things, which were made rich by her, shall stand afar off for the fear of her torment, weeping and wailing,

16 And saying, Alas, alas, that great city, that was clothed in fine linen, and purple, and scarlet, and decked with gold, and precious stones, and pearls!

17 For in one hour so great riches is come to nought. And every shipmaster, and all the company in ships, and sailors, and as many as trade by sea, stood afar off,

18 And cried when they saw the smoke of her burning, saying, What city is like unto this great city!

19 And they cast dust on their heads, and cried, weeping and wailing, saying, Alas, alas, that great city, wherein were made rich all that had ships in the sea by reason of her costliness! for in one hour is she made desolate.

20 Rejoice over her, thou heaven, and ye holy apostles and prophets; for God hath avenged you on her.

21 And a mighty angel took up a stone like a great millstone, and cast it into the sea, saying, Thus with violence shall that great city Babylon be thrown down, and shall be found no more at all.

22 And the voice of harpers, and musicians, and of pipers, and trumpeters, shall be heard no more at all in thee; and no craftsman, of whatsoever craft he be, shall be found any more in thee; and the sound of a millstone shall be heard no more at all in thee;

23 And the light of a candle shall shine no more at all in thee; and the voice of the bridegroom and of the bride shall be heard no more at all in thee: for thy merchants were the great men of the earth; for by thy sorceries were all nations deceived.

24 And in her was found the blood of prophets, and of saints, and of all that were slain upon the earth.

Revelation 19:1-4

1 And after these things I heard a great voice of much people in heaven, saying, Alleluia; Salvation, and glory, and honour, and power, unto the Lord our God:

2 For true and righteous are his judgments: for he hath judged the great whore, which did corrupt the earth with her fornication, and hath avenged the blood of his servants at her hand.

3 And again they said, Alleluia. And her smoke rose up for ever and ever.

4 And the four and twenty elders and the four beasts fell down and worshipped God that sat on the throne, saying, Amen; Alleluia.

D&C 1:11-16

11 Wherefore the voice of the Lord is unto the ends of the earth, that all that will hear may hear:

12 Prepare ye, prepare ye for that which is to come, for the Lord is nigh;

13 And the anger of the Lord is kindled, and his sword is bathed in heaven, and it shall fall upon the inhabitants of the earth.

14 And the arm of the Lord shall be revealed; and the day cometh that they who will not hear the voice of the Lord, neither the voice of his servants, neither give heed to the words of the prophets and apostles, shall be cut off from among the people;

15 For they have strayed from mine ordinances, and have broken mine everlasting covenant;

16 They seek not the Lord to establish his righteousness, but every man walketh in his own way, and after the image of his own God, whose image is in the likeness of the world, and whose substance is that of an idol, which waxeth old and shall perish in Babylon, even Babylon the great, which shall fall.

D&C 35:11

11 But without faith shall not anything be shown forth except desolations upon Babylon, the same which has made all nations drink of the wine of the wrath of her fornication.

D&C 64:24

24 For after today cometh the burning—this is speaking after the manner of the Lord—for verily I say, tomorrow all the proud and they that do wickedly shall be as stubble; and I will burn them up, for I am the Lord of Hosts; and I will not spare any that remain in Babylon.

D&C 86:3

3 And after they have fallen asleep the great persecutor of the church, the apostate, the whore, even Babylon, that maketh all nations to drink of her cup, in whose hearts the enemy, even Satan, sitteth to reign—behold he soweth the tares; wherefore, the tares choke the wheat and drive the church into the wilderness.

D&C 88:105

105 And again, another angel shall sound his trump, which is the sixth angel, saying: She is fallen who made all nations drink of the wine of the wrath of her fornication; she is fallen, is fallen!

D&C 133:5

5 Go ye out from Babylon. Be ye clean that bear the vessels of the Lord.

D&C 133:7

7 Yea, verily I say unto you again, the time has come when the voice of the Lord is unto you: Go ye out of Babylon; gather ye out from among the nations, from the four winds, from one end of heaven to the other.

D&C 133:14

14 Go ye out from among the nations, even from Babylon, from the midst of wickedness, which is spiritual Babylon.

CHAPTER TEN

JOHN & DANIEL'S VISIONS

"Daniel was informed of the history of nations and kingdoms by the beasts and figures shown him representing those kingdoms. In contrast, John the Revelator saw actual beasts in heaven to establish in his mind the truth that animals are resurrected and dwell in heavenly spheres." (Bruce R. McConkie, Mormon Doctrine, p. 824.)

Joseph Smith, History of the Church, Vol. 5, p. 324.

"I read the 5th chapter of Revelation, referring particularly to the 6th verse, showing from that the actual existence of beasts in heaven. Probably those were beasts which had lived on another planet, and not ours. God never made use of the figure of a beast to represent the kingdom of heaven. When it is made use of, it is to represent an apostate church."

Joseph Smith, History of the Church, Vol. 5, p. 341.

"When God made use of the figure of a beast in visions to the prophets He did it to represent those kingdoms which had degenerated and become corrupt, savage and beast-like in their dispositions, even the degenerate kingdoms of the wicked world; but He never made use of the figure of a beast nor any of the brute kind to represent His kingdom."

Joseph Smith, History of the Church, Vol. 5, p. 342.

"The revelations do not give us to understand anything of the past in relation to the kingdom of God. What John saw and speaks of were things which he saw in heaven; those which Daniel saw were on and pertaining to the earth.

I am now going to take exceptions to the present translation of the Bible in relation to these matters. Our latitude and longitude can be determined in the original Hebrew with far greater accuracy than in the English version. There is a grand distinction between the actual meaning of the prophets and the present translation. The prophets do not declare that they saw a beast or beasts, but that they saw the image or figure of a beast. Daniel did not see an actual bear or a lion, but the images or figures of those beasts. The translation should have been rendered 'image' instead of 'beast,' in every instance where beasts are mentioned by the prophets. But John saw the actual beast in heaven, showing to John that beasts did actually exist there, and not to represent figures of things on the earth. When the prophets speak of seeing beasts in their visions, they mean that they saw the images, they being types to represent certain things. At the same time they received the interpretation as to what those images or types were designed to represent.

I make this broad declaration, that whenever God gives a vision of an image, or beast, or figure of any kind, He always holds Himself responsible to give a revelation or interpretation of the meaning thereof, otherwise we are not responsible or accountable for our belief in it. Don't be afraid of being damned for not knowing the meaning of a vision or figure, if God has not given a revelation or interpretation of the subject."

Joseph Smith, History of the Church, Vol. 5, p. 344-345.

"Again, there is no revelation to prove that things do not exist in heaven as I have set forth, nor yet to show that the beasts meant anything but beasts; and we never can comprehend the things of God and of heaven, but by revelation. We may spiritualize and express opinions to all eternity; but that is no authority.

Oh, ye elders of Israel, harken to my voice; and when you are sent into the world to preach, tell those things you are sent to tell; preach and cry aloud, 'Repent ye, for the kingdom of heaven is at hand; repent and believe the Gospel.' Declare the first principles, and let mysteries alone, lest ye be overthrown. Never meddle with the visions of beasts and subjects you do not understand."

Teachings of the Prophet Joseph Smith, Section Six, 1843–44, p. 287.

"It is not essential for the elders to have knowledge in relation to the meaning of beasts, and heads and horns, and other figures made use of in the revelations; still, it may be necessary, to prevent contention and division and do away with suspense. If we get puffed up by thinking that we have much knowledge, we are apt to get a contentious spirit, and correct knowledge is necessary to cast out that spirit."

JOHN'S VISION

Joseph Smith, History of the Church, Vol. 3, p. 396.

"The horns of the beast, the toes of the image, the frogs, and the beast mentioned by John, are not going to save this generation; for if a man does not become acquainted with the first principles of the Gospel, how shall he understand those greater mysteries, which the most wise cannot understand without revelation?"

Joseph Smith, History of the Church, Vol. 5, p. 341.

"There is a grand difference and distinction between the visions and figures spoken of by the ancient prophets, and those spoken of in the revelations of John. The things which John saw had no allusion to the scenes of the days of Adam, Enoch, Abraham or Jesus, only so far as is plainly represented by John, and clearly set forth by him. John saw that only which was lying in futurity and which was shortly to come to pass. See Rev. 1:1-3, which is a key to the whole subject: 'The revelation of Jesus Christ, which God gave unto Him, to show unto his servants things which must shortly come to pass; and He sent and signified it by His angel unto His servant John: who bare record of the word of God, and of the testimony of Jesus Christ, and of all things that he saw. Blessed is he that readeth, and they that hear the words of this prophecy, and keep those things that are written therein: for the time is at hand.' Also Rev. 4:1. 'After this I looked and, behold, a door was opened in heaven; and the first voice which I heard was as it were of a trumpet talking with me; which said, Come up hither, and I will show thee things which must be hereafter.'

The four beasts and twenty-four elders were out of every nation; for they sang a new song, saying, 'Thou art worthy to take the book, and to open the seal thereof: for thou wast slain, and hast redeemed us to God by thy blood out of every kindred, and tongue, and people, and nation.' (See Rev. 5:9.) It would be great stuffing to crowd all nations into four beasts and twenty-four elders.

Now, I make this declaration, that those things which John saw in heaven had no allusion to anything that had been on the earth previous to that time, because they were the representation of 'things which must shortly come to pass,' and not of what has already transpired. John saw beasts that had to do with things on the earth, but not in past ages. The beasts which John saw had to devour the inhabitants of the earth in days to come. 'And I saw when the Lamb opened one of the seals; and I heard, as it were the noise of thunder, one of the four beasts saying, Come and see. And I saw, and beheld a white horse: and he that sat on him had a bow; and a crown was given unto him: and he went forth conquering, and to conquer. And when he had opened the second seal, I heard the second beast say, Come and see. And there went out another horse that was red: and power was given to him that sat thereon to take peace from the earth, and that they should kill one another: and there was given unto him a great sword.' (Rev. 6:1-4.) The book of Revelation is one of the plainest books God ever caused to be written."

Joseph Smith, History of the Church, Vol. 5, p. 341.

"John saw curious looking beasts in heaven; he saw every creature that was in heaven, —all the beasts, fowls and fish in heaven,—actually there, giving glory to God. How do you prove it? (See Rev. 5:13.) 'And every creature which is in heaven, and on the earth, and under the earth, and such as are in the sea, and all that are in them, heard I saying, Blessing, and honor, and glory, and power, be unto Him that sitteth upon the throne, and unto the Lamb for ever and ever.'

I suppose John saw beings there of a thousand forms, that had been saved from ten thousand times ten thousand earths like this,—strange beasts of which we have no conception: all might be seen in heaven. The grand secret was to show John what there was in heaven. John learned that God glorified Himself by saving all that His hands had made, whether beasts, fowls, fishes or men; and He will glorify Himself with them.

Says one, 'I cannot believe in the salvation of beasts.' Any man who would tell you that this could not be, would tell you that the revelations are not true. John heard the words of the beasts giving glory to God, and understood them. God who made the beasts could understand every language spoken by them. The four beasts were four of the most noble animals that had filled the measure of their creation, and had been saved from other worlds, because they were perfect: they were like angels in their sphere. We are not told where they came from, and I do not know; but they were seen and heard by John praising and glorifying God.

The popular religionists of the day tell us, forsooth, that the beasts spoken of in the Revelation represent kingdoms. Very well, on the same principle we can say that the twenty-four elders spoken of represent beasts; for they are all spoken of at the same time, and are represented as all uniting in the same acts of praise and devotion."

Joseph Smith, History of the Church, Vol. 5, p. 345.

"He then read Rev. 13:1-8. John says, 'And I saw one of his heads as it were wounded to death; and his deadly wound was healed; and all the world wondered after the beast.' Some spiritualizers say the beast that received the wound was Nebuchadnezzar, some Constantine, some Mohammed, and others the Roman Catholic Church; but we will look at what John saw in relation to this beast. Now for the wasp's nest. The translators have used the term 'dragon' for devil. Now it was a beast that John saw in heaven, and he was then speaking of 'things which must shortly come to pass;' and consequently the beast that John saw could not be Nebuchadnezzar. The beast John saw was an actual beast, and an actual intelligent being gives him his power, and his seat, and great authority. It was not to represent a beast in heaven: it was an angel in heaven who has power in the last days to do a work.

'All the world wondered after the beast,' Nebuchadnezzar and Constantine the Great not excepted. And if the beast was all the world, how could the world wonder after the beast? It must have been a wonderful beast to cause all human beings to wonder after it; and I will venture to say that when God allows the old devil to give power to the beast to destroy the inhabitants of the earth, all will wonder. Verse 4 reads, 'And they worshiped the dragon which gave power unto the beast; and they worshiped the beast, saying, Who is like unto the beast? Who is able to make war with Him?'

Some say it means the kingdom of the world. One thing is sure, it does not mean the kingdom of the Saints. Suppose we admit that it means the kingdoms of the world, what propriety would there be in saying, Who is able to make war with my great big self? If these spiritualized interpretations are true, the book contradicts itself in almost every verse. But they are not true.

There is a mistranslation of the word dragon in the second verse. The original word signifies the devil, and not dragon, as translated. In chapter 12, verse 9, it reads, 'That old serpent, called the devil,' and it ought to be translated devil in this case, and not dragon. It is sometimes translated Apollyon. Everything that we have not a key-word to, we will take it as it reads. The beasts which John saw and speaks of as being in heaven, were actually living in heaven, and were actually to have power given to them over the inhabitants of the earth, precisely according to the plain reading of the revelations. I give this as a key to the elders of Israel. The independent beast is a beast that dwells in heaven, abstract [apart] from the human family. The beast that rose up out of the sea should be translated the image of a beast, as I have referred to it in Daniel's vision."

Orson Pratt, Journal of Discourses, Vol. 7, p. 219, August 14, 1859.

"John, the Revelator, in describing this same power under the figure of a beast, says—'And all the world wondered after the beast.' 'And it was given unto him to make war with the Saints, and to overcome them; and power was given him over all kindreds, and tongues, and nations.' (Revelation, chapter 13.) Therefore, instead of the ancient Church overcoming the image, it was itself to be overcome by the image. History shows the sad fulfillment of these predictions. Therefore the former-day kingdom was not the stone of the mountain. The ancient kingdom being overcome, fled to heaven, and the priesthood was caught up to God and to his throne; and there the Saints are reserved in heaven until the coming of the Son of God to reign on the earth, according to the predictions of the Prophets. Then he will bring that kingdom which is in heaven with him. He has to set up a kingdom on earth preparatory to that which will come from heaven. This preparatory kingdom must be established on the earth, where men-made governments exist. It will be a kingdom increasing in greatness and power and glory on the earth for many years preparatory to the coming of the King with the heavenly kingdom, at which time both the heavenly and earthly will be united in one, under their great Head and Lawgiver."

Orson Pratt, Journal of Discourses, Vol. 15, p. 337, January 26, 1873.

"I will turn now to the revelations of St. John, and will refer first to a few sayings contained in the 14th chapter, commencing at the 6th verse:—And I saw another angel fly in the midst of heaven, having the everlasting Gospel to preach unto them that dwell on the earth, and to every nation, and kindred, and tongue, and people. Saying with a loud voice, Fear God, and give glory to him; for the hour of his judgment is come.

It seems that the dispensation in which the Angel should fly was to be characterized as a dispensation of judgment. Immediately after the Angel brought the Gospel, judgment was to be poured out on the nations of the earth. In the 8th verse we read, 'And there followed another Angel, saying, 'Babylon is fallen, is fallen, that great city, because she made all nations drink of the wine of the wrath of her fornication.' And a third Angel followed, saying with a loud voice, 'If any man worship the beast and his image, and receive his mark in his forehead or in his hand, the same shall drink of the wine of the wrath of God, which is poured out without mixture into the cup of his indignation and he shall be tormented with fire and brimstone in the presence of the holy Angels and in the presence of the Lamb.'

To show that this preaching of the Gospel and the pouring out of these judgments upon spiritual Babylon the Great, was a work which should precede the coming of the Son of Man, I will read the 14th verse and to the end of the chapter."

Charles W. Penrose, Journal of Discourses, Vol. 24, p. 208-210, May 18, 1883.

"This revelation that was given to John will seem very strange to a great many people, who are under the impression that the everlasting Gospel has been upon the earth ever since it was taught by Jesus Christ and His Apostles. But if that were so, what need would there be for the Lord to send an angel with it? As I before explained, John saw the time when the whole earth would be under the influence of that wicked power which he saw sitting on a scarlet colored beast, and out of the cup which she held in her hand, all nations were to drink—not merely the heathen nations, but all the nations of the earth without exception. I am well aware that this will not sit very comfortably on the bosoms of some of our Christian friends. But what we are after, or should be after, is truth; and we should be desirous to obtain the truth notwithstanding that it may come in contact with our preconceived notions. John saw that the whole earth would go astray; and all the Apostles spoke more or less of the time when people would depart from the Church, when they would 'not endure sound doctrine, but after their own lusts they would heap to themselves teachers having itching ears;' and says the Apostle, 'they shall turn away their ears from the truth, and shall be turned into fables;' their teachers shall 'preach for doctrine the commandments of men;' and the Apostle might have added, that if they did not preach to suit the people, they would discharge them and hire others. The time was to come when 'darkness would cover the earth, and gross darkness the people,' but preceding the destruction of Babylon the great archangel was to come to earth with the everlasting Gospel to preach to all nations; and the burden of his message was to call upon the people with a loud voice, saying, 'Fear God, and give glory to Him, for the hour of His judgment is come; and worship Him that made heaven and earth, and the sea, and the fountains of water,' signifying that the people had gone astray and were worshiping some other god or gods."

Joseph Fielding Smith, Answers to Gospel Questions, Vol. 2, p. 97.

"The cherubim on the Ark of the Covenant were placed there as symbolic figures, representing guardians, whose wings protected the altar. These, like the figures seen by Ezekiel, were symbolic, not necessarily living beings, and by them the Lord was teaching Ezekiel a lesson in relation to his mission to Israel. The same is true in relation to the several beasts seen by the Revelator John. All of these visions by symbolic representation had something to do with history which the Lord was revealing, the full meaning of which has not been made clear to our understanding."

Teachings of Ezra Taft Benson, p. 399-400.

"We live in that time of which the Lord spoke when He said that 'peace shall be taken from the earth, and the devil shall have power over his own dominion' (D&C 1:35). We live in that day which John the Revelator foresaw when 'the dragon was wroth with the woman, and went to make war with the remnant of her seed, which keep the commandments of God and have the testimony of Jesus Christ' (Revelation 12:17). The dragon is Satan; the woman represents the Church of Jesus Christ. Satan is waging war against the members of the Church who have testimonies and are trying to keep the commandments. And while many of our members are remaining faithful and strong, some are wavering. Some are falling. Some are fulfilling John's prophecy that in the war with Satan, some Saints would be 'overcome' (Revelation 13:7). ('The Power of the Word,' Ensign 16 [May 1986]: 81.) (CR April 1986)."

DANIEL'S VISION

Teachings of the Prophet Joseph Smith, Section Two, 1834–37, p. 103-104.

"Daniel has told us that he is to stand in his proper lot, in the latter days; according to his vision he had a right to shut it up, and also to open it again after many days, or in latter times. Daniel's image, whose head was gold, and body, arms, legs and feet, were composed of the different materials described in his vision, represents different governments. The golden head was to represent Nebuchadnezzar, King of Babylon; the other parts, other kings and forms of governments which I shall not now mention in detail, but confine my remarks more particularly to the feet of the image. The policy of the wicked spirit is to separate what God has joined together, and unite what He has separated, which the devil has succeeded in doing to admiration in the present society, which is like unto iron and clay.

There is confusion in all things, both political and religious; and notwithstanding all the efforts that are made to bring about a union, society remains disunited, and all attempts to unite it are as fruitless as to attempt to unite iron and clay. The feet of the image are the government of these United States. Other nations and kingdoms are looking up to her for an example of union, freedom, and equal rights, and therefore worship her as Daniel saw in the vision; although they are beginning to lose confidence in her, seeing the broils and discord that rise on her political and religious horizon. The image is characteristic of all governments."

Teachings of the Prophet Joseph Smith, Section Five, 1842–43, p. 253.

"The earth is groaning under corruption, oppression, tyranny and bloodshed; and God is coming out of His hiding place, as He said He would do, to vex the nations of the earth. Daniel, in his vision, saw convulsion upon convulsion; he "beheld till the thrones were cast down, and the Ancient of Days did sit;" and one was brought before him like unto the Son of Man; and all nations, kindred, tongues, and peoples, did serve and obey Him. It is for us to be righteous, that we may be wise and understand; for none of the wicked shall understand; but the wise shall understand, and they that turn many to righteousness shall shine as the stars for ever and ever."

Teachings of the Prophet Joseph Smith, Section Six, 1843–44, p. 289.

"Daniel says (7:16) when he saw the vision of the four beasts, 'I came near unto one of them that stood by, and asked him the truth of all this,' the angel interpreted the vision to Daniel; but we find, by the interpretation that the figures of beasts had no allusion to the kingdom of God. You there see that the beasts are spoken of to represent the kingdoms of the world, the inhabitants whereof were beastly and abominable characters; they were murderers, corrupt, carnivorous, and brutal in their dispositions. The lion, the bear, the leopard, and the ten-horned beast represented the kingdoms of the world, says Daniel; for I refer to the prophets to qualify my observations which I make, so that the young elders who know so much, may not rise up like a flock of hornets and sting me. I want to keep out of such a wasp-nest."

Brigham Young, Journal of Discourses, Vol. 5, p. 76, July 26, 1857.

"The God of heaven showed Nebuchadnezzar that this kingdom would never be destroyed; and that is my testimony. This is the kingdom of heaven—the kingdom of God which Daniel saw. This is the kingdom that was revealed to King Nebuchadnezzar and interpreted to him by the Prophet Daniel. This is the kingdom that was to be set up in the last days. It is like a stone taken from the mountain without hands, with all its roughness, with all its disfigured appearance—uncomely—even a stumbling-block and a stone of offence to the nations of the earth. This is the kingdom that is set up; and the history of the kingdoms of this world all understand, or can read and understand it."

Parley P. Pratt, A Voice of Warning, p. 17-18.

"In this great view of the subject, we have presented before us in succession, first, the kingdom of Nebuchadnezzar; second, the Medes and Persians, who took Babylon from Belshazzar, and reigned over all the earth; third the Greeks, under Alexander, who conquered the world, and reigned in the midst of Babylon; and fourth, the Roman empire, which subdued all things; fifth, its division into eastern and western empires, and its final breaking up or subdivision into the various kingdoms of modern Europe, represented by the feet and toes, part of iron and part of clay.

And lastly, we have presented before us an entirely new kingdom, organized by the God of heaven in the last days, or during the reign of these kings, represented by the feet and toes. This last kingdom was never to change masters, like all the kingdoms which had gone before it. It was never to be left to other people. It was to break in pieces all these kingdoms, and stand forever.

Many supposed that this last kingdom alluded to was the kingdom of God which was organized in the days of Christ or his apostles. But a greater blunder could not exist. The kingdom of God set up in the days of Christ or of his apostles, did not break in pieces any of the kingdoms of the world; it was itself warred against and overcome, in fulfillment of the words of Daniel, 7th chapter, 21st verse: 'I beheld, and the same horn made war with the saints, and prevailed against them;' also 22nd verse, 'Until the Ancient of Days came, and judgment was given to the saints of the most High; and the time came that the saints possessed the kingdom'; also verse 27th, 'And the kingdom and dominion, and the greatness of the kingdom under the whole heaven, shall be given to the people of the saints of the most High, whose kingdom is an everlasting kingdom, and all dominions shall serve and obey him.'"

Orson Pratt, Journal of Discourses, Vol. 13, p. 125, April 10, 1870.

"All the governments which have hitherto had a place on our earth, excepting those now in existence, have had an end. Human governments have been very changeable in their nature. The Lord has raised up a nation here and a nation there, a kingdom here and a kingdom there, and He has suffered them to live and flourish for a few centuries, and some, perhaps, even for one or two thousand years; then He has caused them to pass away. But He spoke to His ancient servant, who is called Daniel, whose prophecy is written in this book (the Bible), and said that in the latter days He would set up a government or kingdom which should have no end. This government will differ from all preceding governments set up from the Creation down to the period of its establishment. Daniel says it shall become universal and shall cover the whole earth. He calls the citizens of that government Saints. He beheld that the stone cut out of the mountain without hands should roll forth and become a great mountain and fill the whole earth, and that all earthly governments, kingdoms and empires should become like the chaff of the summer threshing floor, and no place should be found for them; while the stone that was cut out of the mountains should have dominion over the whole earth, and the Saints of the Most High should have dominion under the whole heaven.

Now there will have to be a beginning to that work. The Lord will not make such a wonderful revolution as the one I have named, all in one day, or in one year. Jesus made his appearance on the earth in the meridian of time, and he established his kingdom on the earth. But to fulfill ancient prophecies the Lord suffered that kingdom to be uprooted; in other words, the kingdoms of this world made war against the kingdom of God, established eighteen centuries ago, and they prevailed against it, and the kingdom ceased to exist. The great beast that John saw made war with it and prevailed against it, and human institutions, without prophets or inspired men, usurped the place of the ancient kingdom of God. But God has promised that the latter-day kingdom shall stand for ever. Though the heavens and earth be wrapped together as a scroll and pass away, yet the kingdom that was to be set up in the latter days will have no end, but will prevail among all people under the heavens and will have dominion for one thousand years. After that, when the earth passes away, the kingdom will be caught up; it will not perish, be annihilated or overcome, but be caught up into the heavens while the earth is undergoing its last change; and when the Lord shall resurrect the earth, the same as He will our bodies, and make it a new earth, wherein shall dwell righteousness, He will then bring down out of Heaven to the new earth this latter-day kingdom, with all the former kingdoms that He has built up in other dispensations, and they will stand for ever, for the new earth will never pass away."

Orson Pratt, Journal of Discourses, Vol. 15, p. 47-48, April 7, 1872.

"Let me refer now to another prophecy. Daniel the Prophet has told us that in the latter days after the great image that was seen in dream by Nebuchadnezzar, the king of Babylon, representing the various kingdoms of the world, should be destroyed, and those nations should pass away and become like the chaff of the summer threshing floor, the Lord would establish an everlasting Government here upon the earth. The Lord God saw proper to reveal to his servant Daniel the nature of this Government. He represented it as having a very small beginning—as a stone cut out of the mountain without hands, which stone should fall upon the feet of the image, and they should be broken in pieces. After the destruction of the feet all the image should fall—the legs of iron, the belly and thighs of brass, the breast and arms of silver, the head of gold—representing the remnants of all those ancient nations—the Babylonians, Medes and Persians, and the Greeks; also the remnants of those that once constituted the great Roman empire—those now in Europe and those of European origin which have come across the great ocean and established themselves here on the vast continent of the west, all, all were to be destroyed by the force of this little kingdom to be established by the power of truth, and by the authority that should characterize the nature of the stone cut out of the mountains. 'In the days of these kings,' says the Prophet, 'shall the God of heaven set up a kingdom that shall never be destroyed, neither shall it be left to any other people, but it shall stand for ever,' etc. The Prophet Daniel uttered the prophecy; Joseph Smith, by authority of the Almighty, fulfilled it, so far as the organization or setting up of the kingdom was concerned."

Orson Pratt, Journal of Discourses, Vol. 15, p. 70-72, February 4, 1872.

"King Nebuchadnezzar was so earnest in regard to this matter that he sent forth a decree that unless the wise men of Babylon would interpret to him his dream and also tell the dream itself, he would destroy the whole of them. I suppose he had not much confidence in them, and consequently concluded that if they could not tell the dream he could not put confidence in their interpretations. When Daniel heard of the decree of the king, to destroy all the wise man, he sent in a request that the king would not be quite so hasty in his measures, but give him a little time, during which he and his fellows besought the God of heaven that they might know concerning the dream and the interpretation thereof. The Lord heard the prayers of his servants and revealed to Daniel concerning the dream, and also gave him the interpretation. Daniel requested to be brought before his majesty the king, and he promised to give the dream and the interpretation. He was brought in before him, and addressed him in language something like the following—'The wise men, astrologers, soothsayers, magicians, etc., can not interpret the dream, O king, neither is there any wisdom in me that I can; but there is a God in heaven who is able to give the interpretation thereof. Thou, O king, art a king of kings, and the God of heaven hath given thee a kingdom, and dominion over all the nations. Thou art a part and portion of the dream; or, in other words, you represent a portion of the dream you had. Thou, O king, sawest and beheld a great image. This image's head was of fine gold, the breast and the arms of silver, the belly and the thighs of brass, the legs were of iron, the feet were part of iron and part of potter's clay. Thou sawest until that a stone was cut out of the mountain without hands, which smote the image upon the feet that was part of iron and part of clay, and brake them to pieces, then was the iron, the clay, the silver, the brass and the gold all broken to pieces together, and became like the chaff of the summer threshing floor, and the wind carried them away, and there was no place found for them, but the stone that smote the image became a great mountain and filled the whole earth. This was the dream—he then gives the interpretation. 'Thou, O king, art this head of gold.' That is, the kingdom of Nebuchadnezzar, that bore rule over all the earth, was considered the head of gold. 'After thee shall come another kingdom represented by the breast and the arms of silver.' That is the Medo-Persian kingdom. After that another kingdom still inferior, called the kingdom of brass, forasmuch as gold is better than silver, silver more precious than brass, so these kingdoms that were to arise, to succeed each other, were to be inferior as time should pass along. The third kingdom, of brass, represented the Macedonian empire; then after that another kingdom, great and terrible, whose legs were of iron, strong and powerful. The fourth kingdom bore rule over the earth; that is admitted, by all commentators, to be the great Roman Empire, and by the division of the Roman empire into two divisions, representing the legs, and afterwards into the feet and toes. I shall not go through and bring up historical facts to show the particular divisions that grew out of the Roman empire, but will merely state that the present modern kingdoms of Europe that have grown out from the Roman empire represent the last vestiges of that great and powerful empire of Rome; that is, it fills up and makes the image complete. First the head of gold—the Babylonian empire; second, the breast and arms of silver—the Medo-persian empire; third, the belly and thighs of brass, the Macedonian kingdom; fourth, the great Roman empire represented by the two legs of iron, the eastern and the western empires of Rome. Afterwards a division of the Roman empire into feet and toes, constituting all the modern European governments and those, governments that have grown out of the European governments located in North and South America.

Do we wish to understand the geographical position of the great image? if we do, we must consider the head located in Asia; the breast and the arms of silver a little west of the great Babylonian Empire, the belly and thighs of brass still westward; the legs of iron and the modern kingdoms composing the feet and toes, part of iron and part of clay, as extending throughout Europe and branching across the Atlantic Ocean, and extending from the East Sea even to the West, from the Atlantic unto the Pacific. This will constitute the location of the great image, running westward.

The image being now complete, all that we need now is to find something that will represent the stone cut out of the mountain without hands, something distinct entirely from the image, having no fellowship with it, that has not grown out of it, and that has no authority that comes from it, but a distinct and entirely separate government that should be established in some mountain. 'Thou sawest until that a stone was cut out of the mountain without hands.' What shall that stone do? It shall smite the image upon the feet and toes. Not upon the head, at first, not upon the breast and arms of silver, not upon the belly and thighs of brass, not upon the modern kingdoms of Europe that have grown out of the legs of iron, but shall smite upon the feet and toes of the great image; there is where it is to commence its attack.

Now let us inquire, for a few moments, how or in what manner this kingdom, called the stone cut out of the mountain, commences this severe attack. Is it to be with weapons of a carnal nature, with sword in hands and weapons of warfare to wage a war against the kingdoms or governments of the earth? No, indeed! Connected with the kingdom or stone cut out of the mountain without hands is a power superior to that of carnal weapons—the power of truth, for the kingdom of God cannot be organized on the earth without truth being sent down from heaven, without authority being given from the Most High; without men again being called to the holy Priesthood and Apostleship, and set forth to publish the truth in its naked simplicity and plainness to the inhabitants of the earth. This truth will be the weapon of warfare, this authority and power sent down from heaven will go forth and will proclaim the message of the everlasting Gospel, the Gospel of the latter-day kingdom, publishing it first among the nations that compose the feet and toes of the great image. Will they be broken to pieces? Yes, when this message is published to them. When they are sufficiently warned, when the servants of God have gone forth in obedience to his commandments, and published in their towns, villages, cities, states and governments these sacred and holy principles that God Almighty has sent down from heaven in the latter times, it will leave all people, nations and tongues that hear the Gospel, and the principles and message pertaining to that kingdom, without any excuse. It will be a warning that will be everlasting on the one hand, or on the other, either to the bringing of the people to repentance, reformation and obedience to the Gospel of the kingdom, or the judgments which are predicted in this prophecy of Daniel will be poured out upon the heads of those nations and kingdoms, and they will become like the chaff of the summer threshing floor, even all those kingdoms that compose the great image; for be it known that the remnants of the Babylonish kingdom, represented by the head of gold, still exist in Asia; the remnants of the silver kingdom, of the brass kingdom, and the kingdom of iron still have their existence; but when the Lord Almighty shall fulfil this prophecy, the toes and feet and legs of iron of that great image, or all these kingdoms, will be broken in pieces, and they will become like the chaff of the summer threshing floor; the wind will carry them away and no place will be found for them.

This prophecy of Daniel will give a true understanding of the matter to our wise men and statesmen, and all who desire to know the future destiny of the American government, the European governments, and all the kingdoms of the earth. Their destiny is total destruction from our earth, no matter how great or powerful they may become. Though our nation may grasp on the right hand and on the left; though it may annex the British possessions, and extend its dominions to the south and grasp the whole of this great western hemisphere, and although our nation shall become as powerful in population as in extent of territory, its destiny is foretold in the saying of the Prophet Daniel, 'They shall become like the chaff of the summer threshing floor, the wind shall carry them away and no place shall be found for them.' So with the kingdoms of Europe, so with the kingdoms of Western Asia and Eastern Europe.

Let us now say a few words in regard to this stone which shall be cut out of the mountain without hands. Now there must be something very peculiar in regard to the organization of the Latter-day kingdom that is never to be destroyed. All these other governments that I have named have been the production of human hands, that is, of human ingenuity, human wisdom; the power of uninspired men has been exerted to the uttermost in the establishment of human governments, consequently all has been done by human ingenuity and power. Not so with the little stone. Man has nothing to do with the organization of that kingdom. Hear what the Prophet has said: 'In the days of these kings the God of heaven shall set up a kingdom.' It is not to be done by human means or power, or by the wisdom of man, neither by mighty conquests by the sword; but it is to be done by him that rules on high, who is King of kings and Lord of lords; by him that suffered and died upon the cross that we might live; by him whose right it is to reign and govern the nations of the earth. He it is that will give laws; he it is that will give commandment; he it is that will organize that kingdom, and it will be done according to the pattern in all things. Has there been any such kingdom organized since the day that the Prophet Daniel delivered this prophecy? I know that there are some who believe that the kingdom spoken of under the name of the 'little stone' was organized 1800 years ago by our Savior and his Apostles. I do not know why they believe this, unless because it is fashionable. There is no evidence to prove any such thing. Indeed that kingdom that was organized 1800 years ago was organized altogether too soon to accomplish the prophecies that are here given. The two legs of iron, and the feet and toes were not yet formed, and remember that the stone is not cut out of the mountain without hands, until this great image is complete, not only the head, breast, arms and the legs, but the feet and the toes also; they all become complete before the kingdom called the 'stone' is made manifest. Now the feet did not exist, and did not begin to exist until many centuries after the days of Christ. What did that kingdom do that was built up by our Savior and his Apostles? Did it break in pieces any part of that great image? No. What did that image do to that kingdom? It accomplished the prophecies of Daniel—made war with the Saints and overcame them. Very different from the latter-day kingdom! The powers of this world, under the name of the great image, made war with Jesus, with the Apostles, with the former-day Saints, with the kingdom that was then established and overcame them, not only in fulfillment of what is declared by the Prophet Daniel, but also what is declared by John the Revelator; and those powers obtained dominion over all people, nations and tongues, and made them drink of the wine of the wrath of the fornication of Great Babylon, and they became drunken with her abominations. Instead of the kingdom of God then being built up in fulfillment of the prophecy of Daniel 1800 years ago, the nations of the earth overcame it and rooted it out of the earth. But mark the words of the text: 'And in the days of these kings shall the God of heaven set up a kingdom that shall never be destroyed.' Very different from the former-day kingdom; 'and the kingdom shall not be left to other people.' All these human governments have been changing hands, and have been left to some other people. The Babylonish kingdom was left to the Medes and Persians, the Medo-Persian kingdom to the Macedonian, the Macedonian to the Roman; but the latter-day kingdom shall not be left to another people, but it shall break in pieces and consume all these kingdoms, and it shall stand forever. 'Forasmuch as thou sawest that the stone was cut out of the mountains without hands, and that it brake in pieces the iron, the brass, the clay the silver and the gold; and the great God hath made known unto thee what shall come to pass hereafter, and the dream is certain and the interpretation thereof sure.'

Having learned, then, that the kingdom built up by our Savior and his Apostles did not fulfil this prophecy; that that kingdom itself was rooted out of the earth, and every vestige of its authority destroyed, and that nothing in the shape or appearance of the kingdom of God has existed for some sixteen or seventeen centuries past, inasmuch as this is the case and all nations without any such Church, without any such kingdom without any authority to baptize or lay on hands for the gift of the Holy Ghost; without authority to administer the Lord's supper; without the authority to build up the kingdom of God; without Prophets, without Revelators, without inspired Apostles, without angels, without visions, without the revelations and prophecies of heaven, which always characterize the kingdom of God; I say inasmuch as this is the case, and darkness has covered the earth and gross darkness the people for so many generations, no wonder that, in the wisdom of God, the time should at length arrive to send another messenger from heaven. No wonder that an angel should be commissioned from the eternal heavens from the throne of the Almighty with another message to the inhabitants of our globe! For do you suppose that this latter-day kingdom that is to be set up without hands will be set up without any communication from heaven, without any new revelation, without any Prophets, without any Apostles, or inspired men? Do you suppose that God will accomplish a work of this nature and yet the heavens be veiled over our heads like brass? Oh no. When the glad time shall come for God Almighty to organize and set up the latter-day kingdom on the earth, he will make it known by sending an angel—and in no other way, for that is the way pointed out in prophecy."

Orson Pratt, Journal of Discourses, Vol. 18, p. 180-181, March 26, 1876.
        "Come further still, into Europe and you find the feet and toes of the image in the latter-day kingdoms of the earth, which have branched across the great deep and have planted themselves in America. Are they partly strong and partly broken? Yes. Some of them have some strength apparently, and they have among themselves all the characteristics of miry clay with the iron, for they are divided one against another, and they have to keep up their standing armies because they are afraid of one another. But where is the stone from the mountains? Where is that kingdom that is called the stone? In the interpretation the Prophet says—'Thou sawest until the kingdom of God was set up, and it smote the image upon the feet,' and so on. It does not commence its attack away in Asia, where the head of gold or its descendants live, neither in any intermediate part, but it commences at the very extremity of this great image, as it spreads out to the west, and commences upon the feet and the toes; it is there where the stone is cut out of the mountain without hands it is there where the God of heaven should set up a kingdom, as Daniel says, that should never be

destroyed, neither shall it be given into the hands of another people, but it shall stand for ever. Not like the former-day kingdom that was set up, before the Roman empire had attained to its zenith of power. The former-day kingdom of Christ, was set up in the days of the Apostles; that was overcome and destroyed out of the earth. The beasts made war upon them and prevailed against them, and they were banished from the earth, and the woman upon the scarlet-colored beast seems to have had dominion among all the nations, kindred, tongues and people, more or less. But in the latter-days the kingdom of God was to be built up on the earth that should never be destroyed; it was not to be like the former-day one, but it should stand for ever, while all these other kingdoms should not only be destroyed, but, like the chaff of the summer threshing floor, should be carried completely away, and no place should be found for them."

Orson Pratt, Journal of Discourses, Vol. 18, p. 339-340, February 25, 1877.

"Why will this vast assemblage of people stand there? What will be the object of the Ancient of Days, in coming with this vast multitude, and what is to be accomplished? We read that the four beasts, representing the powers of the earth, will exist at the time of the coming of the Ancient of Days. And that the fourth beast, represented by the Roman Empire and the kingdoms that have grown out of it, will be 'slain and his body destroyed and given to the burning flame.' Here then we can read the destiny of that portion of the inhabitants of the earth constituting the fourth beast: or, in other words, the destiny of the kingdoms of Europe, who were to arise and grow out of that fourth power. We can read the final destiny of the kingdoms of Europe, namely, Germany, France, Italy, Spain, Portugal, Scandinavia, and the great northern power, Russia, Austria and Prussia, and all those various nations, that more particularly pertain to this great iron power that once so cruelly oppressed the people; its 'body shall be destroyed and given to the burning flame,' which signifies the nature of the judgment that will befall them. According to other prophecies, contained in Daniel, a succession of judgments, great and terrible in their nature, will overtake them, before the ire spoken of comes. Nation will rise against nation in war, kingdom against kingdom: or in the language of Isaiah, 'Behold, the Lord will come with fire, and with his chariots like a whirlwind, to render his anger with fury, and with his chariots like a whirlwind, to render his anger with fury, and his rebuke with flames of fire. For by fire and by his sword will the Lord plead with all flesh; and the slain of the Lord shall be many.'

It seems then that the body of the fourth power is to be given to the burning flame, that signifies the utter extinction of that power from the face of the earth. The heathen nations representing the other three beasts, will not then be destroyed: but their lives are to be prolonged, and their dominion is to be taken away. Though their lives will be prolonged, yet they will not have power to rule and govern, only as they are permitted. If you will read from the beginning of the 36th to the end of the 39th chapters of Ezekiel, you find much said, in regard to the heathen nations. 'And the heathen shall know that I am the Lord,' etc. But the fourth power represents the nations of modern Christendom. They have not the privilege of the heathen, in having their lives prolonged. Why? Does the speaker mean to say that modern Christendom is more wicked than the heathen? Yes; the people of Christendom possess more light and knowledge than the heathen, and therefore, they are under the greater condemnation; for according to the light and knowledge they severally have, will they be judged. The more enlightened nations, so called, are rejecting the Gospel message which is being sent to them by divine authority; and for that reason their utter destruction is inevitable, and, as had been decreed, they must pass away. Their lives will not be prolonged. Not only the kingdoms and governments of Europe, and the western portion of Asia are to be thus visited, but also those who have grown out of these kingdoms, and that have emigrated to this western hemisphere and elsewhere. For instance, this great republic must pass away in the manner indicated unless the people repent."

Orson Pratt, Journal of Discourses, Vol. 21, p. 279-280, June 20, 1880.

"This same great gathering is characterized also by Daniel, as a stone cut out of the mountain without hands. This stone is represented as a kingdom, and its location is represented as a mountain, showing that there is to be a kingdom of God set up in the last days by the gathering together of his people in an elevated region of country, called a mountain. By and by that stone will roll forth, until the kingdoms of this world are broken in pieces, and as the Prophet Daniel said, the kingdom shall not be left to other people, but shall stand forever; all those other earthly kingdoms, that Nebuchadnezzar saw in his dream, will vanish away, like a night vision, or, in other words, become 'like the chaff of the summer threshing floors; and the wind carried them away, and no place was found for them.' There are many politicians that are trying to foretell the future. They speak of what this government, and that government, and the other government will be, several hundred years hence, or perhaps in ages hence, as though they could see and understand, naturally, the condition of the various governments and kingdoms of the earth, for a long time to come; but Daniel, who was filled with the Spirit of the living God, saw that all these earthly governments—with the setting up of which God had nothing to do particularly, that is, their founders were neither prophets nor revelators so as to found them upon the principles of the everlasting Gospel—were to vanish away, like the chaff of the summer threshing floor. And you know how that vanishes, especially when the wind blows strongly. So shall it be with all the governments, kingdoms, powers, republics, and empires upon the face of this globe, except one government, namely, that government which the God of heaven shall establish in the latter-days upon the mountains. This is the work of God. It is God that causes these kingdoms to vanish away. It is our God that will cleanse the earth from wickedness. 'A fire shall devour before him, and it shall be very tempestuous round about him.' He it is that will speak and the wicked shall melt away. He it is that will cause violent whirlwinds to go forth and destroy this, that, or the other city, according to his own will. He it is that will send forth pestilence and plague, and will perform all that has been spoken by the mouth of his prophets, concerning the destruction that is to take place in the latter days."

John Taylor, The Government of God, Chapter 11.

"It may not be improper here to notice an opinion that has very generally prevailed throughout the christian world, that Christ's kingdom was a spiritual kingdom; that it was set up at the time our Saviour was upon the earth; and that Christianity as it now exists, is that kingdom. After what I have already written on the subject of a literal reign and kingdom, this would seem superfluous; but as this opinion is almost universal in the Christian world, my readers must excuse me, if, in this instance, I digress a little. Several writers in the Catholic church, as well as the Rev. David Simpson, M.A., Bishop Burnett, the Rev. John Wesley, and may others among the Protestants, have advocated the above opinion. The substance of their ideas is as follows: that Daniel, by the figure of an image of gold, silver, brass, iron, clay, in chapter 2—and by the figures of the four beasts, in chapter 7, represented a spiritual kingdom; that this kingdom was set up in the days of the Saviour, and his disciples; that Christianity, as it now exists, is that kingdom, and that it will become universal over all the earth. They state that the four great empires, the Babylonian, Persian, Grecian, and Roman, are represented by the head, breast, belly, and legs of the Image, and by the four Beasts, in chapter 7; and that the kingdom of God was to be set up under the dominion of the fourth, which, as they correctly state, was the Roman. They state, moreover, that the declaration and prophecy of the Angel to Mary, above quoted, were also fulfilled in the first coming of the Messiah; in his preaching, in his Gospel, and in the organizing of the church, etc. Many other passages are made to bear the same signification, which it would be foreign from my present purpose to notice. I have referred to the above, as some of the most prominent. Now, with all deference to the gentlemen who have written on this subject (and education, respectability, and talent, entitle their opinions to some respect) I must beg to leave to differ from them, and consider, that in trying to support a favorite dogma, they have been led into error; for it seems to me that nothing can be more foreign to the meaning of these scriptures than the above interpretation. Now concerning the four great monarchies being represented as above, I consider it is perfectly correct; but to state that the kingdom was to be set up under the fourth monarchy, or under the dominion of the fourth beast, is stretching the thing too far; and putting a construction upon it which it evidently will not bear. The text reads, 'in the days of those kings shall the God of Heaven set up a kingdom.' The question is, What kings? I am answered, during the reign of one of the four; and that as Christ came during the reign and dominion of the Roman empire, it evidently refers to that. But let me again ask a question, Under the reign of what kings was this kingdom to be set up? Under the reign of the fourth? Verily, No. Let Daniel speak for himself. After describing the fourth kingdom, which was the Roman, which is compared to iron, and which in the Image was represented by the legs, he then refers to other kingdoms and powers, as being compared to iron and clay. There were also feet and toes, as well as a body, which were compared to powers or kings. This is clearly exemplified in the seventh chapter of Daniel, for after speaking of the four kings, he describes ten horns, of which the ten toes in the Image above referred to, are typical. Those ten horns, he says, are ten kings. It was, then, in the days of those kings, or while those kingdoms should be in existence, that the God of Heaven should set up a kingdom; and not during the power of the fourth kingdom; to which, with any degree of truthfulness, the figure could not apply in either case. But again, it could not apply to the first coming of our Saviour for the following reasons:

First.—The stone hewn out of the mountain without hands was to smite the Image on the toes; whereas, according to the interpretation of the divines before referred to, the toes were not yet in existence, for they state that this kingdom was set up during the fourth monarchy, which was the Roman, and which is represented in the legs of the Image. Now, as the powers composing the feet and toes were not yet formed, how could the little stone smite that which was not in existence? For it will be observed that after the whole Image was made, the stone was hewn out of the mountains without hands which smote it.

Secondly.—When the kingdom is set up, it is stated 'it shall not be left to other people;' but we are told in Dan. 7, that after the fourth monarchy which was the time, according to the aforesaid interpretation, for the setting up of the kingdom of God, a certain 'horn,' or king, should make war with the Saints, and prevail against them;' and that 'he should think to change times and laws—and that they should be given into his hand.' Nothing can be more obvious than this; for this power, after the first coming of the Messiah, not only thinks to change times and laws, but 'they' are actually 'given into his hand,' which will not be the case, when the kingdom above referred to is set up.

Thirdly.—When the kingdom of God was to be set up, it was to be 'given to the Saints of the Most High;' and all nations, kindreds, people, and tongues, were to obey the Lord, which has not taken place, and never can under the present state of things.

Fourthly.—There is no more similarity between Christianity, as it now exists, with all its superstitions, corruptions, jargons, contentions, divisions, weakness, and imbecility, and this KINGDOM OF GOD, as spoken of in the Scriptures, than there is between light and darkness; and it would compare with the earth, or a pater with the glorious luminary of day.

Fifthly.—The kingdom of God, as spoken of by Daniel, was to become universal, which Christianity has not, and cannot, as it now exists.

Sixthly.—The Angel's testimony to Mary has not yet been fulfilled. It is stated, that 'The Lord shall give unto him the throne of his father David, and he shall reign over the House of Jacob for ever, and of his kingdom there shall be no end;' whereas he did not sit upon David's throne, nor does he now; he did not reign over the house of Jacob, nor does he now, for the ten tribes are yet outcasts; 'the house of Judah is scattered, and without a king,' and Jesus himself, when asked to divide an inheritance, demanded, 'Who made me a ruler or king.' He, indeed was a king; 'but in his humiliation his judgment was taken away.'

From the whole of the above it is very evident that the kingdom, of which these divines speak, was not, and could not be the one referred to by Daniel, or by the angel to Mary; as we have before stated, it was a literal kingdom, and not a spiritual one only. I would further remark here, that a certain power was to 'make war with the Saints, and to prevail against them until the Ancient of Days came; and then, and not till then, was 'judgment given to the Saints of the Most High.'"

John A. Widtsoe, Evidences and Reconciliations, p. 94-95.

"The futility of reducing general prophecy to exact times or places is well illustrated by the famous visions of Daniel. It is conceded that the stone that broke the image to pieces is the Kingdom of God; but there has been and is interminable debate as to the historical kingdoms and meaning represented by the gold, silver, iron, and clay portions of the image; the horns of the beasts; the thousand, three hundred and five and thirty days; and the several other statements of Daniel. (See the Book of Daniel). Hundreds, perhaps thousands, of books have been published and tens of thousands of sermons have been preached in the attempt to interpret Daniel's prophecies. It has been a fruitless effort, at best a doubtful conjecture. There remains only the general meaning of these glorious visions: that righteousness will triumph in its battle with evil."

Teachings of Ezra Taft Benson, p. 168.

"Today The Church of Jesus Christ of Latter-day Saints is extending the heralded message of the restoration of the gospel to every nation which permits us entrance through its borders. This is a fulfillment of the vision and revelation received by Daniel, the prophet (see Daniel 2:34-35, 44). (CR April 1978, Ensign 8 [May 1978]: 32.)"

274

Bruce R. McConkie, The Mortal Messiah, Vol. 2, p. 278.

"Also, the sea—a raging, restless sea—is a symbol of a sinful and wicked world. The beasts seen by Daniel in vision and used as types of worldly kingdoms came up out of the sea, a sea upon which the four winds of heaven strove. (Dan. 7.) And the Lord said to Isaiah: 'The wicked are like the troubled sea, when it cannot rest, whose waters cast up mire and dirt. There is no peace, saith my God, to the wicked' (Isa. 57:20-21)—leaving us to conclude that when Christ calms the seas of life, peace enters the hearts of men."

SCRIPTURAL REFERENCES

Daniel 2:31-45

31 Thou, O king, sawest, and behold a great image. This great image, whose brightness [was] excellent, stood before thee; and the form thereof [was] terrible.

32 This image's head [was] of fine gold, his breast and his arms of silver, his belly and his thighs of brass,

33 His legs of iron, his feet part of iron and part of clay.

34 Thou sawest till that a stone was cut out without hands, which smote the image upon his feet [that were] of iron and clay, and brake them to pieces.

35 Then was the iron, the clay, the brass, the silver, and the gold, broken to pieces together, and became like the chaff of the summer threshingfloors; and the wind carried them away, that no place was found for them: and the stone that smote the image became a great mountain, and filled the whole earth.

36 This [is] the dream; and we will tell the interpretation thereof before the king.

37 Thou, O king, [art] a king of kings: for the God of heaven hath given thee a kingdom, power, and strength, and glory.

38 And wheresoever the children of men dwell, the beasts of the field and the fowls of the heaven hath he given into thine hand, and hath made thee ruler over them all. Thou [art] this head of gold.

39 And after thee shall arise another kingdom inferior to thee, and another third kingdom of brass, which shall bear rule over all the earth.

40 And the fourth kingdom shall be strong as iron: forasmuch as iron breaketh in pieces and subdueth all [things]: and as iron that breaketh all these, shall it break in pieces and bruise.

41 And whereas thou sawest the feet and toes, part of potters' clay, and part of iron, the kingdom shall be divided; but there shall be in it of the strength of the iron, forasmuch as thou sawest the iron mixed with miry clay.

42 And [as] the toes of the feet [were] part of iron, and part of clay, [so] the kingdom shall be partly strong, and partly broken.

43 And whereas thou sawest iron mixed with miry clay, they shall mingle themselves with the seed of men: but they shall not cleave one to another, even as iron is not mixed with clay.

44 And in the days of these kings shall the God of heaven set up a kingdom, which shall never be destroyed: and the kingdom shall not be left to other people, [but] it shall break in pieces and consume all these kingdoms, and it shall stand for ever.

45 Forasmuch as thou sawest that the stone was cut out of the mountain without hands, and that it brake in pieces the iron, the brass, the clay, the silver, and the gold; the great God hath made known to the king what shall come to pass hereafter: and the dream [is] certain, and the interpretation thereof sure.

Daniel 7:7-27

7 After this I saw in the night visions, and behold a fourth beast, dreadful and terrible, and strong exceedingly; and it had great iron teeth: it devoured and brake in pieces, and stamped the residue with the feet of it: and it was diverse from all the beasts that were before it; and it had ten horns.

8 I considered the horns, and, behold, there came up among them another little horn, before whom there were three of the first horns plucked up by the roots: and, behold, in this horn were eyes like the eyes of man, and a mouth speaking great things.

9 I beheld till the thrones were cast down, and the Ancient of days did sit, whose garment was white as snow, and the hair of his head like the pure wool: his throne was like the fiery flame, and his wheels as burning fire.

10 A fiery stream issued and came forth from before him: thousand thousands ministered unto him, and ten thousand times ten thousand stood before him: the judgment was set, and the books were opened.

11 I beheld then because of the voice of the great words which the horn spake: I beheld even till the beast was slain, and his body destroyed, and given to the burning flame.

12 As concerning the rest of the beasts, they had their dominion taken away: yet their lives were prolonged for a season and time.

13 I saw in the night visions, and, behold, [one] like the Son of man came with the clouds of heaven, and came to the Ancient of days, and they brought him near before him.

14 And there was given him dominion, and glory, and a kingdom, that all people, nations, and languages, should serve him: his dominion [is] an everlasting dominion, which shall not pass away, and his kingdom [that] which shall not be destroyed.

15 I Daniel was grieved in my spirit in the midst of [my] body, and the visions of my head troubled me.

16 I came near unto one of them that stood by, and asked him the truth of all this. So he told me, and made me know the interpretation of the things.

17 These great beasts, which are four, [are] four kings, [which] shall arise out of the earth.

18 But the saints of the most High shall take the kingdom, and possess the kingdom for ever, even for ever and ever.

19 Then I would know the truth of the fourth beast, which was diverse from all the others, exceeding dreadful, whose teeth [were of] iron, and his nails [of] brass; [which] devoured, brake in pieces, and stamped the residue with his feet;

20 And of the ten horns that [were] in his head, and [of] the other which came up, and before whom three fell; even [of] that horn that had eyes, and a mouth that spake very great things, whose look [was] more stout than his fellows.

21 I beheld, and the same horn made war with the saints, and prevailed against them;

22 Until the Ancient of days came, and judgment was given to the saints of the most High; and the time came that the saints possessed the kingdom.

23 Thus he said, The fourth beast shall be the fourth kingdom upon earth, which shall be diverse from all kingdoms, and shall devour the whole earth, and shall tread it down, and break it in pieces.

24 And the ten horns out of this kingdom are ten kings that shall arise: and another shall rise after them; and he shall be diverse from the first, and he shall subdue three kings.

25 And he shall speak great words against the most High, and shall wear out the saints of the most High, and think to change times and laws: and they shall be given into his hand until a time and times and the dividing of time.

26 But the judgment shall sit, and they shall take away his dominion, to consume and to destroy it

unto the end.

27 And the kingdom and dominion, and the greatness of the kingdom under the whole heaven, shall be given to the people of the saints of the most High, whose kingdom is an everlasting kingdom, and all dominions shall serve and obey him.

Revelation 4:6-9

6 And before the throne there was a sea of glass like unto crystal: and in the midst of the throne, and round about the throne, were four beasts full of eyes before and behind.

7 And the first beast was like a lion, and the second beast like a calf, and the third beast had a face as a man, and the fourth beast was like a flying eagle.

8 And the four beasts had each of them six wings about him; and they were full of eyes within: and they rest not day and night, saying, Holy, holy, holy, Lord God Almighty, which was, and is, and is to come.

9 And when those beasts give glory and honour and thanks to him that sat on the throne, who liveth for ever and ever,

Revelation 5:6

6 And I beheld, and, lo, in the midst of the throne and of the four beasts, and in the midst of the elders, stood a Lamb as it had been slain, having seven horns and seven eyes, which are the seven Spirits of God sent forth into all the earth.

Revelation 6:12-17

12 And I beheld when he had opened the sixth seal, and, lo, there was a great earthquake; and the sun became black as sackcloth of hair, and the moon became as blood;

13 And the stars of heaven fell unto the earth, even as a fig tree casteth her untimely figs, when she is shaken of a mighty wind.

14 And the heaven departed as a scroll when it is rolled together; and every mountain and island were moved out of their places.

15 And the kings of the earth, and the great men, and the rich men, and the chief captains, and the mighty men, and every bondman, and every free man, hid themselves in the dens and in the rocks of the mountains;

16 And said to the mountains and rocks, Fall on us, and hide us from the face of him that sitteth on the throne, and from the wrath of the Lamb:

17 For the great day of his wrath is come; and who shall be able to stand?

Revelation 7:1-4

1 AND after these things I saw four angels standing on the four corners of the earth, holding the four winds of the earth, that the wind should not blow on the earth, nor on the sea, nor on any tree.

2 And I saw another angel ascending from the east, having the seal of the living God: and he cried with a loud voice to the four angels, to whom it was given to hurt the earth and the sea,

3 Saying, Hurt not the earth, neither the sea, nor the trees, till we have sealed the servants of our God in their foreheads.

4 And I heard the number of them which were sealed: [and there were] sealed an hundred [and] forty [and] four thousand of all the tribes of the children of Israel.

Revelation 7:11

11 And all the angels stood round about the throne, and about the elders and the four beasts, and fell before the throne on their faces, and worshipped God,

Revelation 8:1-2

1 AND when he had opened the seventh seal, there was silence in heaven about the space of half an hour.

2 And I saw the seven angels which stood before God; and to them were given seven trumpets.

Revelation 8:6-13

6 And the seven angels which had the seven trumpets prepared themselves to sound.

7 The first angel sounded, and there followed hail and fire mingled with blood, and they were cast upon the earth: and the third part of trees was burnt up, and all green grass was burnt up.

8 And the second angel sounded, and as it were a great mountain burning with fire was cast into the sea: and the third part of the sea became blood;

9 And the third part of the creatures which were in the sea, and had life, died; and the third part of the ships were destroyed.

10 And the third angel sounded, and there fell a great star from heaven, burning as it were a lamp, and it fell upon the third part of the rivers, and upon the fountains of waters;

11 And the name of the star is called Wormwood: and the third part of the waters became wormwood; and many men died of the waters, because they were made bitter.

12 And the fourth angel sounded, and the third part of the sun was smitten, and the third part of the moon, and the third part of the stars; so as the third part of them was darkened, and the day shone not for a third part of it, and the night likewise.

13 And I beheld, and heard an angel flying through the midst of heaven, saying with a loud voice, Woe, woe, woe, to the inhabiters of the earth by reason of the other voices of the trumpet of the three angels, which are yet to sound!

Revelation 9:1-21

1 AND the fifth angel sounded, and I saw a star fall from heaven unto the earth: and to him was given the key of the bottomless pit.

2 And he opened the bottomless pit; and there arose a smoke out of the pit, as the smoke of a great furnace; and the sun and the air were darkened by reason of the smoke of the pit.

3 And there came out of the smoke locusts upon the earth: and unto them was given power, as the scorpions of the earth have power.

4 And it was commanded them that they should not hurt the grass of the earth, neither any green thing, neither any tree; but only those men which have not the seal of God in their foreheads.

5 And to them it was given that they should not kill them, but that they should be tormented five months: and their torment [was] as the torment of a scorpion, when he striketh a man.

6 And in those days shall men seek death, and shall not find it; and shall desire to die, and death shall flee from them.

7 And the shapes of the locusts [were] like unto horses prepared unto battle; and on their heads [were] as it were crowns like gold, and their faces [were] as the faces of men.

8 And they had hair as the hair of women, and their teeth were as [the teeth] of lions.

9 And they had breastplates, as it were breastplates of iron; and the sound of their wings [was] as the sound of chariots of many horses running to battle.

10 And they had tails like unto scorpions, and there were stings in their tails: and their power [was] to hurt men five months.

11 And they had a king over them, [which is] the angel of the bottomless pit, whose name in the Hebrew tongue [is] Abaddon, but in the Greek tongue hath [his] name Apollyon.

12 One woe is past; [and], behold, there come two woes more hereafter.

13 And the sixth angel sounded, and I heard a voice from the four horns of the golden altar which is before God,

14 Saying to the sixth angel which had the trumpet, Loose the four angels which are bound in the great river Euphrates.

15 And the four angels were loosed, which were prepared for an hour, and a day, and a month, and a year, for to slay the third part of men.

16 And the number of the army of the horsemen [were] two hundred thousand thousand: and I heard the number of them.

17 And thus I saw the horses in the vision, and them that sat on them, having breastplates of fire, and of jacinth, and brimstone: and the heads of the horses [were] as the heads of lions; and out of their mouths issued fire and smoke and brimstone.

18 By these three was the third part of men killed, by the fire, and by the smoke, and by the brimstone, which issued out of their mouths.

19 For their power is in their mouth, and in their tails: for their tails [were] like unto serpents, and had heads, and with them they do hurt.

20 And the rest of the men which were not killed by these plagues yet repented not of the works of their hands, that they should not worship devils, and idols of gold, and silver, and brass, and stone, and of wood: which neither can see, nor hear, nor walk:

21 Neither repented they of their murders, nor of their sorceries, nor of their fornication, nor of their thefts.

Revelation 12:3

3 And there appeared another wonder in heaven; and behold a great red dragon, having seven heads and ten horns, and seven crowns upon his heads.

Revelation 12:7-9

7 And there was war in heaven: Michael and his angels fought against the dragon; and the dragon fought and his angels,

8 And prevailed not; neither was their place found any more in heaven.

9 And the great dragon was cast out, that old serpent, called the Devil, and Satan, which deceiveth

the whole world: he was cast out into the earth, and his angels were cast out with him.

JST Revelation 12:13-17

13 For when the dragon saw that he was cast unto the earth, he persecuted the woman which brought forth the man child.

14 Therefore, to the woman were given two wings of a great eagle, that she might flee into the wilderness, into her place, where she is nourished for a time, and times, and half a time, from the face of the serpent.

15 and the serpent casteth out of his mouth water as a flood after the woman, that he might cause her to be carried away of the flood.

16 And the earth helpeth the woman, and the earth openeth her mouth, and swalloweth up the flood which the dragon casteth out of his mouth.

17 Therefore, the dragon was wroth with the woman, and went to make war with the remnant of her seed, which keep the commandments of God, and have the testimony of Jesus Christ.

JST Revelation 13:1

1 And I saw another sign, in the likeness of the kingdoms of the earth; a beast rise up out of the sea, and he stood upon the sand of the sea, having seven heads and ten horns; and upon his horns ten crowns; and upon his heads the name of blasphemy.

Revelation 13:1-18

1 And I stood upon the sand of the sea, and saw a beast rise up out of the sea, having seven heads and ten horns, and upon his horns ten crowns, and upon his heads the name of blasphemy.

2 And the beast which I saw was like unto a leopard, and his feet were as the feet of a bear, and his mouth as the mouth of a lion: and the dragon gave him his power, and his seat, and great authority.

3 And I saw one of his heads as it were wounded to death; and his deadly wound was healed: and all the world wondered after the beast.

4 And they worshipped the dragon which gave power unto the beast: and they worshipped the beast, saying, Who is like unto the beast? who is able to make war with him?

5 And there was given unto him a mouth speaking great things and blasphemies; and power was given unto him to continue forty and two months.

6 And he opened his mouth in blasphemy against God, to blaspheme his name, and his tabernacle, and them that dwell in heaven.

7 And it was given unto him to make war with the saints, and to overcome them: and power was given him over all kindreds, and tongues, and nations.

8 And all that dwell upon the earth shall worship him, whose names are not written in the book of life of the Lamb slain from the foundation of the world.

9 If any man have an ear, let him hear.

10 He that leadeth into captivity shall go into captivity: he that killeth with the sword must be killed with the sword. Here is the patience and the faith of the saints.

11 And I beheld another beast coming up out of the earth; and he had two horns like a lamb, and he spake as a dragon.

12 And he exerciseth all the power of the first beast before him, and causeth the earth and them which dwell therein to worship the first beast, whose deadly wound was healed.

13 And he doeth great wonders, so that he maketh fire come down from heaven on the earth in the sight of men,

14 And deceiveth them that dwell on the earth by the means of those miracles which he had power to do in the sight of the beast; saying to them that dwell on the earth, that they should make an image to the beast, which had the wound by a sword, and did live.

15 And he had power to give life unto the image of the beast, that the image of the beast should both speak, and cause that as many as would not worship the image of the beast should be killed.

16 And he causeth all, both small and great, rich and poor, free and bond, to receive a mark in their right hand, or in their foreheads:

17 And that no man might buy or sell, save he that had the mark, or the name of the beast, or the number of his name.

18 Here is wisdom. Let him that hath understanding count the number of the beast: for it is the number of a man; and his number is Six hundred threescore and six.

Revelation 14:9-12

9 And the third angel followed them, saying with a loud voice, If any man worship the beast and his image, and receive his mark in his forehead, or in his hand,

10 The same shall drink of the wine of the wrath of God, which is poured out without mixture into the cup of his indignation; and he shall be tormented with fire and brimstone in the presence of the holy angels, and in the presence of the Lamb:

11 And the smoke of their torment ascendeth up for ever and ever: and they have no rest day nor night, who worship the beast and his image, and whosoever receiveth the mark of his name.

12 Here is the patience of the saints: here are they that keep the commandments of God, and the faith of Jesus.

Revelation 15:5-8

5 And after that I looked, and, behold, the temple of the tabernacle of the testimony in heaven was opened:

6 And the seven angels came out of the temple, having the seven plagues, clothed in pure and white linen, and having their breasts girded with golden girdles.

7 And one of the four beasts gave unto the seven angels seven golden vials full of the wrath of God, who liveth for ever and ever.

8 And the temple was filled with smoke from the glory of God, and from his power; and no man was able to enter into the temple, till the seven plagues of the seven angels were fulfilled.

Revelation 16:1-21

1 And I heard a great voice out of the temple saying to the seven angels, Go your ways, and pour out the vials of the wrath of God upon the earth.

2 And the first went, and poured out his vial upon the earth; and there fell a noisome and grievous sore upon the men which had the mark of the beast, and upon them which worshipped his image.

3 And the second angel poured out his vial upon the sea; and it became as the blood of a dead [man]: and every living soul died in the sea.

4 And the third angel poured out his vial upon the rivers and fountains of waters; and they became blood.

5 And I heard the angel of the waters say, Thou art righteous, O Lord, which art, and wast, and shalt be, because thou hast judged thus.

6 For they have shed the blood of saints and prophets, and thou hast given them blood to drink; for they are worthy.

7 And I heard another out of the altar say, Even so, Lord God Almighty, true and righteous [are] thy judgments.

8 And the fourth angel poured out his vial upon the sun; and power was given unto him to scorch men with fire.

9 And men were scorched with great heat, and blasphemed the name of God, which hath power over these plagues: and they repented not to give him glory.

10 And the fifth angel poured out his vial upon the seat of the beast; and his kingdom was full of darkness; and they gnawed their tongues for pain,

11 And blasphemed the God of heaven because of their pains and their sores, and repented not of their deeds.

12 And the sixth angel poured out his vial upon the great river Euphrates; and the water thereof was dried up, that the way of the kings of the east might be prepared.

13 And I saw three unclean spirits like frogs come out of the mouth of the dragon, and out of the mouth of the beast, and out of the mouth of the false prophet.

14 For they are the spirits of devils, working miracles, which go forth unto the kings of the earth and of the whole world, to gather them to the battle of that great day of God Almighty.

15 Behold, I come as a thief. Blessed is he that watcheth, and keepeth his garments, lest he walk naked, and they see his shame.

16 And he gathered them together into a place called in the Hebrew tongue Armageddon.

17 And the seventh angel poured out his vial into the air; and there came a great voice out of the temple of heaven, from the throne, saying, It is done.

18 And there were voices, and thunders, and lightnings; and there was a great earthquake, such as was not since men were upon the earth, so mighty an earthquake, [and] so great.

19 And the great city was divided into three parts, and the cities of the nations fell: and great Babylon came in remembrance before God, to give unto her the cup of the wine of the fierceness of his wrath.

20 And every island fled away, and the mountains were not found.

21 And there fell upon men a great hail out of heaven, [every stone] about the weight of a talent: and men blasphemed God because of the plague of the hail; for the plague thereof was exceeding great.

Revelation 17:1-18

1 And there came one of the seven angels which had the seven vials, and talked with me, saying unto me, Come hither; I will shew unto thee the judgment of the great whore that sitteth upon many waters:

2 With whom the kings of the earth have committed fornication, and the inhabitants of the earth have

been made drunk with the wine of her fornication.

3 So he carried me away in the spirit into the wilderness: and I saw a woman sit upon a scarlet coloured beast, full of names of blasphemy, having seven heads and ten horns.

4 And the woman was arrayed in purple and scarlet colour, and decked with gold and precious stones and pearls, having a golden cup in her hand full of abominations and filthiness of her fornication:

5 And upon her forehead was a name written, MYSTERY, BABYLON THE GREAT, THE MOTHER OF HARLOTS AND ABOMINATIONS OF THE EARTH.

6 And I saw the woman drunken with the blood of the saints, and with the blood of the martyrs of Jesus: and when I saw her, I wondered with great admiration.

7 And the angel said unto me, Wherefore didst thou marvel? I will tell thee the mystery of the woman, and of the beast that carrieth her, which hath the seven heads and ten horns.

8 The beast that thou sawest was, and is not; and shall ascend out of the bottomless pit, and go into perdition: and they that dwell on the earth shall wonder, whose names were not written in the book of life from the foundation of the world, when they behold the beast that was, and is not, and yet is.

9 And here is the mind which hath wisdom. The seven heads are seven mountains, on which the woman sitteth.

10 And there are seven kings: five are fallen, and one is, and the other is not yet come; and when he cometh, he must continue a short space.

11 And the beast that was, and is not, even he is the eighth, and is of the seven, and goeth into perdition.

12 And the ten horns which thou sawest are ten kings, which have received no kingdom as yet; but receive power as kings one hour with the beast.

13 These have one mind, and shall give their power and strength unto the beast.

14 These shall make war with the Lamb, and the Lamb shall overcome them: for he is Lord of lords, and King of kings: and they that are with him are called, and chosen, and faithful.

15 And he saith unto me, The waters which thou sawest, where the whore sitteth, are peoples, and multitudes, and nations, and tongues.

16 And the ten horns which thou sawest upon the beast, these shall hate the whore, and shall make her desolate and naked, and shall eat her flesh, and burn her with fire.

17 For God hath put in their hearts to fulfil his will, and to agree, and give their kingdom unto the beast, until the words of God shall be fulfilled.

18 And the woman which thou sawest is that great city, which reigneth over the kings of the earth.

Revelation 19:19-20

19 And I saw the beast, and the kings of the earth, and their armies, gathered together to make war against him that sat on the horse, and against his army.

20 And the beast was taken, and with him the false prophet that wrought miracles before him, with which he deceived them that had received the mark of the beast, and them that worshipped his image. These both were cast alive into a lake of fire burning with brimstone.

Revelation 20:1-4

1 And I saw an angel come down from heaven, having the key of the bottomless pit and a great chain

in his hand.

2 And he laid hold on the dragon, that old serpent, which is the Devil, and Satan, and bound him a thousand years,

3 And cast him into the bottomless pit, and shut him up, and set a seal upon him, that he should deceive the nations no more, till the thousand years should be fulfilled: and after that he must be loosed a little season.

4 And I saw thrones, and they sat upon them, and judgment was given unto them: and I saw the souls of them that were beheaded for the witness of Jesus, and for the word of God, and which had not worshipped the beast, neither his image, neither had received his mark upon their foreheads, or in their hands; and they lived and reigned with Christ a thousand years.

D&C 77:2-4

2 Q. What are we to understand by the four beasts, spoken of in the same verse?

A. They are figurative expressions, used by the Revelator, John, in describing heaven, the paradise of God, the happiness of man, and of beasts, and of creeping things, and of the fowls of the air; that which is spiritual being in the likeness of that which is temporal; and that which is temporal in the likeness of that which is spiritual; the spirit of man in the likeness of his person, as also the spirit of the beast, and every other creature which God has created.

3 Q. Are the four beasts limited to individual beasts, or do they represent classes or orders?

A. They are limited to four individual beasts, which were shown to John, to represent the glory of the classes of beings in their destined order or sphere of creation, in the enjoyment of their eternal felicity.

4 Q. What are we to understand by the eyes and wings, which the beasts had?

A. Their eyes are a representation of light and knowledge, that is, they are full of knowledge; and their wings are a representation of power, to move, to act, etc.

INDEX

Aaron, 1:226, 1:228, 2:230, 3:90, 3:142

Aaronic Priesthood, 1:6, 1:17, 1:112, 3:10, 3:12, 3:90

Abominable church. *See* Great and abominable church.

Abomination, 1:131, 1:142, 1:255, 1:275, 1:283, 2:4, 2:vi, 2:3, 2:27, 2:37, 2:107, 2:115, 2:117, 2:153, 2:241, 3:19, 3:35, 3:38, 3:40, 3:54, 3:294, 3:352

Abomination of desolation. *See* Desolation of abomination.

Abominations, 1:7, 1:50, 1:131, 1:156, 1:213, 1:253, 1:256, 1:273, 2:3, 2:11, 2:13, 2:25, 2:34- 2:35, 2:46, 2:62, 2:70-2:72, 2:76-2:77, 2:98, 2:112, 2:129, 2:138, 2:140-2:141, 2:164, 2:190, 2:230, 2:234-2:236, 2:239, 2:244, 2:246, 2:251-2:252, 2:269, 3:54, 3:81, 3:101, 3:212, 3:231, 3:324, 3:328

Abortion, 1:107, 1:109, 1:201

Abraham, 1:1, 1:1, 1:5, 1:7, 1:8, 1:11, 1:16, 1:63, 1:64, 1:122, 1:136, 1:176, 1:200, 1:274, 2:82, 2:91-2:92, 2:104-2:105, 2:125, 2:127, 2:131, 2:151, 2:246, 2:259, 3:22, 3:72, 3:109, 3:121, 3:149, 3:162, 3:171, 3:185, 3:201, 3:225, 3:270, 3:326, 3:352

Acton, Lord, 1:209

Adam, 1:1, 1:4, 1:8, 1:10, 1:11, 1:13, 1:17, 1:26, 1:32, 1:35, 1:121, 1:161, 1:266, 2:14, 2:160, 2:163, 2:166, 2:170, 2:221, 2:224, 2:226, 2:235, 2:259, 2:4, 3:8, 3:45, 3:66, 3:86, 3:139, 3:151, 3:153, 3:155, 3:158, 3:160, 3:163-3:164, 3:191, 3:196-3:199, 3:201, 3:203, 3:245, 3:248, 3:273, 3:302, 3:307-3:308, 3:311, 3:313, 3:320, 3:331, 3:332, 3:334-3:335, 3:347, 3:348

Adams, John, 1:196, 1:211, 3:241

Adam-ondi-ahman, 2:4, 3:151

Adultery, 1:216, 3:132, 3:260

Adversary, 1:41, 1:78, 1:80-1:81, 1:85, 1:109, 1:115, 1:143, 2:vii, 2:151, 2:171, 2:173, 2:183, 2:192, 2:211, 2:220, 2:234, 3:285

Adversity, 1:114, 1:126, 2:179, 2:183, 2:193

Affection, 1:21, 1:102, 2:15, 2:178, 3:117, 3:260

Affliction, 1:65, 1:89, 1:143, 1:176, 2:10, 2:62, 2:157, 2:159, 2:170, 2:188, 2:190, 3:98, 3:107

Afflictions, 1:17, 1:50, 1:57, 1:72-1:74, 1:81, 1:83, 1:118, 1:121, 1:133, 1:134, 1:237, 1:245, 2:v, 2:33, 2:138, 2:155-2:156, 2:158, 2:175, 2:188, 2:190, 2:193, 3:v, 3:166, 3:260, 3:278

Africa, 1:225, 1:228, 1:232, 1:267, 2:7, 2:9, 2:139, 2:149, 3:4, 3:19, 3:155, 3:179, 3:241

Age, 1:3, 1:7, 1:14, 1:16, 1:30, 1:57, 1:98, 1:101-1:102, 1:109, 1:117, 1:122, 1:160, 1:179, 1:187, 1:211, 1:228, 1:234, 1:236, 1:239, 1:247, 2:3, 2:11, 2:16, 2:40, 2:74, 2:80, 2:158, 2:159, 2:171, 2:174, 2:176, 2:202, 3:vi-3:7, 3:11, 3:21, 3:43, 3:52, 3:108, 3:124, 3:129, 3:152, 3:154, 3:164, 3:189, 3:191, 3:202, 3:203, 3:206, 3:212, 3:213, 3:242, 3:296, 3:311, 3:318-3:319, 3:331

Agency, 1:31, 1:47, 1:56, 1:89, 1:103, 1:151, 1:165, 1:167-1:168, 1:192, 1:199, 1:211, 1:219, 2:17, 2:44, 2:73, 2:150, 2:154, 2:182-2:183, 2:224, 2:234, 3:81, 3:136, 3:201, 3:205, 3:219, 3:234, 3:238, 3:240, 3:247, 3:287, 3:292, 3:342

Ages, 1:vii, 1:3, 1:10, 1:18, 1:42, 1:48, 1:49, 1:91, 1:97, 1:152, 1:166, 1:191, 1:261, 1:266, 1:278, 2:8, 2:50, 2:184, 2:226, 2:235, 2:259, 2:272, 3:vi, 3:5, 3:14, 3:73, 3:138, 3:162, 3:164, 3:220, 3:235, 3:277, 3:315, 3:330, 3:340, 3:347

Albany, 2:136, 2:143, 2:153

Alliance, 1:174

Alliances, 1:175, 1:205, 2:88

America, 1:33, 1:35, 1:101, 1:150, 1:164, 1:172, 1:173, 1:185, 1:189-1:191, 1:193, 1:197, 1:202, 1:206, 1:209, 1:210, 1:238, 1:246, 1:280, 2:7, 2:55, 2:64, 2:79, 2:122, 2:136, 2:139, 2:147, 2:152, 2:267, 2:270, 3:3-3:4, 3:16, 3:18, 3:68, 3:76-3:77, 3:93, 3:115, 3:123, 3:127, 3:135, 3:168, 3:170, 3:289, 3:296, 3:299, 3:305

Anarchy, 1:99, 1:155, 1:156, 1:170, 1:190, 1:210-1:211, 1:220, 2:1, 2:11, 3:133

Ancient of Days, 1:260, 2:1, 2:8, 2:187, 2:264, 2:265, 2:274, 2:277, 3:8, 3:63, 3:153, 3:157, 3:159, 3:235, 3:237, 3:308

Ancients, 1:8, 1:29, 1:46, 2:48, 3:24, 3:31, 3:96, 3:225, 3:340

Angel, 1:17-1:18, 1:53, 1:66, 1:87, 1:133, 1:150, 1:223-1:224, 1:227, 1:236, 1:241, 1:243, 1:252, 1:256-1:257, 1:259, 1:270, 1:272, 1:276, 2:1, 2:12, 2:28, 2:40, 2:46, 2:58, 2:59, 2:87, 2:101, 2:102, 2:116, 2:132, 2:140,

287

Creature, 1:59, 1:201, 1:230, 1:253, 1:255, 1:257, 2:145, 2:188, 2:208, 2:259, 2:260, 2:285, 3:27, 3:145, 3:196, 3:335

Creatures, 1:106, 1:140, 1:191, 2:28, 2:56, 2:57, 2:177, 2:246, 2:279, 3:81, 3:199, 3:298, 3:302, 3:304

Creed, 1:161, 3:318

Creeds, 1:145, 1:261, 2:66, 2:196, 2:241, 3:63, 3:206, 3:228

Crime, 1:87, 1:194, 1:211, 2:21, 2:33, 2:208, 2:221

Crises, 1:97, 1:98, 1:102, 1:114, 2:151

Crisis, 1:32, 1:104, 1:126, 1:177, 1:190, 1:198, 1:207, 1:208, 2:viii, 2:150, 3:vii, 3:222

Criticism, 1:190, 1:190, 2:184

Critics, 1:197

Crops, 1:30, 2:2, 2:21, 2:35, 2:41, 2:64, 2:141

Crown, 1:106, 1:188, 2:54, 2:119, 2:170, 2:182, 2:259, 3:7, 3:49, 3:148, 3:164, 3:298, 3:302, 3:304, 3:335

Crowns, 1:31, 1:223, 1:250, 2:21, 2:179, 2:203, 3:46, 3:49

Crumble, 1:46, 1:58, 1:59, 1:62, 1:153, 1:229, 3:71

Crystal, 2:278, 3:351, 3:355

Cult, 2:217

Cults, 1:283, 2:203

Culture, 1:125, 1:280, 3:290

Cumorah, 1:26, 3:306, 3:311

Curse, 1:2, 1:11, 1:21, 1:34, 1:90, 1:128, 1:250, 1:255, 1:284, 2:23, 2:24, 2:32, 2:34, 2:36, 2:48, 2:57-2:58, 2:64, 2:65, 2:76, 2:96, 2:187, 2:188, 2:193, 2:228, 3:30, 3:56, 3:67, 3:72, 3:86, 3:122, 3:158, 3:177, 3:181, 3:189, 3:199, 3:204, 3:220, 3:253, 3:263-3:264, 3:278, 3:294, 3:303, 3:332, 3:335, 3:343-3:344

Curses, 1:117, 2:94, 3:111, 3:345

Curtain, 1:41, 1:256, 3:22, 3:55

Curtain of heaven, 1:256, 3:22, 3:55

Cycle(s), 1:96, 1:200

Cyclone(s), 1:71, 2:16, 2:64

Damnation, 1:199, 2:19, 2:72, 2:73, 3:328

Damned, 1:60, 1:139, 1:224, 2:206, 2:228, 2:258, 3:64

Dan, 1:250, 2:202, 2:273, 2:275, 3:8, 3:13, 3:159, 3:162, 3:237

Danger, 1:33, 1:47, 1:57, 1:77, 1:80, 1:92, 1:166, 1:168, 1:172, 1:173, 1:179, 1:189, 1:190, 1:202, 1:204, 1:208, 2:15, 2:69, 2:166, 2:181, 2:183, 2:213, 2:215, 2:225, 3:vii, 3:115

Daniel, 1:2, 1:40, 1:76, 1:78, 1:128, 1:245, 1:260, 1:275, 2:8, 2:27, 2:45, 2:98, 2:108, 2:112, 2:115, 2:123, 2:155, 2:169, 2:171, 2:187, 2:246, 2:265, 2:267, 2:270, 2:272, 2:274, 2:277, 3:8, 3:13, 3:35, 3:38, 3:40, 3:63, 3:85, 3:135, 3:151, 3:154, 3:156, 3:158-3:161, 3:163, 3:164, 3:217, 3:220, 3:228, 3:231, 3:233, 3:236-3:237, 3:240-3:241, 3:254, 3:258, 3:307, 3:313

Dark Ages, 1:191, 2:235

Darkness, 1:viii, 1:3, 1:8, 1:21, 1:31, 1:66, 1:75, 1:79, 1:85, 1:86, 1:93, 1:95, 1:98, 1:105, 1:108, 1:110, 1:128, 1:130, 1:138, 1:143, 1:145, 1:146, 1:159, 1:215, 1:226, 1:253, 1:254, 1:261, 1:288, 2:2, 2:7, 2:18, 2:25, 2:27, 2:30, 2:32, 2:33, 2:35, 2:36, 2:39, 2:59, 2:66, 2:76, 2:123, 2:128, 2:136, 2:149, 2:154, 2:155, 2:158, 2:173, 2:191, 2:192, 2:201, 2:213, 2:219, 2:239, 2:262, 2:274, 2:283, 3:vi, 3:viii, 3:7, 3:28, 3:33, 3:43-3:44, 3:49, 3:59, 3:99, 3:101, 3:113, 3:126, 3:130, 3:199, 3:200, 3:204, 3:211, 3:219, 3:222, 3:225, 3:237, 3:241, 3:244, 3:312, 3:314, 3:317, 3:325, 3:327, 3:328, 3:333, 3:353

Daughter, 1:38, 2:2, 2:24, 2:161, 2:250, 3:103, 3:154, 3:201

Daughters, 1:viii, 1:13, 1:21, 1:39, 1:55, 1:128, 1:161, 1:261, 1:267, 1:270, 1:271, 2:2, 2:113, 2:178, 2:235, 3:33, 3:77, 3:85, 3:95, 3:99, 3:164, 3:181, 3:194, 3:263, 3:307, 3:339

David, 1:166, 1:169, 1:230, 1:245, 1:278, 2:44, 2:50, 2:55, 2:88, 2:91, 2:122, 2:146, 2:180, 2:185, 2:201, 2:272, 2:274, 3:viii, 3:23, 3:80, 3:86, 3:91, 3:115, 3:117, 3:121, 3:125, 3:134, 3:171, 3:232, 3:235, 3:237, 3:248, 3:250, 3:253-3:256, 3:307

  root of David, 3:251

Index

3:221, 3:222, 3:243, 3:266, 3:267, 3:270, 3:288, 3:304, 3:307, 3:313, 3:329, 3:342

Minister, 1:17, 1:28, 1:46, 1:116, 1:274, 2:50, 2:93, 2:234, 3:17, 3:90, 3:140, 3:177, 3:184, 3:232, 3:310

Ministers, 1:223, 1:235, 1:278, 2:84, 2:173, 2:203, 3:74, 3:81

Ministry, 1:11, 1:18, 1:121, 1:142, 1:231, 1:239, 1:248, 1:255, 1:259, 2:37, 2:95, 2:103, 2:123, 2:199, 2:220, 3:11, 3:49, 3:140, 3:160, 3:179, 3:184, 3:194, 3:290, 3:295, 3:313, 3:318

Miracle, 1:51, 1:95-1:96, 1:250, 2:92, 2:125, 3:24, 3:79, 3:130

Miracles, 1:viii, 1:23, 1:39, 1:135, 1:136, 1:238, 1:265, 1:266, 2:59, 2:83, 2:92, 2:116, 2:191, 2:233, 2:282-2:284, 3:47, 3:180, 3:325, 3:328, 3:344, 3:345

Miraculous, 1:117, 3:130

Mission, 1:vii, 1:8, 1:11, 1:17, 1:26, 1:48, 1:59, 1:68, 1:71, 1:92, 1:95, 1:98, 1:119, 1:122, 1:142, 1:156, 1:181, 1:195, 1:212, 1:224, 1:228, 1:239, 1:242, 1:243, 1:250, 1:255, 1:279, 1:292, 2:14, 2:15, 2:79-2:80, 2:150, 2:262, 3:10, 3:169, 3:186, 3:197, 3:318

Missionaries, 1:50, 1:101, 1:110, 1:227, 1:249, 2:13, 2:138, 3:7, 3:169, 3:175, 3:190

Missionary work, 1:3, 1:101, 1:223, 1:231, 1:278, 1:280, 2:121, 3:201

Missouri, 1:viii, 1:33, 1:51, 1:151, 1:278, 1:279, 1:291, 1:292, 2:4, 2:121, 2:124, 2:132-2:133, 2:144-2:145, 2:181, 2:233, 2:234, 3:65, 3:89, 3:91, 3:104, 3:115, 3:120, 3:123, 3:126, 3:129, 3:131, 3:133, 3:136, 3:137, 3:143, 3:144, 3:148, 3:153, 3:155, 3:158, 3:160, 3:162, 3:248, 3:267, 3:269, 3:274, 3:277, 3:278, 3:311, 3:313, 3:331

Missouri River, 2:145, 3:313, 3:331

Mistake, 1:vii, 1:10, 1:51, 1:54, 1:91, 1:97, 1:123, 1:173, 1:234, 2:7, 2:217, 3:9, 3:76, 3:274, 3:287

Mistakes, 1:184, 1:184, 3:239

Moab, 2:45

Mob, 1:30, 1:36, 1:71, 1:148, 2:134, 2:136, 2:162, 3:64

Mobocracy, 1:79, 1:151, 2:134, 2:141, 3:263

Mobs, 1:29, 1:79, 1:80, 1:148, 1:155, 2:134, 2:150, 2:157, 2:159, 2:164

Mock, 2:160

Model, 1:198, 3:346

Moderation, 3:281, 3:281

Modesty, 2:199

Monetary System, 1:197, 1:198, 1:202, 1:207, 1:209

Money, 1:85, 1:92, 1:162, 1:183, 1:187, 1:192, 1:194, 1:197, 1:201, 1:202, 1:208, 1:209, 2:230, 3:92, 3:99, 3:102, 3:190, 3:263, 3:268, 3:272, 3:278, 3:283, 3:284, 3:286, 3:297, 3:328

Monroe Doctrine, 1:179

Moon, 1:8, 1:21, 1:50, 1:122, 1:124, 1:128, 1:228, 1:234, 1:247, 1:251, 1:256, 1:260, 2:7, 2:12, 2:18, 2:21, 2:23, 2:25, 2:27-2:28, 2:36, 2:38, 2:52, 2:68, 2:107, 2:108, 2:113-2:115, 2:278, 2:279, 3:19-3:21, 3:24, 3:30, 3:36-3:40, 3:42, 3:43, 3:51, 3:58, 3:64, 3:76, 3:77, 3:79, 3:80, 3:96, 3:99, 3:129, 3:130, 3:140, 3:146, 3:149, 3:200, 3:201, 3:223, 3:305, 3:331, 3:334, 3:352

turn to blood, 1:260

Moral, 1:60, 1:97, 1:119, 1:121, 1:167, 1:178, 1:179, 1:184, 1:188, 1:191, 1:193-1:194, 1:196, 1:197, 1:202, 1:206, 1:208, 1:219, 2:151, 2:154, 2:223, 3:136, 3:238

Morality, 1:60, 1:112, 1:116, 1:185, 1:208, 1:210, 1:212, 2:133, 2:152, 3:288

Mormon, 1:7, 1:14, 1:26, 1:45, 1:46, 1:78, 1:82, 1:97, 1:99, 1:102, 1:104, 1:125, 1:193, 1:196, 1:200, 1:210-1:211, 1:235, 1:236, 1:238, 1:245-1:247, 1:260, 1:264, 1:265, 1:280, 1:289, 2:5, 2:15, 2:34, 2:43, 2:47, 2:50, 2:59, 2:61, 2:79, 2:84, 2:88, 2:104, 2:108, 2:120-2:121, 2:123-2:126, 2:142, 2:147, 2:185, 2:202, 2:213, 2:218, 2:220, 2:230, 2:233, 2:235, 2:240, 2:257, 3:vi, 3:5, 3:9, 3:48, 3:70, 3:82, 3:85, 3:106, 3:117, 3:136, 3:137, 3:140, 3:157, 3:167, 3:172, 3:173, 3:175, 3:179, 3:217, 3:229, 3:248, 3:251, 3:273, 3:283, 3:286, 3:293, 3:298, 3:299, 3:306, 3:310, 3:318, 3:338, 3:343, 3:349

Moroni, 1:17, 1:18, 1:26, 1:101, 1:105, 1:108, 1:134, 1:196, 1:197, 1:214, 1:246, 2:20, 2:35, 2:128, 2:208, 2:235, 3:162, 3:298

Mortal, 1:11, 1:13, 1:31, 1:72, 1:184, 1:232, 1:246, 1:247, 1:250, 2:151, 2:179, 2:184, 2:185, 2:202, 2:203, 2:226, 2:236,

312

Nephites, 1:45, 1:99, 1:113, 1:117, 1:136, 1:178, 1:215-1:216, 1:231, 1:264, 2:4, 2:35, 2:65, 2:88, 2:93, 2:94, 2:129, 2:136, 2:169, 2:220, 3:93, 3:140, 3:161, 3:172, 3:175, 3:179, 3:183, 3:272, 3:273, 3:283, 3:286, 3:293, 3:300, 3:305, 3:326, 3:349

Nephities, three. *See* Three Nephites.

Net, 1:116, 1:260, 1:267, 1:271, 2:224

New Jerusalem, 1:viii, 1:32, 1:39, 1:127, 1:138, 1:274, 1:280, 1:290, 2:48, 2:91, 2:121-2:122, 2:124-2:126, 2:135, 2:145, 2:151, 3:47, 3:58, 3:59, 3:62, 3:66, 3:68, 3:92, 3:93, 3:103, 3:106, 3:112, 3:115, 3:118, 3:120-3:122, 3:124, 3:129, 3:131, 3:133, 3:136, 3:142, 3:146, 3:150, 3:160, 3:177, 3:185, 3:210, 3:267, 3:271, 3:274, 3:275, 3:290, 3:300, 3:312, 3:336, 3:341, 3:344, 3:346-3:348, 3:352

New name, 3:146

New York, 1:180, 1:204, 1:270, 2:136, 2:137, 2:143, 2:145, 2:153, 3:123

Newspaper, 2:51

Newspapers, 2:225

Night vision, 1:9, 1:24, 1:271, 2:164, 2:272, 3:70, 3:71, 3:80, 3:90, 3:102, 3:228

Nile (River), 2:84-2:84, 3:193

Noah, 1:vii, 1:4, 1:11, 1:16, 1:20, 1:31, 1:55, 1:69, 1:74, 1:97, 1:103, 1:111, 1:117, 1:123, 1:125, 1:133, 1:230, 2:3, 2:7, 2:9-2:12, 2:16, 2:31, 2:63, 2:68, 2:69, 2:76, 2:190, 3:2-3:4, 3:14, 3:29, 3:59, 3:66, 3:113, 3:142, 3:162, 3:204, 3:280, 3:308, 3:313, 3:319, 3:336

Noble, 1:16, 1:183, 1:197, 1:209, 2:199, 2:217, 2:260, 3:83, 3:280

North countries, 1:249, 2:39, 2:65, 2:104, 2:106, 3:167-3:169, 3:185-3:186, 3:313, 3:352

North country, 1:235, 1:241, 2:45, 2:83, 2:133, 2:249, 3:21, 3:98, 3:155, 3:165, 3:169, 3:172-3:173, 3:178, 3:253, 3:312

North Pole, 3:167

Nuclear, 1:206, 1:209

Numbers, 1:52, 1:81, 1:252, 2:56, 2:91, 2:92, 2:174, 2:218, 2:220, 2:225, 2:238, 3:62, 3:76, 3:116, 3:175, 3:221, 3:225, 3:311

Oath, 1:20, 1:127, 1:152, 1:164, 1:197, 1:217, 2:235, 3:29, 3:59, 3:113, 3:204

Oaths, 1:210, 1:218, 2:76

Obedience, 1:32, 1:58, 1:78, 1:93, 1:95, 1:96, 1:113, 1:114, 1:188, 2:19, 2:164, 2:218, 3:6, 3:63, 3:89, 3:93, 3:94, 3:110, 3:119, 3:132, 3:202, 3:235, 3:239, 3:264, 3:275, 3:292, 3:293, 3:295, 3:343

Obey, 1:36, 1:56, 1:60, 1:81, 1:82, 1:95, 1:130, 1:157, 1:194, 1:214, 1:265, 1:268, 1:272, 1:278, 1:284, 2:41, 2:73, 2:86, 2:142, 2:155, 2:168, 2:174, 2:195, 2:212, 2:214, 2:218, 2:264, 2:265, 2:274, 2:278, 3:24, 3:26, 3:72, 3:128, 3:163, 3:181, 3:198, 3:237, 3:240, 3:247, 3:254, 3:265, 3:273, 3:277, 3:284, 3:291, 3:294, 3:295, 3:314, 3:317

Obligation, 1:13, 1:103, 1:110, 1:187, 1:194, 2:225, 3:288

Ocean, 1:1, 1:159, 1:271, 2:106, 2:120, 2:244, 2:266, 2:268, 3:57, 3:112, 3:155, 3:167, 3:180, 3:229, 3:241, 3:314, 3:342

Atlantic Ocean, 2:268, 3:155, 3:180

Pacific Ocean, 2:120, 3:127

Oceans, 3:117, 3:180

Offering, 1:94, 1:170, 1:193, 1:226, 2:48, 2:231, 2:235, 3:17, 3:22, 3:47, 3:126, 3:158

Offerings, 1:93, 1:128, 2:80, 2:181, 3:291

Official, 1:191, 1:204, 3:160, 3:261

Officials, 1:174, 1:182, 1:190, 1:205, 2:92

Offspring, 1:72, 1:148, 1:156, 1:275, 2:13, 2:160, 3:134, 3:208, 3:256, 3:345

Oil, 1:36, 1:47, 1:63, 1:95-1:96, 1:129, 1:249, 2:99, 2:119, 2:253, 3:viii, 3:17, 3:99, 3:126, 3:166, 3:168, 3:169

Old Testament, 1:125, 1:259, 3:24, 3:311

Olive tree, 1:240, 1:288, 3:172

Omaha, 1:269

One hundred forty-four thousand, 1:3, 1:250

One mighty and strong, 2:202, 3:78, 3:303

Schemers, 3:281

School, 1:43, 1:56, 1:171, 1:187, 3:5, 3:124, 3:276, 3:282

Schools, 1:107, 1:121, 1:178, 1:183, 3:61, 3:125, 3:127

Science, 2:44, 2:108, 3:83, 3:86, 3:117, 3:141

Scoffers, 1:21, 2:69, 3:8, 3:45

Scorn, 1:120

Scourge, 1:36, 1:42, 1:43, 1:49, 1:52, 1:100, 1:102, 1:176, 1:255, 1:3, 2:6, 2:19, 2:21, 2:22, 2:36, 2:56, 2:61, 2:64, 2:133, 2:136, 2:137, 2:220, 3:96, 3:106

Scripture, 1:vi, 1:6, 1:54, 1:68, 1:200, 1:241, 1:261, 1:273, 1:274, 1:280, 2:44, 2:108, 2:136, 2:179, 2:215, 3:2, 3:6, 3:117, 3:132, 3:192, 3:199, 3:215, 3:312, 3:316, 3:320

Scroll, 1:256, 2:5, 2:23, 2:28, 2:52, 2:131, 2:266, 2:278, 3:5, 3:6, 3:22, 3:45, 3:55, 3:166, 3:227

Scrolls, 3:320

Sea, 1:26, 1:51, 1:64, 1:73, 1:85, 1:115, 1:130, 1:140, 1:217, 1:234, 1:236, 1:237, 1:243, 1:255, 1:260, 1:271, 1:276, 1:291, 1:294, 2:3, 2:5, 2:11, 2:15, 2:21-2:22, 2:25, 2:27, 2:38, 2:39, 2:52, 2:66, 2:79, 2:81, 2:84, 2:87, 2:96, 2:102, 2:106, 2:127, 2:138, 2:153, 2:222, 2:245, 2:253, 2:260-2:262, 2:268, 2:275, 2:279, 3:4, 3:21, 3:34, 3:42, 3:46, 3:54-3:55, 3:57, 3:59, 3:64, 3:82, 3:96, 3:111, 3:112, 3:122, 3:150, 3:166, 3:170, 3:173, 3:180-3:181, 3:185, 3:192, 3:197, 3:202-3:204, 3:208, 3:210-3:211, 3:245, 3:252, 3:308, 3:310, 3:322, 3:327, 3:330, 3:338, 3:340, 3:341, 3:347, 3:351, 3:355

    sea of glass, 2:29, 2:29, 2:278, 3:192, 3:338, 3:353, 3:355

Seal, 1:15, 1:38, 1:90, 1:140, 1:142, 1:224, 1:230, 1:241, 1:255, 1:293, 2:2, 2:28, 2:37, 2:38, 2:52, 2:59, 2:147, 2:169, 2:202, 2:285, 3:1, 3:12, 3:15, 3:46, 3:53, 3:54, 3:108, 3:110, 3:185, 3:186, 3:190, 3:192, 3:209, 3:210, 3:324, 3:339, 3:350

Sealed, 1:8, 1:14, 1:18, 1:23-1:24, 1:26, 1:53, 1:69, 1:71, 1:84, 1:116, 1:130, 1:140, 1:226, 1:244-1:245, 1:248-1:249, 1:251, 1:258, 1:291, 1:292, 2:2, 2:136, 2:179, 2:195, 2:278-2:279, 3:53, 3:137, 3:185, 3:191, 3:192, 3:194, 3:211, 3:295, 3:306, 3:311, 3:313, 3:324, 3:327, 3:329-3:330, 3:339

Sealed in their foreheads, 1:53, 1:226, 1:248-1:249, 2:2, 3:194

Sealed records, 3:311

Sealing power, 1:14

Seals, 2:259, 3:195

Season, 1:7, 1:56, 1:117, 1:121, 2:18, 2:65, 2:74, 2:141, 2:158, 2:185, 2:240, 2:277, 2:285, 2:3, 3:1, 3:36, 3:38, 3:44, 3:82, 3:90, 3:92, 3:107, 3:118, 3:125, 3:139, 3:143, 3:191, 3:204, 3:209, 3:211, 3:213, 3:334, 3:336, 3:340, 3:348-3:350, 3:354

    Season, little. *See* Little season.

Seasons, 1:29, 1:75, 1:96, 1:279, 2:38, 2:43, 2:58, 2:186, 3:11, 3:14, 3:44, 3:69, 3:180, 3:212, 3:213, 3:226, 3:314

Second Coming, 1:vii, 1:14, 1:18, 1:51, 1:54-1:55, 1:62, 1:68, 1:75, 1:76, 1:87, 1:90, 1:97, 1:99, 1:101, 1:110, 1:112, 1:116, 1:117, 1:119-1:120, 1:122, 1:124-1:126, 1:199, 1:227, 1:259, 1:269, 1:280-1:282, 2:vi, 2:3, 2:21, 2:28, 2:44, 2:50, 2:59, 2:69, 2:74, 2:92, 2:94, 2:95, 2:108, 2:126, 2:0, 3:vii, 3:2, 3:1, 3:3, 3:8, 3:9, 3:12, 3:15, 3:17-3:19, 3:21-3:24, 3:28, 3:30, 3:34, 3:35, 3:46, 3:49, 3:52, 3:94, 3:96, 3:136-3:137, 3:143, 3:162, 3:206, 3:297, 3:318, 3:333

Secret, 1:23, 1:28, 1:67, 1:99, 1:102, 1:110, 1:154, 1:163, 1:166, 1:168, 1:178, 1:185-1:186, 1:213, 1:216, 1:218, 1:221, 1:253, 1:290, 2:2, 2:20, 2:32-2:33, 2:36, 2:49, 2:76, 2:108, 2:129, 2:140, 2:141, 2:149, 2:175, 2:191, 2:202, 2:220, 2:230, 2:260, 3:1, 3:6, 3:35, 3:38, 3:40, 3:48, 3:101, 3:162, 3:211, 3:213, 3:260, 3:262, 3:312, 3:327, 3:328

Secret combination, 1:178, 1:185, 1:186, 1:217-1:218

Secret combinations, 1:23, 1:99, 1:154, 1:166, 1:184, 1:186, 1:290, 2:191, 3:328

Secret societies, 1:110, 1:178, 2:175

Sect(s), 1:145, 1:149, 1:230, 2:viii, 2:160, 2:173, 2:186, 3:63, 3:64, 3:221, 3:334

Secular, 1:119, 1:211, 3:247, 3:295, 3:317

Security, 1:92, 1:105, 1:115, 1:116, 1:132, 1:149, 1:151, 1:167, 1:172, 1:176, 1:177, 1:179-1:181, 1:183, 1:190, 1:198, 1:200, 2:149, 2:151, 2:183, 2:213, 2:229, 3:92, 3:102

331